# BLACKS AND SOCIAL JUSTICE

# BLACKS AND SOCIAL JUSTICE

### Revised Edition

*Bernard R. Boxill*

ROWMAN & LITTLEFIELD PUBLISHERS, INC.

**ROWMAN & LITTLEFIELD PUBLISHERS, INC.**

Published in the United States of America
by Rowman & Littlefield Publishers, Inc.
4720 Boston Way, Lanham, Maryland 20706

British Cataloging in Publication Information Available


**Library of Congress Cataloging-in-Publication Data**

Boxill, Bernard R.
Blacks and social justice / Bernard R. Boxill. — Rev. ed.
p.  cm.
Includes bibliographical references and index.
1. Afro-Americans—Civil rights.  2. Afro-Americans—Race
identity.  3. Social justice.  4. Busing for school integration—
United States.  5. Affirmative action programs—United States.
I. Title.
E185.615B63   1992
305.896'073—dc20   92–12819 CIP

ISBN 0–8476–7757–5 (cloth : alk. paper)
ISBN 0–8476–7710–9 (pbk. : alk. paper)

Printed in the United States of America

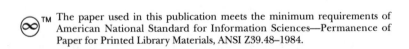 ™ The paper used in this publication meets the minimum requirements of
American National Standard for Information Sciences—Permanence of
Paper for Printed Library Materials, ANSI Z39.48–1984.

# Contents

# Introduction

In recent years, black people have marked with deepening apprehension the development of a certain trend in the nation's racial policies. There is nothing really new about the trend, for in many ways it is a return to traditional attitudes. But it had seemed, for a time, that these attitudes had softened. The first alarms were set off by the patronage and good will extended to Marco DeFunis and Allan Bakke, when their suits against preferential admissions reached to the Supreme Court. But it was left for the Reagan administration, which had consistently backed off the issues of busing, affirmative action, and housing discrimination, to show clearly the direction in which the nation's policies on race are heading. In January of 1982, in one of its more conspicuous reversals of federal civil rights policy, it moved to end the practice of denying tax-exempt status to private schools which discriminate against minorities. The conceit of institutions like Bob Jones University, in propounding that God commands the separation of the races, was apparently deemed a genuine religious belief to be protected by the First Amendment.

Civil rights groups have denounced these changes in policies they fought so long and hard for. But others, including whites who stood with blacks against legalized segregation, and whose credentials and good will are not to be doubted, maintain that the retired or endangered policies are as unjust as the racist policies whose harmful effects they were designed to combat. If it was wrong to discriminate against black people on the basis of their color, these critics maintain, it must be equally wrong to discriminate in favor of black people on the basis of their color. Their slogan is Justice John Marshall Harlan's aphorism, formulated in his dissent in *Plessy* v. *Ferguson*, that "our Constitution is color-blind." There are blacks too, who welcome the changes and who, perhaps because of their color, feel entitled to speak with a forthrightness few whites have dared to emulate. According to these black critics, affirmative action, busing, and the other color-conscious policies instituted to speed black progress suggest that blacks cannot succeed without special help, and so are belittling and insulting, as well as unjust.

The assumption behind color-conscious policies, according to these critics, is that blacks are poor because of racism. They maintain that this "race theory" is false and pernicious. Blacks are poor, they argue, because their class determines that they lack the skills and attitudes to work that the market will pay for. And this "class theory" of black inequality, they conclude, demonstrates that color-conscious policies are both unjust and counter-productive.

The first aim of this book is to rebut or defuse these and other charges being leveled against the color-conscious policies that have been threatened by Ronald Reagan's administration. I will first take up the views of the economist Thomas Sowell, the best-known advocate of the class theory, who declares that color-conscious policies are decisively invalidated by their lack of utility, and that, in any case, philosophers exaggerate the importance of the justice of social policies and institutions. However, as I demonstrate in Chapter 2, far from showing color-conscious policies to be unjust and unproductive, his class theory suggests that they are both just and productive. His opposition to these policies stems not from his class theory, as he imagines, but from inconsistent fragments of a philosophical theory of justice—the very kind of consideration he depreciates—from the far right.

But there are others, of a far different ilk, who also believe that philosophers exaggerate the importance of justice, and who maintain that the subject of the justice of color-conscious policy is of little moment politically. Impressed by Karl Marx's attack on rival socialists' proposals for economic justice, these critics argue that the ideas of moral and legal rights, just deserts, and equality which determine the justice of social practices are designed to legitimize bourgeois society and that preoccupation with the question of the justice of color-conscious policies diverts energy from the proletariat revolution. I take this charge seriously, not only because the Marxist attack on justice raises fundamental questions, but also because many black people are attracted to Marxism. On the one hand, they are disillusioned by the failure of piecemeal reforms to make significant inroads on racism, and therefore welcome the Marxist theory that racism will be eradicated only by a radical revolution. On the other hand, they are anxious to find a basis for an irrepressible optimism, and are consequently heartened by Marx's confident prophesy that the required revolution is inevitable. But I recommend skepticism. As I argue in Chapter 3, the Marxist polemic against justice tends to subvert social revolution. Unless the Marxist strategy makes an explicit appeal to the ideal of justice, it gives well-off white workers every reason to use the desperate black underclass as cannon fodder in outbreaks of urban unrest that can snatch only trifling concessions from the capitalist class.

But are color-conscious policies just or unjust? Some are certainly unjust. It goes without saying that Jim Crow legislation is unjust. But critics cannot as a result infer that all color-conscious policy is unjust. Jim Crow legislation was insulting to black people and its intention was to degrade them. The color-conscious policies that are threatened by the Reagan administration are not insulting to white people, and their intention is to elevate black people. The differences in the nature, intent, and presumed result of these two kinds of policy are so deep that it is presumptuous to conclude that because they resemble each other in being color-conscious, they resemble each other in being unjust. The question of the justice or injustice of color-conscious policies cannot be decided in the abstract. Each policy must be judged on its own merits.

The two most widely applied and controversial color-conscious policies designed to elevate black people which the Reagan administration seems most determined to dismantle are busing and preferential treatment in education and jobs. I will take up the question of busing before that of preferential treatment because it became an issue first.

During the years in which it was enforced, most black people opposed segregated schooling. They couldn't help seeing that white children were better taught than black children. Understandably, they reasoned that if black children were in the same schools as white children they would be taught as well. But school desegregation became a national issue only in 1954, when, in *Brown* v. *Board of Education of Topeka* the Supreme Court ruled that segregating black children deprives them of "equal protection of the laws guaranteed by the Fourteenth Amendment." The arguments for and against *Brown* remain, at bottom, the arguments for and against busing. For some the issue was and is equal educational opportunity; for others the injustice of de jure segregation and the harmfulness of either de jure or de facto segregation; and for others still whether it is the right of parents or of the community to control childrens' education.

I analyze and assess these various arguments in Chapters 4, 5, and 6. Since my concern is moral and philosophical rather than legal, I do not attempt to decide whether desegregation policies and laws are constitutional, nor whether the Supreme Court should, in making its decisions, rely or not rely on social science statistics that show busing to be beneficial. I attempt only to decide whether desegregation policies and laws are morally justifiable. My conclusions are modest. Although

I show that busing is not unjust, I cannot conclude that it is justified. The root of the problem is the empirical uncertainty about the benefits of busing. Even if busing equalizes educational opportunities and transgresses against no rights, it is surely foolish and wrong if it confers no benefits and avoids no harm.

The case for preferential treatment may have at one time been similarly dependent on social science. For example, in their early, enthusiastic response to a policy of preferential treatment, certain prestigious colleges and universities admitted grossly unprepared black students. Predictably, many of these students either failed ignominiously or got blatantly undeserved passes. Some cynics hinted—an intriguing thought—that the universities had aimed at this demonstration of black incompetence all along, while others alleged that the well-advertised militancy of the preferentially admitted students was only frustration with work too hard for them.

But because the costs of university education are too high to squander on useless gestures—or on proving black incompetence—university officials began to admit only the most qualified black students. Though these students still had generally lower test scores than white students, they could, and did, profit from the universities' courses. A degree in medicine confers virtual certainty of affluence, and degrees in law or in the sciences and arts, especially if they are granted by prestigious universities, are keys to innumerable opportunities.

But while this development in the administration of preferential treatment seems to mitigate the charge that the policy benefits no one, it exposes it to the charge that it especially benefits those who deserve no special benefit. This is the most common criticism of preferential treatment, and is prized as a masterstroke. All it needs to make its case is the assumption that the most qualified black students are precisely those least harmed or wronged—or those not harmed or wronged at all—by racial discrimination.

Since the most qualified blacks are likely to come from the black middle class, this argument joins forces with the argument that preferential treatment benefits the comfortable black middle class instead of, and perhaps at the expense of, the needy black lower class and underclass. But it is a different argument, and the people who oppose preferential treatment on philosophical grounds, and who do not appear to be notably moved by appeals to need, prize it for reasons more congenial to their outlook. To many, the heart of the case for preferential treatment is that blacks deserve it as compensation for the harms inflicted on them by racial discrimination. Consequently, its opponents argue, if preferential treatment benefits only those who have escaped the harms of racial discrimination, then the practice is indeed unjustified.

The various forms this criticism of preferential treatment has taken have had a fatal attraction for philosophers, including some very able advocates of preferential treatment. Yet, as I demonstrate in Chapter 7, they are a mishmash of gratuitous assumption, poor analogy, and plain logical blunder, fueled by resentment, not reason.

Whatever may be the ultimate fate of those arguments for preferential treatment, which, looking back to the past, view it as compensation for the injuries of racial discrimination, certain philosophers feel that a better, less contentious argument for preferential treatment looks forward to the future. The most persuasive case for treating blacks preferentially, they say, is that the policy is a means to a happier, more equal society in the future. "Let bygones be bygones" appears to be their motto.

While I admit that this approach is an eminently agreeable one, I must add that it is especially so to the unscathed. To those who bear the scars of racial discrimination, its invocation is apt to seem a convenient and sanctimonious ploy, even if it is coupled with a commitment to produce a more equal society. They might well want to know how a commitment to equality is compatible with repudiating the moral relevance of their injuries. Indeed, they might feel that proposals urging their advancement which proclaim that the causes of their inequality are irrelevant, and might be accident, their own laziness, or genetic inferiority as well as the color bar, are insulting to their abilities as well as to their status as moral equals. For these reasons, I resist the tendency common even among advocates of preferential treatment to dismiss backward-looking arguments in favor of forward-looking arguments.

In the remaining chapters of the book I take up questions of a more general nature. The first of these questions, addressed in Chapter 8, is the long-standing issue of black self-segregation as opposed to integration. Practically every important black thinker, including as staunch an assimilationist as Frederick Douglass, has conceded that black self-segregation may at times be necessary or desirable. W. E. B. Dubois, however, felt that this, as a strategy against discrimination, confronts blacks with a dilemma. The "only effective defense," he wrote, that a "segregated and despised group has against complete spiritual and physical disaster is internal self-organization." But internal self-organization involves "more or less active segregation and acquiescence in segregation." Thus, to combat the evil of segregation, we must acquiese in the very evil we wish to combat.

Black history can, to some considerable degree, be interpreted as a history of attempts to seize this dilemma by one of its horns. The assimilationists (William Monroe Trotter is the most extreme) disdain self-segregation and urge protest. The separatists (here Booker T. Washington is the most extreme) disdain protest and urge self-segregation.

And then there is Dubois. Although he thought the dilemma "complete " and "without issue," he bravely seized both its horns. Trotter and Washington were both right and wrong. We must self-segregate, Dubois insisted, but we must also never acquiesce to forced segregation. We must forever protest it.

The resolution of Dubois's dilemma takes us far afield, to a discussion of the concepts of race and racism, of "black pride," and of the ideals of authenticity and integrity. My conclusions will appear, at first, to support Dubois's conviction that there is a deep dilemma inherent in policies of self-segregation. I show, however, that this appearance is misleading. There is, in fact, no dilemma, and the doctrine which makes it appear that there is—that of cultural or ethnic pluralism—is spurious and subverts the ideal of authenticity.

Dubois's belief that injustice must be protested against leads us to our next topic—black self-respect and dignity. The insults and injustice of racism are well known, of course, to undermine self-respect. But this is not the issue I consider. The issue I consider is: What is the self-respecting response to the insults and injustices of racism? Dubois thought it should involve protest and agitation. Yet—and Dubois himself admits this—there seems something undignified about insistent protest. Dignity suggests reserve and self-restraint, and these qualities are not the hallmark of the agitator.

This problem is related to an objection often made to preferential treatment. Part of this objection is that, if a policy of preferential treatment is in operation, black people must ever be uncertain about how competent they really are. But unsettling as this incertitude must be to self-esteem and self-confidence—and to those who feel they must know where they stand, to peace of mind—it may be only the beginning. There is a darker possibility. Preferential treatment, warns frequently-quoted black critic Thomas Sowell, makes black achievement "synonymous" with "charity" and undermines black "self-respect" and the "respect of others." A white commentator, J. Harvie Wilkinson, approvingly explained and improved on this: Preferential treatment, he writes, is, like charity, both a "temptation" and a source of "resentment." Another commentator, Michael Levin, makes a different, though in many ways similar, point. Anyone who is publicly known to have been preferentially hired, he writes, must feel himself to be a "fraud" and intensely "embarrassed."

These observations may be independent of any argument that black people have a right to preferential treatment. Even if a person has a right to something, he may not be doing the correct or self-respecting thing in taking it. Most contemporary analyses of self-respect ignore this point. Conceiving of self-respect exclusively in terms of its opposition to servility, and therefore as a kind of assertiveness, they analyze it in terms of rights. In truth, however, self-respect is as often opposed to underhandedness and meanness as it is to servility, and is as often manifested by a disdain for exacting one's pound of flesh as it is by assertiveness. The elaboration of a conception of self-respect which takes these facts into account, and of cognate ideas like dignity and self-esteem, is the subject of Chapter 9.

Chapter 10 considers the problem of how color-conscious policies even if they are useful, just, and not subversive of self-respect, can be enacted or sustained in the face of growing popular disapproval. Martin Luther King, Jr., used civil disobedience successfully against Jim Crow. The question therefore arises of whether the same means are appropriate in the present circumstances.

King saw civil disobedience as an appeal to the nation's conscience. On the basis of this assumption he reasoned that the civilly disobedient should accept the penalty for their disobedience, and should steadfastly refrain from violence. Both of these conclusions have since been challenged. King thought that the civilly disobedient should accept the penalty for disobedience in order to establish their sincerity and conscientiousness. Certain liberal critics (I have in mind chiefly Ronald Dworkin) have cast doubt on the validity of this contention, on the one hand by urging leniency for certain kinds of civil disobedience, and on the other by implying that it is only the cogency of the disobedient's arguments that counts, and not the sincerity of his belief in them. These critics mean well, but their theory is inconsistent. They cannot deny leniency to segregationists who practice civil disobedience and be consistent; nevertheless, they do. And, as I argue, when they try to avoid this inconsistency, the modification of the theory which results is elitist, because it makes civil disobedience the prerogative of the well-to-do, the well-educated, and well-connected, and therefore irrelevant to the black struggle.

King believed that his view that the disobedient should refrain from violence was consistent with putting "pressure on the merchant," as he put it, by disrupting business. But philosopher John Rawls has argued that even this kind of non-violent disruptiveness detracts from the effectiveness of civil disobedience as an appeal to the country's sense of justice. Though I have general reservations about how widely civil disobedience is likely to be used in future black struggles for equality, I argue that Rawls's proscription of the kind of pressure King recommended is based on an unfounded, ultimately Platonic idea—that justice and harmony are naturally associated—and makes civil disobedience practically useless as a means of black advancement.

But any examination of the issue of blacks and social justice must begin with the fundamental question of whether or not law and morality should be color-blind. It is to this question that I now turn.

# 1

# *The Color-Blind Principle*

## Plessy

In 1892, Homer Plessy, an octoroon, was arrested in Louisiana for taking a seat in a train car reserved for whites. He was testing a state law which required the "white and colored races" to ride in "equal but separate" accommodations, and his case eventually reached the Supreme Court.

Part of Plessy's defense, though it must be considered mainly a snare for the opposition, was that he was "seven-eighths Caucasian and one-eighth African blood," and that the "mixture of colored blood was not discernible in him." The bulwark of his argument was, however, that he was "entitled to every right, privilege and immunity secured to citizens of the white race," and that the law violated the Fourteenth Amendment's prohibition against unequal protection of the laws.[1] Cannily, the court refused the snare. Perhaps it feared—and with reason—that the ancestry of too many white Louisianans held dark secrets. But it attacked boldly enough Plessy's main argument that the Louisiana law was unconstitutional. That argument, Justice Henry Billings Brown wrote for the majority, was unsound. "Its underlying fallacy," he averred, was its "assumption that the enforced separation of the two races stamps the colored race with a badge of inferiority." "If this be so," Brown concluded, "it is not by reason of anything found in the act, but solely because the colored race chooses to put that construction upon it."[2]

Only one judge dissented from the court majority—Justice John Marshall Harlan. It was the occasion on which he pronounced his famous maxim: "Our Constitution is color-blind." In opposition to Justice Brown,

Justice Harlan found that the "separation of citizens on the basis of race [was a] badge of servitude . . . wholly inconsistent [with] equality before the law."[3]

Plessy's is the kind of case which makes the color-blind principle seem indubitably right as a basis for action and policy, and its contemporary opponents appear unprincipled, motivated by expediency, and opportunistic. This impression is only strengthened by a reading of Justice Brown's tortuously preposterous defense of the "equal but separate" doctrine. It should make every advocate of color-conscious policy wary of the power of arguments of expediency to beguile moral sense and subvert logic. Yet I argue that color-conscious policy can still be justified. The belief that it cannot is the result of a mistaken generalization from *Plessy*. There is no warrant for the idea that the color-blind principle should hold in some general and absolute way.

## "I didn't notice" Liberals

In his book *Second Wind*, Bill Russell recalls how amazed he used to be by the behavior of what he called "I didn't notice" liberals. These were individuals who claimed not to notice people's color. If they mentioned someone Russell could not place, and Russell asked whether she was black or white, they would answer, "I didn't notice." "Sweet and innocent," Russell recalls, "sometimes a little proud."[4] Now, the kind of color-blindness the "I didn't notice" liberals claim to have may be a worthy ideal—Richard Wasserstrom, for example, argues that society should aim toward it—but it is absolutely different from the color-blind principle which functions as a basis for policy.[5] Thus, while Wasserstrom supports color-conscious policies to secure the ideal of people not noticing each others' color, the principle of color-blindness in the law opposes color-conscious policies and does not necessarily involve any hope that people will not notice each others' color. Its thesis is simple: that no *law* or *public policy* be designed to treat people differently because they are of a different color.

## Color-blind and Color-conscious Policies

The essential thing about a color-conscious policy is that it is designed to treat people differently because of their race. But there are many different kinds of color-conscious policies. Some, for example the Jim Crow policies now in the main abolished, aim to subordinate blacks, while others, such as busing and preferential treatment, aim at elevating blacks.

Some color-conscious policies explicitly state that persons should be treated differently because of their race, for example the segregation laws at issue in *Plessy*; others make no mention of race, but are still designed so that blacks and whites are treated differently, for example, the "grandfather clauses" in voting laws that many states adopted at the turn of the century. To give one instance, in Louisiana this clause stated that those who had had the right to vote before or on 1 January 1867, or their lineal descendants, did not have to meet the educational, property, or tax requirements for voting. Since no blacks had had the right to vote by that time, this law worked effectively to keep blacks from voting while at the same time allowing many impoverished and illiterate whites to vote—yet it made no mention of race.

My object in this chapter is to demonstrate that the color-blind principle, which considers all color-conscious policies to be invalid, is mistaken. I do not deny that many color-conscious policies are wrong. Jim Crow was certainly wrong, and, for different reasons, proposals for black control of inner cities and inner city schools are probably wrong. But this is not because they are color-conscious, but for reasons which indicate that color-conscious policies like busing and affirmative action could be correct.

Advocates of the belief that the law should be color-blind often argue that this would be the best means to an ideal state in which people are color-blind. They appeal to the notion that, only if people notice each other's color can they discriminate on the basis of color and, with considerable plausibility, they argue that color-conscious laws and policies can only heighten people's awareness of each other's color, and exacerbate racial conflict. They maintain that only if the law, with all its weight and influence, sets the example of color-blindness, can there be a realistic hope that people will see through the superficial distinctions of color and become themselves color-blind.

But this argument is not the main thesis of the advocates of legal color-blindness. Generally, they eschew it because of its dependency on the empirical. Their favorite argument, one that is more direct and intuitively appealing, is simply that it is wicked, unfair, and unreasonable to penalize a person for what he cannot help being. Not only does this seem undeniably true, but it can be immediately applied to the issue of race. No one can help being white or being black, and so it seems to follow that it is wicked, unfair, and unreasonable to disqualify a person from any consideration just because he is white or black. This, the advocates of color-blindness declare, is what made Jim Crow law heinous, and it is what makes affirmative action just as heinous.

The force of this consideration is enhanced because it seems to account for one peculiar harmfulness of racial discrimination—its effect on self-respect and self-esteem. For racial discrimination makes some black people hate their color, and succeeds in doing so because color cannot be changed. Furthermore, a racially conscious society has made color seem an important part of the individual's very essence, and since color is immutable it is easily susceptible to this approach. As a result, the black individual may come, in the end, to hate even himself. Even religion is here a dubious consolation. For if God makes us black or white, to the religious black that by which he is marked may come to seem a curse by the Almighty, and he himself therefore essentially evil.

Of course, there are strategies that attempt to circumvent these effects of racial discrimination, but their weaknesses seem to confirm the need for color-blindness. For example, some black people concede that black is bad and ugly, but attempt to soften the effects of this concession by insisting that black is only "skin deep," we are all brothers beneath the skin, and the body, which is black and ugly, is no part of and does not sully the soul, which is the real self and is good. Thus, black people sometimes protested that although their skins were black, their souls were white, which is to say, good. There is truth to this feeling, in that nothing is more certain than that neither a black nor a white skin can make a person good or bad. Yet it is not a wholly successful approach to the problem of color. It requires that the black person believe that he is in some sense a ghost, which he can believe only if he is a lunatic. Another strategy is put forth by Black Nationalism. The black nationalist agrees with the racists' view that his color is an important and integral part of his self, but affirms, in opposition to the racists, that it has value. This strategy, which is exemplified by the slogans "black is beautiful" and "black and proud," has the obvious advantage of stimulating pride and self-confidence. Nevertheless, it is no panacea. For one thing, it has to contend with the powerful propaganda stating that black is *not* beautiful. And there is a more subtle problem. Since the black cannot choose *not* to be black, he cannot be altogether confident that he would choose to *be* black, nor, consequently, does he really place a special value in being black. Thus, some people, black and white, have expressed the suspicion that the slogan "black is beautiful" rings hollow, like the words of the man who protests too loudly that he loves the chains he cannot escape. In this respect the black who can pass as white has an advantage over the black who cannot. For, though he cannot choose not to be black, he can choose not to be *known* to be black.

## The Responsibility Criterion

A final argument in favor of legal color-blindness is related to, and further develops, the point that people do not choose to be, and cannot avoid being, black or white. This links the question of color-blindness to the protean idea of individual responsibility. Thus, William Frankena writes, that to use color as a fundamental basis for distributing "opportunities, offices, etc." to persons is "unjust in itself," because it is to distribute goods on the basis of a feature "which the individual has not done, and can do nothing about; we are treating people differently in ways that profoundly affect their lives because of differences for which they have no responsibility."[6] Since this argument requires that people be treated differently in ways which profoundly affect their lives only on the basis of features for which they are responsible, I call it the responsibility criterion.

The responsibility criterion also seems to make the principle of color-blindness follow from principles of equal opportunity. Joel Feinberg takes it to be equivalent to the claim that "properties can be the grounds of just discrimination between persons only if those persons had a fair opportunity to acquire or avoid them."[7] This implies that to discriminate between persons on the basis of a feature for which they can have no responsibility is to violate the principle of fair opportunity. But color (or sex) is a feature of persons for which they can have no responsibility.

The responsibility criterion may seem innocuous because, though, strictly interpreted it supports the case for color-blindness, loosely interpreted it leaves open the possibility that color-conscious policies are justifiable. Thus, Frankena himself allows that color could be an important basis of distribution of goods and offices if it served "as [a] reliable sign[s] of some Q, like ability or merit, which is more justly employed as a touchstone for the treatment of individuals."[8] This sounds like a reasonable compromise and is enough to support some arguments for color-conscious policies. For example, it could support the argument that black and white children should go to the same schools because being white is a reliable sign of being middle-class, and black children, who are often lower-class, learn better when their peers are middle-class. Similarly, it might support the argument that preferential hiring is compensation for the harm of being discriminated against on the basis of color, and that being black is a reliable sign of having been harmed by that discrimination.

But however loosely it is interpreted, the responsibility criterion cannot be adduced in support of all reasons behind color-conscious policies. It cannot, for example, sustain the following argument, sketched by Ronald Dworkin, for preferential admission of blacks to medical school. "If quick hands count as 'merit' in the case of a prospective surgeon this is because quick hands will enable him to serve the public better and for no other reason. If a black skin will, as a matter of regrettable fact, enable another doctor to do a different medical job better, then that black skin is by the same token 'merit' as well."[9] What is proposed here is not that a black skin is a justifiable basis of discrimination because it is a reliable sign of merit or some other factor Q. A closely related argument does make such a proposal, viz., that blacks should be preferentially admitted to medical school because being black is a reliable sign of a desire to serve the black community. But this is not the argument that Dworkin poses. In the example quoted above what he suggests is that being black is in *itself* merit, or, at least, something very like merit.

According to the responsibility criterion, we ought not to give A a job in surgery rather than B, if A is a better surgeon than B only because he was born with quicker hands. For if we do, we treat A and B "differently in ways that profoundly affect their lives because of differences for which they have no responsibility." This is the kind of result which puts egalitarianism in disrepute. It entails the idea that we might be required to let fumblers do surgery and in general give jobs and offices to incompetents, and this is surely intolerable. But, as I plan to show, true egalitarianism has no such consequences. They are the result of applying the responsibility criterion, not egalitarian principles. Indeed, egalitarianism must scout the responsibility criterion as false and confused.

Egalitarians should notice first, that, while it invalidates the merit-based theories of distribution that they oppose, it also invalidates the need-based theories of distribution they favor. For, if people are born with special talents for which they are not responsible, they are also born with special needs for which they are not responsible. Consequently, if the responsibility criterion forbids choosing A over B to do surgery because A is a better surgeon because he was born with quicker hands, it also forbids choosing C rather than D for remedial education because C needs it more than D only because he was born with a learning disability and D was not.

At this point there may be objections. First, that the responsibility criterion was intended to govern only the distribution of income, not jobs and offices—in Feinberg's discussion, for example, this is made explicit. Second, that it does not mean that people should not be treated differently because of differences, good or bad, which they cannot help, but rather that people should not get less just because they are born without the qualities their society prizes or finds useful. This seems to be implied in Frankena's claim that justice should make the "same proportionate contribution to the best life for everyone" and that this may require spending more on those who are "harder to help"—probably the untalented—than on others. Qualified in these ways, the responsibility criterion becomes more plausible. It no longer implies, for example, that fumblers should be allowed to practice surgery, or that the blind be treated just like the sighted. But with these qualifications it also becomes almost irrelevant to the color-blind issue. For that issue is not only about how income should be distributed. It is also about how jobs and offices should be distributed.

Most jobs and offices are distributed to people in order to produce goods and services to a larger public. To that end, the responsibility criterion is irrelevant. For example, the purpose of admitting people to medical schools and law schools is to provide the community with good medical and legal service. It does not matter whether those who provide them are responsible for having the skills by virtue of which they provide the goods, or whether the positions they occupy are "goods" to them. No just society makes a person a surgeon just because he is responsible for his skills or because making him a surgeon will be good for him. It makes him a surgeon because he will do good surgery.

Accordingly, it may be perfectly just to discriminate between persons on the basis of distinctions they are not responsible for having. It depends on whether or not the discrimination serves a worthy end. It may be permissible for the admissions policies of professional schools to give preference to those with higher scores, even if their scores are higher than others only because they have higher native ability (for which they cannot, of course, be considered responsible), if the object is to provide the community with good professional service. And, given the same object, if for some reason a black skin, whether or not it can be defined as merit, helps a black lawyer or doctor to provide good legal or medical service to black people who would otherwise not have access to it, or avail themselves of it, it is difficult to see how there can be a principled objection to admissions policies which prefer people with black skins— though, again, they are not responsible for the quality by virtue of which they are preferred.

## Justice and the Responsibility Criterion

A further point needs to be made in order to vindicate color-conscious policies. The principles of justice are distributive: Justice is concerned not only with increasing the total amount of a good a society enjoys, but also with how that good should be distributed among individuals. Generally, judicial principles dictate that people who are similar in ways deemed relevant to the issue of justice, such as in needs or rights, should get equal amounts of a good, and people who are dissimilar in these regards should get unequal amounts of the good. In terms of these principles certain laws and rules must be considered unjust which would not otherwise be thought unjust. Consider, for example, a policy for admitting persons to medical school which resulted in better and better medical service for white people, but worse and worse medical service for black people. This policy would be unjust, however great the medical expertise—certainly a good—it produced, unless color is relevant to the receiving of good medical attention.

In a case like this, where it is not, the theoretical circumstance outlined by Dworkin, in which black skin might be considered a "merit," becomes viable. It is true, of course, that color is not, precisely, merit. But to insist on strict definition in this context is to cavil. The point is that if black clients tend to trust and confide more in black lawyers and doctors, then color—functioning as merit—enables a good to be produced and distributed according to some principle of justice.

If these considerations are sound, then the responsibility criterion thoroughly misconstrues the reasons for which racial discrimination is unjust. Racial discrimination against blacks is unjust because it does not enable goods to be produced and distributed according to principles of justice. It is not unjust because black people do not choose to be black, cannot *not* be black, or are not responsible for being black. This is completely irrelevant. For example, a policy denying university admission to people who parted their hair on the right side would be unjust because the way in which people part their hair is irrelevant to a just policy of school admission. It does not matter in the least, in relation to the nature and object of education, that they choose how they part their hair. Similarly, even if black people could choose to become white, or could all easily pass as white, a law school or medical school that excluded blacks because they were black would still act unjustly. Nothing would have changed.

The arguments in support of color-blindness tend to make the harmfulness of discrimination depend on the difficulty of avoiding it. This is misleading. It diverts attention from the potential harmfulness of discrimination that *can* be avoided and brings the specious responsibility criterion into play. Suppose again, for example, that a person is denied admission to law school because he parts his hair on the right side. Though he, far more easily than the black person, can avoid being unfairly discriminated *against*, he does not thereby more easily avoid being the object, indeed, in a deeper sense, the victim, of unfair discrimination. If he parts his hair on the left side he will presumably be admitted to law school. But then he will have knowingly complied with a foolish and unjust rule and this may well make him expedient and servile. Of course, he will not be harmed to the same extent and in the same way as the victim of racial discrimination. For example, he probably will not hate himself. Unlike color, the cause of his ill-treatment is too easily changed for him to conceive of it as essential to himself. Moreover, if he chooses to keep his hair parted on the right side and thus to forego law school, he *knows* that he is not going to law school because he freely chose to place a greater value on his integrity or on his taste in hairstyles than on a legal education. He knows this because he knows he could have chosen to change his hairstyle. As I noted earlier, this opportunity for self-assertion, and thus for self-knowledge and self-confidence, is denied the black who is discriminated against on the basis of his color.

Nevertheless, as I stated earlier, the considerations that stem from applying the responsibility criterion to a judgment of racial discrimination are secondary to understanding its peculiar harmfulness. Suppose, for example, that a person is not admitted to medical school to train to be a surgeon because he was born without fingers. If all the things he wants require that he have fingers, he may conceivably come to suffer the same self-hatred and self-doubt as the victim of racial discrimination. Yet his case is different, and if he attends to the difference, he will not suffer as the victim of racial discrimination suffers. The discrimination that excludes him from the practice of surgery is not denigrating his interests because they are his. It is a policy that takes into account a just object—the needs of others in the community for competent surgery. Allowing him to be a surgeon would rate other, equally important, interests below his. But racial discrimination excludes its victims from opportunities on the basis of a belief that their interests are ipso facto less important than the interests of whites. The man without fingers may regret not being born differently, but he cannot resent how he is treated. Though his ambitions may be thwarted, he himself is still treated as a moral equal. There is no attack on his self-respect. Racial discrimination, however, undermines its victims' self-respect through their awareness that they are considered morally inferior. The fact that racial discrimination, or any color-conscious policy, is difficult to avoid through personal choice merely adds to its basic harmfulness if it is in the first place unjust, but is not the *reason* for its being unjust.

It remains to consider Feinberg's claim that if people are discriminated for or against on the basis of factors for which they are not responsible the equal opportunity principle is contravened. This I concede. In particular, I concede that color-conscious policies giving preference to blacks place an insurmountable obstacle in the path of whites, and since such obstacles reduce opportunities, such policies may make opportunities unequal. But this gives no advantage to the advocates of color-blind policies. For giving preference to the competent has exactly the same implications as giving preference to blacks. It, too, places obstacles in the paths of some people, this time the untalented, and just as surely makes opportunities unequal. Consequently, an advocate of color-blindness cannot consistently oppose color-conscious policies on the grounds that they contravene equal opportunity and at the same time support talent-conscious policies. Nor, finally, does my concession raise any further difficulty with the issue of equal opportunity. As I argue later, equal opportunity is not a fundamental principle of justice, but is derived from its basic principles. Often these basic principles require that opportunities be made more equal. Invariably, however, these same principles require that the process of equalization stop before a condition of perfect equality of opportunity is reached.

To conclude, adopting a color-blind principle entails adopting a talent-blind principle, and since the latter is absurd, so also is the former. Or, in other words, differences in talent, and differences in color, are, from the point of view of justice, on a par. Either, with equal propriety, can be the basis of a just discrimination. Consequently, the color-blind principle is not as simple, straightforward, or self-evident as many of its advocates seem to feel it is. Color-conscious policies can conceivably be just, just as talent-conscious policies can conceivably be—and often are—just. It depends on the circumstances.

# 2

# *Black Progress and the Free Market*

## The Legacy of Booker T. Washington

Booker T. Washington once told the story of an old colored doctor who employed somewhat peculiar methods of treatment. One of the doctor's patients was a rich old lady who thought she had cancer, and who for twenty years had enjoyed the luxury of being treated by the doctor. As the doctor became—mainly thanks to the cancer—pretty rich himself, he decided to send one of his boys to medical school. After graduating the young doctor returned home, and his father took a vacation. While he was away, the old lady called in the young doctor. He treated her, and within a few weeks the "cancer" was cured. When the old doctor returned and found his patient well, he was outraged. He reminded his son that he had put him through high school, college, and medical school on that cancer. "Let me tell you, son," the old man concluded, "you have started all wrong. How do you expect to make a living practicing medicine in that way?"[1]

Now Booker T. was not in the habit of telling amusing stories just for the fun of it. He always told them to make a point. The point he was making in this case was, as he went on to put it, "there is a certain class of race-problem solvers who don't want the patient to get well, because as long as the disease holds out they have not only an easy means of making a living, but also an easy medium through which to make themselves prominent before the public."[2] The worst offenders, Washington thought, were certain colored people. These people, he charged, make "a business of keeping the troubles, the wrongs and the hardships of the Negro race before the public . . . partly because they want sympathy, and partly because it pays. [They] do not want the Negro to lose his grievances because they do not want to lose their jobs."[3]

This barbed observation, the result of Washington's philosophy of stoicism and self-help, suitably coarsened for late 20th-century wrangles, continues to be the weapon of choice in the armory of his contemporary representatives. Walter E. Williams, one-time student of Thomas Sowell's and now professor of economics at George Mason University, recently swung this roundhouse: ". . . a whole lot of people have their livelihoods staked on the existence of a so-called 'disadvantaged' class of people. I'm not only talking about the 'poverty pimps' who administer and manage these programs. I'm also talking about professors who get federal grants to study poverty, and then meet in Miami in the winter to discuss the problems of the poor."[4]

This outburst was ignited by a theory about racial subordination and racial progress, shared by Sowell and Williams, that is virtually identical to Washington's. The centerpiece of that theory is the proposition that the free market system is the only sure road to black elevation, and correspondingly, that governmental interference in the free market is the chief cause of black subordination. Williams puts this most clearly: The "basic problem of blacks in America," he writes, is "severe government-imposed restraints on voluntary exchange. Or put another way: the diminution of free markets in the United States."[5]

Surrounding this fundamental proposition are various other propositions of a consequential, ancillary, and supportive nature. Perhaps the most provocative of these is that racial discrimination does not explain, and is not even an important part of the explanation, of black subordination; according to this theory, after governmental interference in the economy, the most important explanation of black subordination is that black people lack those valuable personal qualities the economy demands. This has the corollary that, if blacks are subordinated, it is because of their own inadequacies. While this inference does not blame the victim, as some have misleadingly charged, it does succeed in absolving everyone from blame. Washington expressed his allegiance to this view as well as his faith in the free market eloquently, if obliquely, in his famous "Atlanta Exposition Address": "No race that has anything to contribute to the markets of the world," he declared, "is long in any degree ostracized."[6] And even Thomas Sowell, who is not noted for his delicacy, hides the unpleasant truth in a bland generality: "What determines how rapidly a group moves ahead," he writes, "is not discrimination but the fit between the elements of its culture and the requirements of the economy."[7]

If this proposition is true, it follows at once that an essential condition of black progress is that blacks acquire what the market demands. When he wanted to, Washington could strip away the frills as well as anybody: "Harmony will come," he observed, "in proportion as the black man gets something the white man wants."[8] Sowell, the professional economist, makes the same point less trenchantly: "To get ahead," he writes, "you have to have some ability to work, some ability at entrepreneurship or something else that the society values."[9]

Now, among the things the "white man wants," or, if you will, "the society values," will be certain skills, and accordingly, Washington and Sowell both stress the need for blacks to acquire such skills.[10] But, they explicitly deny that blacks must have a *high level* of skills in order to progress. According to them, even a low level of saleable skills—or incompetence—cannot explain black unemployment. Competence and incompetence are relative matters. Hardly anyone is so incompetent that there is no work he can do, and no one ready to pay him to do it. Consequently, even assuming black incompetence, black advocates of the free market must still explain the disproportionately high rate of black unemployment. Part of their explanation is that it is the fault of government interference. For example, Williams accuses the government, through its minimum-wage laws (and these are, perhaps, the chief bugbear of black free market supporters), of interfering with the freedom of blacks to work for wages employers are prepared to pay for the use of their skills. They admit, of course, that these wages will be low. But this dovetails neatly with their partiality for the rags-to-riches approach to life. Low-paying jobs, they argue, are the bottom rung of the ladder on which countless European and Asian immigrants have climbed out of poverty.

Washington first outlined the essentials of this theory of progress. It was one of his favorite themes that the acquisition of basic, humble skills would be sufficient to start blacks on the road to elevation. Black radicals, usually from a relatively safe berth in the North, accused him of "accommodating" his theory to white prejudice, but the fact that Sowell, who accommodates no one, makes the same claim shows that they were mistaken. While Washington evidently arrived at this view intuitively, Sowell comes to it via the study of history. According to Sowell, history reveals that a high level of education is not a necessary condition of progress. Even the immigrant Jews, he argues, who did arrive in the country with a long tradition of learning, did not rise from poverty because of that learning.[11] And, he continues, education, past a basic minimum, being unnecessary to social elevation, much compulsory education is unjustified. "Everyone recognizes," he writes, "the need for literacy and other educational basics. But compulsory attendance laws have been applied to keep youths in school long past the time necessary to learn these things."[12] Their effect, he asserts, is simply to keep black youths out of the labor force, and blacks as a whole from starting the long march to affluence.

But although higher education and greater skills may not be necessary to advancement, it does not follow that they cannot accelerate it. Why then, the skeptic may ask, cannot black youths use compulsory secondary education and the opportunities for higher education, to acquire skills which will enable them to steal a march on history? Sowell's negative response to this idea reveals the most dismaying aspect of his theory. Most black youths, he argues, do not and cannot use their years in school to acquire exceptional skills and learning. They simply lack the discipline for it. Learning "many of the most valuable intellectual skills," he writes, is "dry, tedious, frustrating" and a cause of "headaches." "How many black students are prepared to accept headaches after twelve years of coasting through inferior public schools?" he asks, and he things that the question "answers itself."[13] Moreover, he believes, the universities know this very well. They recruit black students only to "keep government money coming in" and with no real hope of educating them. At many universities which have drives to recruit more minority students, those students "are flunking out in droves," or else special easy courses are cooked up for them. The result: "Never has it been easier to graduate from college as a complete ignoramus." Moreover, he opines, basically the same process occurs during secondary education.[14]

Sowell believes that this problem of attitude and discipline has hampered black education since emancipation. Though the newly-freed slaves eagerly sought education, teaching them was a "trial." They were convinced that "education was a good thing" but they had no conception of the "disciplined work" it required.[15] If Sowell's theory of what hinders black progress is sound, there is no question of their stealing a march on history. Blacks as a group must start at the bottom. As Washington had warned prophetically: "it is at the bottom of life we must begin and not at the top."[16] Opportunities for education can speed a group's progress, but education cannot allow them to skip a stage of that progression. What a generation can learn in school is limited by the attitude to education it has absorbed from its parents. There is hope, for the "first generation to break out of the vicious cycle of undereducation tends to raise the next generation to still higher levels," but the process, which is thus cumulative, is also gradual.[17] Sowell aptly describes it as an "intergenerational relay race," and, like a die-hard Marxist denying that the "stages of society" can be skipped, he is consistently emphatic about his law of history.[18]

But as Sowell realizes, minimum wage laws, compulsory school attendance, and other policies through which do-gooders in government try, and predictably fail, to circumvent history, cannot explain black backwardness. Since these laws did not always exist, why, unlike other groups, did not blacks climb the free market ladder when it was there? Part of Sowell's answer is that many blacks *did* climb the ladder when it was there. Their descendants are most of the middle-class blacks of today. The majority· of blacks did not climb the ladder because they lived in the rural South, and only relatively recently migrated to the great urban centers in the North. The chance to get on the ladder used to be found there, but after the great wave of European immigrants the government had taken away the ladder. The rest of Sowell's answer is, however, at a more fundamental level and involves blacks' attitudes to menial jobs.

And, as always, Washington said it first. Because of two hundred years of slavery, he lamented, for generations the "Negro's idea of freedom" was "freedom from restraint and work."[19] We must learn, he resolved, "to dignify and glorify common labor."[20] Sowell adds little to Washington's diagnosis: ". . . blacks who suffered from slavery," he writes, "also suffered from its aftermath in that many became hypersensitized against menial jobs. That's tragic because most of the groups in America that started out destitute and rose to affluence began in menial jobs."[21]

## Black Libertarianism

There are, of course, differences between Washington and his disciples. The one which emerges most clearly in Sowell's work is his belief that it is wrong for government to interfere in the liberties of its citizens, even when this may seem the way to secure some valuable end. This fundamental view is obscured because Sowell usually advances empirically based arguments to the effect that the end in question will best be secured by policies which do not interfere with citizens' liberties. But when these empirical arguments are challenged, he invariably falls back on the moral argument that it is morally wrong to interfere with citizens' liberties. For example, Sowell is a strong advocate of the voucher system, an idea originally popularized by economist Milton Friedman, one of Sowell's mentors.[22] The system is one whereby, for each school-age child, parents receive a voucher worth the average cost to the taxpayer of educating a child, and use these vouchers to pay for the education of their children at any school that is willing to accept them, public or private, and at any location. Advocates of this scheme defend it both on the moral ground that it breaks the monopoly of the public school system, thus widening the range of choices open to parents and increasing their liberty, and on the empirical ground that it makes schooling more effective. Sowell, at least, seems to feel that the moral justification alone is sufficient. Thus, when Hugh Price of the *New York Times* opposed the voucher system, arguing that management improvements could make public schools more effective, Sowell conceded the point, but fell back on the idea of liberty as the basis of his defense of the system. "I am not sure," he responded to Price, "whether that's an argument against vouchers versus compelling people to go to a particular monopoly."[23]

What is so controversial about this? It is part of conventional wisdom, seemingly enshrined, moreover, in the U.S. Constitution, that a government ought not to transgress on individual liberties for utilitarian advantages. But before anyone thinks of invoking this truism in order to render Sowell's view comfortably commonplace, he should be clear of the nature and extent of the individual liberties Sowell believes in.

These liberties are the liberties of a night watchman state. Walter Williams puts this clearly: "I would confine government to performing only its legitimate function," he notes, "namely defending us against foreign and domestic adversaries who would like to take our lives and our private property."[24] In this view, the right to private property, in particular the right to keep what one has, as Locke put it, "mixed one's labor with," becomes the main concern of justice. No one could have put this better than Williams, when, for all the world like Thrasymachus showing Socrates the plain truth about justice, he stunned a panel on social justice held in New York by the Manhattan Institute for Policy Research with this blunt definition of justice: "I keep what I produce, and you keep what you produce."[25]

Given this account of the nature of individual rights, many of the functions people have become used to government performing, and ostensibly performing to secure their rights—to education and welfare, for example—are really instances of transgression, for utilitarian purposes, against individual liberties. Again I quote from Williams, who has, more than Sowell, inherited Washington's gift for the earthy example: "Here is a poor lady that needs teeth. I could walk up to you with a gun and say, 'Give me your money so I can give this old lady some teeth.' That is robbery and it's unjust. It doesn't change anything when, poof! the government comes to me and says, 'Mr. Williams that money you were going to spend to plant trees you will now give to me and it will go to that toothless old lady'—it's pretty callous to forcibly deprive me of the fruits of my labor for the benefit of some other individual who didn't sweat my sweat. I don't consider that social justice."[26]

What is more, argue Sowell and Williams—and here both their moral and their economic arguments against governmental intervention in the economy happily coincide—even when government transgresses against individual rights from benevolent motives, it is usually not successful in delivering the utilitarian advantages it has transgressed against rights to secure. And, they remind us—who should not need reminding—as often as not government transgresses against rights, or permits transgression, from malevolent motives. "Black people were enslaved in the United States," Williams notes, "because government did not do its proper job of protecting their individual rights."[27] On these grounds Sowell and Williams echo what is perhaps the most characteristic aspect of Washington's social program—his opposition to political activism and to enlisting government help for black progress. "I would urge people not to look at government as the benefactor of blacks," Williams warns. But he cannot resist a dig at the "poverty pimps." Government, he allows, is "the benefactor of elite blacks who get jobs controlling other blacks." But, these opportunists apart: ". . . for blacks in particular, and Americans in general, what is needed is less government and more freedom."[28]

Now, since governmental enforcement of color-conscious policies interferes with the free market, when Sowell and Williams attack governmental interference on the grounds that it transgresses rights and is counter-productive, they are, by inference, attacking the enforcement of color-conscious policies. And, indeed, they are among the most potent forces against special treatment for blacks. Their views have received enormous attention in newspapers and magazines and they have become pundits of race relations and racial policies. Sowell, in particular, has become the most quoted man in America on racial issues, with white conservatives using his candid words about black laziness and incompetence to tell the kind of harsh truth delicacy forbids them from telling themselves.

Of course, all this is part of an intellectual and popular revival of conservative and libertarian philosophies. The election of Ronald Reagan made unmistakable the fact that the revival was on a popular level, but more significant was the publication in 1975 of Robert Nozick's *Anarchy, State and Utopia*, which made the intellectual respectability of the revival equally unmistakable. In this book, Nozick, a professor of philosophy at Harvard, presents a series of brilliant and sophisticated arguments in defence of the once distained libertarian philosophy, of a minimal state—one in which government is limited to protecting its citizens from fraud, force, and violence, and to securing contracts—and by implication of Williams's "I keep what I produce and you keep what you produce" definition of social justice. As Randall Rothenberg observed in *Esquire*,

Nozick is "the intellectual bedrock behind latter-day libertarianism, a do-your-own-thing, laissez-faire capitalist darling of the Right."[29]

However, there is a fundamental difference between Nozick's projects, on the one hand, and those of Sowell and Williams on the other. Nozick can respond to certain objections to his libertarianism with sangfroid. When, for example, opponents ask what his minimal state would do about poor people, Nozick answers comfortably, "charity." But Sowell and Williams cannot give this answer. They are proud men and they scorn the idea of charity for blacks. Indeed, their most vehement denunciations of color-conscious policies are based on the conviction that they are charity. Accordingly, the task they have set themselves is different, and in many ways more difficult, than the task Nozick set himself. Nozick is concerned with demonstrating that "the minimal state is the most extensive state that can be justified. Any state more extensive violates people's rights."[30] He does not have to demonstrate that the minimal state provides the best opportunity for a subordinated minority like blacks to progress. Sowell and Williams, however, have to demonstrate just that. I believe that this task is too much for even their considerable powers. They are not able to prove their empirical claims, they do not adhere to their moral claims, and their moral claims—both those they hold ostensibly and those they retreat to—are unacceptable. My object, in this chapter, is to confute black conservatism and the whole Booker T. Washington philosophy of racial uplift, once and for all.

## Discrimination and Black Subordination

As I noted earlier, perhaps the most provocative of the claims Sowell and Williams make in support of their theory that the free market system is the only sure path to black advancement, is that racial discrimination is not a decisive cause of black subordination. But although this is their official view, the one trumpeted to the press,[31] it is not their real view. Their real view, at least the view for which they provide argument, is that *in a free market*, racial discrimination is not a decisive cause of black subordination. And this shows how careless—and misleading—their official view is. For since, as they frequently insist and lament, markets have rarely been free, their real view provides absolutely no support for their official view. On the contrary, it suggests that their official view is false.

Sowell and Williams imply that it is the absence of free markets that permits racial discrimination to have its effects, and, consequently, that it is the absence of a free market that is the real cause of black subordination in this country. But, even if it is true that a free market tends to eliminate the effects of discrimination, as they say, it does not follow that the absence of a free market is the cause of black subordination since rigidly enforced equal opportunity laws might, equally, tend to eliminate the effects of discrimination. Ideology, not logic, seems to determine Sowell's and Williams's choice of the main cause of black subordination.

Consider the *piece de resistance* of their argument: the free market tends to eliminate the effects of discrimination. Sowell distinguishes two main kinds of discrimination. In the first—pure discrimination—"people are treated differently because of group membership as such."[32] This is the kind of discrimination in which blacks are not hired because, although they are the most qualified, employers view them with "antipathy or hostility." Williams, in a more perspicuous discussion of the same phenomenon, calls it "racial preference."[33] In the second kind of discrimination Sowell distinguishes—perceptual discrimination—people are treated differently because "the group is perceived as less capable or less responsible by employers, landlords or other potential transactors."[34] This is the kind of discrimination which results in blacks not being hired because, although they may be the most qualified, and although employers may not view them with antipathy or hostility, they are considered generally less capable or less responsible than whites. Williams calls this kind of discrimination racial prejudice, using the word "prejudice" to stress that this kind of discrimination involves essentially an "attempt to minimize information costs,"[35] that is, to minimize the cost of actually obtaining information about individuals.

Sowell and Williams have no difficulty in demonstrating that the free market tends to eliminate pure discrimination and some kinds of perceptual discrimination. If an employer engages in these kinds of discrimination, he hires inferior workers for the same wage he would pay superior workers. If all employers do this, none gains an edge on the others. But if some don't, even if for no better reason than that their greed outweighs their prejudice, they, by hiring the superior workers other employers reject, gain a considerable edge over the others. These will either have to change their policies or drop out of business. Since few employers want to discriminate more than they want to stay in business, most come to their senses. In this way the competitive free market functions to remove the effects of discrimination.

This argument, as Sowell observes, "assumes that (1) employers are attracted by prospects of unusually high profits and that (2) there is no effective collusion against a particular group."[36] Objections can hardly be raised to either assumption. The first is obviously true, and the second is part of the definition of a free market. Moreover, Sowell argues, attempted collusions are not likely to be effective for long. It is costly to police a hiring system so it is certain to exclude the unwanted group, though Sowell allows that these costs would be relatively low for blacks because their color makes them easy to identify; and there are temptations to break such agreements, for profits can be made by hiring the superior workers of the excluded group.[37]

Sowell and Williams believe, however, that government interference in the free market, even with the best of intentions, is likely to be far more effective than collusion in suppressing the beneficient effect of the market in eliminating discrimination, and is for that reason much more to be feared. Their favorite example is a government-imposed minimum wage. "A higher wage rate," Sowell writes, "simultaneously attracts more job applicants and reduces the number of persons whom it is profitable to hire. . . . The net result is that the number of jobs decreases as the number of applicants increases. One consequence of this is that ethnic discrimination becomes less costly—perhaps free—to the employer, even in a profit-seeking business."[38]

These arguments are supposed to have the sort of effect on common sense that so many arguments in physical science have. Common sense gives its verdict on a particular phenomenon, but science magisterially controverts that verdict, and, bowing before its logic, ordinary mortals must abandon their belief in common sense. However, unfortunately for Sowell and Williams we do not have to give up the commonsensical view that discrimination is an important cause of black subordination, because their logic is not the logic of science. There are instances and kinds of discrimination which are not likely to be cured by the panacea of the free market.

The first and most obvious is discrimination in the non-profit sector, which includes universities and government-regulated industries, and most important, government itself, both local and national. Sowell is, of course, aware of this case. For government, he observes, "racial discrimination is free."[39] Indeed this fact is his *coup de grace* against advocates of government regulation of industry and a more than minimal state. But it does not support his conclusion. There are reasons for expanding government regulation of industry and government itself, in particular reasons that stem from moral principles to which he ostensibly holds allegiance, for example, taking citizens' liberties seriously. I hope to demonstrate that, as a result, even if Sowell is right that discrimination is free in government, he still cannot consistently urge the abolishment of government regulation of industry and the idea of a minimal state. On the contrary, I will argue that the principles he ostensibly holds imply that there should be an increase in government regulation of industry, and a more than minimal state, and that we should depend on methods other than those of the free market, perhaps even the hated color-conscious policies, to eliminate discrimination.

Another kind of discrimination that is resistant to the influence of the free market is discrimination—either pure or perceptual—against highly trained blacks. Sowell also acknowledges this. He writes, "In situations where long and costly preparations are necessary to be able to enter an excluded area [or] years of training to become a skilled craftsman or a classical musician—the very fact that the exclusion exists tends to prevent any backlog of qualified people from building up, and therefore reduces the cost of those who maintain the exclusion." What is more, he admits that this consideration, which gains in importance in "blue-collar skills which are highly specific," may also explain why "Negroes have had far less success in breaking into skilled blue-collar fields."[40] How anyone can make these admissions, and simultaneously proclaim that "culture, not discrimination decides who gets ahead," boggles the mind. One's equanimity returns only after one reminds oneself of the power of an ideology to confuse thought.

Sowell and Williams focus their gaze, unaccountably, on the tendency of the employer to discriminate. But what of the tendency of the public to discriminate? The idea that employers may be racially prejudiced but that the public is color-blind is perfectly ludicrous. As anyone knows, who has even the slightest acquaintance with the significance of race in America, the public is as prone to pure or perceptual discrimination as the employers. Because of this the employer may have to engage in a type of discrimination which has not, so far, been defined. An employer may decide that he had better not hire blacks, even if he neither dislikes them nor believes them to be incompetent, because he perceives that the public would rather not be served by blacks, either because *it* dislikes them (pure discrimination) or thinks them incompetent (perceptual discrimination). What is worse, precisely the same argument that Sowell and Williams use to show that the free market compels employers not to discriminate can be used to show instead that the free market compels employers to discriminate. For, just as there are situations in which the free market makes it costly to discriminate, in the situation cited the free market makes it costly not to discriminate.

It could be objected that discrimination is not as widespread among the public as this argument assumes. But, whether or not this is true, it is not an option available to Sowell and Williams, because they insist that discrimination *is* widespread. In fact, confusingly, they see its prevalence as the cornerstone of their case against the efficacy of discrimination. "Oxygen is so pervasive in the world," Williams observes, "that it alone cannot explain very much. Similarly with discrimination. Discrimination is so pervasive that it alone cannot explain much."[41]

Given the pervasiveness of discrimination—a point on which, as I noted, Sowell and Williams are consistently emphatic—the situation outlined above is more crucial to the issue than the cases of employer discrimination that Sowell focuses on. He ignores it in *Markets and Minorities,* but does note it in his earlier book, *Race and Economics.* "If a group is paid less, or employed or promoted less often, because it is disliked by employers, co-workers and customers," he writes there, "then it may continue to suffer low wages and higher unemployment rates even if its current capabilities are equal to those of others." And how does the champion of the free market deal with this most pertinent point? I will let him rebut his own views: "The functioning of the market," Sowell admits, "will not tend to eliminate such differentials."[42]

Less ideologically laced arguments for the harmlessness of discrimination are no more persuasive. Consider for example the views of William Julius Wilson in his book *The Declining Significance of Race,* published in 1978, which, for a brief time, stole the limelight from Sowell.[43] According to Wilson, because of recent complex changes in government, the economy, and society, racial discrimination is not now an obstacle to black progress. His view must not be identified or confused with that of Sowell and Williams. Wilson does not share Sowell's and Williams's faith in the free market. In particular, he does not believe that the market eliminates discrimination, nor, accordingly, that government intervention in the market is always counter-productive. Indeed, he believes that sometimes government intervention in the market decisively enhances a group's progress. Thus, while Wilson shares Sowell's view that it is "class-related disabilities," that is, lack of skills and poor attitudes to work, not race, which hold back blacks, and that special treatment for blacks is mistaken and wrong, he does not share Sowell's view that the best policy is for the government to step back and let the market work its magic. On the contrary, he calls for massive government intervention in the market. Sowell is the darling of the color-blind right, and Wilson is the darling of the color-blind left.

What then are the arguments Wilson uses to support his view? He admits that racial discrimination persists unabated in the sociopolitical system—that is in the competition for "public schools, municipal political systems and residential areas"—but he thinks that it is harmless because it has virtually disappeared in the economic order, that is, in the competition for jobs, and discrimination in the sociopolitical order "has far less effect on individual or group access to those opportunities and resources that are centrally important to life survival than antagonism in the economic order."[44]

This is a terrible argument. From the assumption that discrimination in the sociopolitical order is less important than discrimination in the economic order, it cannot be inferred that discrimination in the socio-political order is not important. Further, the implication that school and residential segregation, though persistent, is harmless is contradicted by Wilson's own view. Even if he is right in his belief that job discrimination harms more than school or residential discrimination, if black children are restricted to poor schools and ghettos, where they are poorly educated and exposed to bad influences, they will not acquire the skills or attitudes which would enable them to get and hold jobs. Hence, if, as Wilson seems to believe, it is not having decent jobs which fundamentally destroys the black members of the underclass, then school and residential discrimination is—indirectly—just as harmful as job discrimination.

## Justice and Discrimination

We have seen that there are numerous gaps, often admitted, as well as flaws and contradictions, in the arguments Sowell, Williams, and Wilson make in support of the claim that discrimination is not an important cause of black subordination. And a closer study of their account of discrimination reveals subtler confusions in their discussion of discrimination and the inconsistency of their moral position.

We recall that, in "perceptual discrimination," or "prejudice" to use Williams's preferred term, persons perceive the group discriminated against as "less capable or less responsible." This perception could be mistaken. It might be that the group discriminated against is as capable and responsible as other groups. But we cannot assume that it is. As Sowell notes, "There is too much evidence of group differences . . . to arbitrarily assume that they are homogenous in all the relevant variables when they transact in labor, housing or other markets. It is an empirical question not an axiom."[45]

And we know, of course, how Sowell answers the empirical question about black group differences. Blacks, he maintains, are, as a group, not as capable and responsible as other groups. They earn low wages because "their share of the human capital of the country" is "desperately small," not only in saleable skills and formal education, but, more importantly, in "basic traits" such as "punctuality, efficiency and long term planning" which are valued by the economy. Blacks lack these traits in the first place because of the effects of slavery, and second because of being "limited to menial jobs for generations."[46] In many if not all cases of perceptual discrimination against blacks, therefore, the discrimination is based, as Williams puts it, on "the recognition of real differences."[47]

Much perceptual discrimination is immune to free market pressures. Indeed, according to the account of Sowell and Williams, it is the market which often engenders this kind of discrimination. This is because of the cost, to a potential employer, of acquiring knowledge of any individual's productivity level. Since, by assumption, blacks are on the average less productive than whites, it may pay employers not to consider blacks for employment. As Williams observes, "physical attributes are easily observed and hence constitute a cheap form of information."[48] And, on the other hand, employers who take the trouble to acquire knowledge of individual productivity incur costs the others avoid, and put themselves at a competitive disadvantage. Hence, on precisely the same basis on which Sowell concludes that the market eliminates discrimination—the economic considerations of the employers—in this case, the market engenders discrimination.

Sowell tries to camouflage this further gap in his argument by maintaining that, although discrimination may be deleterious to exceptional blacks, it does not harm blacks as a group. "Where employment, renting, lending, or other transactions decisions are based on assessments that are accurate for the group average but inaccurate for the individual under consideration," he writes, "the windfall losses of those individuals underestimated by applying the group average are offset by windfall gains by those individuals over-estimated by applying the group average."[49] In this way Sowell hopes to bolster his claim that discrimination is not a barrier to black progress. But what of justice? Isn't the individual black who is excluded by this kind of discrimination unjustly treated? Significantly, Sowell agrees. "Choosing cost bearers on the basis of race or ethnicity," he concedes, "goes counter to general conceptions of justice."[50] Yet, he resists suggesting that employers bear the costs of acquiring the knowledge of individuals which would preclude this injustice. "No one does that in real life," he notes, "because costs of knowledge make it prohibitive."[51]

Now this is a fine thing for the senior partner of black libertarianism's dynamic duo to be saying! One would have expected Sowell to insist on the primacy of rights, and let efficiency go to the wall. But no, he insists on efficiency, and lets rights—black rights—go to the wall.[52]

Consequently, Sowell's position on this issue is, simply, that utility outweighs justice, and sometimes he makes the point explicitly. Thus, he thinks that John Rawls, a professor of philosophy at Harvard and author of the influential book *A Theory of Justice*, exaggerates the importance of justice. The proper attitude to justice, Sowell believes, is that of Adam Smith, whose *Wealth of Nations* spawned modern economics. "To Smith," Sowell observes, "some amount of justice was a prerequisite for any of the other features of society to exist." But Smith did not, in Sowell's view, countenance the "doctrinaire" view suggested by Rawls that "all increments of justice invariably outweighed increments of other things."[53] Sowell postulates an extreme case to show that sometimes utility outweighs justice and tries to use it to discredit Rawls. According to Rawls, he notes, "a policy that benefitted all of the human race except one person should not be adopted" because it would be unjust. But the extreme and farfetched nature of such arguments is their weakness. They cannot show that in less extreme cases utility outweighs justice. And the case of discrimination is among the less extreme cases. Surely, even if legislation compelling employers to be fairer does reduce efficiency, it does not spell disaster. On the contrary, by giving incentives to blacks to become productive—a possibility Sowell notes—it may in the long run increase efficiency.

It may be objected that since by assumption most blacks are unproductive relative to whites, perceptual discrimination only risks not employing the most productive, and so only risks being unfair. One response to this objection is that, in terms of decency, it is unfair not to treat a person as an individual. But Sowell's argument can be undone even if we concede that it is only unfair to deny the most productive employment. Let us look at how a fairly consistent libertarian treats the question of policies that risk unfairness of this kind.

Robert Nozick believes that it is not enough that those who engage in risky behavior compensate those whose rights they violate. A system which allows this still "has a cost in the uncompensated for fear of those potential victims who were not actual victims."[54] Because he takes rights seriously, as a libertarian should, Nozick thinks that people have a right to be free from fear that their rights will be trangressed against, and to protect that right Nozick argues that the state may prohibit behavior which risks violating rights. Now, employers who engage in the kind of discrimination which Sowell approves of on utilitarian grounds are certainly engaged in behavior which risks violating blacks' rights—even if we concede for the moment that no one can expect to be treated as an individual when he is looking for a job. For, since the correlation between blackness and low productivity is not exact, discrimination on those grounds risks violating the right of the black who happens to be the most productive person in a pool of applicants. Nor, since the average productivity of different pools of applicants varies, does it risk violating the rights only of truly "exceptional" blacks. Every black would be subject to the possibility that, no matter how poor his competition, his rights might be violated. And this means, in Nozick's terms, the right of every black not to fear that his rights are going to be violated would be traduced. This result doesn't even depend on the assumption that all employers practice discrimination. As Nozick acknowledges, for the general case the fact that society permits it at all is enough.[55] Every black person would have to live with the fear that his rights might be violated. (However, as I point out later in this chapter, Nozick's libertarian conception of "rights" may still be invidious to the idea of justice for blacks.)

Now this fear, and the violation of rights it involves, are, of course, the sources of that loss of self-confidence which advocates of preferential treatment have noted and tried to combat.[56] To deal with these effects one of two alternative policies—both of which are suggested by Nozick—is necessary. On the one hand, discrimination could be prohibited. On the other hand, if discrimination results in great savings for employers and industry, it could be permitted if its beneficiaries pay compensation to those whose rights they have violated. A libertarian who takes rights seriously must adopt either one of these alternatives. But black libertarians adopt neither, and so we must conclude that they do not take rights—especially black rights—seriously. They are ready to sacrifice black rights on the altar of efficiency, and they do not even ask for compensation. Furthermore, if they did adopt one of the alternatives they would seriously undermine their position on free market efficacy. For either alternative would require government expansion, the first by increasing government's regulation of industry, and the second by requiring the creation of a government department to oversee the payment of compensation.[57] This would also mean that Sowell and Williams would have to withdraw their contention that discrimination in government is unimportant. Their support for this view was their thesis that, although discrimination in government is unchecked by the market, government ought, in any case, to be minimal. But we have seen that even if government sticks to the libertarian definition of its function as protector of rights it is still apt to expand.

However, it will surely be objected that the whole of my attempt to show black libertarianism as contradictory rests on the assumption that libertarianism allows that blacks—and people in general—have the right to be considered for positions on the basis of their individual merits, or that the best candidate has a right to a position. This, it may be pointed out, is utterly false. The libertarian view rejects the idea that applicants for jobs have rights to be considered. These merit-based rights are liberal rights. But they are not libertarian rights. They conflict with the rights libertarianism holds sacrosanct—property rights—and hence do not exist for libertarians. The property owner, and therefore the employer, says the libertarian, has a right to hire whom he pleases. In this particular case he has a right to hire—deliberately—unproductive whites instead of productive blacks if he so wishes. If Sowell is right, if he does this he will bankrupt himself. But this too, libertarians say, is his right. Thus, it may seem that what I have shown is that libertarianism does not take liberal rights seriously but that I have not shown that libertarianism does not take libertarian rights seriously.

I admit that libertarianism gives the employer, or property owner, the right to hire whom he pleases, and specifically, if he desires, the right to discriminate invidiously against blacks. Although Sowell conceded that discrimination based on statistical generalizations was contrary to general "conceptions of justice," Williams, who is in many respects more consistent that Sowell, does say, quite explicitly, that if the employer is a property owner he can hire at his own discretion. "Trespassing across somebody else's lawn," he writes, "violates their property rights, but failing to hire a person, or failing to lend money to a person does not. I have every right not to lend you money if I don't want to, for whatever reason."[58]

Now, the main source of the attractiveness of the libertarian principles of justice is that, as Nozick observes, they are rooted in historical principles—what is just depends on what has happened. For this reason libertarians must, and do, take the right to compensation very seriously. Paradoxically, these are precisely the rights black libertarians reject. Among the main targets of their attack on color-conscious policies is the idea that they can be justified as compensation for past transgressions against black rights.

If libertarianism is correct in its belief that employers should be able to hire whomever they please, the transgressions for which blacks should be compensated should not include pure and perceptual discrimination, as these are often the bases for employers' decisions. But pure and perceptual discrimination are not, and have not been, the only transgressions against black rights: slavery, and state-enforced discrimination against blacks—interferences in the free market according to libertarian principles—are also transgressions against black rights. And accordingly libertarians, including black libertarians, should insist that these are transgressions. As I have noted, Williams denounces government for not doing its job in protecting black rights during slavery, and goes on to point out that after emancipation government continued not to do its job. Similarly, as part of his polemic against government, Sowell reminds us that it has been "quite active in suppressing the advancement of blacks in the United States," and gives civil rights organizations some credit for "getting the government off the backs of blacks, notably in the South with the Jim Crow laws, but in other parts of the country with other kinds of laws and other kinds of practices."[59] In view of these observations, it is somewhat surprising that he and Williams so vehemently condemn the claims of advocates for compensation for blacks.

Evidently sensing the contradiction in his argument, Sowell tries to show that he opposes the idea of compensating blacks for the harmfulness of slavery and the Jim Crow laws not because he opposes the idea of compensation, but because compensation is not owed in this case. One of the reasons for which blacks claim the right to compensation for slavery is that, since the property rights of slaves to "keep what they produce" were violated by the system of slavery to the general advantage of the white population, and, since the slaves would presumably have exercised their—libertarian—right to bequeath their property to their descendants, their descendants, the present black population, have rights to that part of the wealth of the present white population derived from violating black property rights during slavery. Against this reasoning Sowell argues that "much evidence" suggests that it is false to assume that the "white population as a whole derived economic benefits from the enslavement of blacks," and that it may even be false that slaveholders "actually profited by investing in slaves as compared to other investment opportunities available."[60]

His first point is irrelevant. A thief cannot rebut claims for compensation by arguing that his thievery was unprofitable, and even less by arguing that he could have found more profitable things to do with his time. Whether or not the white population as a whole benefited from slavery, it did support slavery. And Sowell's second point, by implying that several generations of slaveholders might have persisted in incurring needless costs threatens the very foundation of his theory that considerations of cost-effectiveness tend to eliminate discrimination. In fact, all that remains of Sowell's appeal to history to undo claims for compensation is the possibility that these claims should be small because economic output was small under slavery. But even that may be false. As Sowell himself allows, some contemporary economists argue that "slavery achieved more output than other economic systems under comparable circumstances."[61]

Sowell's objections aside, the actual property the slaves might have bequeathed to their descendants if their rights to keep and dispose of what they produced had been respected is the most modest of the bases for the claims to black compensation. If I am kidnapped and forced to work for subsistence at a primitive machine, and my meager earnings are then confiscated, I am not only owed compensation for the confiscation of those earnings. Far more importantly, I am also owed compensation for what I would have produced had I not been kidnapped; and if I am not around to claim my compensation, my descendants, to whom I would have bequeathed it, can claim it as their right. And this is the case in relation to the slaves and their descendants.

Sowell is aware of this but thinks that the claim can be confuted because no suitable baseline exists from which to measure the losses of the descendants of slaves. "Is that baseline where these descendants would be if their ancestors had never been enslaved?" he asks. If so, he writes, since the standard of living in black Africa is lower than that of black America, the "grotesque conclusion of this arithmetic might be that blacks pay whites compensation." On the other hand, he continues, if the "baseline if premised on the assumption that blacks would have voluntarily immigrated to the United States and would have earned the national average income in the absence of slavery and discrimination then it makes two highly unlikely assumptions:" Africans would have voluntarily immigrated to America, and, if they did, they would have earned at the national average income.[62]

This argument is riddled with confusion. In the first place, even if contemporary American blacks might still be in Africa and have a lower standard of living had their ancestors never been enslaved, it does not follow that they might have to pay whites compensation. Compensation is owed those whose rights are transgressed. Whites' rights are not transgressed because blacks in America have a higher standard of living than blacks in Africa. Sowell's "grotesque conclusion" is based on his misunderstanding of the concept of compensation. Furthermore the premise of his argument—contemporary American blacks would still be in Africa except for slavery—is false too. Contemporary American blacks would not exist if their ancestors had never been enslaved. As James S. Fishkin has observed, "If Kunta Kinte, Alex Haley's ancestor portrayed in *Roots*, had not been brutally kidnapped and sold as a slave, there is virtually no likelihood that the author of *Roots* would have come to exist in the twentieth century."[63]

But pointing out Sowell's error here seems, at first, to support his conclusion. Since—save, perhaps, for a few exceptions—it is better to exist than not to exist, those who would not have existed but for injustice enjoy a net profit from injustice. Consequently, if compensation requires that we use as a baseline what they would have been had the injustice never occurred, any demands they might make for compensation have been satisfied by the fact of their existence.

This is a vacuous conclusion which confounds the injustice but for which present-day blacks would not have existed with the injustice for which compensation is claimed. The injustice but for which present-day blacks would not have existed is the injustice committed against their ancestors by the slave trade and slavery. But the injustice for which present-day blacks claim compensaion is the injustice committed against *present-day blacks*.

This does not imply that blacks deserve compensation only for present-day discrimination. The people who enslaved Kunta Kinte's children did not wrong them only by enslaving them. They also wronged them by depriving them of their inheritance—of what Kunta Kinte would have provided them with, and passed on to them, had *he* been compensated— a stable home, education, income, and traditions. Similarly today's blacks deserve compensation not only for present-day discrimination, but also for being deprived of their just inheritance.

Returning to Sowell, what *is* the baseline from which to measure the losses of the descendants of slaves? Contrary to his belief, I argue that this baseline must be set at or near the national average income, and moreover, that this conclusion proceeds logically from Sowell's own position.

To suggest that we should calculate on the basis of some much lower standard could be supported by the momentous assumption that slavery did not hold back black progress. But Sowell does not make that assumption. He emphasizes the morbid "legacy of slavery," the "foot-dragging, work-avoiding patterns " of today's blacks, their "duplicity and theft," and their "tragic" hostility to "menial jobs."[64] Since these are among the main traits he blames for holding back blacks, his own theory suggests that the baseline from which to measure black losses should be much higher than blacks earn and perhaps near the national average.

And there is an even more obvious inconsistency in his argument. One of his most striking points is that middle-class blacks are in large majority the descendants of blacks who were freed before the Emancipation and who, therefore, gained a head start on other blacks. He has, indeed, instanced this to show how far removed, in tradition and condition, "elite blacks" are from the masses, singling out Andrew Young in particular as being out of touch with the problems of the black poor.[65] Moreover, this "head start" conception is central to his theory that progress is a cumulative process, an "intergenerational relay race." If so, it is difficult to see why he denies that, had the descendants of enslaved Africans been freed and given compensation, *their* descendants would not be earning income near the national average. Why would these blacks not have passed the baton?

Ultimately Sowell's arguments against blacks' right to compensation come to nought. His own theory of the causes of black backwardness entails the conclusion that blacks do have this right. Why, then, does he so strongly resist the idea? The answer seems to be that he thinks compensation, at least in the form of color-conscious policies, is counter to more financially and industrially oriented ideals of production. Taking this into account, and reviewing the other contradictions in Sowell's writing, the possibility begins to dawn that, despite his press coverage, behind his libertarian facade Sowell embraces that crude utilitarianism which proposes to maximize welfare by maximizing the production of goods and services.

## Utilitarianism and Discrimination

On the face of it, the idea of Sowell being a utilitarian seems unlikely. Sowell opposes busing, minimum wage laws, preferential treatment, and welfare measures in general, all of which are often defended on utilitarian grounds, on the grounds that they invade individual liberties. It is for this reason that he is called conservative or libertarian. But it may be argued that Sowell's defense of individual liberties shows that, like John Stuart Mill, he is a utilitarian who takes the long view, and who conceives of utility "in the largest sense grounded on the permanent interests of man as a progressive being." Let us consider this possibility.

As a utilitarian who understood that utility in the largest sense required individual liberty, Mill set an important limit on how the state could pursue utilitarian ideals. This limit depended on his concept of self-regarding conduct. Self-regarding conduct he defined as conduct which "affects only" the agent, or "if it also affects others" does so "only with their free voluntary and undeceived consent and participation."[66] The state, Mill's thesis implies, is never justified in interfering with self-regarding conduct. "The only part of the conduct of any one, for which he is amenable to society," he wrote, "is that which concerns others. In the part which merely concerns himself, his independence is, of right absolute." Mill did not deny that self-regarding conduct could be immoral. His point was that even if it was, the liberty to engage in it conduced, ultimately, to utility in the largest sense.

If racial discrimination by private employers can be interpreted as self-regarding conduct, the argument above may appear to provide the grounds for a utilitarian defence of Sowell's toleration of racial discrimination. Sowell, it is true, gives no hint himself of such a defence, he gives only crude, short-term reasons for tolerating racial discrimination, for example, because it saves information costs. However, there may be reasons for toleration if racial discrimination, from the more sophisticated utilitarian point of view, is considered self-regarding conduct. This view was expounded by Williams in an address he gave in New York in 1982. Williams does not deny that racial discrimination is immoral. But he maintains that, just as it would not be justified to outlaw "certain forms of voluntary consenting sexual behavior among adults" on the grounds that they were immoral, it would not be justified to outlaw racial discrimination on the grounds that it is immoral.[67] "We do not need," he says, "laws that prohibit discrimination in private activities."[68] And to nail down his point, he implies that equal employment opportunity laws are as misguided as would be laws against individual discrimination in the matter of choosing a mate. "When I was choosing a wife," he reveals, "I discriminated against Chinese women, Japanese women, white women, fat women, and women who did not bathe regularly. I'm quite sure none of my tests for choosing a wife would ever meet the Equal Opportunity Commission (EEOC) validation criteria."[69] However, it should be stressed that William's opposition to laws against racial discrimination applies only to discrimination in "private activities." It does not apply to discrimination in "public sector, taxpayer supported jobs." Williams is quite prepared to "eliminate racial discrimination in those kinds of jobs."[70]

The most plausible argument that private discrimination is self-regarding depends on a distinction between causing harm and failing to prevent harm that can be illustrated by the example of the drowning person. A pushes B into a river. C sees B drowning and could throw him a line but doesn't. A caused B harm. C failed to prevent harm to B. In terms of discrimination, this argument claims that, although private acts of discrimination often fail to prevent harm, they do not necessarily cause it. A typical example of the argument would be something like the following: B is harmed because he needs but does not have an apartment. A has an apartment for rent but refuses to rent it to B because B is black. A has failed to prevent harm to B but he has not caused it. Or: Students attending all-black schools may be harmed because their schools are poorly funded and have no middle-class students. Whites refuse to allow integration. Whites have failed to prevent harm to black students but they have not caused it.

It can be argued that because discrimination and segregation offend and insult blacks they do cause harm and are thus other-regarding and liable to state intervention. But if the psychic toll of segregation on blacks can be weighed against the reasons for segregation, then by implication it seems that the psychic cost to racists of integration should also be weighed against the benefits of integration. In theory—and possibly in practice—this could tip the scales in favor of segregation.

However, Richard Wollheim, a professor of philosophy at London University, has proposed an interpretation of Mill's concept of self-regarding action which seems to promise a way out of these difficulties.[71] Although there are ambiguities in his presentation, it can be summarized as follows: Self-regarding actions are actions which "affect either the agent alone or other people solely insofar as they believe such actions to be right or wrong."[72] Therefore, the belief that a self-regarding action is wrong is always false because an action is wrong only if it causes pain and, by assumption, the only pain the action causes comes as a result of the belief that it is wrong and consequently cannot be grounds for the belief. For this reason, the weighing of pleasures and pains caused by an action to determine whether, in utilitarian terms, it is right or wrong must, Wollheim reasons, "be made as if in a world prior to the adoption of moral attitudes."[73] Otherwise, any action could be right or wrong if enough people believed strongly that it was right or wrong. According to Wollheim, Mill offered two reasons why the pain caused as a result of such false moral beliefs should not be taken seriously. First, says Wollheim, he believed that "with the progress of intellectual inquiry false moral beliefs were likely to disappear;"[74] second, that they are not in any case moral beliefs at all, i.e., they are "not about what all should or ought to do," but are merely preferences, i.e., about what the individual himself "would like to do or be, or sees himself doing or being."[75] Wollheim recognizes that the first argument, as things stand, is weak, and he devotes far more space to developing the second.

According to Wollheim, this argument proceeds from the utilitarian view that a genuine moral belief about an action must be supported by reasons and the only thing that counts as a reason is a painful or pleasurable consequence of the action. But if so, if the only painful consequences of A's action stem from B's belief that it is wrong, the belief cannot be based on a genuine reason and so cannot be a moral belief. Consequently, it cannot be about A's actions—for moral beliefs are about everyone's actions—but must be only about how B prefers to act himself. Hence, A's action cannot "run counter to B's belief"[76] and thus cannot be "the cause of B's pain."[77]

Although Wollheim himself does not do so, this argument might be adduced to show that discrimination is not self-regarding. Suppose that a utilitarian weighing of the pleasures, pains, and harms resulting from segregation and from integration were made as if in a world prior to the adoption of moral attitudes, and the result was that segregation caused harm and pain and integration did not. Then, by Wollheim's account, the belief that segregation is wrong would be true, and the belief that integration is wrong would be false, and indeed not a moral belief at all but a mere preference. Accordingly, to return to our original paradox, though integration may seem to impose psychic costs on the racist because he claims to believe it to be wrong, it does not really do so because his belief is not a moral belief at all but only a preference. Hence, the psychic costs of integration to the racist cannot be attributed to integration and cannot be held against it.

But this argument is highly suspect. First, it is not clear that the racists' beliefs about integration are really just preferences in Mill's and Wollheim's sense. For racists have, or claim to have, grounds—and often good utilitarian grounds—for condemning integration. Of course, these grounds are often not true, but that does not affect the nature of the objection. For what makes a belief a preference rather than a moral belief is not that the agent believes something on false grounds, but that he believes something on no grounds at all. To counter this we must fall back either on Mill's optimistic view that false beliefs tend to be replaced eventually by true ones, or on Wollheim's observation that though reasons are often cited in support of a belief, such beliefs are often only "beliefs reinforced by rationalizations and such beliefs must count as preferences."[78]

This last possibility is plausible because we know that racism is often supported by rationalization, but even if it can be substantiated difficulties remain. Wollheim argues that self-regarding conduct, as he defines it, does not cause pain to those other than the agent himself because it does not run counter to their beliefs. As C. L. Ten has pointed out, this assumes, groundlessly, that we cannot have moral beliefs about how others should act.[79]

Nor is Wollheim on solid ground when he argues that as we learn more about the mind of someone pained by another's self-regarding action we come to see that it has a "larger part to play in the etiology of his pain" than does the action.[80] This is as faulty an argument as one that states that as we learn more about the nerves in the nose that we come to see that they have a larger part to play in the etiology of pain than a blow to the nose. Wollheim probably means that those other than the agent are pained by self-regarding actions only because they have incorrect, nonutilitarian attitudes. But even if we grant this questionable claim, his conclusion is still erroneous. Even if sick people in hospitals are pained by ordinary street noises only because their bodies are not functioning properly, it may still be justifiable—and on utilitarian grounds—to restrict ordinary street noises around hospitals.

However, racial discrimination is not self-regarding conduct. To understand why it isn't, we must go back to the suggestion made hypothetically earlier, that an inspection of the results of segregation and integration as if in a world without moral attitudes would reveal that segregation causes pain and harm and integration does not. If this is true, as I will attempt to prove, not only is racial discrimination not self-regarding, there are also good utilitarian reasons to weigh the psychic cost to blacks of segregation against it, and *not* to weigh the psychic cost to racists of integration against integration. For, from a utilitarian perspective, good utilitarian attitudes should be encouraged, and bad, nonutilitarian attitudes should be discouraged. The former help to produce happiness, the latter help to produce misery. Giving importance to the pain experienced by racists through their false belief that integration is wrong would encourage these nonutilitarian attitudes; giving credence to the pain segregation causes blacks through their true belief that segregation is wrong would encourage the good utilitarian attitudes.

Of course, this argument depends on the assumption that segregation causes harm independent of the belief that it is wrong, and we have seen that assumption can be challenged. I wish now to reconsider that challenge by focusing on a key philosophical point: the contention that private discrimination causes no harm, which depends on the belief that there is a distinction between causing harm and failing to prevent harm. Mill himself seemed to reject this distinction. He affirmed, for example, that "a person may cause evil to others not only by his actions, but by his inactions."[81] Certain contemporary philosophers, such as John Harris and John Kleinig, appear to agree with Mill.[82] Others, such as Eric Mack, appear to disagree with him.[83]

Eric Mack maintains that failing to prevent harm is not causing harm, and demonstrates that, in many cases where we are tempted to speak of "nondoings being responsible" for harm, we can "reconstrue the case in a way that does not involve negative causation." Sometimes, he points out, we can say that it is the agent's prior actions, not his later inaction, which causes the harm. Other times we can say that ascribing responsibility of this kind is "just a way of ascribing blameworthiness and does not involve a genuine causal judgment at all."[84]

Mack realizes, however, that he cannot prove his case in this way, and he therefore attempts a more positive argument against what he isolates as the key claim of his opponents—viz., that "refraining from an action which would have prevented a human harm causes that harm."[85] Suppose Smith is drowning, and Jones sees this and refrains from helping. Mack must prove false the possibility that Jones's inaction caused Smith to drown in the sense that it was a necessary condition for Smith's drowning. Mack rejects this possibility on the grounds that if Jones were 1,000 miles away from the beach where Smith drowned he could not be said to have refrained from helping Smith. Given that the tide and Smith's distance from shore are "jointly sufficient for Smith's aquatic demise," Smith would have drowned anyway and consequently Jones's refusal to help cannot be a necessary condition for Smith's drowning. The flaw in this argument is Mack's assumption that the tide and Smith's distance from shore are jointly sufficient for Smith's drowning. This may be true in the case where Jones is 1,000 miles away, but it is false in the case where Jones is on the beach and sees Smith drowning. For in that case, Jones could have helped Smith, and therefore the tide and distance could not have been jointly sufficient for Smith's drowning. If Mack were right, the tide and distance would also be jointly sufficient for Smith's drowning in a case where there is a floating spar which Smith seizes in order to save himself. But this is logically absurd because in that case Smith would not drown. The point in general is that, like the floating spar, Jones's presence makes a difference to the causal conditions for Smith's drowning. Suppose Brown is in exactly the same situation as Smith but survives because he has throughout his life refrained from drinking, smoking, and debauchery and is therefore very physically fit. Mack's argument that Jones's refraining did not cause Smith to drown is as flawed as would be the argument that Brown's refraining did not cause Brown to survive.

If, as we seem to be able to prove, refusal to prevent harm causes harm, we can dismiss, without raising controversial empirical questions, the argument that private discrimination and segregation cause no harm. For clearly, private discrimination does not merely fail to prevent harm, but abstains from preventing harm. A does not discriminate against blacks if he fails to rent his apartment to blacks because no blacks apply. He discriminates only if blacks apply and he refuses to rent to them because they are black. Similarly, whites are not guilty of segregation simply because of the existence of all-white and all-black schools. They practice segregation only if they refuse to integrate.

Thus, the traditional interpretation of Mill's view of what causes harm does not, after all, support the view that only the state should be forbidden from acting in a discriminatory manner. Instead, it supplies us with considerable reasons for saying that individuals should also be forbidden from acting in a discriminatory manner. What is more, there is no utilitarian argument, based on the concept of utility in the larger sense, which justifies condoning private racial discrimination. Black libertarians, or utilitarians, are faced with a dilemma: If they are libertarians they cannot—though they do—dismiss compensation arguments. And if they are utilitarians they cannot—though they do—tolerate racial discrimination.

## The Alleged Disutility of Color-conscious Policies

One of Sowell's deepest misgivings about color-conscious policies, and in this he is joined by Wilson, is that they will exacerbate racial conflict. Sowell, for example, has warned in the popular press that if the "government continues to hand out goodies on a racial or ethnic basis" it may not take long for "people to be at each others' throats—and for blood to be in the streets."[86] And Wilson writes that "if there is an imminent potential for racial conflict in the industrial order it would most probably be related to the affirmative action program."[87] However, even if these warnings are well-founded, they cannot, on Sowell's and Wilson's own accounts, be the basis of an independent argument against color-conscious policies. Suppose that color-conscious policies are just and useful to black progress. Then, if we refrain from implementing them because of fear of racial conflict, racism *would* be an important barrier to justice and to black progress—contrary to the class theory to which Sowell and Wilson adhere. Consequently, they cannot, on pain of self-contradiction, use predictions about racial conflict as independent arguments against color-conscious policies. They must first prove such policies pernicious.

Wilson's argument, in brief, is this: There is no competition for jobs in the underclass. Jobs exist, but because they are low-paying and menial, blacks and whites don't compete for them. (They are taken by illegal aliens.) Consequently, since there is no racial competition for jobs, and therefore no opportunity for racial discrimination over jobs, racial discrimination cannot be the factor keeping blacks in the underclass from getting jobs. Finally, he concludes, because racial discrimination is not the factor keeping these blacks from getting jobs, color-conscious policies are irrelevant to their ability to get jobs, and hence irrelevant to their progress.[88]

The final step in this argument is a giant non sequitur. From the claim that racial discrimination is not what keeps blacks in the underclass from getting jobs, it does not follow that color-conscious policies are not necessary for the progress of these blacks. The inference is as faulty as would be the argument that, since no one unfairly discriminates against the musically gifted, or the artistically or mathematically gifted, special programs for them are irrelevant to their progress. Yet, Wilson's opposition to color-conscious policies in this area is adamant. He concludes *The Declining Significance of Race* with the observation that the problems of the underclass must be tackled "on a broad class front" which goes "beyond the limits of ethnic and racial discrimination."[89]

But, as I observed, not only is Wilson's dismissive attitude toward color-conscious policies unjustified, his own class theory suggests that his advocacy of color-blind policies is ill-considered.

Wilson suggests a color-blind policy which will make available to the black and white underclass "jobs that pay decent wages and that provide opportunities of advancement—jobs that will enhance an individual's self-respect and feelings of self-worth," and he properly stresses that this is in "sharp contrast" to Sowell's suggested policy which would create low-paying, menial jobs—jobs which already exist.[90] But if, as Wilson assumes, this kind of color-blind policy will solve the problems of the black and white underclass, there is a large gap in his argument—implied by his own theory. According to Wilson's theory "jobs that pay decent wages" already exist, just like low-paying, menial jobs. The problem is that these decently paying jobs are not within the reach of the underclass. As he himself repeatedly stresses, decently paying jobs "are decreasing in the central cities of our nation" and exist more in the suburbs. The solution to the problem then would seem to be to move blacks to the suburbs. But Wilson also repeatedly stresses that opposition to residential integration in the country continues unabated. Consequently, given that residential integration would require a deliberate color-conscious policy, it would seem that if Wilson's proposal is to succeed, it cannot, after all, be color-blind.

This conclusion blunts the point of Wilson's version of Washington's attack on "race problem solvers." The black intelligentsia, Wilson charges, "has a vested interest in keeping race as the single most important issue in developing policies to promote black progress."[91] This is because it achieved, and maintains, its present comfortable position largely through color-conscious policies like affirmative action which are based on the assumption that race *is* the most important issue. Consequently, in pursuit of what Wilson perceives as self-interest, the black middle class advertises the miseries of the black underclass while promoting and sustaining the illusion that these miseries are due to racism.[92] In this way it hopes to expand color-conscious programs which create more opportunities for itself. Carl Gershman, a follower of Wilson's, takes this suggestion further. According to Gershman, not only does the black middle class falsely insist on race being the most important consideration in developing policies for black progress but, perceiving that its advantages depend on the deprivation of the black lower class, it actually *blocks* policies that would help the black lower class. Using Wilson's version of the class theory, Gershman, among other things, argues that black leaders at a national conference in Richmond, Virginia, in 1979 urged policies seriously opposed to the interests of the black lower class. But, this charge assumes precisely what Wilson's version of the class theory denies—that racial discrimination is an important impediment to black progress. Gershman concedes this point without realizing it. To illustrate his thesis about the self-serving and destructive nature of the policies urged by the new leadership of the black middle class, he relates how, at a hearing on urban policy conducted by the House Committee on Banking Currency and Housing, Paul R. Porter, an urban specialist, proposed that poor blacks wishing to relocate to areas of industrial growth be assisted by the government. According to Gershman, Representative Parren J. Mitchell (a Democrat from Maryland) opposed this proposal on the grounds that by relocating blacks—moving them out of the central cities—such a policy would "destroy the political base that we blacks have begun to develop in this country."[93] Gershman presents this as evidence of the way in which the black middle class blocks the progress of the black lower class to selfish advantage. But if, as Wilson says, opposition to residential integration has not declined, the exchange is also evidence for the importance of racial discrimination—a view that Gershman, as Wilson's disciple, rejects.

Sowell's argument about the counter-productiveness of color-conscious policies has two phases. First, there is a frontal attack on the effectiveness of those policies. Second, there is a rearguard action in which he concludes that in the long run government intervention creates social and political instabilities.

The frontal attack is simply the accusation that, in Sowell's words, color-conscious policies like affirmative action "have produced little over-all pay or employment changes for blacks relative to whites."[94] He backs up this claim with the argument that affirmative action makes it difficult for employers to fire incompetent blacks and so discourages them from hiring blacks in the first place.

But, there is a gap in Sowell's argument. He has completely overlooked another effect of affirmative action. Because the policy carries penalties for noncompliance, affirmative action also makes it costly for an employer to hire no blacks at all. Therefore, a fairer assessment of the net effect of affirmative action is that it forces employers to intensify their search for the "right" blacks, that is, as Christopher Jencks notes, "young blacks with educational credentials and mature blacks with steady work histories."[95] Empirical studies suggest that in this respect affirmative action has been productive. Jencks reports that three of the four studies conducted to estimate the effect of affirmative action on employment concluded that it "increased minority employment by 6 to 13 percent," and, while he allows that the effect of affirmative action on income is "less clear cut," he also demonstrates that in this case too the evidence makes it difficult to deny, as Sowell does with assurance, that affirmative action "increased black workers' earnings." The most that Sowell can say, Jencks concludes, is that while affirmative action improved black workers wages, "it also may have made it harder for some blacks to find jobs."[96]

## The Attack on Politics and Protest

Sensing, perhaps, the weakness of his frontal attack on the effectiveness of affirmative action, and by extension of all government interference in the free market on behalf of blacks, Sowell invariably falls back on his rearguard argument—that government interference in the market creates instabilities. At this point he admits that this interference is sometimes effective. "At particular historic junctures," he writes, "governmental policy may be beneficial to particular ethnic groups." But he goes on to object that it is unreliable in the long run. "It is the long-run reliance on political action" he warns, "that is questionable in view of the unpredictability of political trends in general."[97] And to drive home his point about the "sheer volatility of governmental policy toward ethnic groups" he reminds us not only of the shifts in U.S. government attitude toward blacks, but of Idi Amin's "brutal mass expulsions of East Indians" from Uganda, "the slaughter of the Ibos in Nigeria," "the severe current official discrimination against the Chinese in Indonesia," and, of course, "Hitler and the Holocaust."[98]

Of Thomas Sowell's many strange arguments, this one is the most bizarre and perverse. The evidence he cites to support his conclusion in fact supports the very opposite. Consider his claim that political activity does not help a minority's progress. His reasons for this are that although political activity may help enact favorable government policy, there are usually economic incentives tempting individuals to "behave at variance with government policy."[99] And Sowell thinks that history proves him right. "The high tide of black political power during Reconstruction," he reminds us, "was not a period of notable economic advance, and in fact included some important retrogressions."[100] And more generally he maintains that "political success is not only relatively unrelated to economic advance, those minorities that have pinned their greatest hopes on political action—the Irish and the Negroes, for example—have made some of the slowest economic advances. This is in sharp contrast to the Japanese-Americans, whose political powerlessness may have been a blessing in disguise, by preventing the expenditure of much energy in that direction."[101] Here, of course, he is following Booker T. Washington, whose opposition to engaging in politics to achieve advancement is legendary: "The best course to pursue in regard to the civil rights bills in the South," Washington advised, "is to let it alone."[102]

The most curious property of tunnel vision is not that it blinds. It is that it distorts. Weaknesses appear to be strengths. Washington and Sowell both have a bad case of tunnel vision. Consider again the examples Sowell cites to prove the volatility of government policy in relation to minorities—the Indians in East Africa, the Ibos in Nigeria, the Chinese in Indonesia, and the Jews in Germany. To support Sowell's belief in the ineffectiveness of political power and political action these groups should have been groups with political power and a history of political activity. But the very opposite is true. The Indians in East Africa kept a low political profile, as do the Chinese in Indonesia, and by Sowell's own account the Jews only slowly became involved in politics in this country because they were apolitical in the European countries from which they came originally. Of the groups Sowell mentions, only the Ibos were politically active, and their problems would have been worse had they been less politically involved. Furthermore, these groups were or are doing exactly what Sowell recommends black America do. They kept or keep out of politics, and made or make a lot of money. So if their fate is anything to go by, this is what Sowell plans for us: keep out of politics and make a lot of money, and one day we'll be "brutally expelled," "slaughtered," or suffer a "Holocaust"!

The obvious point to be made here, is, if a person plans to acquire something of value, he had better also plan to acquire a way to keep it, or others will take it away from him. That Washington and Sowell overlook this is amazing. Why else are there locks on doors and guards in banks? And that they overlook it is more amazing still when we recall that their policies are based on the assumption that man is self-interested. For if man is self-interested, what can protect the valuables of the weak from others so motivated? Their oversight literally boggles the mind when we recall that they claim to be examining the experience of black people. I confess that my mind was boggled when I first read Washington's pronouncement that "Harmony will come in proportion that the black man gets something the white man wants." For there was a time when the black man had something the white man wanted. And it did not bring harmony, or even less, justice. It brought the death of 100 million black people—the number estimated to have died as a result of the slave trade—and two hundred years of slavery.[103] Washington knew this. After noting that the country's immigration laws were framed to keep out people who "might prove a burden upon the tax-payers, because of their poverty and inability to sustain themselves," he boasts that "for two centuries or more it was the policy of the United States to bring in the Negro at almost any cost," concluding rhetorically, "Would any individual or any country have gone to the expense during so many years to import a people that had no economic value?"[104]

Now this boast completely demolishes, of course, the centerpiece of Washington's, and Sowell's, theory—their conviction that all you need to get ahead is to get "something the white man wants " or "something the society values." This really stupid and dangerous idea, which is of a piece with their admonition to eschew politics, does not even state a necessary condition for getting ahead. If you have enough weapons, as kings and conquerors have proved throughout history, you do not need to have something the society values to get ahead. Unless, of course, it is the power to refrain from killing when you can kill.

Every black political thinker worth his salt, with the exception of Washington and his disciples, has acknowledged these elementary truths and has correspondingly concluded that the problem for blacks in America is and has been the problem of the vulnerability of the weak and inarticulate—especially the weak and inarticulate with something the strong want. For example, Martin Delany, the first and wisest of the black nationalists was acutely aware of this. It is the basis of his analysis of black subordination and enslavement. Blacks were subordinated and enslaved, he argued, first because they were weak. They were "least potent in urging their claims."[105] Added to and exacerbating this weakness was the fact that blacks had something whites wanted. Blacks were enslaved, Delany argued, because of their "superior skill and industry."[106] And there was a final factor that determined the enslavement of blacks and made those who practiced it almost immune to moral dissuasion. He observed that those who proscribe others select those who "differ as much as possible . . . from themselves" for this "ensures the greater success" of their proscription as "it engenders the greater prejudice, or in other words, elicits less interest on the part of the oppressing class."[107] And because he supposed that only one of these causes of black subordination could or should be altered—the lack of power—Delany argued that the future of black elevation lay in blacks acquiring power by emigrating to Africa and establishing a great black nation there. A long line of black thinkers, from Marcus Garvey to Stokely Carmichael and Charles V. Hamilton, have endorsed his Black Power solution to the problem of subordination, though they have not always endorsed his idea that emigration was the way to get it.

Assimilationists, for example Delany's great contemporary Frederick Douglass, have, of course, proposed a different solution to the problem of black subordination. But Douglass did not analyse the causes of black subordination any differently than Delany. In particular, he did not deny that part of the cause of their subordination was their powerlessness, and their inability to arouse the whites' sense of justice. He refused to endorse Delany's solution of emigration because he though it was unrealistic and an evasion of a duty to expose, protest, and combat injustice, and his followers today reject the idea of Black Power for similar reasons. Accordingly, Douglass and his contemporary representatives propose to solve the problem of black subordination by attacking another of its causes, viz., the white majority's belief that blacks differ in some fundamental way from whites. Thus, on the grounds that congregation made blacks more noticeable, and accentuated their difference from whites, Douglass at one time condemned the idea that unity is strength, at least in every circumstance, and urged blacks to disperse themselves among whites.[108] And to back up the effects of this dispersal, since it alone would not solve the problem, Douglass mounted a relentless attack on the idea that prejudice is "natural" and that there is a moral difference between blacks and whites. He employed all his enormous intellectual and oratorical powers to prove and persuade people that "it is all false this talk about the invincibility of prejudice against color," and that despite obvious physical differences, and even differences in origin, "a man's a man for a' that."[109]

It is difficult to say which strategy, that of Black Power, or that of the assimilationists, is superior. Both have advantages and both have disadvantages. The advantages of the Black Power approach include the well-established efficacy of power. Its disadvantages include its tendency to degenerate into cultural chauvinism, to strike poses and to become infected with the racism of black racial superiority. Finally, of course, its goals may simply be impossible to achieve. Many of these disadvantages are precisely the advantages of assimilation. Assimilation utterly rejects racism and concedes nothing to injustice. However, it too has disadvantages. With some advocates, it tends to involve a depreciation of those characteristics which distinguish blacks from whites, and in this way may undermine black self-esteem. Also, it may lead to a preoccupation with protesting injustice and a corresponding disregard for the importance of achievement—there is this much foundation to Washington's fears about political involvement. Finally, of couse, like those of Black Power, its aims, too, may be unachievable. Neither strategy is guaranteed to succeed, and each has dangers. Perhaps the best policy would be a judicious combination of the best parts of both. Certainly the worst policy would be to eschew both power and protest. To urge black people to make money, or to acquire skills that will enable them to make money, while at the same time urging them to avoid all means of self-defence, as Washington and Sowell do, is a prescription for disaster.

As I have observed, their recommendations are especially perverse because they are based on a theory which assumes that self-interest is the prime motivation for human beings. Here it should be noted that Washington comes off as less confused than Sowell. For he at least allows that the self-interest of human beings includes an interest in their moral betterment. Thus he could, and did, urge justice by reminding whites of their interest in their souls.[110] But Sowell will have none of this "higher," though still prudential, reasoning. For him, bewildered by his own "causal analysis," it is all "dollars and cents." His saying this, and his urging of policies for blacks of enrichment without self-defence—and this among a people whose history demonstrates the lengths they will go to get dollars and cents—is not mere intellectual blunder. It is reprehensible folly.

# 3

# Marxism, Justice, and Black Progress

## The Alleged Irrelevance of Justice

On 25 March 1931, nine black teenagers were arrested and jailed in the small town of Scottsboro, in rural Alabama. They were accused of raping two white women and, in short order, were found guilty and sentenced to die in the electric chair. Although the defendants were lucky that lynchers even let them get to trial, the sheer haste of the proceedings, and the incompetence of the defense attorney, a white lawyer from Chattanooga, Tennessee, quickly made the Scottsboro case famous as an example of American injustice to blacks. The international communist movement quickly recognized the case as a propaganda windfall, and, since the NAACP had hesitated to come to the defense of the Scottsboro boys, as a golden opportunity to replace that organization as the champion of the black masses. *The Daily Worker* accused the NAACP, which was by then making a belated attempt to get involved in the case, of surrendering the boys, who were lower class, to mob violence in order to keep its respectable middle-class image, and many blacks were impressed by this accusation.

Not satisfied with this advance, doctrinaire communists tried to apply their theories to the case. W. E. B. Dubois quoted this diagnosis from a Moscow pundit: "Again as in the case of Sacco and Vanzetti, the American bourgeoisie is attempting to go against proletarian social opinion. It is attempting to carry through its criminal provocation to the very end." Responding to this attack in *Crisis*, the official organ of the NAACP, W. E. B. Dubois described this piece of Marxist orthodoxy as a "ludicrous misapprehension of local conditions." The Sacco-Vanzetti case did, he conceded, represent "the fighting of prejudiced entrenched capital against radical opinion"; but in rural Alabama something altogether different was going on; there, it was the "white proletarian mob" which was determined to kill the Scottsboro boys, and the capitalists who were trying to curb the "blood lust."[1]

Moscow had excellent reasons for playing down the racism of the white proletarian mob, for it raises a serious problem for the Marxist theory of revolution. According to that theory, workers will succeed in overthrowing capitalism because they will be unified. But the racism of white workers directed against blacks of the same class suggests that workers will not be unified. Dubois was well aware of this problem: "No revolt of a white proletariat could be started," he wrote, "if its object was to make black workers their economic, political and social equals."[2] The "lowest and most fatal degree" of the suffering of black workers, Dubois continued, comes "not from the capitalists but from fellow white workers. It is white labor that deprives the Negro of his right to vote, denies him education, denies him affiliation with trade unions. . . ."[3]

The sanguine Marxist may respond that, whatever may have been the case when Dubois wrote, things are very different now. Not so. Marxist scholars continue to blame race issues and racism for undermining the working-class movement in America. Thus, in his important book *Racial Inequality*, Michael Reich finds that the absence of a socialist or working-class movement and racism and racial inequality in this country are "not just parallel developments," but are "inextricably linked and must be understood jointly."[4]

Given that racial discrimination is an especially virulent form of injustice, one would expect Marxists, who want to achieve working-class unity, to stress the importance of justice. Strangely enough, however, they do the exact opposite. And Marx himself set the pattern for their reactions, mercilessly castigating socialists when they made appeals to justice and such cognate ideas as equal right. The most famous example of his hostility to such appeals is his vitriolic marginal notes to the draft of a social program presented to him in 1875 by one of the factions of the German social democratic movement. Marx considered the program to be fundamentally flawed because of its dependence on ideas like "equal right," "fair distribution," and "the undiminished proceeds of labor." "I have dealt more at length [with these ideas]" he fumed, ". . . to show what a crime it is to attempt, on the one hand, to force on our Party again, as dogmas, ideas which in a certain period had some meaning but have now become obsolete verbal rubbish, while again perverting on the other, the realistic outlook, which it cost so much effort to instill into the Party but which has now taken root in it, by means of ideological nonsense about right and other trash."[5]

His reasons for taking this position, later Marxists have explained, is that he thought capitalism just, and accordingly, that demands for justice do not call capitalism into question, and that therefore such demands are ameliorative and counterrevolutionary. Marx, these Marxists say, condemned capitalism for reasons far more radical than possible injustice, denied that justice was an important ideal, and conceived of communist society as a society "beyond justice." His revolutionary program therefore called for the Communist party to eschew appeals to the "ideological nonsense" of justice, and to maintain a "realistic outlook." It was simply to teach the workers that it was in their interests to rise up against capitalism and abolish it. As Marx wrote, the role of the party is to "point out, and bring to the front, the common interests of the entire proletariat independently of nationality."[6]

If these considerations are sound, a case can be mounted for the belief that Marxists should oppose color-conscious policies, both because they are urged as being just, and because they are urged as being to the advantage of blacks in particular. First, if they are urged as being just they are urged on the basis of "ideological nonsense," and do not call capitalism into question. Second, if they are instituted they will ameliorate the hardships of black workers and therefore take the edge off their motivation to revolt, and, because they are not in the "common interest of the entire proletariat independently of nationality," but in the interest only of the black proletariat, they will divide the working class.

Since I am defending color-conscious policies in this book, both on the grounds that they are just and on the grounds that they are to the advantage of blacks, I am constrained to rebut these Marxist attacks on justice. This is especially necessary since many black people are sympathetic to Marxism but also feel deeply that color-conscious policies are both just and beneficial. I demonstrate in this chapter that these attitudes are not inconsistent. The Marxist denigration of justice is unjustified. Indeed, it is self-defeating. Appeals to justice, especially in a racist society, are necessary if the working class is ever to be unified. Nor will such appeals be counterrevolutionary. Marxist theory does not imply that capitalism is, or can be, just. On the contrary, it implies that capitalism is not, and cannot be, just, and, moreover, that the workers can come to realize this. Finally, while it is true that Marx conceived of communist society as a society beyond justice, workers should not therefore be discouraged from thinking in terms of justice, for the idea of a society beyond justice is utopian.

## Racial Antagonisms in the Working Class

Marxists, of course, are very aware of racial and ethnic antagonisms in the working class. Marx himself noted the antagonism between English and Irish workers in England, and explicitly drew a parallel between it and racial antagonism in America which Dubois believed was a local peculiarity requiring a modification of Marxist theory.[7] The attitude of the English worker to the Irish worker, Marx remarked in a letter to S. Meyer and A. Vogt, "is much the same as that of the 'poor whites' to the 'niggers' in the former slave states of the U.S.A." Thus, he wrote, England is "divided into two hostile camps, English proletarians and Irish proletarians. The ordinary English worker hates the Irish worker as a competitor who lowers his standard of life. In relation to the Irish worker he feels himself a member of the ruling class."[8] But Marx denied that this antagonism had to be overcome by appeals to the sense of justice of the English worker. It could and would be overcome, he insisted, simply by showing English workers that it was not in their interest to feel this hatred. His comments imply that he thought that English workers *mistakenly* believed that Irish workers lowered their standard of living. And, of course, he located the source of this mistake in the machinations of capitalists. The antagonism between English and Irish workers, Marx wrote, "is artifically kept alive and intensified—by all means at the disposal of the ruling class. This antagonism is the secret of the impotence of the English working class. It is the secret by which the capitalist class maintains its power. And that class is fully aware of it."[9]

However, a moment's reflection reveals that this argument is blatantly inconsistent with a fundamental point of the Marxist revolutionary theory—that the reserve army of the unemployed permits the capitalist to lower wages. For, if this is so, English workers were utterly correct in seeing Irish workers as competitors who lowered their standard of living. And exactly the same rule operates for white workers and black workers. As a result, certain theorists, for example Edna Bonacich, have devised what is known as the split labor market theory. According to this theory, highly paid white workers use their political power and the ideology of racism to prevent capitalists from hiring lower-paid black workers.[10] Dubois anticipated this theory, employing it to explain socialism's poor political showing. "Socialism," he wrote, "meets no response from the white proletariat because it offers no escape to wealth and no effective bar to black labor, and a mud-sill of black labor is essential to white labor's standard of living."[11]

Marxists sometimes argue that the white aristocracy of labor which gains by racism exists because of colonial exploitation. With the liberation of the colonies, the capitalists of the industrialized world will be compelled to step up the exploitation of the domestic proletariat. They will break the unions of the white aristocracy of labor in order to hire cheaper black labor. Eventually the black and the white proletariat will be ground down to similar conditions.

With this end in view, Marxists always support colonial liberation movements. Marx himself suggested this strategy to give impetus to the revolution. He acknowledged that he believed at first that Ireland would be liberated by the ascendancy of the working class in England. But, he recounts, "deeper study" convinced him that the "opposite" was true, viz., that Ireland had to be liberated before there could be an ascendancy of the working class in England. "The sole means of hastening it—the social revolution in England," he wrote "is to make Ireland independent." And he reiterated that an appeal should be made not to the workers' sense of justice, but to their self-interest. Thus, he maintained that "it is the special task of the Central Council in London to awaken a consciousness in the English workers that for them the national emancipation of Ireland is *no question of abstract justice or humanitarian sentiment* but the first condition of their own social emancipation."[12]

But the strategy of generating colonial liberation makes no advance on the previous strategy. On the one hand, according to the theory of colonial exploitation, colonies are in the best interests of highly paid white workers. On the other hand, Marx proposed appealing to these workers' self-interest to support the liberation of colonies. Clearly, if the theory is true, the strategy must fail. Engels saw the difficulty when, in a letter to K. Kautsky, he wrote, "You ask me what the English workers think about colonial policy. Well, exactly the same as they think about politics in general: the same as the bourgeois think . . . the workers gaily share the feast of England's monopoly of the world market and the colonies."[13]

It may seem, however, that the world-wide liberation of colonies after World War II, often as a result of the action of the working class in the imperialist countries, vindicates Marx's belief in his strategy. Alan Gilbert, a professor at the University of Denver for example, maintains that "internationalism" was the "hallmark" of Marx's political theory.[14]

Gilbert illustrates his point by instancing English working-class opposition to British support of the South in the American Civil War, the eventual French working-class opposition to the maintenance of the Algerian colony, and Portuguese working-class opposition to colonialism in Africa. According to Gilbert, these examples show how "working class internationalism" can move the working classes to defend their "long-range common interests" against "short-lived economic gain."[15] They show nothing of the sort. The colonies are liberated because the *colonial peoples fought for it.* They, and only they, deserve credit. Did not Frantz Fanon, major spokesman for the Algerian peasant revolution, and the most brilliant of the Third World theorists, accuse the European working class of playing the "Sleeping Beauty"?[16] The colonies were not liberated because the working classes in imperialist countries saw that they had "long-range common interests" with the colonial peoples. This is Panglossaian nonsense. There was nothing long-range about the interests of the working classes in opposing colonial domination. They opposed colonial domination because they were tired of their sons and brothers being sent to die in some distant corner of the world, and afraid of being sent to the same fate themselves. Gilbert mentions this motive for working-class opposition to colonialism, but he does not attempt to tell us why it is not the whole motive, nor what it has to do with what he refers to as "social emancipation."

There are Marxist economists who deny the existence of a substantial class of white workers who profit from racism. For example, in *Racial Inequality* Michael Reich claims to demonstrate that racism "works against most whites' economic interests," conceding only that it benefits a "few privileged workers."[17] And Reich thinks that his results indicate how racial antagonism can be overcome, and unity achieved, for at least a major part of the working class. "The finding that racism works against most whites' economic interests" he writes, "suggests that most whites need not be hostile to campaigns against racism. On the contrary, it should be possible to mobilize a coalition against racism that encompasses broad segments of the American population."[18] If he is right, Marx's claim that workers will unite because they will see that it is in their interests to do so is forgivable hyperbole. It is enough that most will unite for this reason.

But how is this conclusion compatible with the Marxist theory that a reserve army of the unemployed allows capitalists to lower wages? If that theory is correct, it follows inexorably that if whites reduce the army of unemployed by excluding blacks from the labor force they will then raise their wages. If racism pits white and black workers against each other then it is fairly clear that overcoming racism will raise the wages of both sets of workers. But if racism pits white workers and capitalists against black workers, it would seem to follow that, while overcoming racism would raise black workers' wages, it would *lower* white workers' wages.

It may be objected that such a cartel, between white workers and capitalists, could not be maintained. Sowell takes this line in his argument that the free market eliminates discrimination. Thus, while he allows that if whites organized into one giant monopoly discrimination could be made profitable, he denies that such a cartel could be sustained. "As long as each individual is seeking to maximize his individual gains," he argues, "each individual white has incentives to violate the agreement, and can be prevented from doing so only by various means of policing the agreement, of widely varying effectiveness and cost."[19]

When Reich comes to consider the possibility of a combination of white capitalists and white workers against blacks, he uses the same argument to show why the cartel couldn't work. He considers it the most decisive refutation of the discrimination model of Lester Thurow, which assumes a white monopolistic cartel, writing, "even if all whites benefit from the existence of the cartel, it will still be in the interests of individual whites to cheat on the cartel agreement."[20]

But while Sowell uses this argument consistently, Reich cannot. As we have seen, Reich thinks that an interracial coalition of workers is possible. But precisely the same observation that undermines the plausibility of a white monopolistic cartel, undermines the plausibility of an interracial coalition of workers. For the problem from which that argument draws its conclusions—the free-rider problem—infects all attempts to create cartels or coalitions. If the organization is large, no individual's participation will significantly increase the chances of it succeeding; and if it does succeed individuals will receive its benefits even if they didn't participate. Consequently, if individuals act in self-interest no one will participate and no cartels or coalitions will form or be maintained.

Reich is aware of the difficulty the free-rider problem raises for his proposals for class unity, and he tries to make short shrift of it. The "free-rider analysis," he writes, "leads to such absurdities as predicting that individuals will never want to vote, join unions or fight in a war."[21] But Reich has missed the point. Free-rider analysis does not predict that individuals will never vote, join unions, or go to war. If it did, even bourgeois thinkers could not be so blind as to fail to see that it is totally refuted by the fact that individuals do vote, join unions, and go to war. What free-rider analysis does predict is that under certain conditions, individuals do not vote, join unions, or go to war *from motives of self-interest*. And Reich admits as much when he writes that people form solid coalitions because of "retaliation against noncooperators," and because they are "social beings imbued with ideologies that motivate their actions as much as self-interest does."[22]

But now Reich has defeated his own argument. For, if retaliation against noncooperators and shared ideologies can save his interracial coalition of workers from destruction by free-riders, why may they not save the cartel of white capitalists and workers from a similar fate?[23] And here the capitalist–white worker coalition has a decided advantage since, according to the Marxists anyway, the capitalists control the state.

Indeed, Marx's claim that "The executive of the modern State is but a committee for managing the affairs of the whole bourgeoisie"[24] suggests that even at the time he was writing capitalists had formed a loose coalition, and employed legal means to sustain it. That such means can be employed to sustain racist coalitions is proved by the existence of Jim Crow laws.[25]

I may be suspected of creating a bogeyman. Racism, it may be protested, is on the wane, and there are, in any case, laws against the kind of cartel I fear. As Reich puts it, "Civil rights legislation and antidiscriminatory agencies prohibit the existence of formal cartels in the United States today."[26] Now I do not, in the first place, believe that I am raising a bogeyman. A white cartel exists today in South Africa, and it existed, not very long ago, in this country. Reich notes these points but still seems to take the view that it cannot happen here and now.[27] I certainly hope he is right. The question, however, is "Why?"

Why, then, has racism waned, and have antidiscrimination laws been enacted? The comfortable Marxist view is that as an ideology, racism must necessarily wane as conditions change because ideologies arise from specific economic conditions and wane when these conditions change. But this is a dangerous line. With their penchant for blaming all ills on capitalism, Marxists almost unanimously blame racism on capitalism. Reich endorses this view. "Modern racism" as opposed to "casual color-prejudice," he writes, "must be understood as originating in the context of the development of capitalism."[28] But if this is true, then it is hardly consistent of Marxists to predict that racism will subside before capitalism is destroyed.

But suppose that racism is a product of early and mature capitalism and wanes with the changing conditions of late capitalism? This is not an impossible theory. But is it consistent with Marxist dialectic's account of how ideas change and develop, and, in particular, with the view that interracial unity among workers will come from worker self-interest alone and without an appeal to justice?[29]

Although Marx maintained, in the *Manifesto* and elsewhere, that capitalism provides the necessary conditions for the union of the proletariat—for example, "by the improved means of communication" among workers it created[30]—he did not maintain that it provided *sufficient* conditions for the union of the proletariat. The workers are self-interested, but their self-interest is not, in the beginning, so enlightened that they see at once that they must unite. Their enlightenment is the result of struggle. Consequently, the workers' attempts at unity, though facilitated by the processes of capitalist production, are, Marx writes, "continually being upset" by "competition between the workers themselves."[31] However, he believed that in the end this competition will be allayed by a unifying ideology that will help them secure their collective interests.

This account is not implausible. It does not, however, explain why racism has waned, or will wane in the future. On the contrary, it raises the specter of the possibility that racism might increase. The argument's flaw, as it applies to the issue of racism, is that it assumes that racism will wane because white workers will finally realize that they must unite with black workers to secure their interests. But, as I have noted, this begs the question. White workers may just as easily conclude that they must unite with white capitalists—and against black workers—to secure their interests.

I do not deny that considerations of self-interest and the problem of free-riding had much to do with the breakdown of the white cartel and Jim Crow laws in the South. My point is that Marxist arguments fail to prove that appeals for justice—of which there were plenty during the breakdown of Jim Crow—did not also play an important part. And I suspect that in the future, the concept of justice will assume increased importance in the fight against discrimination. During the breakdown of Jim Crow, capitalism was still in its youth and demand for labor was high. The economic incentive for workers to break away from the coalition was strong. Capitalism has now come of age, and the demand for labor is low. There is a reserve army of the unemployed, and this, together with the minimum wage laws, should make the incentive to break a coalition—if it should form—weak. Therefore, self-interest and the difficulties posed by free-riding can no longer be depended on to be major factors undermining racism. More and more we must appeal explicitly to the need for justice.

## The Revolution

It will surely be objected, however, that throughout the last section I have overlooked the radical nature of the Marxist account of why workers unite. I have assumed that they unite in order to secure their interests under capitalism. The Marxist view is that workers unite to *overthrow* capitalism.

But this view is inconsistent with the great weight Marxists give to the claims of self-interest. If it is unlikely that all workers will have higher incomes if racism is overcome, it is even more unlikely that all workers will have higher incomes if capitalism is overcome. Lower-paid workers in a capitalist system may be better off in a socialist system, but surely not *highly paid* workers. This would be the case only if productivity increased dramatically under socialism. Marx, of course, predicted that in a socialist country "the springs of cooperative wealth would flow more abundantly."[32] But, as is usually the case in his accounts of the benefits of socialism, apart from the suggestion that this will result from the democratic control of the means of production—a system that has proved to be fraught with difficulties—he does not try to justify his prediction.[33]

Whenever I have expressed these doubts to Marxists, I have been accused of reading Marx simplistically. Marx, they protest, did not condemn capitalism and praise socialism because workers get low wages under capitalism and would get high wages under socialism. Indeed, he laid little emphasis on this. He condemned capitalism and praised socialism because workers are *unfree* under capitalism and *free* under socialism. To prove this they cite Marx's claim that "the system of wage labor is a system of slavery, and indeed of a slavery which becomes more severe in proportion as the social productive forces of labor develop, whether the worker receives better or worse payment."[34] Finally, they argue that workers will come to realize this fact about capitalism, and will topple it for that reason. Allen Wood, a leading advocate of the view that Marx allowed that capitalism could be just, makes this argument explicit. Wood argues that Marx believed his unmasking of the imprisoning nature of capitalism "made it possible for the workers to understand their condition of poverty, frustration and discontent for what it is: a condition of servitude."[35]

Perhaps, then Marx stressed material self-interest only as the motive which would get workers *started* in their struggle against capitalism. Perhaps he believed, as Wood suggests, that, both through the success of their struggle, and through its educational effects, they would come to realize that they are miserable because they are slaves, and that they would, accordingly, revolt to take collective control of their destiny. There are passages which suggest this reading. For example, in a letter to Fredich Bolte, a prominent figure in the American labor movement, Marx stressed that the "political movement of the working class"—a movement to take collective control of matters—arises "precisely from its economic struggles."[36] And in a speech to German trade unionists he made the same point: ". . . once the worker's material situation has become better, he can consecrate himself to the education of his children; his wife and children do not need to go to the factory, he himself can cultivate his mind more, look after his body better, and he himself becomes a socialist without noticing it."[37]

But this supposition flatly contradicts one of the arguments some Marxists use against appeals for justice according to which justice, in particular distributive justice, undermines the workers' motive to revolt by ameliorating the worst cases of material need and inequality.[38] In the passages above, however, Marx seems to be telling us that ameliorating material need does not undermine the determination to revolt. Marxists cannot have it both ways. If justice is counterrevolutionary because it is ameliorative, then material self-interest is the major motive for revolution. But if so, proletarian unity may not be achieved and the revolution may never come off. On the other hand, if the major motive for revolution is one higher than material self-interest, then demands for justice are not counterrevolutionary because justice is ameliorative. And if this is the case, no objection can be raised to color-conscious policies on the grounds that they are counterrevolutionary because they are just and therefore ameliorative.

Furthermore, whatever motive we impute to workers, their revolution would run into the problem of the free-rider as I outlined it earlier: On the one hand, participating in a revolution is costly, and on the other, no individual's participation will signifcantly increase the chances of the revolution succeeding. If the revolution does succeed, individuals will receive its benefits even if they didn't participate in it. Consequently, if each worker reasons from the point of view of self-interest, no worker will participate in the revolution and the revolution will not occur.

Both Marxists and liberal theorists have offered solutions to this application of the free-rider factor. The question is, "What do these solutions show?" As I have emphasized, the free-rider problem does not demonstrate that revolutions do not occur. Revolutions do occur. What an analysis of the free-rider problem makes clear is that under certain conditions revolutions do not occur if people are motivated by rational self-interest—if this is understood as something that increases the agent's overall advantage. The solutions acknowledge this, and they either point to conditions in which revolutions may occur even given that people reason rationally and from self-interest in the usual sense of the word, or else they appeal to a different conception of rationality. My argument is that, while these solutions may apply to a society without racial antagonisms, unless they involve an appeal to justice they will not work in a society with racial antagonisms.

Consider first solutions to the free-rider problem which attempt to show how revolutions occur even when people are motivated by self-interest in the usual sense. Marx seems to have anticipated one of these theories when, at the end of the *Manifesto*, he declared, "The proletarians have nothing to lose but their chains."[39] Since this implies that participating in a revolution is not costly for the proletarian, if it is true the free-rider problem cannot apply to the revolution since that problem assumes that participating in the revolution *is* costly to the proletarian. It is for this reason that Fanon's revolutionary theory is not vulnerable to the free-rider problem. His theory applied to a peasant revolution in the Third World—particularly in Algeria. Participating in a revolution was not costly to the peasants he was describing. They were precisely the kind of desperate beings who have nothing to lose but their chains. It is unlikely, however, that this holds true for the proletarians of advanced capitalist countries. The fact that the proletariat in the advanced Western capitalist countries was not becoming progressively impoverished, at least in an absolute sense, may have forced Marx to abandon his theory that the system is responsible for the absolute pauperization of the proletariat for the theory that the difference in wealth between the proletariat and the bourgeoisie progressively widens. But if the latter theory is more plausible, it also makes Marx's revolutionary theory less plausible, because it implies that the proletariat do have more to lose than their chains.[40]

However, the economist Matthew Edel and the philosopher Gregory Kavka have suggested a way out of the difficulty. Edel applies his solution to explain how unions form even if people reason from self-interest, and then expands it to apply to revolutions. All that is necessary, he argues, is that a few are willing to take the risk initially. If a signal such as "an accident at the workplace . . . triggers risk taking by enough individuals," he writes, "others will see the swelling of union ranks itself as a signal to join; they will realize that their joining can make a difference by maintaining the growth momentum."[41] Kavka has generalised the argument in his paper "Two Paradoxes of Revolution," and applied it directly to the issue of revolution. The root idea of the argument is, as he puts it, that "rational agents expected utility calculations about participation in revolution will change as they observe others joining the revolutionary struggle." It may be, he concedes, that at time $t_0$ only a few will revolt. But these few, he suggests, may "alter the expected utility calculations of others at time $t_1$, so that it now maximises expected utility for some of the latter to join the movement. And their recruitment into the movement may, in turn, affect the calculations of the others at $t_2$, and bring them into the fray, and so forth."[42]

Now, as Kavka acknowledges, for this process to get started, there must be at least a few at time $t_0$ who are desperate enough to revolt. And who are these likely to be? The question answers itself. The evidence of events like the riots in the Watts section of Los Angeles in the 1960s and in Miami in the early 1980s leads us to believe that it will be the black underclass. And now we can see why the process Kavka describes is likely to be stymied in America. White workers are likely to see revolting blacks as a threat. Dubois, commenting on the communists' handling of the Scottsboro case, was in effect observing a form of Kavka's process at work. Into this "delicate situation," Dubois wrote, "the Communists hurl themselves" and "seizing leadership of the poorest and most ignorant blacks, head them toward inevitable slaughter and jail-slavery." And he also anticipated the weakness of Kavka's solution to the free-rider problem in a racist context. "There is no conceivable idea," he wrote, "that seems to the present overwhelming majority of Americans higher than keeping Negroes 'in their place'." And because black Americans know this Dubois feared that they would be chary of striking the spark. "American Negroes," he observed, "do not propose to be the shock troops of the Communist Revolution, driven out in front to death, cruelty and humiliation in order to win victories for white workers." They "know perfectly well that whenever they try to lead a revolution in America, the nation will unite as one fist to crush them and them alone."[43]

But loyal Marxists maintain that a model of rationality of the kind presupposed in the Kavka's solution is inadequate to explain "mass action." John Roemer, for example, claims that such solutions are "bankrupt."[44] They overlook, he argues, the Marxist insight that "the individual's framework for making decisions emerges from his class position,"[45] and duplicate Adam Smith's error in presuming that "all economic agents think like capitalists."[46] This is a conceivable presumption he allows, since "workers too under capitalism have adopted a self-interested outlook," but he insists it is rebuttable. At crucial points Roemer maintains a new "paradigm" of rationality appropriate to the workers' class position emerges; in particular, "collective rationality replaces individual rationality," and in this way "significant collective action becomes possible."[47]

Unfortunately, although Roemer insists on the existence of a new paradigm of "collective rationality," he does not describe it, lending weight to Edel's remark that solutions to the free-rider problem based on new concepts of rationality "may appear mystical." But Kavka, in the same paper referred to earlier, has made good the lack. According to Kavka, "adopting a collectivist perspective involves evaluating acts according to the consequences that would ensue if everyone in the relevant group performed such acts." And, since we are assuming that "the expected consequences for each and all of them of a successful revolt are much better than the consequences of living under the existing regime," it is "obvious," Kavka notes, that "if a sufficient number of potential revolutionaries . . . reason collectively, a revolution will occur."[48]

Kavka also offers a "speculative explanation of the evolutionary origin of collective reasoning." It is based on the argument that, as a result of the free-rider problem, groups of collectivist reasoners have a competitive edge over groups of individualist reasoners. Accordingly, the extinction rate of groups of individualist reasoners will be higher than the extinction rate of groups of collectivist reasoners, and, as a result,

Kavka concludes, "over a long period of time we would expect collectivist reasoning to become the dominant mode of human reasoning."[49]

Considered in general, this theory is plausible. However, applied to the case of the emergence of collectivist reasoning in the black and white proletariat, it is implausible. Because it is racist, the white proletariat treats the black proletariat unfairly. As a result, if the black proletariat reasoned collectively with respect to the proletariat as a whole, its extinction rate would be even higher than if it reasoned individualistically. And the facts bear this out: Capitalists can use black workers as strikebreakers precisely because black workers do not reason collectively with respect to the proletariat as a whole.

And there is a further difficulty. Kavka assumes that there are initially groups of collectivist reasoners and groups of individualist reasoners, and explains how the former will come to displace the latter. But what needs to be explained is how collectivist reasoning *emerges* in a group of individualist reasoners. For one of Marx's bitterest indictments of capitalism is that it makes people—including workers—egoistic. And although Roemer says that workers will learn to abandon individualist reasoning he admits that they start with it. Accordingly, he states that the possibility of "workers learning to discard the individualist model and adopting a collective rationality" depends on their "realization that their (individual) lots shall improve only to the extent that they struggle to improve the lot of the collective."[50] But if this is the mechanism by which collective rationality arises, it will *not* arise among black workers. For white workers treat them unfairly, and this means that their lot does not improve when they struggle to improve the lot of the collective.

Furthermore, Roemer's mechanism does not even explain why collective reasoning emerges among white workers. For it is false to insist that their individual lots shall improve only to the extent that they struggle to improve the lot of the collective. Their individual lots will improve even more if *others* struggle to improve the lot of the collective and they play the free-rider. Roemer's model really implies only that they will become wilier individualists, pretending to reason collectively and urging others to do so. Kavka's thesis shows why it is unlikely that such "sophisticated individualists" could become dominant in a group of collectivist reasoners. But his argument is not available to Roemer, for Roemer has to show why such sophisticated individualists could not become dominant in a group of *individualist* reasoners.

The most plausible account of a transition of this kind depends on a belief in the workers' sense of fairness and justice. As David Lyons has demonstrated, the compelling nature of the paradigm of collective reasoning can be accounted for only by an appeal to considerations of justice and fairness.[51] That is, for people with a sense of justice, the compelling argument against individualist reasoning in the context of certain kinds of action is that because it promotes free-riding it is unfair and unjust, and the compelling argument for collectivist reasoning is that since it rules out free-riding it is fair and just. And, given the structure of our society, and the fact that workers are initially individualist reasoners, we can assume that they will have a sense of justice. To people who reason individualistically, free-riding will seem rational, and the moral notions of justice and fairness have to be brought in to balance the claims of rationality and to forestall the collapse of their society. Consequently, in such societies, a sense of justice is functional, and sure to be endemic. And Marx concurs. "The ideas of the ruling class," he declared—and among such ideas he must have included the idea of justice, as he believed it legitimized capitalist society and the existence of the ruling class—"are in every epoch the ruling ideas."[52]

## Harold Cruse and Domestic Colonialism

Even the more imaginative analyses of the race-class issue in America cannot avoid the conclusion that the problem of racism requires a revision of Marxist theory. For example, Harold Cruse, a long-time student of Marxist theories about the race question and author of *The Crisis of the Negro Intellectual*, would probably argue that I have overlooked the fundamental error in the line of argument I have examined. That error is the assumption that the next important revolution in America is or should be a combined black and white proletariat revolution. The next important revolution in America, according to Cruse, is, or should be, a black bourgeois revolution. American Marxists fail to see this, says Cruse, because they insist on seeing black people as proletarians with black skins. But this is a blunder. Black people are not just proletarians with black skins. They are a *colonized* people. "The position of the Negro in America," Cruse affirms, is "nothing less than a Western form of domestic colonialism."[53]

If he is right about the position of the Negro, he may also be right that the next important revolution in America is or should be a black bourgeois revolution. At least this claim can be shown to be based on a most impeccable source—Lenin himself. According to Lenin—in a passage quoted by Cruse—in colonial and semi-colonial countries "the working class suffers not so much from capitalism as from the lack of capitalist development. The working class is therefore interested in the widest, freest, and speediest development of capitalism. . . . Therefore, the bourgeois revolution is in the highest degree advantageous to the proletariat."[54] Cruse argues that this is exactly the position of the black working class in America. The black working class, he says, suffers not "so much from capitalism in America, but from a lack of capitalistic development."[55] And this dims the prospect that a socialist revolution— even if it should occur—would be to the advantage of blacks. We must, Cruse observes, "educate for the essentials of socialism by educating in the essentials of capitalism."[56] For this reason Cruse maintains that "Marxist socialists must support all pro-capitalistic aspirations of Negroes in terms of economic institutions."[57] And in this, he believes, they would get the support of the black working class, for its support of black capitalist institutions, Cruse writes, shows that it is "interested in the widest development of capitalistic free-enterprise ventures for the black minority."[58] Finally, Cruse notes that a spontaneous black bourgeois revolution, which would make up for the lack of capitalist development and meet that interest, has from the first struggled to get under way. Its most recent incarnation was the Black Power conference in Newark, New Jersey, in 1968, but its roots reach back even to the period of slavery, when Martin Delany preached black capitalism.

It is irrelevant to object that there is no sizeable black bourgeoisie. Cruse is well aware of this. His point is that if the hoped-for proletarian revolution is to occur, there *must* be one. A more germane objection is that black capitalism is not in the cards. As W. A. Lewis, who won a Nobel prize for his work on development economics, points out, most new businesses, white or black, go bankrupt within twelve months.[59] Cruse is also fully aware of these obstacles, and his response to them reveals how ineluctably racism requires a revision of Marxist theory.

The spontaneous impulse of a bourgeois movement, Cruse argues, is nationalist and separatist. The bourgeoisie want power and wealth, and the way to achieve these is normally to control the resources and market of an area. But because the aspiring black bourgeoisie in America are inside the greatest capitalist power in the world, their efforts to control the resources and market of their area have been, as Cruse observes, "incomplete, frustrated and aborted."[60] Accordingly, from the first, there has emerged, alongside the nationalist-separatist black bour- geoisie, an integrationist black bourgeoisie. The split between the ideas of Martin Delany and Frederick Douglass, between those of Booker T. Washington and of W. E. B. Dubois, between Marcus Garvey and Dubois, and between the goals of the Black Power movement and the NAACP are, Cruse believes, instances of the split between the nationalist- separatist black bourgeoisie and the integrationist black bourgeoisie. The integrationist black bourgeois class does not try to develop black cap- italism, or, Cruse observes, to "achieve economic and political domination over the black community (which, historically should be its natural func- tion. . . )." Instead it uses a rationale based on "social equlaity" and "equal opportunity" and tries to integrate itself into the existing white capitalist society, and to "disavow any special responsibility toward developing the economic and political autonomy of the black community." This, Cruse charges, is "social opportunism." When the bourgeois integrationists oppose "the economics of Black Power," he maintains, "the real motivation is their unwillingness to assume responsibility for building group institutions."[61]

Teetering anxiously on the brink of the ghetto, the black middle class makes an attractive target for criticism, and black intellectuals—those blacks, usually middle class themselves, who theorize about the function and legitimacy of a black middle class—have long aimed their barbs at it. In the last chapter we observed Washington, Sowell, Wilson, and Williams castigating sections of it for being "poverty pimps." Now we see Cruse castigating it for shirking its responsibilities to the black lower class. In his book *Black Bourgeoisie*, published in 1957, Franklin Frazier, the greatest black sociologist since Dubois, had anticipated Cruse, and in 1982 Martin Kilson, professor of government at Harvard, reported that it had not reformed. According to Kilson, the arguments of black historian Nell Painter and Afro-American lawyer and journalist Roger Wilkins that "the black bourgeoisie will revitalize its relationship to lower-class blacks" are "phony."[62] It is not my concern here to judge the validity of these charges. Neither is it to judge whether the black middle class has a responsibility to the black lower class, nor to say whether it will heed that responsibility and succeed in establishing black capitalism. It is only to point out that, insofar as that claim of responsibility is used to appeal to the black middle class to develop capitalism for the benefit of the black lower class, and as a means to class unity and eventually the revolution, it demands a momentous alteration in Marxist theory. For Marx never even hinted that capitalists develop countries *from a sense of responsibility*. Capitalists, Marx said, seek profit, and in seeking and making profit sometimes unintentionally develop a country. That motive alone, the motive of self-interest, was, he thought, sufficient to bring about the development necessary for a socialist movement. The fact that Cruse has to appeal to the sense of responsibility of the black bourgeoisie to bring about this condition shows—if he is right—how fundamental a revision in Marxist theory is necessary in considering the problem of racism.

## Is Justice Counterrevolutionary?

Even if workers will unite only if there is justice among them, appeals for justice may yet be counterrevolutionary in Marxist terms. That is, while justice may unite workers, it may unite them only in an effort to wring concessions from capitalism, but not to overthrow it. Thus we move from the argument that appeals for justice are counterrevolutionary because justice ameliorates need and inequality, thereby deflecting the workers from the revolutionary course, to the argument that appeals for justice are counterrevolutionary because capitalism can be just. The leading proponent of this theory is Allen Wood. According to Wood, Marx held that societies with different modes of production have different standards of justice. A standard of justice rationalizes and expedites the mode of production to which it corresponds and can be applied only to that mode of production. Accordingly, the only standard of justice that can be applied to capitalism is the capitalist standard of justice, and capitalism is necessarily just by that standard. In particular, the wage-relation between capitalists and worker is just because the capitalists pay the workers a wage equivalent to the exchange value of the workers labor-power, and the capitalist system of justice is one in which equivalents are exchanged. On these grounds, Wood concludes that Marx allowed that capitalism could be just, and to clinch his theory cites Marx's famous remark to the effect that, though the buyer of labor-power (the capitalist) exploits the seller of labor-power (the worker) this is "by no means an injury to the seller."[63]

The theory that Marx condemned capitalism for reasons other than its injustice seems also to get support from his early essay, "On the Jewish Question." In that essay, Marx allows that the modern capitalist state can accord everyone his political and human rights but maintains that it must nevertheless be condemned. Assuming, then, that according people their rights is just, Marx seems to suggest that he believes that capitalism might be just. Accordingly, since he certainly condemned capitalism, he must have condemned it on other grounds.

Perhaps these considerations show that Marx thought that—by its own lights—capitalism *as a practice* is just, or alternatively, that, again by their own lights, capitalist societies *can* be just. But they certainly do not show that capitalist societies *are* just, nor, in particular, that capitalist societies are just to black people. If they are not, and if, as would be natural in such societies, black workers resent white workers for accepting the benefits of their subordination, then, whether or not appeals for justice are ultimately revolutionary, justice would be necessary to the revolution since it would be necessary to assuage feelings of resentment which undermine class unity.

But *did* Marx argue that capitalism could be just? If he did, appeals for justice are, *ultimately*, conservative, and on that basis a Marxist might maintain that the best strategy for the revolution is to avoid appeals to justice for blacks even when these are well-founded. But the theory that Marx believed capitalism just has been subjected to searching criticism. As Nancy Holmstrom points out, Marx remarked of the wage-relation in capitalism that "the free laborer . . . agrees, i.e. is compelled by social conditions to sell the whole of his active life, his very capacity to work, for the price of the necessities of life, his birthright for a mess of pottage," and also that "surplus labor always remains forced labor— no matter how much it may appear to result from free contractual agreement." Accordingly, she concludes that Wood views "the exchange between capitalist and workers too narrowly." Even if equals are exchanged for equals, the exchange is not equal because each party to it is not equally free; since the capitalist controls the means of production, the worker is not free not to sell his labor power. Thus, on the basis of the plausible assumption that equal freedom to exchange is as necessary to justice as equal exchange, Holmstrom concludes that Marx's observation of the wage-relation was just "tongue-in-cheek."[64]

Wood is, of course, fully aware of the passages Holmstrom cites, but he thinks they show only that Marx condemned capitalism as a "form of servitude." "It is only a prejudice," he maintains, to suppose that "servitude necessarily 'connotes' injustice," noting that Aristotle did not share this prejudice.[65] But Wood seems to have forgotten that the justice Marx was discussing was not Aristotelian, but bourgeois, and by the lights of the bourgeois, servitude *does* necessarily connote injustice.

Similarly, Wood's claim that Marx held that capitalism conceals the servitude it involves behind a "mask of universal liberty" may also be sound. However, it too may entail that Marx also held that capitalism conceals the injustice it involves behind that same mask. This conclusion suggests an interpretation of "On the Jewish Question." In it, Marx may not be saying that capitalism is just. He may be saying that capitalism *pretends* to be just: It accords everyone "equal rights" but this is only a mask. Behind that mask it is unjust because, by allowing some to own the means of production, it makes the rights of others worthless.

If these considerations are cogent, the ideas of right and justice, far from being counterrevolutionary, are very revolutionary indeed. For, if capitalism is unjust because the parties to the wage-relation—workers and capitalists—are not equally free, then, since the wage-relation is essential to capitalism, demands for justice would be ultimately, demands for the dissolution of capitalism. It may be that Marx underestimated the power of his own dialectic. For, although appeals to the "mask" of bourgeois justice—equal rights before the law—may be conservative, why should we believe that, as a result of their educative struggles, the workers cannot penetrate to the reality behind the mask? Indeed, if Wood is right that Marx believed that his unmasking of capitalism would make it possible for the workers to understand that their misery was due to their "servitude," then the workers will do precisely that.

The final Marxist objection to appeals for racial justice, and justice and rights generally, stems from Allen Buchanan's account of the Marxist critique of justice and rights. According to Buchanan, Marx believed that capitalism is necessarily unjust on its own terms, but did not stress this because he believed, as we observed earlier, that the future communist society would be "beyond justice."[66] According to this theory, a Marxist could admit that the idea of justice and the importance of rights are potentially revolutionary, but insist that a revolutionary should not appeal to them because they will be obsolete and counterproductive in the society that replaces capitalism.

But will every conception of justice and rights be obsolete and counterproductive in communist society? Especially if we keep the race problem in mind, there is every reason to answer this question in the negative.

The Marxist would argue that it would be foolish to wait for racist tendencies in society to disappear before calling for class unity. He would argue, reasonably, that class unity is possible if workers see that it is in their interest to suppress manifestations of racism in order to overthrow capitalism. But this raises a problem: If workers suppress manifestations of racism among themselves in order to overthrow capitalism, there is no reason to suppose that they will continue to suppress manifestations *after* they overthrow capitalism. The philosopher Karl Popper made the general point in his criticism of Marx's revolutionary theory. "There is no earthly reason," Popper observes, "why the individuals who form the proletariat should retain their class unity once the pressure of the struggle against the common class enemy has ceased."[67] And the implications of this possibility for the race question have not been lost on black students of Marx: "What guarantee," Harold Cruse asks, "do Negroes have that socialism means racial equality any more than does capitalist democracy?"[68]

The Marxist should be wary of the facile answer that communism or socialism means the transcendence of racism. I am ready to admit that because there would be no classes under communism, the members of a communist society would not hold different opinions because they belonged to different classes. And I concede too that, for the same reason, the members of a communist society would not persist in mistaken opinions because their class interest blinds them to the truth. But because it is false to insist that only class interest blinds people to the truth, it does not follow that the members of a communist society would not— and do not—have vehement differences of opinion, and would not believe falsehoods.

According to philosopher G. A. Cohen, Marx believed that a capitalist society disguises the fact that the market values of commodities are determined by the quantity of necessary labor time required for their production, but in a socialist society, in which production proceeds according to a democratically formulated plan, the appearance and reality of labor are one. As Cohen summarizes the view he attributes to Marx, "Socialism dissolves the mysteries by abolishing the market."[69] This account implies that there can be no basis in a socialist society for serious disagreement about social reality. If reality always appears to be exactly what it is, if, as Cohen puts it, the relations between human beings are "transparent" and "intelligible," then, when people disagree about these relations, all they have to do to dissolve their disagreement is to look again. Needless to say, this theory is quite implausible and naive, and Cohen has no difficulty in showing that even under socialism a gulf will persist between reality and appearance. And if this is so, then there will still be a basis for serious theoretical disagreements about the relations between human beings under socialism.

Cohen underplays this problem when he remarks that "It is surely reasonable to regret the fact that experience induces a propensity to believe falsehoods about important social matters, even when the propensity is restrained by theoretical knowledge."[70] If Cohen means by this, as I suspect he does, that under socialism the propensity in question will remain only a propensity, then I think that his remark is misleading. If there is a gulf between social reality and its appearance, then claims of theoretical knowledge may come into conflict with other claims of theoretical knowledge.

Consequently, since racism involves claims of theoretical knowledge about relations between human beings, we cannot—on Marxist grounds—expect that the emergence of socialism would mean the end of the false beliefs of racism. At most, Marxist thought implies that communism is a necessary condition for the transcendance of racism. It cannot mean that communism is a sufficient condition for the transcendance of racism. To think that is to succumb to economic determinism, the "undialectical" view, already rejected, that economic structures mechanically determine peoples' ideas without the intervention of the lessons and effects of their political struggles.[71] But if socialism or communism are only necessary conditions for the transcendence of racism, or more precisely, racist tendencies, then these tendencies could still manifest themselves under socialism. If this is true, and they can be finally rooted out only dialectically, through the political struggles of black and white workers, then it is absolutely clear that, since black workers will be in a minority, they will need to insist on their rights, and consequently, that justice will not be obsolete or counterproductive in a communist society.

# 4

# Busing: The Backward-looking Argument

## *Brown* and Its Aftermath

In the course of a powerful polemic against busing, the columnist Ross Mackenzie stressed how it "has required children to spend long hours on buses," adding that this burden falls especially on black and Hispanic children.[1] To this kind of sudden solicitude, Shirley Chisholm, congresswoman and one-time Presidential candidate, has given an apt if somewhat ungracious rejoinder. "What about black children who had to get up at 4:30 A.M. to be bused right past their own neighborhood schools? Where were the voices then? Hypocrites."[2] But although some opponents of busing are certainly hypocrites they can still respond with the old saw, "if it was wrong then, it is wrong now." Their hypocrisy does not relieve their opponents of the need to construct arguments for busing.

The modern controversy over school desegregation and busing began with the famous *Brown* v. *Board of Education of Topeka* decision of 1954, when the Supreme Court announced that "segregation in pubic education" is a "denial of the equal protection of the laws."[3] Thurgood Marshall, who had argued the case before the Supreme Court, and who is, of course, himself now a member of the court, apparently experienced two moods when he heard it. The *Times* quoted him as predicting that school segregation in America would be entirely stamped out in no more than five years.[4] But Harvard law professor Derrick Bell reports that at an ecstatic celebration at the NAACP's Manhattan headquarters, Marshall wandered through the party frowning and said: "You fools go ahead and have your fun, but we ain't begun to work yet."[5]

Twenty-eight years later we know what we might have opined from the first—that Marshall's pessimistic mood was the realistic one. According to many accounts (Bell, for example, takes this view), most black children today still attend "racially isolated" schools.

Part of the explanation is that many white citizens and leaders were, and are, determined to keep schools segregated. Five weeks after *Brown*, Thomas Stanley, the governor of Virginia declared "I shall use every legal means at my command to continue segregated schools in Virginia."[6] Even then he was only one of a chorus, and in the years since a veritable army of politicans, parents, pundits, pharisees, and racists have followed him, and they have not always used only legal means. Their "recruiting division" has even managed to convert some blacks to their cause and in that unlikely soil has struck black gold, for certain of these recruits have gone so far as to ridicule the *Brown* decision itself. The history of all-Jewish schools, writes one star recruit, Thomas Sowell, reduces the court's finding that separate schools are inherently inferior to a "laughingstock."[7]

But black credulity and white intransigence are not the only reasons why *Brown* failed to desegregate schools. Another reason is to be found in *Brown* itself. It condemned the traditional dual school system, but such systems had two distinct aspects, which the decision did not distinguish, and which hindsight has taught us are crucially different. On the one hand, students were assigned to schools on the basis of their race—on the other hand, their schools were all-black and all-white. Brown did not say clearly which of these aspects of segregation it condemned, or whether it condemned both of them. This was all the segregationists needed.

They saw at once that they could salvage most of what they wanted—separation of the races—by assuming that the court condemned only the assigning of students to schools on the basis of their race. The reason is obvious: all-black and all-white schools could be secured by means other than assigning students to schools on the basis of race. And among these means, one could be dressed up to seem particularly pure—assigning students to schools closest to where they lived. Because of residential segregation, this would be almost as effective a means of maintaining segregation as assignments made on the basis of race.

Unfortunately for the segregationists, this stratagem was squashed. In a series of cases, beginning with *Green* v. *New Kent County* in 1968, and continuing with *Swann* v. *Charlotte-Mecklenberg Board of Education* in 1971, and *Keyes* v. *District No. 1, Denver, Colorado* in 1973, the Supreme Court has made it increasingly clear that while the law forbids racial assignments designed to segregate schools, it does not forbid, and in fact may require, racial assignments intended to integrate schools. In desperation the segregationists have reached for their enemies' weapons, and have brandished vigorously Justice Harlan's powerful aphorism "our Constitution is color-blind." But to no avail. In the law, at least, however it may appear in moral terms, it is sometimes permissible to take a person's color into account.

But while the law has become clearer, it remains controversial. Some commentators argue that it is bad; others argue that it is good; all appear to agree that the Court has not justified either the original *Brown*, or subsequent decisions.

To some, of course, *Brown* was anathema. But even among those who thought it was good law, there were legal scholars who maintained that it was badly argued. Their main criticism was the apparent grounds for the court's main finding. Chief Justice Warren had written that the court's finding that segregation harms black children was "amply supported by modern authority," and in the famous footnote 11 of the opinion had cited seven works by social scientists as that authority.[8] The segregationists used the footnote in a manner typical of their style and abilities: the social scientists listed, they charged or implied, were either communists or foreigners and therefore not to be trusted. But legal scholars had a different axe to grind. Part of their objection was that the court claimed to have relied on what they considered poor social science to prove what was in any case obvious. For example, New York University law professor Edmund Cahn gave the first work cited in the footnote, a paper by Kenneth B. Clark, a rough going over. Proving that segregation is harmful, Cahn concluded impatiently, was like proving that "fire burns."[9] But the more serious and considered part of the scholars' objection was that the court should not have relied on social science at all.

Having said this, the scholars felt it incumbent upon them to reveal what they thought the court should have relied on. But their disclosures are no more than suggestive. Cahn seemed to think that anyone who understood what segregation was would see that it was wrong, and he compared it eloquently to the isolation of lepers, but this is as far as he got.[10] Charles L. Black, Jr., a law professor at Yale, thought the question deserved even less consideration. If asked whether segregation offends against equality, he wrote, "I think we ought to exercise one of the sovereign prerogatives of philosophy—that of laughter."[11] Others took the question more seriously. Some thought the court's decision depended on the ideal of equality and elaborated ingenious arguments to show that—independent of the findings of social science—separate schools are inherently unequal. One at least thought that it depended on a question of rights. In the quaintest and most equivocal of the endorsements of *Brown*, Herbert Wechsler, one of the nation's leading legal scholars and a professor of law at Columbia, wrote that the case rested on the fact that segregation was a denial of the right of freedom of association, though he allowed that integration raised problems too because it forced an association on those to whom it was repulsive.[12]

These main positions in relation to the issue of desegregation were staked out in the original controversy over *Brown*, and remain the foci of the present controversy over school desegregation. Most advocates of school desegregation believe that their position is justified because segregated schools are harmful or violate the ideal of equal educational opportunity. Opponents of desegregation, on the other hand, contend that the concept of equal educational opportunity is meaningless. Making use of the concept that Wechsler had outlined to throw scholarly doubt on the *Brown* decision, they maintain that desegregating schools violates the right of parents to determine their children's education. And in a characteristically novel and provocative essay, Ronald Dworkin retrieves Cahn's idea that the case for desegregation lies in the transparently insulting nature of segregation and, welding it to his own powerful moral theory, fashions a case for desegregation which, he says, is independent of the causal judgments of social science.[13]

I will examine these arguments in the next few chapters of this book. In the present chapter I analyze what is perhaps the most immediately appealing argument for school desegregation. I call it the backward-looking argument, because it looks backward to the past.

## The Backward-looking Argument

School segregation may be either de jure or de facto. This is a fundamental, though contested, distinction in the busing controversy. The distinction does not lie in the racial composition of the schools, for in both kinds of segregation schools are all-black or nearly all-black, and all-white or nearly all-white. The distinction lies in the cause. In de jure segregation the school board intentionally assigns black and white students to different schools because they are black and white. De facto segregation is caused by other factors; the school board does *not* intentionally assign black and white students to different schools because they are black or white.

The backward-looking argument can now be summarized as follows: Past unjust de jure segregation is one of the causes of present de facto segregation. De facto segregation is harmful. Justice demands that a harmful condition caused by injustice be undone. Consequently, justice may demand that de facto segregation cease.

This argument crucially depends on the premise that de jure segregation is unjust. This is its main tactical advantage over other arguments in favor of busing. The most intellectually respectable opponents of desegregation, the advocates of color-blindness, accept that premise, but do not accept similarly central premises of any of the other arguments. Furthermore, the other key premises of the backward-looking argument are also highly plausible: De jure segregation did actually exist, it probably did cause de facto segregation; and justice does demand that harmful conditions caused by injustice be altered.

Perhaps for these reasons, the Supreme Court has always appealed to the backward-looking argument in its desegregation cases. In *Swann*, for example, the court ruled that a North Carolina school district had to integrate its all-black and all-white schools because, although the school board did not currently practice de jure segregation—it assigned students to schools on the basis of geographical proximity—it *used* to practice de jure segregation, and this was considered an essential link in the sequence of causes that brought about all-black and all-white schools. Similarly, in *Keyes* the court ruled that the Denver public school system had to integrate its schools again because, although the school board did not currently practice de jure segregation, it used to do so. Finally, in *Columbus* and *Dayton II* in 1979, the court ordered a system-wide remedy of de facto segregation on the grounds that the school boards in question had practiced de jure segregation and that a causal connection to the current condition of segregation could be presumed.

If the strength of the backward-looking argument is its foundation on an indisputable past injustice, its weakness is that this same injustice seems long past. Even if past de jure segregation generally does cause de facto segregation, it need not continue to do so throughout time. The court acknowledged this in *Swann*, allowing that the passage of time could weaken the causal effectiveness of past de jure segregation, though it did not say when this might happen. Further, even if past de jure segregation generally does tend to cause a pattern of all-black and all-white schools, it need not have been the cause of *every* segregated pattern. This seems so obviously true to certain people, even some advocates of busing, that they deem it a decisive point against the backward-looking argument. Ronald Dworkin, for example, points out that denying it implies that "if there had not been *de jure* segregation in the past there would now be *de facto* integration," and argues that this is so implausible that the backward-looking argument must fail.[14]

But the crucial assumption of the first part of this objection, viz., that de jure segregation is a thing of the distant past, is utterly gratuitous. When the Supreme Court outlawed school segregation in 1954, school boards did not universally comply. Some openly defied the Court, others chose subterfuge. For example, some school boards said they assigned students to the schools in the zones nearest to where they lived, then drew school zone lines so that black and white students were always assigned to different schools. Other boards introduced "transfer plans," which allowed students to transfer out of schools they had been assigned to, and still others instituted "freedom of choice" plans, knowing full well that many black parents were being intimidated into not sending their children to white schools.[15] Moreover, there is reason to believe that many school boards continue to practice some kind of covert de jure segregation, or have only recently stopped doing so.[16] If this is so, the backward-looking argument is less vulnerable to doubts about the causal relationship between de jure and de facto segregation.

But appeal to the practice of covert de jure segregation raises a peculiar problem. There is no question that when a school board practices de jure segregation covertly it is being unjust. The problem is in telling when it is practicing de jure segregation covertly. Since the board does not state its intentions, they must be inferred from its actions. But inferring intention from action is hazardous. Consequently, proving the existence of covert de jure segregation is likely to be difficult, and many cases are likely to be unprovable. In *Keyes* the Supreme Court took steps to minimize this problem. Speaking for the majority, Justice Brennan argued that "a finding of intentionally segregative school board actions in a meaningful portion of a school system creates a presumption that other segregated schooling within the system is not adventitious. It establishes, in other words, a *prima facie* case of unlawful segregative design on the part of school authorities, and shifts to those authorities the burden of proving that other segregated schools within the system are not also the result of intentionally segregative actions."[17]

Critics have objected to this argument on the grounds that the burden of proof it places on *petitioners* is unfair, and that it tends to make school authorities responsible for too *little*. Thus, in a separate opinion, Justice Powell wrote that he would relieve "petitioners of the initial tortuous effort of identifying 'segregative acts' and deducing 'segregative intent.' I would hold, quite simply, that where segregated public schools exist within a school district to a substantial degree, there is a *prima facie* case that the duly constituted public authorities . . . are sufficiently responsible to warrant imposing on them a nationally applicable burden to demonstrate that they nevertheless are operating a genuinely integrated school system."[18] Only a slight extension of this argument—that where segregated schools exist within a school district to a substantial degree, there is a prima facie rebuttable case that the public authorities intended it—considerably mitigates the force of Dworkin's objection.

## Intentions, Motive, and Dignitary Harm

Owen Fiss, a professor of law at Yale, who cites Justice Powell's view approvingly, at one time argued that, although proof that a school board intends to segregate students may be sufficient to hold it liable for any segregation its policies cause, such a proof should not be necessary.[19] Whether or not a school board intends to segregate, he argued, it should be held liable for any segregation its policies cause, if that segregation was foreseeable and avoidable.[20]

But, from denying that proof of a school board's intention to segregate is necessary to a case for desegregation, Fiss has moved to denying that such a proof is *relevant* to a case for desegregation. He can find no point in trying to impute an intention to segregate to school boards. "The concept of segregative intent," he writes, "gives very little direction to educational administrators,"[21] fails to distinguish that "harm which is certain from that which is uncertain,"[22] and does not make "any contribution to the resolution of the state action problem."[23] Finally, as if to nip in the bud all discussion of school boards' intentions to segregate, Fiss affirms that there can be no such thing. "An organization," he writes—and it is clear that he considers school boards organizations— "has neither an intention nor a will."[24]

Fiss developed this view with the best of intentions. Proving a case of an initial intent to segregate, even in part of a school system, as the court requires, is tedious, difficult, and often impossible. To insist that such proofs be a necessary condition for holding school boards liable for segregation would leave many forms of harmful segregation intact. It is therefore understandable that Fiss, who is concerned with abolishing harmful segregation, wants to dismiss considerations about school boards' intentions. But this move is unnecessary. We can avoid the problem Fiss seeks to avoid—proving intent to segregate—without denying that school boards have intentions or that their intentions are relevant to the desegregation issue. All that is necessary to avoid the problem is to point out that an agent, and thus a school board, may justly be held responsible for the foreseeable harms it causes, even if it did not intend those harms. And dismissing school boards' intentions has even more serious drawbacks. By denying the relevance of their intentional wrongdoing, we would deny the necessity of their having to acknowledge that wrongdoing. This is not only unfair to the black students who are intentionally and wrongfully segregated, but also, as I will show, depreciates or ignores the most important harm of intentional segregation— the dignitary harm caused by the perception that one has been intentionally segregated.

Following the ideas of H. L. A. Hart, I distinguish among certain classes of action: (1) "intentionally doing something," (2) "doing something with a further intention," and (3) "bare intention."[25] (1) "intentionally doing something": A person intentionally does something if he sets out to do it, and he does not intentionally do something if he does not set out to do it. Suppose A aims a gun at B, pulls the trigger and wounds B. A has wounded B intentionally if he set out to wound B. If, however, A believed the gun was unloaded, A has not wounded B intentionally because he could not have set out to wound B. Whether or not a person performs an act intentionally depends on how the act is defined. If, in the above example, the relevant act is defined as "aiming the gun at B and pulling the trigger," then A may have performed this act intentionally both when it has the consequence that B is wounded, and when it does not have this consequence. (2) "doing something with a further intention": A person does something with a further intention when he does it intentionally in order to cause something else to happen. If A intentionally aims a gun at B and pulls the trigger, and if he does so in order to cause B to be wounded, then he does so with the further intention of wounding B. It is clear from these examples that a person can perform the same act both when he intentionally does something, and when he does something with a further intention. However, the distinction is important because it is often easy to distinguish an act that has been performed intentionally, but less easy to identify a further intention. For example, while it may be clear that a school board has intentionally assigned students to schools nearest to where they live, it may be unclear whether it has done so with the further intention of segregating blacks. (3) "bare intention": A person has a bare intention of doing something if he plans to set about doing it in the future but takes no present steps toward its execution. For example, A has a bare intention to shoot and wound B if he plans to do so next month, but has not yet bought the gun with which to do it.

A person does not necessarily intend the result that he foresees his action will cause. A may foresee that firing a gun at B will make a noise, but he does not necessarily intentionally make a noise, because he may not have set out to make a noise. Indeed, he might well prefer that his firing the gun not make a noise. But it also does not follow that in firing the gun A makes a noise unintentionally. This would be so only if A had put a silencer on his gun and did not foresee that in firing the gun he would make a noise. To do something unintentionally is not simply not to do it intentionally. If someone does something unintentionally he is surprised when it happens because he did not foresee it. On the other hand, someone can not intend to do something, yet not be surprised when he does, because he has foreseen that it would be the result of some act he did intend.

However, as Hart points out, the legal use in English of the word "intentionally" differs from its ordinary use. In English law a person is held to have killed intentionally if he foresaw someone would die as a result of his actions, even if killing was not what he set out to do. Similarly, George Graham, among other philosophers, proposes the notion that, although a person need not intend all the consequences of his actions which he can foresee he nevertheless intentionally brings about all of these consequences. His argument is that, if a person foresees that an act will have certain consequences, and acts anyway, he "decides" to bring about these consequences.[26] Other philosophers, such as Anthony Duff, propose the concept that, although a person need not intend all of the consequences of his actions which he can foresee, he nevertheless intentionally brings about those consequences which he might have considered reasons for not acting.[27] These philosophers are concerned with maintaining a connection between intentionality and responsibility. But as I noted earlier, it is not necessary to do something intentionally in order to be responsible for it; it is only necessary to be in a position to determine whether it will occur. Thus, a person may be held responsible for something even though he did not intend it or do it intentionally, and, indeed, even if he did not foresee it.

Given the above accounts of the nature of intention, it is obvious why it is necessary to attribute intentions to school boards. For if a school board can intend to segregate, and if to intend to segregate is to set out to segregate, we can tell school boards not to set out to segregate. Contrary to what Fiss has claimed, this is a relevant issue that gives considerable direction to school administrators. Furthermore, if a school board intends to segregate, segregation is more likely to result from its policies, other things being equal, than if it does not intend to segregate. For, if a board intends to segregate, then it will design policies that cause segregation, and if it does not intend to segregate it will not design policies that cause segregation. Consequently, assuming that, generally, policies designed to cause an end are more likely to cause it than policies not designed to cause it, it follows that, contrary to Fiss's theory, believing that school boards can intend to segregate may help to mark off harm that is certain from harm that is not certain.[28]

In order to prevent harm, other things being equal, government must curb policies certain to cause harm before it curbs policies not certain to cause harm. One way for government to do this is for it to hold agents—for instance school boards—liable for the harm which is certain to result from their policies and not liable, or less liable, for the harm which is not certain to result from their policies. If this is so, then, given the conclusions we reached above, supposing that school boards can intend to segregate can help solve the problem of when to hold school boards liable for segregation.

The difficulty with this argument is that other things may not be equal. Suppose, for example, that the policy designed to segregate causes a kind of segregation that is only trivially harmful, while a policy not designed to segregate causes a segregation that is gravely harmful. Or suppose that segregation is as likely to result from policies not designed to segregate as from policies designed to segregate. In neither case is it clear that the most efficient strategy for preventing this harm would be to hold school boards more liable for the kind of segregation they intend than for the kind of segregation they do not intend. However, I argue that this kind of problem arises only because neither consideration of segregation allows for the importance of dignitary harm—the sense of wounded dignity, inferiority, and stigma experienced by the victims of school segregation.

If they are rational, people tend to see what is there, and not to see what isn't there. Policy design *is* something that is "there." It is an objective fact in the world. Consequently, policies designed to secure a particular end are not only more likely to secure that end but are also— an entirely different thing—more likely to be *perceived* as designed to secure that end than policies not so designed.

Now these truths apply to black people. That is, black people tend to recognize policies designed to segregate them. But the intentions of a school board determine how it designs its policies. It if intends to segregate, they will have a certain design. If it does not, its policies will have another design. Consequently, segregation which is intended is more likely to be perceived as intended than segregation which is not intended, and, if it is the perception of discrimination, of intentional segregation, which causes stigma, more likely to cause that harm.

Fiss rejects this argument on the grounds that, in schools that are all-black and all-white, students will perceive themselves to be intentionally segregated whether or not they are, and, as a cause of stigma, "The perception of the victim is more important than the attitude of the perpetrator."[29] But if I am right, this objection can be sustained only by the presumption that black people are not rational. I do not mean that every rational person always immediately sees the truth. I mean that if we respect people we cannot *presume* that they cannot be rationally convinced of the truth. This implies that if they have harmful false beliefs, and we would save them from harm, we must show them that their beliefs are false, not pretend that they believe the truth. But this falsehood is exactly what Fiss's position commits him to. For, suppose that black students believe falsely that they are intentionally segregated. Fiss cannot attempt to persuade them by rational means that their belief is false. To do so he would have to appeal to the fact that the school board did not intend to segregate, and this would contradict his belief that what the school board intends makes no difference. Consequently, if Fiss admits that their belief may cause them to feel stigmatized and that this harm is serious, he must attempt to deal with this harm and their belief by ordering desegregation. That is, he must act as if their false belief were true.

But Fiss appears not to accept the idea that the harm of stigmatizing is serious. Thus he objects to the view I have proposed on the grounds that it does not account "for the special status it must accord stigmatic harm."[30] My analysis of the concept of harm contains a defense of this view, but for our purposes here I submit that it is intuitively clear that a feeling of moral inferiority is a far graver harm than the other harm attributed to segregation—loss of significant educational contacts. The black child who grows up feeling that he is less worthy of consideration than a white person just because he is black is psychologically sick. He is as certainly harmed as if he had cancer.

To return to the issue of intentions, suppose a school board intends, and designs its policies in order to secure, some end other than segregation, but segregation is nevertheless a certain consequence of those policies, and suppose that by adopting the same policies, another board can completely disguise its deliberate intention to segregate. Since the design of the two school boards' policies will be identical, they will be likely to be perceived as equally intending to segregate, and consequently as being equally likely to cause harm to dignity. But suppose nevertheless that the intentions of the school boards *do* differ. Then, contrary to my view, it might seem that intentions *are* irrelevant to how and what harm is caused.

But this difficulty can be resolved. Suppose on the one hand that the end the first school board intends is unfair to blacks. In that case, although the school boards may not both intend to segregate blacks, they both intend to wrong them. Consequently, since it is the perception of being intentionally wronged which tends to cause a sense of stigma or dignitary harm, although the intentions of the school boards differ, they do not differ in that they both cause dignitary harm. Therefore it doesn't weaken my position that the policies of the two boards are equally likely to cause dignitary harm.

Now, suppose on the other hand that the end the first school board intends is fair to blacks. Given that segregation harms black students by depriving them of significant educational contacts and advantages, this kind of case must be rare, but it is crucial that we consider it. For if it occurs, though one school board intends to act justly and another to act unjustly their policies are equally likely—or unlikely—to cause dignitary harm, and this suggests that an intention to wrong is not necessarily a cause of dignitary harm, though it may be related to a factor that is.

Fiss suggests that this factor could be motive. Thus, he writes that the claim that the intention to segregate causes stigmatic harm "rests on a confusion of motive and purpose."[31] Since Fiss uses "intent" and "purpose" interchangeably, I assume that he means that the claim in question confuses intention and motive.

Now, there is a distinction between intention and motive. Mill puts it this way: Intention is "what the agent wills to do," motive is "the feeling which makes him will to do so."[32] Or, in the terms I have used, a person intends what he sets out to do, and his motive is why he sets out to do it. Of course, citing a person's intentions often indicates why he did something. For example, if A fires a gun at B and kills him, determining that A's intention was to kill B tells us why he fired the gun at B. Still, killing B was A's intention and not his motive, for it was something A set out to do, while his motive must be what made him set out to do it. A's motive could be greed, or vengeance, or cowardice. These are not things that people set out to do but they are attitudes and desires which, when we discover them, tell us why people set out to do what they set out to do.

How then does the idea that intentional segregation causes stigma confuse intention and motive? Fiss may have the following in mind.

The perception of being intentionally segregated is not, in itself, likely to cause stigmatic harm. What is likely to cause that harm is the perception of being intentionally segregated because of a particular kind of motive. When there is intentional racial segregation, for example, white children are probably as aware of being intentionally segregated as black children. Yet they do not suffer harm. This suggests that it is not the perception of being intentionally segregated which causes harm to black children, but the perception of the demeaning racist motives behind intentional segregation.

This argument, if it is Fiss's, is flawed. No one is likely to feel stigmatized just because he divines others' evil motives. To have such an effect evil motives must give rise to evil actions, and, I would add, evil actions performed with impunity. If this assumption is correct, the perception that a school board has racist motives is not by itself likely to be sufficient to cause blacks to suffer harm. Neither, for the same reason, will the perception that a school board has an intention to segregate unjustly which it cannot or dare not put into action. Such bare intentions cause no harm, stigmatic or otherwise. Thus a school board's intention to segregate unjustly does not matter if it must completely disguise that intention by implementing policies which segregate, but are defensible. For in that case, though the board segregates, it does not segregate unjustly, and therefore its intention to segregate unjustly is a bare intention. If this is correct, the factor, other than motive, which is related to an intention to wrong, and which is a cause of dignitary harm, is the design of policies which wrongly segregate what we recognize as determined by an intention to wrongly segregate. But the intention to segregate is part of that factor. Consequently intention cannot be dismissed as irrelevant to the issue of segregation if dignitary harm is taken seriously.

But, even if these arguments are valid, they come to nothing if, as Fiss says, school boards cannot have intentions. For if school boards have no intentions, they can have no intention to segregate, and consequently their intention to segregate cannot be made responsible for the harm of stigmatization. But the idea that school boards have no intentions has strange consequences. According to Fiss, wrong-doing presupposes on the agent's part "a capacity to have an intention."[33] But Fiss believes that school boards cannot have intentions, and consequently that they cannot have "done wrong," and, in particular, cannot have done wrong even when they practiced de jure segregation. This startling conclusion demands that we look even more carefully at his notion that school boards cannot have intentions.

Fiss apparently believes that school boards cannot have intentions because they have many members. This makes it difficult, he says, not only "to find out what is in the mind of any single member," but also "to know whose purpose is to count for that of the board." Suppose two members of a school board support a policy because it segregates while others support it for "educational reasons." "Whose purpose," Fiss asks, "should count as the purpose of the board?"[34]

However, if my conclusions about the causes and nature of dignitary harm are correct, we should seek an intention to segregate insofar as it is a cause of that harm, not in the intentions of individual members of the board, but in the design of the board's policies. If these are designed to segregate and this is not wrong, the intentions of the board are defensible, or if they are not they are bare intentions—they do not determine policy—and therefore do not cause harm. On the other hand, if the board's policies are designed to segregate and this is wrong, then the board's intentions are indefensible, and because they determine policy, are a cause of harm.

## Policies: Foreseeable and Avoidable Consequences

Of course, attempts to demonstrate that a school board intended to segregate may not succeed easily, and even when they do succeed they may leave the question of the extent of the school board's liability unclear. But Fiss's proposal, that boards, regardless of their intentions, be held responsible for foreseeable and avoidable harms, is not free of these problems either. Part of the difficulty lies with the words "foreseeable" and "avoidable." They are far more ambiguous, and give far less direction to school boards, than Fiss is aware.

What, then, does foreseeable mean, and, in particular, to whom must the consequent segregation be foreseeable? To God, everything is foreseeable. However, surely this is not the standard we must apply to the school boards. If we did, we would hold them liable for *every* pattern of segregation which flowed from their policies, and thus put no limit on their responsibilities to desegregate. Perhaps, then, the standard we should apply to the school boards is that segregation is foreseeable if it is reasonable to assume that the boards foresaw it. Now, however, the problem is what it is reasonable to assume the board foresaw. Some cases will be clear—the consequences of a board's policies will be so immediate that no one could suppose that it might reasonably have overlooked them—and others will be so improbable that no one could suppose that it could reasonably have foreseen them. But between these extremes will be a penumbra. There will be many cases where some will argue that a board could not reasonably have foreseen that its policies would result in a segregated pattern, and others will argue the opposite. Much will depend on which experts the board consulted and heeded, and, given the controversial nature of social science, this will depend, in turn, on judgments that are subjective.

Nor is the problem made any simpler by the stipulation that segregation must be a direct consequence of the boards' policies. There will be few cases where it will be absolutely clear that segregation is—or is not— a direct consequence of a board's policies. As Justice Powell stresses, because of the pervasive influence of the school boards' policies there will be few, if any, segregated patterns in which the boards by their "acts or omissions" are not implicated.[35]

Furthermore, the claim that a segregated pattern would have resulted whatever a board's policies is not independent of the question what constitutes reasonable foresight. A board can probably prevent almost any segregated pattern from emerging if it is prepared to be sufficiently extreme. Here again, although a few cases would be clear, most would not. Those who believe that segregation is very bad and integration very good will contend that it is reasonable to insist that a board do far more to foresee and prevent segregation than others with more moderate views, and, again, only subjective judgments will settle the dispute. This shows that "avoidable" is as elastic a word as "foreseeable." What is avoidable depends on how much we are willing or able to spend to avoid it. With little money, or little willingness to spend it avoiding segregation, little segregation will be avoidable. With more money, or more willingness to spend it avoiding segregation, more segregation will be avoidable.

The problem of resolving these ambiguities becomes very pressing for Fiss because his theory undermines one clear system for fixing the limits of responsibility. Fiss suggests that certain court decisions requiring the school board in question to take all possible steps to eliminate segregation were based on the rule which "holds an intentional wrongdoer accountable for *all* the consequences of his actions," and thus assumed that the board intentionally segregated. If his proposal to dispense with a consideration of intentions is adopted, he thinks that courts might then require boards to "take all reasonable rather than all possible steps to eliminate the segregation," basing their decisions on the rule which holds a "nonintentional wrongdoer . . . accountable only for the proximate consequences of his action."[36]

But there is something obviously wrong about this. If intentional wrongdoers should be held accountable for all the consequences of their actions, and if some school boards are intentional wrongdoers, then Fiss's proposal gets them off the hook. Thus the proposal is inadequate for dealing with boards that intentionally segregate, even if it is adequate for dealing with boards that do not intentionally segregate. Furthermore, by denying that a proof of intentional wrongdoing is ever relevant to a decision about how much desegregation to require, Fiss would deny us the one solid guide to making this decision, setting us afloat, without paddles, on the treacherous sea of what is "reasonable."

According to the backward-looking argument for school desegregation, harmfully segregated schools should be desegregated if they are the result of de jure segregation, that is, of school boards' intentional assignment of black and white students to different schools because of their color. As we have seen, the most serious objection to this argument, which, interestingly enough, is made by some *advocates* of school desegregation such as Fiss on the grounds that the backward-looking argument narrows the scope of permissible desegregation policies, is that school boards' intentions to segregate are irrelevant to the case for desegregation. These critics perceive as relevant only the actual design of school policies, and whether any harms caused by them were foreseeable and avoidable. In this chapter I have tried to rebut this objection. I argued that dismissing school boards' intentions to segregate is offensive to the dignity of segregated black students and their parents, depreciates the importance of dignitary harm, and leads away from the one reasonable way we have of determining the extent of school boards' responsibility to desegregate schools. However, it does not follow from my argument that determining the boards' intentions is necessary to justify a case for the desegregation of schools. In particular, my argument does not attack the forward-looking argument that schools may have to be desegregated even when intentional color-based segregation cannot be proved. This forward-looking argument is the subject of the next chapter.

# 5

# Busing: The Forward-looking Argument

## Kenneth B. Clark

According to John Stuart Mill, "the only purpose for which power can be rightfully exercised over any member of a civilized community against his will is to prevent harm to others."[1] This famous harm prevention principle is the essential moral premise behind what I call the forward-looking, utilitarian, argument that, because segregated schools are harmful they ought to be desegregated. If this premise is sound, the most important question in the busing issue may be the empirical one of whether or not segregated schools are harmful. Fiss, as we have seen, thinks that this is *the* question.

Three decades ago, the well-known black psychologist Kenneth B. Clark addressed himself to this question. He was himself convinced that segregated schools were harmful, but, as a scientist, he wanted to test his conviction, and prove scientifically that it was true. He hit upon a series of experiments with dolls which he thought were both simple and persuasive. These experiments were to make him the center of a violent controversy.

In the first of his experiments Clark showed white and brown dolls, otherwise identical, to black children between the ages of six and nine in segregated schools, and asked them to pick the "nice" doll, and the doll that "looks like you." When more children picked the white doll than the brown doll as both the nice doll and the doll that resembled them, Clark concluded that school segregation had harmed them by giving them a negative image of themselves.[2]

Clark's report of his experiments and conclusions was discussed in a White House conference on children and youth in 1950, but as Clark himself recalls, the report received little publicity.[3] But four years later, in 1954, it made him famous when it appeared as the first item in footnote 11 of the *Brown* decision representing the "modern authority," cited by Chief Justice Warren, who supported the thesis that segregation is harmful. Although there are several other works cited, including those of Franklin Frazier and economist Gunnar Myrdal, it was on Clark's work especially that the critics chose to vent their ire. Edmond Cahn, who endorsed the *Brown* decision, felt that the children were "tricked" in Clark's experiment, and that the experiments were, in any case, inept and heavy-handed attempts to prove, as I noted earlier, what he believed was a "fact of common knowledge" such as, "fire burns" or "a cold causes snuffles."[4] Ernest van den Haag, a psychologist who, unlike Cahn, professed himself to "be doubtful of the wisdom of the decision in the desegregation cases," referred to Clark's arguments as "pseudo-scientific," and went so far as to imply that he might have "deceived the Court deliberately."[5] And when Clark's report appeared in the form of a book, *Prejudice and Your Child*, another famous psychologist, Bruno Bettelheim, lectured him sternly on the dangers of basing "the demand for racial equality—on data from the social sciences."[6]

The criticism of Clark's work falls into two parts. On the one hand, it was argued that Clark was confused and mistaken to base recommendations for legal change on the conclusions of social science. On the other hand, the argument was offered that Clark's allegedly scientific experiments demonstrating the harmfulness of segregation were unsound. These are two very different sorts of criticism. The first is philosophical. The second is scientific. Yet both ignore a fundamental question which must be answered before either type of criticism can be assessed, and indeed before Mill's harm prevention principle can be used to support a case for desegregation. That question is: What is the nature of, and what is to count as, harm?

That there was radical, but unrecognized, disagreement about this, and moreover, that this disagreement centered on a question of morality—not science—can be seen by examining the scientific criticism of Clark's work. Perhaps the sharpest of these criticisms was that Clark had conducted another experiment which seemed to contradict the one cited in *Brown*. In that other experiment Clark compared black children in segregated schools in the South to black children in unsegregated schools in the North. Although only a minority of children in both segregated and unsegregated schools preferred and identified with the black dolls, a higher percentage of children in the segregated did so. In a caustic exchange with Clark, van den Haag concluded that "if Professor Clark's tests do demonstrate damage to Negro children, then they demonstrate that the damage is *less* with segregation and greater with congregation."[7]

Clark was, of course, aware of the apparent anomaly in his experiments. But the conclusion he drew was the opposite of van den Haag's. According to Clark, "what the findings show is that the black children of the South were more adjusted to the feeling that they were not as good as whites, and because they felt defeated at an early age, did not bother using the device of denial." However, Clark believed that it is morally better and morally healthier to be the kind of person who rages ineffectually against his subordinate position in an unjust society than the kind of person who acquiesces, "almost cheerfully," to that position.[8] Frantz Fanon said the same thing when he maintained that it was not his business to advise the black man to "keep his place."[9] This is the moral stand of the revolutionary or, at least, of the reformer, who has an ideal of the human being as more than a maximizer of satisfactions and who insists that society should adjust to what is best in human beings, rather than that human beings should surrender what is best in themselves to suit an unjust society.

Not everyone agrees. Herbert Wechsler, for example, thought it relevant to urge against Clark's position the "benefit" of the "sense of security" obtained from segregated schooling, and more recently, the Harvard sociologist Nathan Glazer has extolled the ghetto—and segregated schooling—as a "place of refuge."[10] The moral position implicit in these views came out clearly in a face-to-face exchange between Clark and Wechsler related by Richard Kluger in *Simple Justice*, the best history of the *Brown* case. "Could it not be reasonably argued," Wechsler asked, "that the Negro child attending a non-segregated school would be doubly frustrated by the limited economic and social opportunity that would later confront him in a world where *de facto* segregation prevailed?" To which, according to Kluger, Clark responded "Which is better—to be sick or to be dead? Segregated school is a sort of fatality."[11] Evidently, in Clark's view the sense of security gained in segregated schools comes at too high a price. The black child in a segregated school may feel secure, but he also feels inferior, and what is far worse, he grows up *accepting* his inferiority. To Clark, *that* is harm. It did not matter to him that segregation helps a child avoid later frustration. Wechsler disagrees with Clark, but not on an empirical issue. He does not challenge Clark's empirically established claim that a black child in a segregated school grows up feeling inferior and accepting his inferiority. On the contrary, that claim is the basis of the—essentially moral—objection he makes to Clark's position. He challenges Clark's *moral* claim that a black person who accepts inferiority is harmed. His view is that accepting inferiority cannot harm a black person because, in the circumstances, it helps the black person avoid frustration. It does not seem to matter to Wechsler that this is only because such a person knows and keeps a place created for him by others. His disagreement with Clark is fundamentally a disagreement over the nature of harm.

Or consider van den Haag's view. He raises the possibility that "sanctioned congregation" may make white children "feel humiliated" and this may "impair their personalities." But what is an impaired personality? This is not an empirical but a moral question. In the case in point, perhaps the humiliation the white children feel at being forced to go to school with black children they think inferior erodes a self-esteem based simply on being white; perhaps it destroys their idea of a world compartmentalized into black and white, and so complicates their moral life and makes their judgments about the world less secure and dogmatic; or, finally, perhaps it hampers their ability to succeed by preventing them from growing up as the kinds of adults who can discriminate against blacks with a clear conscience. I do not know whether "congregation" has these effects, but if it does, I imagine Clark would deny that it impairs white children's personalities. On the contrary, I imagine he would think that it was good for their personalities, much as a dose of medicine is good for the man struggling and kicking to avoid it. Perhaps van den Haag would disagree with this assessment. But his disagreement would not be on any empirical point. The disagreement would be over the question of how children should grow up, morally, and concomitantly, over the nature of harm.

Similarly, Thomas Sowell, challenging both the view that segregation is harmful and the busing edicts dependent on that assumption, presents an argument based on a conception of harm drawn from his own libertarian and conservative moral stance. Sowell thinks the Clark study cited in *Brown* has been "devastated as invalid if not fraudulent."[12] Furthermore, he maintains that "The original premise of the historic *Brown* decision—that separate schools are inherently inferior—was neither supported by fact nor would it stand up under scrutiny. Within walking distance of the Supreme Court was an all-black high school [Dunbar High School] whose eighty year history prior to *Brown* denies that principle."[13] But the way Sowell develops his argument shows that he fails altogether to understand the fundamental question at issue. "As far back as 1899," he continues, Dunbar had "higher test scores than any of the white schools in Washington, and its average I.Q. was eleven points above the national average in 1939—fifteen years before the Supreme Court declared such things impossible. There have been other such black schools elsewhere. . . . The history of all-Oriental and all-

Jewish schools would reduce this ponderous finding to a laughingstock, instead of the revered 'law of the land.' "

But what, then, is the cause of the generally lower-than-average performance of black schools? Sowell thinks that this is the "issue" and that segregation cannot be the reason because all-Oriental and all-Jewish schools, which are as segregated as all-black schools have, in general, test scores higher than, or at least equal to, all-white schools. But to suppose that this is knockdown evidence against the claim that segregation is harmful is to unperceptively take a controversial view of the nature of harm.

Specifically, it is to assume either that the only way a school system can harm children is to reduce their scores on standardized tests, or that children who score well on such tests cannot be harmed in some other way. But both these alternatives were clearly anticipated and considered unacceptable by the Supreme Court. Take the first alternative. Neither Clark nor the court understood harm simply as an induced inability to do well on standardized tests in verbal and mathematical skills. The type of harm Clark most often cited as caused by segregation is more encompassing and includes injury to moral capacities. Segregation, he charged, damages "self-esteem," and sets off "a fundamental confusion in the entire moral sphere of their [segregated children's] lives."[14] In fact, in a long series of desegregation cases, the courts have usually made it clear that they subscribed to something like this view. For example, as far back as 1881, in *Board Education of Ottawa* v. *Tinnon*, the Kansas Supreme Court affirmed that in "common schools" where "all kinds of children mingle together, we have the great world in miniature; there they may learn human nature in all its phases, with all its emotions, passions and feelings, its loves and hates, its hopes and fears, its impulses and sensibilities; . . . But on the other hand, persons by isolation may become strangers even in their own country; and by being strangers, will be of little benefit either to themselves or to society. As a rule, people cannot afford to be ignorant of the society which surrounds them; and as all kinds of people must live together in the same society, it would seem better that all should be taught in the same schools."[15]

Furthermore, not only may children be harmed in ways other than in not learning their arithmetic, they may learn their arithmetic and still be harmed in these other ways. Proof of this can be found in the example of all-Jewish schools—the very sort of school Sowell declares turns the *Brown* finding into a "laughingstock." Thus as Dr. Isidor Chein, psychologist and director of the Commission on Community Relations of the American Jewish Congress, testified in one of the four cases consolidated in *Brown*, discrimination has caused the Jews, too, to feel inferior.[16] Granting that such a feeling is a harm, it follows that even if Sowell is right and all-Jewish schools have high test scores, he has not ruled out the possibility that segregation is harmful. He can think that he has only because he has adopted a very controversial conception of harm.

Charles V. Hamilton, a political scientist at Columbia University, has a perspective and takes a stance on these matters very different from the ones already considered. "We cannot," he writes, "focus on verbal and mathematical skills as criteria for educational improvement."[17] Though Hamilton is, like Sowell an opponent of busing, his deemphasis on the importance of verbal and mathematical skills—the very things Sowell emphasizes—clearly indicates that he brings a different conception of harm and a different moral outlook to the issue. And though, like Clark, Hamilton speaks of educational aims broader than mere success on standardized achievement tests, his conception of harm, and consequently his moral outlook, differs also from Clark's. Whereas Clark speaks guardedly of "a healthy and mature pride in race,"[18] Hamilton frankly demands "group solidarity and pride."[19] Whereas Clark is worried about the moral confusion created in the personality of a child in segregated schools when he is taught "democracy, brotherhood, and love of his fellow man"[20]—concepts that are contradicted by segregation—Hamilton is worried about what happens to a black child in an integrated school when he attempts to be "a carbon copy of the culture and ethos of another racial and ethnic group."[21] And, whereas Clark is worried about the "self-esteem" of the child in segregated, all-black schools, Hamilton is worried about the "self-image" of the child in integrated, predominately white schools.

The different moral components which these writers emphasize in their concepts of harm stem from fundamental differences in moral and political philosophy. Clark writes in the liberal-egalitarian-assimilationist tradition of Frederick Douglass. That tradition views the morally healthy person as someone who is cosmopolitan, humanitarian, egalitarian, autonomous, ruled by his reason, proud only about his own achievements, and rising above ties to race, group, and nation. On the other hand, the nationalist tradition started by Martin Delany and Marcus Garvey, and represented today by Charles V. Hamilton, considers the liberal ideal as pallid, insipid, cold, rootless, colorless, uninspired, and untrustworthy. In its view, the healthy person is drawn by strong feelings to particular people, proud of and loyal to his race and group, capable of identifying completely with them, and ruled more by sterling sentiment than cold reason. Finally, the narrow "economic" conception of harm adopted by Thomas Sowell shows him to be the modern representative of Booker T. Washington, viewing the morally healthy person as one who is self-reliant, enterprising, hard-working, ambitious, and willing to and capable of competing and surviving in the marketplace.

If these considerations are persuasive, the criticism of Clark's experiments on scientific and methodological grounds is trite. These experiments may not have satisfied high standards of scientific method, but the criticism was simpleminded, ungenerous, and negligent too, because it involved no serious effort to determine what Clark was trying to prove segregation caused. And the philosophical criticism is also misguided. Clark did not commit a "naturalistic fallacy," in trying to base moral conclusions on scientific evidence. Morality directed his science. He was trying to prove scientifically that segregation caused a condition that he thought odious.

Yet, for those who would apply Mill's harm prevention principle to the issue of desegregation, these considerations are sobering. For they demonstrate, as I stated above, that the empirical question of whether segregation is harmful is not as important or difficult as the question of what harm actually is.

## The Concept of Harm

According to certain philosophers, R. M. Hare of Oxford University, for example, "To harm somebody is to act against his interests," and a person's interests are "tied in some way," to what he wants or desires, so that an act harms a person when it "would or might prevent some desire of his being realized."[22] I call this the invasion-of-interest concept of harm. This account of the nature of harm would allow, as Hare acknowledges, that a Nazi is harmed when his desire to put Jews in the gas chamber is frustrated, and, given a policy of harm prevention, if his desire is stronger than the desires of Jews "not to be got rid of," his desire ought to be satisfied.[23] The disturbing implications of this conception of harm for the question of desegregation need no elaboration, especially when we consider that the desire for segregation is not the desire of a minority but of the *majority*. Hare thinks that it will never be true that catering to fanatics will satisfy more and stronger desires than protecting their intended victims. But members of a minority may be excused for seeking a better guarantee.

Feinberg outlines a version of this interest invasion theory of harm which, in a roundabout way, produces a conclusion similar to Hare's. According to Feinberg, a person is harmed when his interests are invaded, and he has an interest in something if he stands to gain or lose depending on its condition or outcome.[24] But like Hare he ties interests to satisfaction of desire. Thus he suggests that a man has an interest in taking medicine he does not desire to take only because it will cure him and lead to a greater overall satisfaction of his desires.[25] But if this is so, we are back with Hare, who believes that harm is the frustration of the greatest overall satisfaction of desire. We might maintain that preventing Nazis from killing Jews harms Nazis if it frustrates the greatest overall satisfaction of Nazi desires. As I have noted, this is disturbing enough, but the concept of viewing the consideration of "interests" as a wholly want-regarding process has another implication which I find even more ominous.

The *Brown* decision said that segregation harmed black children by making them feel inferior. Does the invasion-of-interest concept of harm make sense of this? Given an account of interests as being wholly want-regarding, the answer depends on whether feeling inferior diminishes the chance for the overall satisfaction of the children's desires. If it does, then it invades their interests and is a harm. If it does not, then it does not invade their interests and is not a harm.

This is alarming. The court was referring to school age, and often very young, children. Such children cannot be said to have an interest, in a wholly want-regarding sense, in not feeling inferior. Hence, according to the conception of harm we are considering, making them feel inferior cannot harm them directly. Furthermore, given the simple and sensual nature of childrens' desires, this conception of harm leaves equally open the question of whether making children feel inferior harms them even indirectly.

Feinberg seems to accept the idea that it does *not* harm them.[26] In his essay "Harm and Self-Interest," arguing against the political philosopher Stanley Benn, who defends the idea that we inflict moral harm on young children by giving them a bad character, Feinberg maintains that since young children cannot actually want good characters, they cannot have an interest in them, and consequently, since harm is the invasion of interest, cannot be directly harmed by being denied them. Therefore, assuming that a feeling of inferiority undermines good character, Feinberg seems committed to the view that, even if segregation makes black children grow up feeling inferior, it is not, at least for that reason, necessarily harmful.

The political philosopher David Miller provides an account of harm which has the same, strange, implication.[27] According to Miller, each person has certain aims and activities centrally important to him which constitute a "plan of life." On this basis he defines needs and harms: Needs are whatever a person must have to successfully carry out his plan of life, and harms are what happens to a person when his needs are unmet.[28] As Miller notes, this makes the determination of a person's needs and possible harms inflicted on him an empirical matter: A person's needs are not what he *ought* to have, irrespective of the plan of life he in fact has. They are what he *must* have given the plan of life he in fact has. Similarly, Miller maintains we cannot determine how a person can be harmed on the basis of an ideal conception of what he ought to have, but by an empirical determination of what his plan of life happens to be, and what he must have to execute it.

Miller thinks that a strong point of his theory is that it makes need and harm relative to the aspirations and ideals of the person concerned. For example, it easily accounts for the unusual case of the philosopher Franz Brentano. Brentano was blind at the end of his life. This enabled him to concentrate on his philosophy in a way which had been impossible for him before. On this ground, he claimed that he was not harmed by his blindness. Given that the major part of Brentano's plan of life was to do philosophy, Miller's analysis makes sense of this claim.[29]

But this supposed strength of Miller's theory is also its weakness. For if blindness may not be a harm, and even a benefit, why not a feeling of inferiority too? Cyrano de Bergerac wanted to be a successful playwright. This was a major part of his plan of life. Yet he acknowledged that he was a failure because he could not bow and scrape and "cultivate a supple spine." If bowing and scraping come more readily to those who feel inferior, this implies that Cyrano would not be harmed by such a feeling and indeed, *needed* to have it.

It would not be enough to object to this conclusion merely on the grounds that Cyrano did not feel inferior. Brentano was not always blind either. One must object that the central part of Cyrano's plan of life, far more important to him than being a successful playwright, was the determination never to feel inferior to anyone. Given this, Cyrano would indeed be harmed by being made to feel inferior. And this reveals the weakness of the unmet-needs analysis of harm—*given* that a person has a plan of life, and that executing it depends on his not feeling inferior, *then* making him feel inferior harms him. But again, what of children who do not yet have plans of life or well-formed ideas of their inferiority, equality, or superiority? As in the previous case, it seems that making them feel inferior might not harm them.

A partisan of either conception of harm might object that I have been too restrictive, that these theories suppose that children are harmed, not only by what invades their current interests or interferes with their current plans of life, but also by what invades their future interests or interferes with their future plans of life. I pose this possibility because Feinberg has considered the idea of the "future interests" of the child. According to him, these are interests the child "will in fact come to have in the future, and also those he will never acquire, depending on the directions of his growth." A child's future interests, Feinberg notes, are protected by his "rights-in-trust," rights which the child cannot exercise as a child but must be saved for him until he is an adult, for they can be violated "in advance," that is, before the child is in a position to exercise them.[30] For example, the infant's right to walk or to exercise his religious beliefs are rights-in-trust. He cannot exercise them, but they can be violated by acts which make it impossible for him to exercise them when he grows older. Now, assuming this theory, it is conceivable that someone could argue that a child can be harmed "in advance" by conduct which invades his future interests and attempt to defend against my objections by defining those interests appropriately. I maintain, however, that this "future interests" or future plan of life theory overlooks a complication, abandons the concept of harm it was meant to secure, and makes an unwarranted assumption.

The complication is that a child's future interests and plan of life are determined, in large part, by the feelings we generate in him now. If we make him feel inferior to others, his interests and plan of life will be of one sort. If we make him feel equal or superior to others, his interests and plan of life will be of a different sort. Consequently, reference to a child's future interests and plan of life cannot tell us what to do now since what we do now will determine what his future interests and plan of life will be.

The theory may seem capable of handling this complication through the inherent stipulation that a child is harmed, not by interference with his future interests and plans of life, but by interference which will lead him to have the kinds of future interests and plans of life that will not be most likely to lead to his greatest overall satisfaction. But if this tack is taken, the future interests theory abandons the account of harm it is meant to secure. I will demonstrate this in relation to the invasion-of-interest concept; the unmet-needs concept suffers from the same difficulty.

According to the future interests theory, we harm a child by preventing him from developing wants that will lead to his greatest overall satisfaction. That is, we invade his interests by not giving him the opportunity to form these wants. Since it is assumed that he does not actually have these desires, it follows that his interests do not depend only on his actual wants. But this contradicts the view that interests should be considered as wholly want-regarding and harm as the invasion of interests. Suppose, however, that the partisan were to maintain that the wants in question are actual wants because they are actual wants of the child's future self. This argument would fail too, because, as I argued earlier, a child's future self largely depends on how we decide to make him feel now. Consequently, if his future self has certain wants, this is because we decided he ought to have these wants. But if this is so, and if, therefore, we harm a child by not creating in him these wants, then his interests depend on wants he *ought* to have—which again contradicts the concept of interests as wholly want-regarding.

But the determined partisan may deny that when he says children ought to have certain wants, he contradicts his conception of interests as wholly want-regarding. He may insist that all he means by talking about the wants children ought to have is that they should have those which tend to lead to their greatest overall satisfaction, not wants which are in any sense superior, morally or otherwise. But this argument also fails to support the desired conclusion that a feeling of inferiority is harm. It can do so only if it can prove that such a feeling diminishes the overall satisfaction of children's present and future desires. But this is unwarranted. Especially in the case of black children who are to grow up among a prejudiced majority, the kinds of desires that feelings of inferiority generate may lead to greater overall satisfaction than the kinds of desires that a feeling of equality generates.

Against this the authority of Rawls may be weighed. In his well-known contract theory of justice, Rawls proposes that principles of justice are best conceived of as principles that free and rational persons concerned to further their own interests would agree to in an initial position of equality. This initial position of equality is not an actual state of affairs. It is a hypothetical situation characterized in such a way that the principles those involved in it will agree to are principles of justice. Among the essential features of this theoretical situation is that no one knows his place in society, his class or social status, or his natural assets and abilities. As Rawls puts it, "The principles of justice are chosen behind a veil of ignorance." This is to prevent anyone from tailoring principles to favor his particular condition.[31] Now, according to Rawls, the parties to his hypothetical agreement will insist on principles of justice which secure self-respect because they will perceive that without it no one can pursue his plan of life with zest, and delight in its fulfillment.[32] Assuming that a feeling of inferiority destroys self-respect, this may seem to imply that a feeling of inferiority always diminishes overall satisfaction.

But the idea that a feeling of inferiority always diminishes overall satisfaction is simply false. If this is what Rawls means he is no more persuasive than Plato was when he tried to connect justice and happiness. What of the contented, happy slave? We may not like to think he existed, but he may have, and what is more, he may well have satisfied more of his desires than the rebellious self-respecting slave. Similarly, who can say that the prosperous Uncle Tom, even if he feels inferior, does not get more satisfaction than the black who is beaten down because he insists on his self-respect? Rawl's argument is plausible only if the contractors desire satisfactions of a *certain sort*, contingent upon feelings of self-respect. If that is so, Rawls is correct in saying that the contractors will insist on the conditions for self-respect. The self-respecting slave has feelings that the contented slave cannot dream of. Plato, we may recall, bolsters his case for a connection between justice and happiness with a similar argument. According to him, the pleasures of the unjust man are spurious and second-rate compared to the pleasures of the just man.[33] And Mill, of course, maintained that it was better to be Socrates dissatisfied than a fool satisfied, but only because he also maintained that there were higher and lower pleasures, and that Socrates enjoyed higher pleasures, and the fool lower pleasures.[34] But if the supporter of the interest-invasion theory of harm seizes on this kind of argument to support his contention that the theory considers a feeling of inferiority a harm it contradicts itself. As I have suggested, feelings of inferiority may, in certain unfortunate circumstances, tend to lead to greater overall satisfaction than feelings of self-respect. Consequently, if we postulate that we harm a child by making him feel inferior because this prevents him from experiencing the "higher" pleasures possible only to persons of self-respect, then, since these pleasures are the satisfaction of "higher" wants, a value judgment about what wants he ought to have *is* implied, and harm is not simply the diminishing of overall satisfaction. Yet this is exactly what the invasion-of-interest theory of harm says harm is.

It may be objected that the interest-invasion theory of harm does not imply that it is not "desirable" to insure that children grow up with good characters, but only that we do not *harm* them by allowing or encouraging them to grow up with bad characters. This is clearly Feinberg's position for example. But it does not provide us with a basis for attacking segregation. If denying a child a good character by maintaining a segregated school system which makes him feel inferior does not harm him, then giving him a good character by abolishing the system cannot be desirable because it avoids harming him. Perhaps, then, it must be considered desirable because it benefits him. But, although this may be true, it is not a basis for desegregation which appeals to the harm prevention principle. That principle says the state may interfere with individual liberty to prevent harm to others. It does not say the state may interfere with individual liberty to benefit others.

But my objection to these analyses of harm is not merely that they fail to provide us with a rationale for attacking segregation. Though this is true, it is not, in itself, a reason to reject them. My objection is that they are, *in general*, conservative. Their fundamental problem is that they have no ideal of human nature—at least, not one more elevated than that of the human being as a satisfaction maximizer. Accordingly, they are ready to countenance as non-harmful any mangling of the human personality that does not reduce its satisfaction, and to view as harmful any dissatisfaction of a mangled personality.

There is, however, a conception of harm that does not have these implications. Consider, for example, a person robbed at gun point or a homeowner escaping from his burning property. If we assume that their interests are invaded, then, in the invasion of interests conception of harm, the persons in both cases are certainly harmed. Yet, it is often reported that a robbery victim was "unharmed," or that a person was, fortunately, able to escape from his destroyed home, "unharmed." On the other hand, though it is not clear whether animals or plants have "interests," and thus whether these interests can be invaded, it is clear that they can be harmed. Fleas can harm a dog, and frost or drought can harm young trees. Similarly, the doctor who warns a pregnant woman that smoking or drugs can harm her unborn baby does not use the word "harm" in any peculiar sense, though of course the baby has no interests—at least in the want-regarding sense.

Accordingly, it seems that we must acknowledge a third conception of harm, distinct from the invasion-of-interest concept, and, as arguments similar to those above readily demonstrate, distinct from the unmet-needs concept as well. This third account of harm assumes that there is a normal and proper way for children's minds and bodies to function and grow, and a normal and proper way for adults' minds and bodies to function. Given this assumption, a harm is defined as something blocking, diverting, or interrupting a child's proper and normal mental or physical growth, or as something impairing the ability or capacity of an adult's or child's body or mind to function in a normal and proper way. Because of its reference to the essentials of growth and functions, this conception of harm deserves to be considered Platonic.

Now "normal," "proper," and "impair," refer to very general concepts, and "growth" and "development" are often used generally as well. Normal and proper growth and development is how a thing ought or should grow and develop. Furthermore, because human beings are moral creatures, the idea of a normal and proper human development implies that when a human being develops properly and normally, he or she should in the end have the ability and disposition necessary to function morally—that is, to draw relevant moral distinctions, to assess moral arguments, and to make sound moral judgments. Since these abilities and dispositions are qualities of intellect and character, and since, in the conception of harm I call Platonic, harm is a blocking of normal development, or the impairing of the ability to function in a proper way, it follows that this conception of harm assumes good character as one of the ends of a normal development, and explicitly allows for moral harm, especially in children. This is its most important distinction from the conceptions of harm previously discussed.

Feinberg rejects it on the grounds that there is "no impossibility that morally inferior persons can be happy, and excellent persons miserable."[35] He is right, of course. Morally inferior persons can be happy and excellent persons miserable. But it does not follow that we must reject the conception of harm as the blocking or impairing of normal growth and functions. We may reject the view that the harm, or sense of moral inferiority leads to misery, and that a sense of excellence or moral health leads to happiness. And we can still maintain, with Feinberg, that moral character is always a good thing to have even in the many circumstances in which it does not advance self-interest. Indeed, though Plato himself never seems to abandon the claim that excellence always leads to happiness, he does acknowledge that there are some circumstances in which it leads to far less happiness than in others.[36]

Earlier I noted that a person can be robbed of his money, but be said to be unharmed. I did not mean that a person cannot be harmed by being deprived of his money, but I meant to do two things: First, by saying that the victim was unharmed, I meant, specifically, to point to a class of very important harms, viz., impairments in proper and normal bodily functions caused, for example, by gunshot wounds. Second, I meant to hint that even when a person is deprived of his money, it is still possible that he has not been harmed at all. Consider a rich man whose pocket has been picked of five dollars. By the invasion-of-interest account of harm the man has been harmed. However, intuition tells us that this does violence to the concept of harm which ought to mean something more serious. Feinberg senses the difficulty and suggests that we speak of the rich man being moved in a "harmful direction."[37] But a generalization derived from the Platonic conception of harm avoids the awkwardness of this approach.

A rich man is not harmed by a loss of five dollars because it does not impair his ability to function in the way he could before the loss. This suggests how the Platonic conception of harm can be applied generally. First, we generalize the notion of functionality. There are some things we do that, essentially, do not involve manipulation of the physical world outside our bodies. Consequently, some of our abilities to function in some ways can be impaired without interference with the physical world outside our bodies. A gunshot wound, for example, may impair our ability to think, or breathe, or digest food. However, the exercise of most of our abilities requires us to handle and use things. Thus our abilities to build, theorize, imagine, and destroy often require us to use drills, sledgehammers, pens, cameras, paints, and computers. And accordingly many of our functional abilities can be impaired by interference with the world outside our bodies as well as by interference with our bodies. For example, a fiddler's ability to fiddle and an artist's ability to paint can be impaired by depriving them of their instruments as well as by breaking their arms. However, before we extend our conception of harm to include impairing of abilities to function in this broader sense of the word, a further distinction must be drawn.

Though the loss of five dollars does not harm a rich man, the loss of ten thousand dollars probably does. But even after losing ten thousand dollars the rich man can probably still do things the average man cannot. How then is one but not the other harmed? Appeal to plans of life or interests does not help. The world is full of poor people who have the interests and plans of life of the rich. But consider a parallel example: by depriving Samson of his strength, Delilah certainly harmed him. Yet, even after his loss, Samson was no weaker than the average man. How then was Samson, but not the average man, the victim of harm? The answer is that Samson possessed, and in that sense had a *right* to extraordinary strength. The average man does not. Similarly, the rich man possesses, and in that sense has a right to, wealth. The average man does not. We can now propose our generally applicable Platonic conception of harm: Assuming the broad definition of function, a person is harmed by the impairment of abilities to function to which he has a right.

This account of harm eliminates the bewildering superfluity of "harms" generated by the accounts we considered previously. For example, the invasion-of-interest account of harm implies that I would harm a burglar by installing effective locks because he has an interest in entering my house and in not feeling frustrated. This kind of absurdity is avoided by the Platonic account. Effective locks prevent the burglar from exercising his abilities. But given that his feelings of frustration do not further impair his already damaged character, effective locks do not impair any ability to function in the normal and proper way to which he has a right. Hence, in the Platonic concept of harms, effective locks do not harm the burglar. Nor is this simply because they prevent him from exercising his abilities in a wrongful way. Suppose that, instead of installing locks, I installed a booby trap that exploded, blowing off the burglar's hands when he attempted to break in. This would still prevent him from acting wrongly, but because people always have a right to their bodies, it would impair his rightful ability to act in normal and proper ways—hands can be used in better ways than for stealing—and consequently would harm him.

The fact that to harm a person is to impair an ability to function to which he has a right does not mean that a harm is necessarily a violation of a right, or that a violation of a right is necessarily a harm. A person who breaks his arm accidentally suffers a harm, though his rights are not violated; and robbing the rich man of five dollars certainly violates his rights, though I have suggested that it does not harm him.

If what I have said is sound, though we may agree on the definition of a harm as the impairing of an ability to function to which a person has a right, we may still disagree over what conditions constitute harms because we disagree over what rights people have. For example, though an egalitarian and someone who advocates the merit system may both accept my account of harm, they will disagree about whether depriving a rich man of his wealth harms him because they disagree about whether anyone can have a right to that much more wealth than others. By the same token, there will be no disagreement about harm where there is no disagreement about rights. Since a person always has a right to his body, and since as Plato noted, a skill is a capacity for opposites, i.e., for right and wrong, a person is always harmed when his skills or capacities are impaired. However, this is not the case in relation to *dispositions* as distinct from skills. A disposition is not a capacity for opposites but a fixed tendency to behave in a particular way, good or bad. Consequently, though it may be *wrong* to transgress a person's rights to his body in order to eradicate an evil disposition, it does not *harm* him because it does not impair his ability to act in a proper way. Thus, though it is theoretically wrong, all else being equal, to transgress a person's rights to his body in order to cure him of a physical illness, this does not harm, but rather benefits, him.

My analysis of the concept of harm explains why theorists disagree about which things are harms and why their disagreements cannot be readily resolved. For the source of their disagreements need not be factual. It may be about what rights people have, how they ought to live, and ultimately, what kind of society—liberal, egalitarian, libertarian, or nationalist—is legitimate or desirable.

Accordingly, without a resolution of these larger issues, the harm prevention principle cannot provide a solid basis for the desegregation of schools. It is not a neutral instrument which, once accepted in the abstract, can be employed in a relatively noncontroversial manner. Even if it is accepted, its use as a justification for desegregation will be controversial. First, people may agree on all the facts about segregated schools, but, because they disagree about which of these facts are harms still disagree about whether segregated schooling is harmful, or more harmful than integrated schooling. Second, people may agree on all the facts about segregated schools, about which facts are harms, and believe that segregated schooling is harmful, but, because certain conditions cannot be plausibly proved to have been caused by segregated schooling, or prevented by desegregated schooling, conclude that the harm prevention principle cannot be invoked to justify desegregation. The second point is more involved than the first and requires illustration.

Suppose, for example, we adopt the view, which, as I have suggested, seems to be that of Thomas Sowell, that an impairment to a person's ability to function effectively in the marketplace is the primary harm that can be inflicted on him. If we do so, we are likely to interpret the claim that segregated schools are harmful to mean that students in segregated schools do not learn to read and write and do arithmetic, and more generally, do not acquire the skills the marketplace demands. In this account of harm, although we may conclude that segregated schools are harmful, it is clear that we need not conclude that they are harmful just because they are segregated. For if that were the case students in all segregated schools fail—and would fail—to acquire the skills the marketplace demands, and we do not need Sowell's example of Dunbar High School to know that this is false. Consequently, according to this view, even if we can invoke the harm prevention to justify improving segregated schools that are harmful, we may not be in a position to invoke it in order to justify desegregating those schools. Everything depends on what, in the circumstances, will help students to acquire marketable skills. Desegregation may help, but so might other reforms.

If to the above, arguably Sowellian, view of harm we add those which I suggested could be attributed to Hamilton, the harm prevention principle actually seems to support a case against desegregating schools. If a harmed person is one who is unable to readily identify with those of his race, and whose racial pride and loyalty is half-hearted or nonexistent; and if, as seems plausible, such inabilities and inhibitions fester in "properly" integrated schools—which normally means schools with a minority of poor, lower-class, academically ill-prepared blacks and a majority of affluent middle-class, academically better-prepared whites—then, especially where reforms other than school integration can help black students to learn to read and write and do arithmetic well, the harm prevention principle might support those reforms rather than school integration.

Only if we endorse the argument of the Kansas Supreme Court that the different races of one country should not be strangers to each other, and take it to imply that impairment of the ability to treat fellow citizens as associates and to some extent even as familiars is a serious harm, can we, by invoking the harm prevention principle, support a strong case for desegregating schools. For only by mutual association do people cease to be strangers to each other and become associates and familiars, and, arguably, this association is most conveniently arranged and most efficacious during the school years. Yet there are uncertainties even in this case. Association may insure that people are not strangers to each other, but it does not insure that they will see each other as associates or familiars. It may insure that they will hate each other. These possibilities are pertinent because, as is painfully evident, forcibly integrating schools often creates, or at least inflames, hostilities between blacks and whites. Of course, against this observation it can be argued that mutual understanding, which can come only through association, is necessary for the eventual overcoming of hostility, and the eventual creation of a nation in which people see each other as fellow citizens and associates. But although it is an undeniable fact that mutual understanding can come only through mutual association, it is possible to deny that school is, under the circumstances, the best place for mutual association.

This last point emphasizes the fact that the application of the harm prevention principle to justify school desegregation depends on the empirical results of social science investigation of segregated and integrated schooling. But if my analysis of the nature of harm is sound, controversy about these empirical results is tied to and exacerbated by controversy about the conceptual issue of harm. And, as I have noted, the resolution of the issue of what is to be considered harm depends on the resolution of the issue of what rights people have, and ultimately, the issue of what kind of society—liberal, egalitarian, or libertarian— is legitimate. In the next section I take up the more immediate question of rights and demonstrate that certain conceptions about the nature of rights that argue against desegregation are bogus.

## The Rights Arguments

Even when the harm prevention principle supports a case for school desegregation, that case is not decisive. Mill did not say, nor could he have reasonably said, that power always is rightfully exercised over individuals in order to prevent harm to others; he said that the only purpose for which power can be rightfully exercised over individuals is in order to prevent harm to others. Harm prevention is therefore a necessary, but not a solely sufficient condition for the state's legitimate exercise of power over individuals. Among the limits on the state's actions for the prevention of harm are the rights of individuals. The state may not rightfully exercise power over individuals in order to prevent harm to others if doing so violates those individuals' rights. In the case of school desegregation this means that the state may not rightfully bus students against their will in order to desegregate schools, if this violates individuals' rights.

Libertarians write as if they believe that parents have rights to determine their childrens' education and that these rights are violated by state-compelled school desegregation. Indeed, they argue that even the traditional school system in which parents must send their children to neighborhood schools, violates this right. Their view is that parents have a right to as wide a choice as possible about how their children are educated, and accordingly they advocate the voucher system described in Chapter 2, which would give parents, for each school age child, a voucher to be used to pay for the education of that child at whatever school is willing to accept him, whether public or private and at any location.

But, assuming that rights exist and are defined in order to protect important interests, the voucher system, and indirectly, the right on which it is based, is open to a telling objection: parents are not the only ones whose important interests are affected by how their children are educated. If children grow up to be criminals, this affects the important interests of their victims, and if they grow up unemployable, this affects the important interests of the taxpayers who must shoulder the costs of supporting them on welfare. Consequently, parents cannot have a complete right to choose their childrens' education with the compliance of other members of society. To protect their interests, the other members of society have a right to impose broad standards on the educational system which parents must meet.

Furthermore, since the voucher system would entitle parents to send their children to whatever schools they please, it would provide little protection for the childrens' rights to a proper education. Some parents are confused or uncaring, and the voucher system would call forth educational entrepreneurs selling all manner of wares, some of them certainly fraudulent. Knowledgeable and caring parents would simply avoid these schools, but many, less vigilant, would be duped, to the lasting detriment of their children.

To guard against this danger, some of the voucher system's less doctrinaire advocates stipulate that parents should be entitled to send their children only to schools that meet state-imposed minimum standards. However, paradoxically, many of them, such as Friedman, have undermined the effectiveness of this stipulation by also stipulating that parents be allowed to add to their vouchers. Since the latter stipulation would allow well-to-do parents to add to their vouchers and send their children to schools with adequate standards, it would give them an incentive to insist on minimum standards that are less than adequate. Consequently, the minimum standards stipulation would not adequately protect the educational rights of children of less than well-to-do parents.

## The Community Control System

The weaknesses in the voucher system may seem nicely answered by another set of opponents to desegregated schooling—the communitarians. Instead of having a voucher system, or the public school system, the communitarians propose that the members of the local community should have the right to control the schools in their area. In *Black Power*, Stokely Carmichael and Charles V. Hamilton put this idea forcefully: "We must begin to think of the black community as a base of organization to control institutions in that community. Control of the ghetto schools must be taken out of the hands of 'professionals'. . . . Black parents should seek as their goal the actual control of the public schools in their community: hiring and firing of teachers, selection of teaching materials, determination of standards, etc."[38]

It may seem that the community control system would better protect children's rights than the voucher system. The voucher system would give parents—without financial penalty—the option of removing their children from bad schools in the community to good schools outside the community. Thus it would give knowledgeable and caring parents little incentive to improve schools in the community, and in the end these may become, to use Sowell's hard words "human dumping grounds." On the other hand, the community control system would deny parents that option, and accordingly give knowledgeable and caring parents every incentive—and opportunity—to improve the schools in their community. Since this works to the advantage of all children of the community, it may seem that the community control system would protect the educational rights even of children whose parents are less knowledgeable, and presumably, less than well-to-do.

Unfortunately, the community control system has serious weaknesses. Just as parents cannot have the complete right to choose their childrens' education, a local community cannot have such a right either, and for the same reason. How children are educated affects the interests not only of the parents or of the members of the community but also of the citizenry in general. Consequently, the members of a local community have no right to exclude the citizenry from a say in how the children of a local community are educated. And the seeming advantages of the system evaporate when they are examined closely. They depend on the assumption that there are enough knowledgeable and caring parents in black communities to insure that the community control system in black communities would produce good schools. But that assumption may be unwarranted. With laws against housing discrimination being enforced, more and more middle-class blacks—those presumably most knowledgeable about what a good education involves—are moving to the suburbs. As a result, the black ghettos are being left to parents and community members who, however caring they may be, may know little about what children need to be taught if they are to break out of poverty.

Certain advocates of community control completely overlook this. According to Charles V. Hamilton, for example, "The school would belong to the community. It would be a union of children, parents, teachers, social workers, psychologists, doctors, lawyers and community planners." This proposal is likely to seem viable until we recall that Hamilton is speaking specifically of the "ghetto school."[39] One wonders how many ghettos have—living within its boundaries—teachers, social workers, psychologists, doctors, lawyers, and community planners!

These criticisms are directed only at the idea of parents or communities literally controlling schools, that is, in the words of Carmichael and Hamilton, controlling the "hiring and firing of teachers, selection of teaching materials, determination of standards, etc." They are *not* directed at the idea of parents or communities actively supporting the work of teachers, and in this way, participating and becoming involved in the educational process. The distinction between parental control of schools, and parental participation and involvement in the educational process is important. Parents who do not know what a good education requires or how to formulate such a system should not control schools, but they may recognize what a good education requires when they see it, and if they do, they can help their children learn by supporting the work of teachers. Suggesting that this argument is sound, many research results have indicated that children learn better when their parents become involved in the educational process while the evidence in favor of community or parental control is, at best, unclear and controversial.[40]

It may be objected that my criticisms of community control rest on an objectionably paternal attitude to black communities. Hamilton, for example, is likely to raise this point.[41] But such a charge would be completely unfounded. I do argue that the freedom of communities to control schools should be restricted, but *not* in order to prevent community members from harming themselves. Rather, it is to prevent them from harming their children. Paternalism is restricting peoples' freedom in order to prevent them from harming themselves or their property. Hence, a charge of paternalism against my argument would depend on the idea that children are the property of the community—an idea of the same ilk, and as unsupportable as, the idea that children are the property of their parents.

But parents do have duties of a paternalistic nature to their children, and such duties give them certain rights over their children. Can these rights weigh against school desegregation?

I admit that paternalistic duties generate rights over those to whom the duties are owed. This is, I think, a peculiarity of such duties. If adult A has a right over adult B, then B has a duty to A, but his duty carries with it no right over A. Suppose, on one hand, that A can waive his right: if he can, he can waive B's duty and consequently if B's duty implies a right, he can also waive B's rights. But no one can waive another's rights. Suppose, on the other hand, that A cannot waive his right because it is the sort conferred by law, particularly in relation to crime, which no one can waive. Since A cannot waive this right, he cannot waive B's duty to him, but B's duty still carries with it no rights in opposition to A since fulfilling duties imposed by the law puts no one in a position to control or make demands on those to whom the duties are owed. The exceptions to this are the duty to prevent suicide, and, outside criminal law, the duty to help those who need help but cannot give consent to it because they are unconscious. In such cases, the individual's right to life imposes a duty to help on others, and this duty carries with it a right to control or make demands on those with rights. Such a duty is, of course, a paternalistic duty.

The rights generated by paternalistic duties are peculiar in their relation to the rights of others. Rights not generated by paternalistic duties are not defined in terms of others' rights. Thus, they can conflict with others' rights because their object is not the protection of those rights. Rights generated by paternalistic duties, however, are defined in terms of the rights of those to whom the duties are owed and hence cannot conflict with those rights. Thus, parents' rights to make choices for their children are, in the first place, determined and limited by their childrens' rights. They have such rights only in order to be able to do their paternalistic duty to protect their childrens' rights. An adult has a right to choose his own fate, and he can therefore choose to waive all his rights and to destroy himself. But he has a right to make only such choices for his children as will protect their rights.

Far from weighing against school desegregation, the rights parents have over their children because of their paternalistic duties to their children suggest that certain arguments against desegregation are even weaker than they at first appear. For example, Wechsler sees the issue of desegregation as a conflict between rights of association and rights of disassociation. At the "heart of the issue," he writes, is "a conflict in human claims of high dimension, not unlike many others that involve the highest freedoms." And, he claims, "if freedom of association is denied by segregation, integration forces an association upon those for whom it is unpleasant or repugnant."[42] This argument is mistaken, regarding both whose rights are centrally involved and what those rights are. Parents, of course, have a right to associate or not to associate with whomever they please. But they do not have the right to compel their children to associate or not to associate with whomever they please. Those whom their children may associate with is determined not by what their rights are but by their childrens' rights. And children have no right to freedom of association. To suppose that they do is to misunderstand the nature of childrens' rights, and in particular of their rights-in-trust. Among those rights-in-trust are the right of self-realization and the right of self-determination or autonomy. Now, the right to freedom of association allows one to choose with whom one will be associated. If children had this right, they would have the right to choose to associate with those who would transgress their rights-in-trust, for example, by undermining their ability to make free choices. Parents have a paternalistic duty, and correspondingly, a right, to prevent this. But they are properly exercising such a right only when they secure their childrens' rights by doing so. They are not properly exercising it when they compel their children to associate with the people they wish to see them with. The philosopher Antony Flew, also giving undeserved weight to parents' rights to determine their children's education, seems to imagine that the liberty the voucher system allows parents is a decisive point in its favor. Thus, he suggests that every lover of liberty should throw his weight in support of the system because it allows freedom of choice. He gives scant notice to the question of whether or not the system would be good for the children's education. "It is the friends of the educational voucher, and of the market generally, who are in truth the friends of individual liberty and individual choice," he proclaims, assuming that opposition to the voucher system can stem only from an attachment to his bugbear—the idea of equality.[43] Thus, he mocks the "educational bureaucracy," which he says opposes vouchers, "on the ground that parental choice, being made in diverse senses, could not but result in—the horror of it!—inequality." But this is confused rhetoric.

First, Flew's obvious contention, that the educational bureaucracy's objective—equality and reduced freedom—has only to be exposed for all good men to oppose it, suggests that he is unclear about whose liberty is at stake and who is to be made equal to whom. All intelligent thinkers oppose paternalistic interference in the liberty of adults for the purpose of saving them from falling below some perceived standard of—that is, becoming equal to—other adults. Adults should be free to choose to reduce their opportunities if they so desire. If the opposition of the educational bureaucracy to the voucher system entailed opposition to this uncontroversial point, then it would certainly deserve Flew's attack. But it does not; for it does not propose to limit the liberty of parents for the sake of making them equal. At worst—and this is not necessarily the case—it proposes to limit the liberty of parents for the sake of equalizing the liberties of their children.

The fact is that opposition to vouchers need not, as Flew assumes, be based on egalitarian premises at all. They may not be concerned with the fact that parental choice "is bound to produce inequalities," but instead with the fact that parental liberty is bound to produce some very poor choices. But this possibility never occurs to him. He plumps for the voucher system without pausing to wonder how it might affect children, and even without the stipulation that schools which redeem vouchers must satisfy minimum standards set by the state.

Though Friedman, unlike Flew, stresses that schools redeeming vouchers should satisfy minimum standards, he commits the same error as Flew because he would allow parents to add on to vouchers. Furthermore, in a less obvious way, he repeats the error in his response to the objection that the use of vouchers at parochial schools could violate the First Amendment. "The present [educational] arrangements," Friedman writes, "abridge the religious freedom of parents."[44] But, although this is far from being obviously true, Friedman offers no argument in support of it. Surely, the present arrangement of the educational system does not directly abridge the religious freedom of parents. A public school system supported by compulsory taxation does not prevent parents from practicing any religion they choose. It would seem that Friedman assumes that the religious freedom of parents includes the right to compel their children to attend parochial schools, an error similar to Wechsler's about the nature of children's rights. Children have a right-in-trust to religious freedom, and to secure that right parents have a paternalistic duty, and, accordingly, a right, to limit childrens' liberty in certain ways. However, it does not follow that they have a right to compel children to attend parochial schools.

If these arguments are cogent, they show that the rights-based arguments against desegregation fail. Parents have no right, either individually or collectively, to keep their children in segregated schools, and no right to the liberty to have their children educated as they please. Consequently, the state does not necessarily act wrongly when it buses children to other schools against their parents' wishes. Whether the state acts wrongly when it buses children against their parents' wishes depends on the nature of the children's rights, not on the nature of the parents' rights.

The nature of children's rights raises harder questions about the case for school desegregation than the nature of parents' rights. Thus, perhaps the most common, and to my mind, most telling objection to busing is that it siphons funds away from things, like laboratories and libraries, which really contribute to education, and thus transgresses against children's right to a good education.

When this argument is pressed, usually the real concern, though it is never admitted, is for the rights of white children. So interpreted, the argument might seem to be further supported by the fact that white parents are taxed to pay for busing. For, even if they do not have a right to determine their children's education, they may well have a right to have their taxes be used to provide their children with a good education.

This objection is readily met by the backward-looking argument. For it is not clear that white children have a right to exactly the level of education they would have if funds were not expended on busing. Perhaps they have a right to that level of education the community is willing to pay for, but if *they* are not liable for the harms caused by de jure segregation, the community is; and the backward-looking argument for busing maintains that the cost to the community of compensating for these harms is exactly the cost of busing.

A response to the objection based on the forward-looking argument would depend on deeper and more controversial considerations which, in their most radical form appeal to egalitarian values. Resort to generalizations based on my analysis of the concept of harm would not suffice. For example, it would be invalid to argue that, because segregated schooling harms black students, and thus impairs the ability to function to which they have a right, they consequently have a compensatory right to desegregated schooling. Since, as I have noted, the fact of a harm does not necessarily involve the violation of a right, the fact that segregated schooling harms black students does not necessarily entail the conclusion that it violates their rights, nor, consequently, the conclusion that they have a right to compensation. If a man can find no water to drink in a desert, he may be harmed, but his rights have not necessarily been violated. Nor would the situation be different if we discovered that, earlier, another man, acting within his rights, drank the last drop of water in the desert's only well. The case of segregated schooling may be the same. Large numbers of people, all acting within their rights, may bring about demographic conditions which result in segregated and harmful schooling, and yet which arguably do not violate the rights of those harmed. Furthermore, putting aside questions of rights violation and compensation, the fact that a condition harms an individual, impairs functional abilities to which he has a right, does not mean that he has a right to better conditions. It depends on whether or not there are available better conditions to which others have no rights. If I am harmed because my land is infertile, it does not follow that I have the right to take or share my neighbor's fertile land.

It follows that, even after dismissing false claims, such as those made by Flew, that parents have a right to the liberty of educating their children as they please, we still cannot incontrovertibly invoke the harm prevention principle in support of school desegregation until we are clearer about what rights children have. For example, if each child has a right to educational facilities as lavish as his parents are willing or able to afford, and the exercise of this right leads to segregated schooling, then, even if this schooling harms black students, we cannot justifiably invoke the harm prevention principle in order to change it. To be able to do so we must be in a position to argue either that children do not have rights to lavish educational facilities if this means that other children will then have poor facilities which harm them, or that children have rights to equal educational opportunities. But either argument—and they are quite distinct—places a limit on parents' right of bequest, and implies that the impairment of certain abilities to function are not harms, because no one has a right to these abilities. Accordingly, if, when the issue of childrens' rights is raised, we wish to utilize the harm prevention principle in support of the forward-looking argument for desegregation we must appeal to more controversial considerations about the nature of, and right to, equality, and to egalitarian ideals.

## Equal Educational Opportunity

Early advocates of desegregation believed that because whites had higher incomes than blacks, they were providing superior educational opportunities for their children. They argued, therefore, that the only way to make sure that black students got equal educational opportunities was to put them in the same schools as white students.

What were these superior educational opportunities? According to conventional wisdom, they were better facilities, such as better libraries and laboratories. But conventional wisdom was mistaken. In 1966 James S. Coleman, a professor of sociology at the University of Chicago, and his associates, published a report, *Equality of Educational Opportunity: Summary Report*, which indicated that, although black schools generally have facilities inferior to those in white schools, the differences are far less than anyone had expected, and these differences do not explain why children in white schools do so much better academically than children in black schools. However, although the report took away the basis for the "better facilities" argument for school desegregation, it supplied another.

According to the report, the factor most strongly correlated to black children's educational performance is the social class of their schoolmates. Black children in schools with children from middle-class homes generally do better than black children in schools with children from lower-class homes. In practice this turned out to mean that black children in predominantly white schools do better than black children in predominantly black schools.

This conclusion provides an essential empirical premise for an argument for desegregation found, though largely ignored in favor of other arguments, in the original *Brown* decision. In striking down the "separate but equal" doctrine declared by the *Plessy* decision the court appealed to two earlier Supreme Court decisions, *Sweatt* v. *Painter* and *McLawrin* v. *Oklahoma State Regents*. In *Sweatt*, the court ordered that Sweatt, a black man, be admitted to a previously all-white law school, relying in "large part," on the argument that the quality of a law school is measured, not by "tangible" factors like buildings, curriculum, and qualifications and salaries of its teachers, but on intangible factors "incapable of objective measurement." Similarly, in *McLawrin*, in ordering that McLawrin, a black student admitted to a previously all-white graduate school, be treated like all other students, the court again appealed to the argument that the quality of school depends on "intangible factors" like the ability to "engage in discussions and exchange views with other students."

This argument can be interpreted in two ways. The legal scholar Ira Michael Heyman takes it to mean that because "the comparative merit of different graduate schools offering similar programs depends in the last analysis on qualities incapable of measurement," different schools are "unique"—hence denying a black person admission to *any* school because of his or her race is inconsistent with equal educational opportunity.[45] This is an intriguing interpretation but it fails because it fails to address the claim that separate black schools are *inferior*. Instead it substitutes the claim that separate schools are *unique*. But if this is so, black and white schools are equally unique, and the educational opportunities for black and white students are not unequal.

The other interpretation of the argument in question draws on empirical data supplied by the Coleman report. The argument maintains that certain intangible factors make for quality in a school, but does not spell out what these intangible factors might be. The Coleman report suggests that they might be the kind of students attending the school.

Many advocates of school desegregation make this the crucial premise in their argument for busing: The kind of students attending a school make it good or bad. A majority of white middle-class students in a school make it good. Hence busing black students to white middle-class schools puts them in good schools. And, ergo, busing blacks to white middle-class schools will equalize their opportunities for education and achievement. Unfortunately, this plausible argument is both invalid and irrelevant.

It is invalid because, even if a majority of middle-class white students makes a school good, it does not follow that busing black students to such a school will improve their achievement. They simply may not respond to it. The Coleman report provides no grounds for denying this possibility. Coleman and his associates made no experiments. They did not put black students in white middle-class schools to see whether this helped them to do better. They simply observed that black students in white middle-class schools generally did better than black students in black schools. But critics pointed out that black students in white middle-class schools are, generally, middle class anyway, and therefore already likely to do better than black students in black schools, who are generally lower class. Skepticism was in order. As a large number of studies has indicated, busing lower-class black students to middle-class schools simply has not, for the most part, helped them to learn better.

Advocates of busing have responded either by impugning the reliability of these studies or by maintaining that school desegregation has not really been tried—meaning that school desegregation has not been conducted properly. But the outcome of the debate may not matter. As Derrick A. Bell has reiterated in numerous papers, "white flight" to the suburbs is making it increasingly difficult, if not impossible, to desegregate schools. And the Supreme Court does not seem prepared to pursue the policy. In *Milliken* v. *Bradely*, twenty years after *Brown*, it prohibited federal courts from using schools in white suburbs to desegregate urban black schools. As Bell concludes reluctantly, *Brown* may become irrelevant to the busing issue.[46]

However, it is of the utmost importance not to let these setbacks stampede us, as some have been, into foolish and pernicious conclusions. The worst of these being the belief that we should abandon the search for equal educational opportunity and equal educational achievement. This dismal idea had its roots in the findings of the Coleman report that a majority of middle-class students in a school make it a good school. As I indicated, some theorists thought this justified integrating schools. Others, however, drew a very different inference. They thought that it showed that "schools make no difference; families make the difference." For example, Seymour Martin Lipset, a professor at the Harvard department of government, is supposed to have "excitedly" reported to Daniel Patrick Moynihan (who taught at Harvard before becoming a Democratic senator from New York) that this was the gist of the Coleman report.[47] If Lipset is right, certain very gloomy proposals seem reasonable. If "schools make no difference; families make the difference," then it seems that there is no point in trying to equalize educational opportunities or achievements by reforming schools—and in particular by desegregating schools.

One can understand that conservatives and neo-conservatives would be excited by this argument. It is, however, a radical and socialist who has made it famous. In his widely discussed book, *Inequality*, Christopher Jencks concludes "Our research suggests . . . that the characteristics of a school's output depends largely on a single input, namely the characteristics of the entering children." According to Jencks, these are determined by their families. "Everything else," he continues, "the school budget, its policies, the characteristics of the teachers—is either secondary or completely irrelevant."[48] And on that basis Jencks argues that there is no point in equalizing educational opportunities in order to equalize achievements.

Intriguingly, however, Jencks shies away from concluding that there is no point in equalizing opportunities. He is quite ready, he says, to equalize opportunities, and indeed to spend more money on schools. *Not* for the purpose of equalizing achievements, but to make schools fun. "There is no evidence," Jencks writes, "that building a school playground, for example, will affect the students' chances of learning to read, getting into college, or making $50,000 a year when they are 50. Building a playground may, however, have a considerable effect on the students' chances of having a good time during recess when they are 8. The same thing is probably also true of small classes, competent teachers, and a dozen other things that distinguish adequately from inadequately financed schools."[49] For a similar reason, Jencks is not against school integration. He accepts it as part of equalizing opportunities. But not to help black children learn better—to give them access to "desirable" schoolmates. "We accept the proposition," he writes, "that equalizing access to desirable schoolmates is part of equal opportunity even though its long-term effects are problematic."[50]

White radicals and leftists are always trying to tell black people that their aspirations to be as competent and achieve as well as whites are doomed to failure, and that they should pin their hopes on a direct redistribution of economic resources or a socialist revolution. In Chapter 3 we discussed Marxist insinuations of this nature, and Jencks is saying it explicitly. "As long as egalitarians assume that public policy cannot contribute to economic equality directly but must proceed by ingenious manipulations of marginal institutions like schools," he declares at the end of his book, "progress will remain glacial. If we want to move beyond this tradition we will have to establish political control over the economic institutions that shape our society. This is what other countries usually call socialism. Anything less will end in the same disappointment as the reforms of the 1960's."[51]

Black people should—and generally have—rejected these lures. Harold Cruse's advocacy of a black capitalist development, which I described in Chapter 3, arose from his sense that socialism would be a false lure. And Jencks's proposal is a lure. It is not that he is wrong in believing that equalizing achievements will not equalize incomes, and that only a direct redistribution of wealth will do so. He may be right about that. It is that *economic equality is not enough*. It should not be enough for genuine egalitarians, and it is certainly not enough for black people. Black people want to hold their fair share of positions at the top— whether or not they are economically equal—and for that, at least, excellence is, and always will be, essential. And, more generally, black people want to leave their mark, and make their contribution to the world, not live off the achievement of others. As the major poet of negritude, Martiniquan Aime Cesaire wrote, "for it is not true that the work of man is finished, that we have nothing to do in the world, that we are parasites in the world."[52]

That being the case, we cannot give up the pursuit of equal achievement. Nor, if we pursue it through the school system are we trying to defy hard scientific fact. For Jencks's grand conclusion, that schools are "secondary or completely irrelevant," is in fact thoroughly unwarranted. He chose to ignore precisely those schools which would falsify it. And he admits to using this question-begging methodology! On page 13 of his book we find this stupendous confession: "We have not tried to explore the effects of the handful of schools that differ drastically from the American norm. This means we cannot say much about the theoretical limits of what can be done in a place called a school."

And there are conceptual confusions in Jencks's argument too. Consider, for example, his claim that equalizing access to "desirable schoolmates"— by which he seems to mean white students—is "part of" equal educational opportunity. This is nonsense. Why *must* black students have "access" to white students if their educational opportunities are to be made equal? Why can't their educational opportunities be made equal in some other way? And, if their presence does not help black students to learn better or broaden their horizons, in what reasonable sense are they an educational opportunity? What Jencks ignores is that school integration is only one way in which it is possible to equalize educational opportunities. When it is not available other ways must be sought. Some of these ways will leave some schools all black. So be it. If children are learning the right things it does not matter in the least what the racial composition of their schools is. And there are effective all-black schools. Derrick A. Bell, Thomas Sowell, and other black authors who take the difficulties and failures of busing seriously have demonstrated that there are all-black schools in typical black ghettoes with students whose average achievement equals or surpasses national standards.

It may be objected that the argument above implicitly endorses the view for which earlier I showed little sympathy—that harm is simply the impairing or stunting of economically valuable abilities, useful in the marketplace, such as the ability to read, write, or do arithmetic. Not so. The argument above simply stresses the absurdity of saying that the presence of white students is an educational opportunity for black students while at the same time admitting that their presence may have little or no effect on the cognitive or moral development of black children.

However, a far more serious objection would be that I have confused equalizing opportunities with equalizing achievements. It may be granted, that I have cited all-black schools with students whose achievements are more or less the same as white students. But I have no grounds, it will be objected, for inferring that the opportunities of those students are in any sense equal to those of white students. My answer to this depends on an analysis of the concept of equal opportunity.

A person has an opportunity to acquire a good either if he can have it if he chooses to, or if he can try to acquire it with some firm, even if small, possibility of success. Thus, if it is impossible for a prisoner to escape from jail, though he may try to escape, he has no opportunity to escape. Usually we must try if we are to realize our opportunities, but this is not essential. Sometimes we can realize our opportunities merely by choosing to. If an instructor offers an A to any student who chooses to have that grade, he offers his students a golden opportunity, but they need not *try* in order to realize it. They need only indicate that they choose to have an A. However, at least that much initiative—choosing or expressing a preference—is essential to realizing an op-portunity. To that extent choosing to satisfy a qualifying condition for acquiring a good is part of realizing an opportunity for acquiring that good. When a person acquires a good, not because he chose to, or because he tried to, but because he was lucky, he did not have an opportunity to get the good, but only a chance. When I win $100 at roulette that is chance. My opportunity came earlier when I chose to play roulette. Even when a person succeeds partly because he tries, we still say that he had only a chance, and not an opportunity, if his success depends overwhelmingly on luck and factors that he cannot control. An impoverished student may have an opportunity to sit in a competitive examination to win a scholarship to go to a college, but he does not have an opportunity to go to that college because he has no control over his competition. A well-to-do student, however, if he is otherwise qualified, has an opportunity to go to the college.

As the foregoing indicates, creating opportunities is essentially making it possible for people to act in certain ways if they choose. Thus, expanding opportunity is the same as expanding freedom. The fact that an opportunity is a freedom to choose or not to choose to have a good, and not the imposition of any particular good, has an important consequence. Though opportunities offer the prospect of a good or goods they need not be seized. The individual offered the opportunity may decide that the effort required is too great, or the good too far off and uncertain, or he may simply be indecisive and let the opportunity slip by. Thus, if a person has an opportunity he may choose not to take advantage of it.

So, because opportunities are freedoms, even if people have equal opportunities to achieve goods, it does not follow that they will have equal goods. People may decide to exercise their freedoms in different ways or to different degrees, or not to exercise their freedoms at all. Therefore there is a clear distinction between equal opportunity and equal achievement, and it is invalid to argue that because achievements are equal, opportunities are equal; or that because achievements are unequal, opportunities are unequal.

This concept of equal opportunity suggests that the ideal of equal opportunity is to a considerable degree irrelevant to education, especially at the basic level. Because a basic education is essential to a good life, children should not be offered *opportunities* for it. As I noted, a person with an opportunity is in a position to secure some good if he chooses to try to have it, but he is free to choose not to try. Hence, offering children opportunities for education means that they will be free to choose not to try to secure it. What is more—and is alarming—many children are apparently making that choice. But this is intolerable. A basic education is too important for children to be free to reject it. But, by definition, they will be free to reject it if they are offered only opportunities for it. Hence, they should not be offered only opportunities for it.

The first part of my answer to the objection that I have confused equal opportunity with equal achievement would be, therefore, that at the basic educational level it is not important that opportunities be equal. What is important is that children achieve. However, as children mature, it becomes increasingly important that they be given the freedom to choose, and accordingly, the question of equal opportunity becomes increasingly pertinent.

But although unequal achievements do not necessarily mean unequal opportunities, they do suggest them. For example, when a child isn't keeping up with his class, his parents do not, if they care for him, simply assume that everything is fine. They check to see whether something is preventing him from learning. Perhaps they check his diet or whether he hears or sees properly. This is the attitude with which theorists should approach the busing controversy. Unfortunately, they do not often display it. Instead, too often we find them making the assumption that because black and white students are in the same school their opportunities are equal. This is a mistake.

In the first place, such schools may not offer the same environment to black and white students. For example, the teachers may be hostile to black students and supportive of white students. And there is a deeper problem. Even if environments are uniform, opportunities may not be equal. This is because obstacles, and therefore opportunities, are relative to abilities. Because abilities differ, what is an opportunity and an advantage to one child is an obstacle and a disadvantage to another. As I defined opportunity a person has an opportunity if he can have a good if he chooses to, or if he can try to have it with some firm, even if small, possibility of success. If my prison wall is ten feet high and I can't climb over it, I have no opportunity to escape. However, if Jim can climb over it, he has an opportunity to escape—though he may choose not to take advantage of it.

Opportunities being thus relative to abilities, it is the sheerest arrogance for any group to propose as the environment offering equal opportunity for all, the environment which offers the best opportunities for itself. Because people are different, they may need different environments in order for their opportunities to be equal. In particular, because the experiences of black lower-class children are so different from those of white middle-class children, they *may* need to be in properly conducted all-black schools in order for their opportunities to be equal.

The opponent of the idea of equality may be waiting for this conclusion. He will agree that different people require different environments in which to flourish. He will argue, however, that this just shows the incoherence of the idea of equal opportunity. Thus, the English philosopher J. R. Lucas points to the ambiguity involved in calling two boys equally intelligent when one is better than the other in Latin, but worse in mathematics. What we should say, he asserts, is that neither is more intelligent than the other because the concept of equality does not apply in such cases.[53] Lucas's point seems to be that for two things to be equal they must be so in some single measurable factor. Thus, while there is no problem with saying, for example, that two women are equally tall, there is a problem with saying that the two boys are equally intelligent, or that a good basketball player is equally good an athlete as a good football player. The problem in the latter two cases is that the factors or qualities which the boys and athletes are supposed to have in equal degrees are both bogus measures of equality. There is no such quality as generalized intelligence, and no such quality as generalized athletic ability.

It may seem that a similar problem exists in comparing educational opportunities. The extent of a person's opportunities depends on the obstacles he must surmount. But because abilities—and therefore obstacles—differ, there seems to be no such factor as a general impediment; the obstacles in students' paths often seem qualitatively and irreducibly different. Consequently, assessments of opportunities as equal or unequal will often be correspondingly incoherent.

This argument can be resisted. An obstacle bars a person from obtaining a good he could otherwise obtain if he chose to. This definition permits considering certain things as obstacles in the order of the degree to which they prevent persons from achieving goods, even if the obstacles are qualitatively different. In diving competitions, for example, different dives are assigned different degrees of difficulty even though the movements are qualitatively different. And there is a similar policy for gymnastics competitions. I do not know the bases for assigning these degrees of difficulty, but several possibilities seem reasonable and not arbitrary. For example, dive A may be assigned a higher degree of difficulty than dive B because a study of how the weight of the human body is distributed and how the muscles are placed suggests that it takes greater strength to do A than to do B. This might be confirmed by comparing the length of time it takes a person to learn to do the dives, the relative number of divers who can do them, and the relative number of people who tried to do them in competition and failed. Moreover, nothing would be changed if we decided to take into consideration the fact that different divers are built differently. The only difference would be that the order of difficulty for dives would be different for different people. We could still say, however, that different dives were of equal difficulty for different people.

I do not see why it is conceptually impossible to use an analogous method to order qualitatively the different obstacles to education, even if obstacles are relative to abilities. The results, of course, will always be approximate. But the ideal of equal opportunity, however approximate, must be saved from incoherence. Otherwise the egalitarian is left with a choice of proposals that are either too strong or too weak. On one hand, he can propose that students be made to achieve equally. But obviously this proposal would be too strong. Some students, whatever their abilities, may choose not to achieve equally with others. Thus, demanding that they do so may require coercing them past the stage in their education where coercion is justified and therefore be inconsistent with the ideal of equal opportunity. On the other hand, the egalitarian can propose that equal funds be spent on each child. But that proposal would be too weak. Removing certain obstacles to children's learning abilities would cost more than removing others, and certain students would encounter more of those costlier obstacles than others would. Consequently, spending equal funds on each child might also be inconsistent with equal opportunity.

Making opportunity relative to ability is, moreover, perfectly consistent with the egalitarian basis of the equal opportunity concept. Equalizing opportunities is justified both because it tends to bring the person of greatest competence to each position, which is in most people's interests, *and* because most people have interests in filling desirable positions. For example, quite apart from their interests in having skilled engineers in a community, individuals may themselves have interests in *being* engineers. Every incompetent who cheats on his examinations attests to this. But many people who could be competent suffer from peculiar handicaps which prevent or inhibit the recognition of their competence, to the detriment of both themselves and society. For example, if no special provision were made for blind people, this would be a loss of opportunity to blind people and for society. Consequently, if we conceived of uniform environments as being able to guarantee equal opportunities, we would fail to serve both sets of interests—public and private—that the equalizing of opportunities is designed to serve.

Although equalizing opportunities is justified because, as indicated above, it satisfies both public and private interests, it is mainly the consideration of the latter which requires that opportunities for desirable positions be made equal. For, if these interests are equally important and equally worthy of satisfaction regardless of who has them, a society may have to secure equal educational opportunities even when this is not necessary to maintain or enhance the level of competence in each position. For example, a community may be able to get as many competent lawyers as it needs from the privileged classes, but sometimes, in deference to the desire of those members of the poorer classes who want to become lawyers, it may have to spend money in order to equalize opportunities so those people can become lawyers, even if this means that it cannot spend as much on enhancing lawyers' general level of competence.

In defending the ideal of equal opportunity, I do not go so far as to deny that it has limits. We cannot, for example, equalize opportunities at every stage of the educational process. As I have noted, choosing to satisfy a qualifying condition for acquiring a good is conceptually part of realizing an opportunity to acquire that good. Now, often the good for which an opportunity is offered is itself an opportunity. If we equalize that opportunity, people would get it who do not satisfy the qualifying condition of the opportunity which has been offered for it. But that would mean opportunities would not have been offered for acquiring that opportunity, *contra* hypothesis. For example, suppose that A and B are offered the opportunity to attend college and A satisfies the qualifying conditions and is accepted and B does not and is rejected. Since attending college is an opportunity, A has an opportunity that B does not have. But B cannot also be accepted. If he were, it would be false to say that the two people were offered *opportunities* to attend college. Hence, we cannot equalize opportunities at every stage of the educational process. If we do, we may revoke opportunities offered at earlier stages of the process.

A central aspect of almost every person's plan of life is his desire to hold a certain kind of job or position. Most jobs or positions require knowledge of some sort. Consequently, almost any person's plan of life involves acquiring knowledge of some sort. But the process of acquiring knowledge is part of the process of education, whether in schools or "on-the-job." Consequently, almost any person's plan of life depends on the educational opportunities he is offered. Part of what it means to respect a person is respecting him as a rational being, which means that we must not subvert the justified assumptions of his plan of life. One of those justified assumptions is that his educational opportunities will not be subverted or revoked. But, as I have shown, in some cases equalizing educational opportunities implies revoking educational opportunities offered at an earlier stage of the educational process. Consequently, in such cases, equalizing educational opportunities would mean failing to respect people, and hence, in such cases, we ought not to equalize opportunities. Or, if people are not justified in assuming as part of their plans of life that their educational opportunities will not be subverted or revoked—if, that is, qualifying conditions change rapidly and without meaning—people are not in fact offered opportunities, but only chances. But if people are offered only chances, then surely they are not being respected as rational beings. For if nothing is fixed, nothing can be planned, and if nothing can be planned, rationality is futile.

However, this limit on the ideal of equal opportunity must not be exaggerated. Its crucial premise is that opportunities—and equal opportunities—might be offered for other opportunities that ought not to be equalized. But, as things are, that crucial premise is hardly ever true. Usually equal opportunities are *not* offered for opportunities. This is self-evident. Most black and white families and schools are too unequal for the alternative to be taken seriously. And if this is true, equalizing opportunities at any stage of the educational process does not revoke equal opportunities offered at earlier stages, for usually equal opportunities were *not* offered at earlier stages. Consequently, since it is the act of revoking earlier opportunities that shows no respect for people, equalizing opportunities does not usually fail to respect them.

A different kind of limit on the equalizing of opportunities stems from the very, egalitarian, concept on which the ideal of equal opportunity is based. As I noted, equalizing opportunities may require spending more on some students than on others. But a society is not required to bankrupt itself in order to institute special facilities for special students. Though this may be required for equalizing opportunities, it is inconsistent with the egalitarian ideal of giving equal weight to each person's like interests. Instead, it would mean giving too much weight to some people's interest in holding desirable positions, and too little weight to the interests of others in the necessities or amenities of a decent life. Consequently, many ostensibly egalitarian views about education must be reconsidered, most obviously the leveller's argument that resources should be allocated to students in inverse proportion to their abilities so that the talented and untalented will achieve equally. Such a policy would not only destroy civilization, but, for the reasons noted, is also thoroughly inegalitarian. Perhaps less obviously defective, but equally unacceptable, is the view expressed by both John W. Gardener and Christopher Jencks, that equal educational opportunity should demand what is "best" for each student, or the "maximum development of individual potentialities at every level of ability," or that "every youngster" should be enabled to "fulfill his potentialities."[54] Or, finally, that "everyone should get as much schooling as he wants."[55] What is wrong with all these views is that they propose either to indulge some students and sacrifice others, or to indulge students in general and sacrifice non-students in general.

Although—insofar as it does remove obstacles to learning—desegregating schools in order to equalize educational opportunities is probably well within the limits of equalization which I have described, these limits do indicate that, even given egalitarian premises, which provide the strongest support for school desegregation the forward-looking argument is controversial. These limits indicate that, even if desegregating schools will equalize educational opportunities, it may, in egalitarian terms, still be unjustifiable. The question can be settled only by an empirical estimation of the costs of desegregating schools, and a conceptual determination, based on egalitarian premises, of the relative importance of those costs and of the interests of the members of society in general in the necessities and amenities of their lives. Even if a conceptual determination can be made, the empirical uncertainties, both in relation to the costs of desegregation and in relation to establishing whether it decreases harm and equalizes educational opportunities, remain, and cast doubt on the forward-looking argument's justification for busing.

# 6

# Ronald Dworkin
# and Busing

## Edmond Cahn

Advocates of busing have responded to the claim that busing students may be unjustified because it fails to produce hoped-for educational results by proposing a radically different kind of argument for their favored policy. The argument for busing, they say, is not educational, but "constitutional, political and moral," or, in short, its purpose is not to educate, but to integrate.[1] Their hope is that this approach will make busing completely independent of controversial social science theories and claims. Moreover, they claim that this argument is the real basis of the *Brown* decision. Edmond Cahn was one of the first to make this point.[2]

Cahn is easy to misunderstand. It might seem that his objection to the social scientists is that they solemnly—and ineptly—set out to "prove" facts about segregation that "most of mankind already acknowledges," for example, that segregation is psychologically injurious. But this is not his real objection. His real objection is that he believes the scientists were profoundly mistaken in principle. They believed that the decision they favored in *Brown* depended on the finding that segregation is harmful. But, according to Cahn, the decision they favored in *Brown* depended on the familiar and universally accepted moral view that segregation under government auspices is humiliating, insulting, and therefore morally evil. More and more advocates of busing are arguing that Cahn's thesis applies, not only to the original *Brown* decision, but also to all later busing decisions. Even Kenneth Clark, at one time perhaps the staunchest defender of the role of social science in desegregation cases, has switched sides.[3]

## Dworkin versus the Backward- and Forward-looking Arguments for Busing

Characteristically, Ronald Dworkin has presented the boldest version of Cahn's thesis.[4] Distinguishing between causal and interpretive judgments in social science—causal judgments assert a causal connection between two independently specifiable social phenomena, and interpretive judgments specify the meaning or significance of a particular phenomenon in a particular society—Dworkin first argues that Cahn was correct in denying that the *Brown* decision rested on the causal judgments of social science, such as that segregated education is poor education, and was correct in affirming that *Brown* rested instead on the interpretive judgments of social science, such as that segregated education is insulting and degrading.

But then Dworkin goes further than Cahn. Cahn said that segregation under "government auspices" is humiliating and insulting. Given that he was writing in support of *Brown*, a decision which outlawed de jure segregation, it is not unreasonable to interpret this as meaning that de jure segregation is insulting and humiliating. But, since Dworkin uses Cahn's thesis in support of *later* busing decisions which have ordered the reversal of de facto segregation in schools, he must be extending that thesis to state that even de facto segregation in schools is insulting and degrading.

If Dworkin is right, both the backward- and forward-looking arguments for busing are unsound. I have dealt with his criticism of the backward-looking argument.[5] I will now take up his criticism of the forward-looking argument, which he summarises in the following syllogism: every child is entitled to an equal educational opportunity. A segregated education, whether de jure or de facto, does not provide an equal educational opportunity. Therefore, every child is entitled to an integrated education.[6] Dworkin's criticism of this argument is that it is unsound because its second premise, the causal judgment of social science, is statistical. Even if it is true, it does not follow that *every* minority child in a segregated school is getting a worse education than he or she would get in an integrated school. According to Dworkin, a minority child who got a better education in a segregated school could argue as follows: "For me, an integrated education does not provide the level of educational opportunity to which I am entitled. Therefore I am entitled to a segregated education."[7] Since the force of this argument is not weakened by the fact that only a few can advance it, Dworkin concludes that the forward-looking argument for busing fails. The crux of his objection is that a black or minority child can make the statement "For me, an integrated education does not provide the level of educational opportunity to which I am entitled." But this statement contains a crucial ambiguity that is easy to miss if one fixes, as Dworkin fixes, on the idea that it is a black child who would make the statement.

Suppose a white child made the same claim: "For me, an integrated education does not provide the level of educational opportunity to which I am entitled." I, for one, would immediately take him to mean that an integrated education does not provide him with the *best* educational opportunity he can have. And I would answer him as follows: "You may be correct in saying that an integrated education does not provide you with the best educational opportunity you can have. But you are not entitled to the best educational opportunity you can have. You are entitled to an educational opportunity equal to that of other children."

But, suppose he objects that what he means is that an integrated education does not provide him with an equal educational opportunity. There are problems with that statement too. To what is his educational opportunity not equal? To what it would be in a segregated setting? I have admitted that this could be true, but pointed out that he has no right to such an educational opportunity. Does he then mean that his educational opportunity is unequal to that of other children. This seems hardly likely. Opportunities are equal when benefits and obstacles are equally distributed. And integration is, precisely, an effort to distribute equally for children the benefits and obstacles that are involved in the educational process.

But clearly, if it is ambiguous for a white child to say that an integrated education does not provide him with the level of educational opportunity to which he is entitled, it is equally ambiguous for a black child to say the same thing. The ambiguity is merely less easy to see because the statement is less likely to be recognized as a possible claim to privilege.

For example, suppose such a child insists on segregated schooling because in that case he would go to Dunbar (in its heyday), whereas in an unsegregated system he would go to a less distinguished integrated school. I admit that his opportunities in the integrated school would be unequal to, i.e., less than, his opportunities at Dunbar. But, as I have already indicated, he has no right to the best educational opportunities he can get. He has a right only to an educational opportunity equal to that of other children. The price of his getting a superior educational opportunity at Dunbar would be other black children, who do not attend schools like Dunbar, getting vastly inferior educational opportunities. Hence, his insistence on a segregated system would be an insistence on privilege and not on the right to an equal educational opportunity. On the other hand, if he claims that an integrated education does not provide him with an equal educational opportunity, then, as I have already argued, what he says is false.

It follows that the persuasiveness of Dworkin's case depends on a failure to perceive that the key claim in his objection may be either a claim to privilege or a claim to equality, and that it succeeds only if the claim is interpreted as a claim of privilege. Dworkin himself seems to have been taken in by it because sometimes he interprets it as a claim about equal educational opportunity and sometimes as a claim to the best possible education.[8]

But perhaps I misunderstand Dworkin. I fear this may be so, because of the way in which he puts the case that some blacks will have a worse education in integrated schools than in segregated schools. He does not, for example, support this possibility, as I have done, by citing the achievement level in schools such as Dunbar. He supports this possibility with the remark, "People differ to that extent."[9]

What Dworkin means is *not* that some black children in a segregated system will be lucky enough to attend a school, like Dunbar, which offers superior educational opportunities. What he means is that people differ to such an extent that there will be some very unusual black children, who will get an excellent education in schools with very inferior educational facilities and staff. Now this is logically possible. There may be some very uncommon children who would be stirred to great and successful efforts by the noise, violence, and distracted teachers in the worst ghetto schools, but lulled into idleness and failure by the diligence of the student body, and the competence of the teachers, in a properly integrated school. This possibility I cannot categorically deny. People do differ to that extent.

But if Dworkin bases on that possibility the claim that some black children can demand a segregated school system, then he makes equal education opportunity, in those instances, logically impossible to implement. This is clear from the following argument: Equal educational opportunity requires that each child get a certain equal level of education. One child will get this only in a segregated school system. Another child will get it only in an integrated school system. Consequently, equal educational opportunity requires that the school system be both segregated and integrated. But this is logically impossible. Hence equal educational opportunities for all are impossible.

Since this unacceptable conclusion apparently stems directly from the use of the causal judgments of social science to calculate levels of opportunity, some may infer that it supports Dworkin's thesis that these judgments play no part in the case for busing. But that inference would be mistaken.

The fallacy in Dworkin's argument is not that he makes opportunities relative to individual differences. I have allowed that this is legitimate.[10] The fallacy in Dworkin's argument is that he does not heed his own sound distinction between the right to equal treatment and the right to treatment as an equal. The right to equal treatment is the right to "the same distribution of goods or opportunities as anyone else has or is given," and presumably includes the right to equal educational opportunity. The right to treatment as an equal, on the other hand, is the right "not to an equal distribution of some good or opportunity, but the right to equal concern and respect in the political decision about how these goods and opportunities are to be distributed," and requires government to take into account, and give equal weight to, the like interests of each person.[11] Now, according to Dworkin, a person's right to treatment as an equal is "fundamental," whereas "the right to equal treatment holds only in those special circumstances in which, for some special reason, it follows from the more fundamental right." This leads us to the fallacy in Dworkin's argument against the use of social science statistics in busing decisions. For, suppose we grant his assumption that people differ to such an extent that although a majority of black students may get a desirable amount of educational opportunities only in an integrated school system, at least one black student might get that amount of opportunity only in a segregated school system. If that assumption were fact, then, as I noted before, since a school system must be either segregated or integrated, it follows that all black students could not get equal educational opportunities. But this situation would not lead us to an impasse. It would mean only that we were not dealing with one of those "special circumstances" in which one person's right to equal opportunity must be granted because it follows from his more fundamental right to treatment as an equal. Dworkin is clear about how he feels government should proceed in these more usual cases. It should refer back to the principles of the fundamental right—which means giving equal weight to the like interests of each person—and this may well mean that the interests of a minority have to be sacrificed. Proceeding in the same way on the question whether the school system should be segregated or integrated, we easily derive the result that it should be integrated.

In his essay "Social Science and Constitutional Rights," in which he directly addresses himself to the issue of school desegregation, Dworkin appears to rule out this conclusion, on the grounds that we cannot "use numbers to adjudicate rights."[12] He means that we cannot violate one person's rights, even to secure an end which would satisfy a great number of people, and even if that end is otherwise justifiable. Rights, he says, are "trumps."[13] But, whether or not this observation is true in other cases, it is inconsistent when applied to the desegregation issue. For the right to equal educational opportunity, he has established, is a right to equal treatment, and he has assured us that such rights exist only in the special circumstances in which they follow from the fundamental right to treatment as an equal. We have demonstrated that this is not the case when, as Dworkin has postulated, only a minority of black students—possibly only one—might achieve a desirable level of educational opportunity only in a segregated school system.

It follows that Dworkin's demonstration against the forward-looking argument for busing was incorrect in its conclusion that the causal judgments of social science cannot be the basis for a sound case for busing, no matter what plausible political morality we supplement them with. For he tested his premise by seeing what would happen when they are supported only by the equal opportunity principle. If he had allowed the results of social science to be supported by the principle he himself has espoused, that equal weight be assigned to the like interests of every person, he would have arrived at a different conclusion.

## Dworkin's Insult-based Argument

In succeeding sections I will show that a valid case for busing *cannot*, as Dworkin argues, be based on the interpretive judgment of social science—its conclusion that segregation is insulting, and that the attempt to seal the case for busing by basing it on this apparently patent fact, rather than on the controversial claim that busing is beneficial, fails.

Dworkin endorses the idea that unjust discrimination differs from just discrimination because the former involves insult and the latter does not. Thus, he maintains that when the University of California at Davis denied Allan Bakke admission to its medical school in 1973–74, this incident differed signally from the traditional color bars against blacks because, whereas he feels it is "absurd" to claim that Bakke was "kept out because his race is the object of prejudice or contempt," traditional color bars were an "insult" to blacks because they were "generated by and signaled contempt."[14] But it is not clear whether, for Dworkin, insult in itself constitutes—or is only the symptom of—the injustice of color bars.

This question arises if we take a closer look at his version of the insult argument. Thus, in his discussion of the case of the University of Washington law school denying admission to Marco De Funis, a case similar to Bakke's, Dworkin rejects the argument that color bars against blacks differ from preferential admissions policies because blacks, being "the victims of slavery and legal segregation," will see any discrimination against them as "insulting," whereas whites will not.[15] In the first place he points out, it is a mistake "to assume that men in the position of De Funis will not take *their* exclusion to be insulting." They are likely, he notes, to see themselves as the members of minorities such as Jews or Poles that "comfortable liberals are willing to sacrifice in order to delay more violent social change." Dworking further argues that "it is not true . . . that any social policy is unjust if those who it puts at a disadvantage feel insulted. . . . Everything depends upon whether the feeling of insult is produced by some more objective feature that would disqualify the policy even if the insult were not felt."[16] What this leaves unclear is whether the more objective quality in question is insult, as a fact rather than a feeling, or whether it is something altogether different.

Nevertheless, Dworkin maintains quite clearly that color bars against blacks are insulting to them. "Any form of segregation that disadvantages blacks is, in the United States, an automatic insult to them," he declares flatly.[17] His argument here depends on his well-known distinction between personal and external preferences. Dworkin defines a personal preference as an individual's preference for an assignment of goods or opportunities to himself, and an external preference as an individual's preference—possibly pernicious—for such assignments to others.[18] He believes that if a utilitarian argument counts the satisfaction of external preferences in calculating social welfare, then its egalitarian character is corrupted; an acceptable utilitarianism, viz., one which is faithful to the egalitarian principle that each person's satisfaction is to be counted as equal to any other's, must count only the satisfaction of personal preferences in calculating social welfare. Now, according to Dworkin, though a representative democracy may be well suited to the formulation of policies based on preference-oriented utilitarianism, it does not discriminate between personal and external preferences; furthermore, given its history and culture, any personal preference concerning blacks in the United States is likely to be dependent, or, as he puts it, "parasitic" upon external preferences about blacks.[19] On these grounds Dworkin argues that, since the United States is a representative democracy, any official policy that segregates and disadvantages blacks will probably be arrived at by giving weight to external preferences about blacks, or personal preferences about them which are dependent or parasitic upon external preferences about them. But giving weight to such preferences is tantamount to treating those about whom others have those preferences, in relation to their assignments, as worthy of less than equal respect and concern. This is to insult them, and consequently Dworkin concludes that to institute any policy in the United States that segregates and disadvantages blacks is to insult them.

But should a law or policy be considered insulting and rejected—if it is arrived at by weighing external preferences—if it is *advantageous* to those the external preferences are about? That it should is implausible, and Dworkin himself seems to sense this. Thus his conclusion, it should be noticed, is not merely that segregation is insulting to blacks, but that segregation is insulting to blacks if it "disadvantages" them. But this proviso is gratuitous. If it is the weighing of external preferences that is insulting, then segregation need not disadvantage blacks in order to be insulting. *Any* policy that proposed special treatment for blacks, including treatment that was advantageous to them, would be equally insulting as long as that policy were arrived at by weighing external preferences. That Dworkin includes the proviso suggests that he is not sufficiently clear about what an insult is; what kind of injustice it is, if it is an injustice; whether it is by itself sufficient to disqualify a policy; or whether, though it often characterizes policies that must be disqualified, it is then only a symptom of a deeper injustice that makes that policy unacceptable.

## The Nature of Insult

I plan to argue that insult is an objective feature of a situation and is a judgmental injustice. Typically, insults are things people *tell* one another. As Owen Fiss interprets the claim that segregation is an insult, segregation conveys the message "We don't want your kind."[20] This suggests that insults are part of that kind of wrong, which involves making false and derogatory statements about people, that Joel Feinberg has called judgmental injustice. But Feinberg himself denies this. Quoting with approval legal scholar William L. Prosser's suggestion that insult is a mere expression of a "low opinion" of another, he notes that judgmental injustice must make some "judgment of fact" that is derogatory, whereas insults make no judgment of fact but are "mere hurling of epithets." And he concludes that, though insults may be unjust because they may make their targets "suffer wrath or humiliation," they are not a form of judgmental injustice.[21]

The philosopher of language Justin Leiber, somewhat similarly, distinguishes insult on the one hand, and libel and slander on the other hand, on the grounds that, whereas the latter have some "very real and literal chance of being thought to be true," insult does not. Insult, he maintains, does not mean to communicate any belief. That is not its purpose. Its purpose is to "wound and humiliate."[22]

Perhaps Feinberg and Leiber take this view because insulting sentences are not only often literally false, but necessarily and obviously so. This seems to have weighed heavily with Leiber in particular. Insulting sentences, he says, are "often and typcially the more successful as they are wildly improbable, redundant, contradictory and senseless;" they "have no literal sense in that it is wholly unclear what state of affairs could make them literally false;" and "it is a serious defect in a purported insult if there is any possiblity that it could literally be true."[23] Leiber's reasoning here seems to be as follows: suppose that I call a man a pig. This is necessarily and obviously false. Yet my calling the man a pig is, or can, in the proper context, be an insult to him.

But Leiber's point is not merely, I imagine, that the insulting sentence is literally and obviously false. This would not suggest strongly enough that insulting sentences do not express judgments. That the famous Harvard logician W. V. O. Quine is the Boston Strangler is obviously and ludicrously false. Yet Feinberg is willing to take such a claim as a genuine judgmental injustice.[24] Consequently, the inference that insulting sentences express no judgments cannot rest merely on the premise that the judgments they express are obviously false. It rests on the premise that the judgments insulting sentences express are *necessarily* false. A man *cannot* be a pig, or a dog, or a son-of-a-bitch. These are necessary truths. Furthermore, they are *obviously* necessary truths. As Leiber puts it, to deny them is "contradictory and senseless." On this basis, assuming, I suppose, that sentences that are contradictory and sense-less cannot be meant to *say* anything, he concludes that insults are not meant to communicate beliefs.

This argument is unsound—its crucial premise is false. Not all insults, or even the most successful ones, are "contradictory and senseless" or have no chance of being considered true. A person can insult another by calling him a buffoon, and this is neither senseless nor contradictory and could easily be true.

J. L. Austin, professor of philosophy at Oxford University before his death in 1960, once raised the question of why one cannot insult someone by saying to him, "I insult you."[25] Commenting on this, Leiber suggests that the answer is that insulting, like alleging, instigating, insinuating, and hinting, is a speech act which is "blocked or flawed when put in explicit performative form."[26] Or,—as another philosopher, Zeno Vendler, put it more catchily—the explicit performative use of such verbs as insult, allege, insinuate, and hint is "illocutionary suicide" because the illocutionary force of the speech action described by these verbs is frustrated if the explicit performative form is used.[27] According to Leiber, this is because these acts are "of their nature insincere, covert, weaseling." Their intent is essentially "malicious and concealed." Consequently, the explicit performative "I insult you" frustrates the act of insulting because insult depends on its deniability.[28]

Now there are really two questions involved in the reasoning above, and Leiber has failed to distinguish them. The first is why one does not usually succeed in insulting by saying "I insult you." The second is why one blocks or defuses a string of insults by leading with "I insult you." But it is false to aver that the announcement "I insult you" defuses a string of insults. Leiber thinks it is true because he thinks that insults are typically deniable. But he is mistaken. If I call a person a pig or a dog or a son-of-a-bitch, or any one of those senseless, contradictory things Leiber thinks generally characteristic of insult, I can hardly deny that I am insulting. Neither do I necessarily blunt a string of such insults by starting with "I insult you."

Not only is Leiber mistaken about the nature of insulting, he is mistaken about the other verbs he compares it to, and it is important and instructive to see why. Take the verb "hint." According to Leiber and Vendler, to use that verb explicitly is to commit "illocutionary suicide." One defeats one's purpose in hinting by announcing that one is hinting. But this is plainly false. For example, in mathematics texts some of the harder problems are followed by the word "hint" and hint at a way to find the answer. Those hints are certainly not frustrated by the fact that they are preceded by the announcement that they are hints!

So, to announce that one is hinting, just as to announce that one is insulting, is not illocutionary suicide. Sometimes one hints better, or insults better, by announcing that one is going to hint or insult. Nevertheless, there is an important point here, though it has been badly described.

In mathematics texts, the hint that follows a difficult problem is not the answer to the problem. It is a proposition from which the student can infer how he should begin looking for the answer to the problem. Or, sometimes, the passage leading the students in the direction of a solution involves educated guesswork and is thus not strictly inference. What is always true, however, is that to hint at something is not to *say* it literally. It is to say something else in order to prompt the other person to conclude for himself whatever one is hinting at.

Accordingly, it is necessary to distinguish between saying *that* one is hinting, and saying *what* one is hinting at. Saying *that* one is hinting does not frustrate hinting. It may enhance it. Saying *what* one is hinting at does frustrate hinting. It *tells* the other person what one wants him to know, whereas the point of hinting is to get the other person to figure out for himself what one wants him to know. Leiber's claim, that saying that one is hinting is illocutionary suicide, depends on mixing up these two aspects.

Now, consider those insults which are of the wildly contradictory and senseless type. These insults are very much like hinting. They do not literally *say* what they want said. Rather, they say something that prompts the insulted person to conclude for himself what they want said. Suppose, for example, we see a very fat and dirty man, obviously already gorged, but still greedily slurping away at a big bowl of greasy mush, and suppose that, in disgust, we go up to him and tell him that he is a pig. Taken literally, the words we utter are unquestionably false. A man cannot be a pig. On the other hand, only the most obtuse would fail to see what we were getting at. For it is also unquestionably true that in many striking ways the man is very much like a pig. The point, however, is that the insult does not literally say this. It gets the man himself to think it, and if it is well aimed, it will get the man to admit, he is like a pig. He will admit this in the sense that he will spontaneously recognize that the epithet means that he is as sloppy and greedy and dirty as a pig. Since no one has literally said this, his spontaneous recognition of the meaning of the epithet is an admission that there is good ground for attributing these pig-like qualities to him. This is the perverse genius of the well-designed insult. It is not that the insulter can deny that it is an insult. It is that it betrays the insulted person into accusing himself. Without saying anything *literally* derogatory, if only because what it says is *literally* contradictory, it impels the insulted person to acknowledge the worst things about himself. Thus it is that often the best response to an insult is to ignore it, and often the most satisfying answer to an angry response to an insult is, "If the hat fits, wear it."[29]

If the argument above is persuasive, it is a mistake to think that, because insults are, if taken literally, obviously false, they do not express judgments and cannot therefore be a form of judgmental injustice. And if insults are judgmental injustices there is really no mystery at all in Leiber's question about why "I insult you" is not insulting. Insulting sentences express some derogatory judgment about their object, but "I insult you" expresses no such judgment. At most it expresses dislike of the object, and an expression of dislike is not an insult. Consequently, while venomously uttering the sentence "You are a pig " while pointing at a greedy man is an illocutionary act of insulting, normally performed with the intention of also performing the perlocutionary act of wounding, shaming, and hurting, similarly uttering the sentence, "I insult you" is not explicitly performative at all because nothing is performed. For we succeed in performing the illocutionary act of insulting only if we also succeed in performing the illocutionary act of suggesting some derogatory judgment.

It may be objected that the insulted person does not necessarily accuse himself. For example, though the fat man will recognize that we are saying that he is like a pig when we say he *is* a pig, this may not be in the least because he admits that he has pig-like qualities, but because he knows that calling a person a pig is an oblique way of saying that he is like a pig. My response is that in such a case the insulter will have failed in his chief purpose, which is to hurt and wound. If we call the fat man a mouse, he may know, by our tone, that we are insulting or trying to insult him, and this alone may anger him. And he may know that we are figuratively saying that he is like a mouse. But if he cannot see in what particular derogatory ways he is like a mouse, the insult will fail to wound. And if we try to explain matters to him we will have failed signally to deliver the strongest blow of insult, which is to make him accuse himself. Thus it is typically a sign of failure for an insulter to have to explain his insult, and one of the best ways to deal with an insult is to pretend not "to get it." Finally, though a person who does not know *how* he is being insulted will not be *hurt* by the insult, if he knows *that* he is being insulted this may hurt him, and he may be *angered* and want to strike out. Thus the insulter who fears the one he insults often designs his insults so that he can deny that he insulted. There is this much substance in Leiber's thesis that insults must be obviously deniable, but it is far from being generally true. When the insulter does not fear his victim, or the reproof of others, he may want to affirm that he is insulting. In this way he more fully expresses his contempt. For an insult hurts in two ways: First because it is a way of treating people contemptuously; second because of what it says. Feinberg and Leiber have viewed insult exclusively as simply an expression of contempt. And in Leiber's hands this concept becomes paradoxical, because the more insult is an *expression* of contempt, the less the insulter can deny he insulted. An insult becomes more deniable when it obliquely says derogatory things about its object, although it is then less clearly an *expression* of contempt.

Some insults are, more than others, expressions of contempt and dislike, and some are almost completely expressions of contempt and dislike. Thus, the insulter who simply hurls standard epithets can almost be said to be expressing only contempt—although not completely, since even standard epithets like "dog," "rat," "pit," and "shark" have distinctive meanings. Perhaps in such cases we should speak of *abuse* as a specific—and inept—form of insult. For, although the violence with which it is uttered may make abuse threatening and disturbing it altogether lacks the stab of insult.

But abuse is only a part, and the less interesting part, of insulting. If abuse were all there was to insult we could not explain the way in which successful insults are different to fit different people, nor why the *Plessy* "separate but equal" decision was an insult, nor, finally, why the most successful insults are not merely abusive. Feminists are correct in saying that the opinion that women should be housewives is insulting to women, although, of course, that opinion is not abusive. Similarly, the opinion that blacks are carefree, happy-go-lucky, etc., is insulting to blacks although it is not abusive and does not consist of a hurling of epithets. Nevertheless, what makes both examples of insult is the way they invite the insulted people to see themselves in a derogatory way—as sex objects, or animals. Thus, the most skillful insult is not a standard epithet. It is a vivid metaphor or locution that takes the victim unaware and makes him see himself in a new light.

## The Insult of Segregation

Actions often insult more successfully than words. Consider the crime of lynching. For as great as is the *injury* it inflicts, both to its victims and to those to whom it is meant to be a lesson, it is an especially mortifying *insult* because of what it says of them. Its perpetrators admit no wrong. Though they may admit illegality they admit no immorality. Though they conceal themselves they make it clear that they do so only for prudential reasons. On the contrary, in the way in which they call attention to what they have done, lynchers seem to invite, and be confident of rebutting, criticism, to be holding themselves up for approval and declaring their righteousness. Clearly then, the symbolic meaning of a lynching is that its victims, and those like them to whom it is meant as a warning, have no rights, and the effectiveness of lynching as an insult lies in the especial vehemence and perverse eloquence with which it makes that point.

The key to this argument then is that, somewhat like lynching, segregation has a symbolic aspect which expresses contempt for black people. In the case of de jure segregation this cannot be doubted. As Cahn notes, de jure segregation of blacks is like the isolation imposed on lepers and criminals, and, like such forms of isolation stigmatizes,— which is to say, not only marks blacks but *declares* that they are inferior and contaminating.[30] Since a determination of the meaning of segregation depends on an examination of the conventions and attitudes of the society—for it is these which give actions, and indeed words, their meaning—the claim that segregation is insulting is what Dworkin calls an interpretive judgment of social science. However it is not, for that reason, any more arbitrary or conjectural than the claim that a sneer is an expression of contempt. Nevertheless because de jure segregation does not express its contempt through words, segregationists who cared about appearances were able to put up a show of denying that de jure segregation was insulting. In *Plessy*, the Supreme Court indulged in that charade. The "underlying fallacy of the plaintiff's argument," Justice Brown wrote, is "the assumption that the enforced separation of the two races stamps the colored race with a badge of inferiority. If this be so, it is not by reason of anything found in the act, but solely because the colored race chooses to put that construction upon it."[31] But, as I have shown, this is a characteristic defense of those who wish to insult with impunity.

In the case of de jure segregation a racist majority expressed its contempt explicitly through the Jim Crow laws. However, in de facto segregation, laws and policies may be color-blind. Consequently, the case for saying that it constitutes insult is more complicated. Yet I think it can be made. Despite the absence of laws explicitly enforcing segregation in housing, this kind of segregation persists because, when blacks move into a neighborhood, whites usually move out. Now I submit that, given the established patterns of the society, the act of moving out of a neighborhood when blacks move in is an expression of contempt for blacks. The blacks know it, and the whites know it too. Of course, a white family may not mean to express contempt by moving. But all common modes of expression may sometimes not mean to express what they are conventionally taken to express—for example, a man may move his hand about over his head, but not intend to wave at anyone.

## A Critique of Dworkin's Argument for Busing

But although I thus agree with Dworkin's view that segregation of any kind is, in the present context, insulting, I contend against his argument that this view of segregation is sufficient to justify busing. "Suppose," Dworkin writes, "that the natural way drawing district lines produces segregated schools because neighborhoods are segregated. The community is faced with a political decision. Would it be in the general interest to adopt extraordinary methods, like busing, to achieve integration? Or would the objective costs of the decision outweigh the gains?"[32] The ideals of democracy seem to demand that the community should let its representatives decide, or should put the question to a vote. The Harvard sociologist Nathan Glazer takes this view. The judges, he says, "should now stand back and allow the forces of political democracy to do their proper work."[33] But Dworkin is suspicious of these solutions. Both are likely to give weight to external preferences about blacks, and we have seen that he thinks that this corrupts political decision. As he puts it,

"There is a high antecedent probability that any community decisions on that issue will be corrupted,"[34] and he argues that, unless "the decision actually produced by the political process was of a sort *itself* to negate the charge of corruption, then we could conclude, for that case, the judgment that the process was too corrupt to allow it to continue."[35] Thus, Dworkin feels, the courts must decide on, and order, integration. "The order," he writes, "speaks to those in political power and says this: 'If you yourself refuse to produce an outcome that negates the antecedent probability of corruption, then we must impose on you such an outcome. The only decision we can impose, given the nature of the problem, is a decision that requires integration on some formula that is evidently not corrupt even if it is just as evidently arbitrary.'"[36]

Dworkin has advanced a justly famous argument to show that this apparent restriction of the democratic process is, in fact, necessary for, and fully consistent with, a pure utilitarian defense of that process. Now, the kind of utilitarianism usually employed in defense of democracy is preference utilitarianism. According to preference utilitarianism through his votes, each person registers his preferences, and the political process in a democracy is a method designed to reach decisions that maximize the satisfaction of the preferences thus revealed. Dworkin's contention is that the utilitarian and democratic demand that everyone count as one, and the utilitarian demand that the satisfaction of preferences be maximized, may be inconsistent. Sometimes in order to maximize the satisfaction of preference we cannot count everyone equally, because to maximize the satisfaction of preferences we may have to satisfy external preferences, and satisfying such preferences requires that some people not be considered equally. Thus, a truly egalitarian, and in this sense pure, utilitarianism should not give weight to the claims for the satisfaction of external preferences along with the satisfaction of personal preferences. If it does, it will not consider each person equally. For example, if it allows for the satisfaction of the external preference of a white law school candidate that blacks not be allowed in law schools, then the satisfaction of the personal preference of a black law school candidate to be allowed into law school must necessarily be considered less important.[37]

It does not follow that in Dworkin's view we can never use the will of the majority to decide social policy. We can, when the majority's vote expresses personal preferences. But we cannot when, as is sometimes the case, there is a high antecedent probability that the vote expresses external preferences. To follow its dictates in such cases would be to count the members of the minority as less than equal. To guarantee that they do count equally we create constitutional rights in order to protect them from the will of the majority.[38]

If this is sound reasoning, we no longer have to be satisfied with the observation that democracy, especially direct democracy, often allows the majority to tyrannize over the minority. We now recognize that when this happens often what has been at work is not a democratic process at all, but an imitation that denies the egalitarian premise of democracy. In particular, given that Dworkin is right that a community decision against busing would be "saturated" with prejudice against blacks, i.e., would involve external preferences, we have, it seems, solid gounds for rejecting Glazer's proposal to let the busing question be settled by the "forces of political democracy."

I agree with this conclusion, and with the argument that supports it. However, I disagree with the conclusion that, because a community decison not to bus would be corrupt, we must impose upon it a decision to bus.

Dworkin's argument against Glazer's proposal depends on his view that external preferences should be given no weight in a democratic decision making process. This view quickly came under attack even from those who shared Dworkin's egalitarian assumptions. Thus, Marshall Cohen argued persuasively that Dworkin's objection to school segregation is "not plausible if it is simply an objection to the registering of external preferences."[39] If Dworkin were right, Cohen noted, then registering the external preferences of the benevolent able-bodied to increase public spending on the handicapped would violate the right to treatment as equals of the self-interested able-bodied whose personal preference was to increase public spending on themselves.

Now, Cohen does not mean that we should always weigh external preferences. He means that if they should not be weighed it should not be their being external which disqualifies them from consideration, but should be some other characteristic.

What is this other characteristic? Philosopher H. L. A. Hart, who, in his own criticism of Dworkin has arrived at a conclusion similar to the one above, argues that it is the characteristic of being "liberty-denying and respect-denying."[40] But Dworkin's argument is that weighing external preferences is always liberty-denying and respect-denying. That argument has force, and can be outlined as follows: Personal preferences make no comparisons between people or the goods they prefer. External preferences do. To consider a personal preference is thus to give no weight to any view about the relative worth of persons or goods, whereas to consider external preferences is to give weight to views about the relative worth of persons and goods. Consequently, when only personal preferences are considered in making a decision the losers are being told only that they are in the minority. But when external preferences are given weight, the losers are being told that they, or their views, are inferior.

Hart is aware of this argument and tries to rebut it. "It is not clear," he writes, "why the rejection of his ideal and allowing a majority's external preferences denying a liberty to prevail is tantamount to an affirmation of the inferior worth of the minority. The majority imposing such external preferences may regard the minority's views as mistaken or sinful; but overriding them, for those reasons (however objectionable on other grounds), seems quite compatible with recognizing the equal worth of the holders of such views and may even be inspired by a concern for them."[41] For example, Hart says, since the Christian view is that all souls are equally precious, no good Christian believes that homosexuals are less precious than heterosexuals. Yet many Christians would, without inconsistency, outlaw homosexuality, and do so out of a concern for homosexuals.

Moreover, Dworkin appears to acknowledge this. In the discussion in his paper, "Liberalism," of his proposition that citizens have a right to equal respect and concern from their government, he allows that there are two legitimate ways of interpreting that idea, the liberal and the conservative. The liberal interpretation is that government should be neutral on the question of the good life, and should treat no one according to some preferred notion of how the good person would wish to be treated. The conservative interpretation is that government should not be neutral on the question of the good life and should treat everyone according to the preferred view of how the good person would wish to be treated.[42] Clearly, the liberal interpretation supports the view that external preferences should not be weighed in political decisions. But the conservative interpretation seems to undermine that view. In particular, in the conservative interpretation, if the good person would wish to be prevented from engaging in homosexual behavior if he were a homosexual, then giving weight to the external preference that such behavior should not be permitted in order to reach a political decision about whether or not to outlaw it *would* seem to be treating homosexuals with equal respect and concern. But if this is the case, and Hart thinks that Dworkin's discussion commits him to it, then considering external preferences in making political decisions is not clearly inconsistent with treating people with equal respect and concern, and Hart is right in saying that this idea is too indeterminate to play the fundamental role it does play in Dworkin's theory of how decisions should be made.[43]

But it may appear that Hart has not met Dworkin on his strongest ground. Dworkin devised his argument that external preferences should not count in decision-making order to protect the rights of black people, and only later generalized it to apply to the protection of the rights of homosexuals. Though the argument appears to fail in its latter application, it may succeed in its original application.

A person is a homosexual because he has certain attitudes and desires, and possibly certain beliefs and mannerisms also. There are, so to speak, two separable, or at least distinct, factors involved—persons, on the one hand, and homosexual attitudes and behavior on the other. If this is true, it is possible, and not inconsistent, to imagine a majority holding homosexual behavior mistaken and sinful, and legislating against it because they have an equal concern and respect for the persons who happen to be homosexuals as for those who don't.

However, race is a very different matter. A person is black simply because that is what he is. His attitudes, desires, beliefs, and mannerisms are irrelevant. There are not two separable or distinct factors involved, persons on the one hand, and their race on the other. A black person would cease to be the same person if he ceased to be black. If this is so, it makes no sense to speak of legislation against black people as being inspired by an equal respect and concern for them as persons.

It might be objected that homosexuality, or heterosexuality, is as much a part of an individual's identity as his race, and that modern theories of the biological and genetic bases of homosexuality support this view. But this would be missing the point. The argument does not deny that a person's sexual preferences can be as much a part of his identity as his race. It denies that a person can cease to be black in the way that he can cease to engage in homosexual behavior. The conservative conception of the nature of equal respect and concern that Hart uses to oppose Dworkin is that one can hate the sin and love the sinner. This allows him to say that outlawing homosexual behavior is compatible with having respect and concern for the homosexual. But it does not allow him to make a similar point about racist legislation. There is no particular behavior that the black person is disposed to engage in that the racist hates. It is the black person himself that the racist hates.

Though this is true as far as it goes, it is the wrong kind of objection to make to Hart's contention. It depends on the sociological fact that racism is hatred and contempt for the black person himself and not for anything he does. Thus it shows that giving weight to some external preferences, i.e., those characterized by racism, is tantamount to treating some people, i.e., blacks, with less than equal respect and concern. But Hart has not in fact denied this, and he can fall back on his argument (which, though he allows that it does not address the main weakness in Dworkin's theory, seems decisive enough) that what disqualifies a preference from consideration is not its "mere externality" but its "liberty-denying and respect-denying content."

But that argument is in fact invalid. Dworkin is correct in maintaining that external preferences should never be given weight in political decisions. But the argument that shows him to be correct also shows him to be mistaken in his belief that this supports the imposition of busing. The fact that external preferences should never be given weight in political decisions, does not mean that busing cannot be justified just because a community's decision *not* to bus will be based on external preferences.

A conservative legislator who believed that good people, heterosexuals as well as homosexuals, would want homosexual behavior outlawed, may outlaw such behavior out of an equal concern and respect for homosexuals. But it does not follow that a legislator who outlawed homosexual behavior just because of the external preferences of the majority can possibly have equal concern and respect for homosexuals. To have equal concern and respect for them, according to the conservative conception of these feelings, he must treat them as he does because *he* thinks this is the way good people would want to be treated. But he treats them as he does because the majority think this is the way they should be treated. If the majority changed their views, he would change his treatment. Consequently he cannot have equal concern and respect for homosexuals. This demonstrates that according to both the conservative and the liberal conceptions of equal respect and concern, it is always wrong to consider external preferences. For, though the right policy may sometimes coincide with the policy that would be chosen if external preferences were counted, this should never be because external preferences were counted, but because the policy is just, or best. Dworkin uses this kind of argument to defend himself against misinterpretations of his view. "The fact that the majority thinks . . . that cruelty to children is wrong," he writes, "should not . . . count as an argument for anything, although, of course, the different fact that cruelty harms children does count very much."[44]

But this observation is the rock that sinks his argument for busing. I admit that a community decison not to bus would involve external preferences and would be corrupt. And I admit that not busing just because of that community decision would fail to treat black people with equal respect and concern. But it does not follow that we must bus. What follows is that we must ignore and discount the external preferences of the racist majority. And having done that, it does not follow that the decision we would arrive at and deem just and best would necessarily conflict with the decision that we would have come to had we considered the external preferences of the majority. Dworkin must concede this. His point about cruelty to children is precisely that, although we cannot give weight to the majority's view that cruelty to children is wrong in making a decision to outlaw cruelty to children, we can nevertheless come to the identical decision on other grounds. But on what grounds are we to base a decision about what is just and best for the education of black children? Presumably on the basis of facts about the respective educational harms and benefits of segregated and intergrated education. But these are facts drawn from social science research. Consequently, if this argument is sound, Dworkin's attempt to make the case for busing independent of the social sciences must fail.

The objection may be raised that, when there is an antecedent probability that community decisions will be corrupted by external preferences, individuals have been granted rights designed to protect them against corrupt community decisions. If this is conceded, then black children have certain rights with respect to their education because there is an antecedent probability that community decisions about their education will be corrupted by external racist preferences. But these rights can only be the right not to be barred from any school because of their race, and at most their existence supports a case for voluntary busing.

To sum up, a sound policy on school desegregation must not be determined by external preferences. It must be determined by the desired end of securing children a good education. Busing may be the way to do this, or it may stand in the way of doing this. And only the causal judgments of social science can say which.

# 7

# Affirmative Action

## Liberals into Former Liberals

As Michael Kinsley has observed in *Harper's*, "No single development of the past fifteen years has turned more liberals into former liberals than affirmative action."[1] This metamorphosis, if it is not merely an unmasking, is ostensibly due to the belief that affirmative action perverts the just goal of civil rights. That goal, protest the disillusioned liberals, is to guarantee that persons be treated as individuals and judged on their merits; but affirmative action, they complain, guarantees that individuals are treated as mere members of racial groups, and their merits disparaged and ignored.

These liberals were not appeased by Allan Bakke's victory in the Supreme Court in 1978. For although the court ruled that Bakke was wrongly denied admission to the medical school at the University of California at Davis, it allowed that race could be used as a factor in considering applicants. As *Time* announced on its cover: "What Bakke Means. Race: Yes. Quotas: No."

As with busing, the arguments for preferential treatment fell into two classes, backward-looking and forward-looking. Backward-looking arguments justify preferential treatment considered as compensation for past and present wrongs done to blacks and their effects. Forward-looking arguments justify preferential treatment considered as a means to present or future goods, particularly equality. Both the assumptions and the aims of these two kinds of argument must be carefully distinguished.

Backward-looking arguments assume that blacks have been, or are being, wronged. Forward-looking arguments assume that blacks are generally inferior to whites in status, education, and income. Backward-looking arguments aim at compensating blacks. Forward-looking arguments aim at improving the status, education, and income of blacks.

## The Backward-looking Argument

The fundamental backward-looking argument is simply stated: Black people have been and are being harmed by racists attitudes and practices. Those wronged deserve compensation. Therefore, black people deserve compensation. Preferential treatment is an appropriate form of compensation for black people. Therefore black people deserve preferential treatment.

Criticism of this argument falls into two main classes: on the one hand, critics charge that the claims to compensation of the black beneficiaries of preferential treatment are unfounded or vacuously satisfied; on the other hand, they charge that these claims are outweighed by other considerations.

The most common version of the first type always uttered by the critic with an air of having played a trump, is that, since those members of groups that have been discriminated against who benefit from preferential hiring must be minimally qualified, they are not the members of the group who deserve compensation. The philosopher Alan Goldman, for example, argues this way: "Since hiring within the preferred group still depends upon relative qualifications and hence upon past opportunities for acquiring qualifications, there is in fact a reverse ratio established between past discriminations and present benefits, so that those who most benefit from the program, those who actually get jobs, are those who least deserve to."[2] But surely a conclusion that preferential hiring is unjustified based on the argument above is a non sequitur. Let us grant that qualified blacks are less deserving of compensation than unqualified blacks, that those who most deserve compensation should be compensated first, and finally that preferential hiring is a form of compensation. How does it follow that preferential hiring of qualified blacks is unjustified? Surely the assumption that unqualified blacks are more deserving of compensation than qualified blacks does not require us to conclude that qualified blacks deserve no compensation. Because I have lost only one leg, I may be less deserving of compensation than another who has lost two legs, but it does not follow that I deserve no compensation at all.

Even Thomas Nagel, one of the country's leading philosophers and a strong defender of preferential treatment on the basis of the forward-looking argument, resorts to this criticism of the backward-looking argument. Thus he labels a "bad" argument, one that maintains that the "beneficiaries of affirmative action deserve it as compensation for past discrimination," because, he says, "no effort is made to give preference to those who have suffered most from discrimination."[3] Indeed, Nagel makes exactly the same point as Goldman: Because the blacks who benefit from preferential treatment are qualfied, "they are not necessarily, or even probably the ones who especially deserve it. Women or blacks who don't have the qualifications even to be considered are likely to have been handicapped more by the effects of discrimination than those who receive preference."[4] But for the reasons given, this criticism is bogus. Furthermore, since Nagel defends preferential treatment on forward-looking, egalitarian grounds, this puts him into deeper trouble than it does those who reject preferential treatment altogether.

For, if preferential treatment makes no effort to give preference to those who have suffered most, neither does it make an effort to give preference to those who are most unequal to whites. In other words, if the qualified have suffered least, they are also least unequal, and it seems a bad strategy, if one is aiming for equality, to prefer them. Nagel could object that preferring the qualified is a good egalitarian strategy because it will lead indirectly to equality. But a variant of the idea is open to the advocate of the backward-looking argument. He could argue that preferential treatment of the qualified also helps to compensate the unqualified insofar as it shows them that if one is qualified, being black is no longer a bar to promotion.

One claim which would make the objection to compensating qualified blacks stick, and which the critics appear not to have made, is that compensation can be made to only one section of a group—either the qualified or the unqualified—but not to both. If this were true, and if the unqualified are most deserving of compensation, then a case could be mounted for claiming that, under the circumstances, a policy of preferential hiring should not be instituted because it takes from those who are most deserving of compensation (the unqualified) to give to those who are less deserving (the qualified). But if the critics are making this assumption, they have not stated it.

But perhaps the critics mean that qualified blacks are not simply less deserving of compensation than unqualified blacks, but that they deserve no compensation at all, precisely because they are qualified.

Why should this be so? I am not questioning the possibility that, on practical grounds, we may be unable to compensate the qualified members of a group generally discriminated against. I am questioning the assumption that, just because a person has overcome his injury, he no longer has a right to compensation. If I am swindled and through time and effort retrieve my money, shouldn't I be compensated for my time and effort? And if I have plenty of money and hire a good lawyer, shouldn't I also claim from my swindlers the money I paid the lawyer?

But in their eagerness to demolish the case for preferential treatment the critics have become extraordinarily careless, and *have* moved from the claim that qualified blacks are the least harmed and wronged blacks to the unsubstantiated claim that qualified blacks are not harmed or wronged at all. Thus Goldman first made the claim in his essay, "Reparations to Individuals or Groups" that in preferential hiring of qualified minority candidates, there is "an inverse ratio established between past discrimination and present benefits." But then, almost immediately, he makes the very much stronger claim—which does not at all proceed logically from the first—that preferential hiring "singles out for benefits within a generally unjustly treated minority just that minority that has not been unjustly treated."[5] And he makes a similar error in his book, *Justice and Reverse Discrimination*. First he says that "those who are not most qualified will tend to be those who have been discriminated against least," then follows this observation with the assertion that blacks "who have altogether escaped harm from previous injustice . . . will be the ones benefitting from preference."[6] These transitions from one argument to another and others like them, embody several confusions. Most obviously, there is the submerged conflation of those least harmed or wronged, slightly harmed or wronged, and not at all harmed or wronged. Less obviously, the distinction between being harmed, and being wronged or treated unjustly, is not taken seriously enough.

The argument I am proposing in support of preferential treatment should be distinguished from another argument which, I admit, has a certain superficial attractiveness. My argument is that qualified blacks deserve compensation for discrimination because even they have been wronged and probably harmed by it, and that preferential treatment is appropriate compensation for them because it suits their objectives and abilities. The other, superficially attractive, argument is that qualified blacks deserve compensation because they are probably the very blacks who would, in the absence of discrimination, have qualified without preferential treatment. But only a moment's reflection is needed to see that this argument is flawed. As James S. Fishkin points out in *Justice, Equal Opportunity and the Family*, "There is no reason to believe that those blacks who are presently 'best prepared' offer even a remote approximation to those blacks 'who in the absence of discrimination probably would have qualified.' "[7]

But this eminently sound observation does not imply that the "best prepared" are not wronged or harmed by discrimination. That is an altogether distinct claim. The best prepared need not be the ones who would have qualified in the absence of discrimination, but they may nevertheless be disadvantaged by discrimination. Thus, I reject Fishkin's concomitant, completely unsupported, claim that, "it is far from clear that the more advantaged members of a racial minority generally are worse off than they would otherwise have been, were it not for discrimination practiced against their forebears in previous generations."[8] This assumes that discrimination does not generally disadvantage those who are discriminated against, and that is an outrageous and gratuitous conclusion.

But suppose I am wrong and many blacks have in fact escaped the effects of discrimination? This is the fundamental objection to preferential treatment, for, if so many blacks have escaped discrimination and its effects that it results in "compensation" being given large numbers of people who did not deserve it, then it would be unfair. However, even if some blacks escape discrimination altogether, it must be admitted that there is a pervasive prejudice against blacks as a group and a tendency to discriminate against them. Consequently, if as I argued in Chapter 2, the realistic threat of transgression is itself transgression, even those who escape discrimination are wronged and possibly harmed by the discrimination against other blacks. This leads us to the argument proposed by Judith Jarvis Thomson that "even those who were not themselves down-graded for being black or female have suffered the consequences of the down-grading of other blacks and women: lack of self-confidence and lack of self-respect."[9] Goldman has taken this argument as the basis for belief in the concept of a kind of "indirect," "vicarious " wrong. Thus he objects that we should reserve "vicarious compensation"—and what he means by this I do not know—"to those who suffer psychologically or vicariously from injustice toward others, and that we should draw the line [past which compensation is no longer called for] at indirect psychological pressures."[10] But his objection misses the point about the harmfulness of discrimination.

Consider, for example, how Goldman illustrates his point: "A traumatized witness," he writes, "does not suffer the harm of the real victim. Similarly, a Jewish millionaire in Scarsdale, no matter how much he suffered vicariously or psychologically from hearing of the German concentration camps, is not owed the reparations due a former inmate."[11] But Goldman fails to distinguish two kinds of witness to injustice. There is the witness who identifies with the victim, and there is the witness who the transgressors identify with the victim. The first suffers vicariously. The second may not suffer vicariously. However, it does not follow that the latter does not suffer at all. He certainly might suffer at the realization that he too was under sentence and could be next. Therefore there are two completely different kinds of suffering that a witness to the persecution of others might endure. The first stems from sympathy for the victims; it is vicarious and could be called indirect. The second stems from the witness's self-interested realization that he may under sentence too and could be the next to be harmed. But, though this suffering may be "psychological," it is not vicarious, and there is nothing indirect about it. The example of the Scarsdale Jew—the stipulation that he is a millionaire is irrelevant—obscures this. Safely ensconced in Scarsdale, any Jew, millionaire or not, was safe from Hitler. Goldman's example insinuates that the Jew who was not himself victimized could feel only vicarious suffering. To make the argument more balanced, I suggest pondering the plight of a Jewish multimillionaire in Berlin.

Failure to distinguish these two kinds of suffering is responsible for the idea that vicarious suffering is relevant to a consideration of the undermining of self-confidence and self-respect to which Judith Jarvis Thomson was presumably referring. For while the realization that, like the actual victim, the witness to discrimination is also under sentence and could be next, has everything to do with the undermining of his self-confidence and self-respect, vicarious suffering has nothing to do with it. Consequently, the vicarious suffering of middle-class blacks for lower-class blacks, if it exists to any appreciable degree, is completely irrelevant to the question of what undermines their self-confidence and self-respect. What does is the uncertainty and ambiguity of their own lives.

But the red herring of vicarious suffering is misleading in yet another way: It suggests that the undermining of self-confidence and self-respect is a consequence of "injustice toward others." Of course, one's vicarious suffering is no indication of injustice to oneself. Though a white person may suffer vicariously at the thought of discrimination against lower-class blacks, the injustice is to them and not to him. However, when black people feel threatened and insulted when other black people are discriminated against because of their color, the injustice is both to those actually discriminated against and to those who are spared. Because the blacks discriminated against are discriminated against because they are black, all black people receive a warning that they too may experience the same treatment. They are wronged, and liable to be wrongfully harmed, in two ways. First, they are wronged because the realistic threat under which they live transgresses their right to equal security. Second, they are wronged by the judgmental injustice that assumes that because they are black they deserve less consideration than others. Justice Thurgood Marshall's comment in *Bakke* is apropos: "It is unnecessary in twentieth century America to have individual Negroes demonstrate that they have been victims of racial discrimination. [It] has been so pervasive that none, regardless of wealth or position, has managed to escape its impact."[12]

To sum up to this point: The criticism of the backward-looking argument for preferential treatment under consideration is unsound in one of its forms, and irrelevant in the other. Insofar as it assumes that many blacks have escaped wrongful harm as a result of discrimination it is unsound. Even if some blacks have escaped harm this would not be sufficient to make preferential treatment unjustified, because the overwhelming majority it benefited would deserve compensation. Insofar as the criticism assumes the black preferred are less wronged or harmed than other blacks it is irrelevant. The backward-looking argument does not exclude compensating unqualified blacks, or deny that they are more deserving of compensation. Neither does it say that qualified blacks must be compensated first. It asserts only that blacks deserve compensation for the wrongful harms of discrimination. Thus, it is unaffected by the claim that qualified blacks may be the least wronged and harmed of blacks. The fact that qualified blacks are wrongfully harmed at all, and that preferential treatment is appropriate compensation, is sufficient justification for it.

Now, I have admitted that it is a weak argument which tries to justify preferential treatment of qualified blacks applying for desirable places and positions on the grounds that, had there been no discrimination, these blacks would probably have qualified for such places and positions without preferential treatment. The key assumption in this argument is simply not plausible. But if we assume that compensation is owed to blacks as a group, then a stronger version of that argument can be advanced, which goes as follows: Blacks as a group have been wronged, and are disadvantaged, by slavery and discrimination. Consequently, blacks as a group deserve compensation. Furthermore, had it not been for slavery and discrimination, blacks as a group would be more nearly equal in income, education, and well-being to other groups who did not suffer from slavery or the extent and kind of discrimination from which blacks have suffered. Consequently, assuming that compensating a group for wrongful disadvantages requires bringing it to the condition it would have been in had it not been wrongfully disadvantaged, compensating blacks as a group requires making them, as a group, more nearly equal to those other groups. But if blacks as a group were more nearly equal in income, education, and well-being to such groups, some blacks would then fill desirable positions. Accordingly, compensating blacks as a group requires putting some blacks in desirable positions. However, only the blacks who are now most qualified can, fittingly, be placed in desirable positions. Hence, even if those blacks are *not* the very ones who would have filled such places and positions had there been no slavery and discrimination, compensating blacks as a group may specifically require preferential treatment of qualified blacks.

Many objections can be raised to this argument. Perhaps the most obvious is that its conception of compensation differs from the conception of compensation used in the argument that blacks, as individuals, deserve compensation. In that argument, I did not contend that compensating blacks requires placing them in positions they would have occupied had there been no slavery and discrimination. I contended that blacks deserve compensation because they are wronged by discrimination, and that places in universities and professional schools are appropriate compensation for qualified blacks because of their interests and objectives. However, in outlining the group compensation argument I am saying that compensating blacks as a group requires placing them in positions they would have occupied had there been no slavery and discrimination. Is this inconsistent? I think I can demonstrate that it isn't.

I endorse the view that, ideally, compensating either individuals or groups for wrongs requires placing them in positions they would have occupied had they not been wronged. The problem is that this ideal conception of compensation cannot be applied in the case of compensation for individual blacks for the wrongs of slavery and discrimination. To place a wronged individual in a position he would have occupied had he not been wronged depends on an estimate of how much the wrong has detracted from his assets, which in turn depends on an estimate of his assets. For an individual's assets—his capacities, abilities, goals, interests, and enjoyments—determine in large part the position he will come to occupy if he is not wronged. For example, if thugs break the basketball player Dr. J's legs, he will receive more compensation than I would if they broke my legs, because it is known that his legs are a greater asset to him than are my legs to me. Similarly, some years ago the newspapers reported that a certain screen star had insured her legs with Lloyd's of London for several million pounds. Whether or not the story was true, it seemed good sense to many people because they thought the star's legs were such an enormous asset that it would take several million pounds to compensate her for them if they were flawed or lost. It should now be clear why the ideal conception of compensation cannot be used to support an argument in favor of compensating black individuals for the wrongs of slavery and discrimination. In most cases, it simply makes no sense to even try to estimate what any black individual's assets might have been before he was wronged by slavery and discrimination. For, from the very start of their lives—while they are yet in the womb—and of their parents' lives, and of the lives of their ancestors, all the way back to the first black slaves born in the New World, blacks have been wronged by slavery and discrimination.

Yet the fact remains that because they have been wronged they deserve compensation. Accordingly, under the circumstances the ideal conception of compensation must be discarded. By way of compensating blacks all that can practically be done is to adopt my proposal and award them some benefit—such as preferential treatment—appropriate to their interests and objectives.

The argument for group compensation does not run into this sort of difficulty. We can form some estimate of the assets blacks as a group had before slavery and discrimination. Consequently, we can apply the ideal conception of compensation, and reasonably propose to place blacks as a group in the position they would have occupied had there been no slavery and discrimination.

It may be objected, however, that placing blacks in the position they would have occupied had there been no slavery and discrimination would not make blacks equal or nearly equal to other groups because blacks are inferior to other groups, especially white groups, in native talent. But this objection begs the question. The claim that blacks are inferior to whites in native talent is an inference based largely on the fact that the average black I.Q. is lower than the average white I.Q. But that inference is highly controversial. Another, possibly sounder inference, is that black I.Q.s have been lowered as a result of slavery and discrimination. If this assumption is sound, and if I.Q.s are as important for determining people's lives as they are said to be, then blacks' lower average I.Q., far from supporting the case against compensation, very must supports the case for it.

A somewhat less radical objection is that the estimate we can form of the assets of blacks as a group before slavery and discrimination suggests that even without slavery and discrimination they would not have been nearly equal to other groups. Thomas Sowell, for example, suggests this. ". . . the wide diversity among American ethnic groups," he argues, "precludes any assumptions that any group—especially from a non-urban, non-industrial background—would earn the national average in income."[13] But this is not only a weak argument in itself, it is also inconsistent with many other points Sowell himself has stressed as important and decisive in relation to the issue of discrimination.

It is a weak argument, first, because some groups from a "non-urban, non-industrial background," for example, the Irish Catholics, earn *above* the national average income.[14] If can Irish Catholics, why not blacks? Sowell's assertion that such groups tend to earn considerably less than the national average income may be true if we look only at relatively recent immigrants such as the Puerto Ricans. But blacks have been in America for three hundred years. It is invidious to assume that, unlike other groups from non-urban, non-industrial backgrounds, they would not have bettered themselves had it not been for slavery and its aftermath. Finally, although blacks originally came from a non-urban, non-industiral background, it does not follow that they lacked economically valuable assets. Earlier I quoted Sowell's master, Booker T. Washington boasting that the policy of importing black slaves proved that blacks had economically valuable skills, and given the importance Sowell attributes to motives of economic self-interest, he is in no position to confound Washington's argument.[15] Given that blacks did have economically valuable skills, surely, in the absence of slavery and discrimination, they would have realized their assets, parlayed their earnings in order to further improve their skills, and, with three hundred years in which to do it, would today be as urbanized and industrialized as anybody else.

Sowell's argument that because of their non-urban, non-industrial origins, blacks, even if there had been no slavery, would be unlikely to be earning near the national average income, is also inconsistent with certain other theories he holds dear. Recall, for example, his view that middle-class blacks are almost always descended from blacks who were freed before emancipation, a view which he uses in support of the theory that progress is an "intergenerational race." As I pointed out in Chapter 2, if this view and theory are correct, it is difficult to advance any reason why most blacks would not be earning much nearer the national average income if there had been no slavery and discrimination. And there is an even more striking inconsistency in Sowell's argument. The fact he most prizes in support of his contention that it is American blacks' culture, not racial discrimination, which holds them back, is that West Indian blacks, who are physically indistinguishable from American blacks, earn just a little less than white Americans. But the West Indies hardly constitute an industrialized region of the world. Consequently, the fact that a group has a non-industrialized background cannot be the basis of an argument that they are unlikely to earn near the national average income. And so it is with much of Sowell's reasoning. He says one thing to support one point, and the opposite to support another point, and never notices anything amiss.

But what if Sowell is right, and "culture—not discrimination—decides who gets ahead."[16] Assuming that a group's culture is what determines the jobs and positions its members are interested in, certain philosophers seem to agree with him. Thus, Barry Gross implies that blacks may simply not be interested in desirable positions, and argues that black under-representation in desirable positions is no clear indication of discrimination: "The members of a group might simply lack interest in certain jobs (for example, Italians in the public school system are in short supply)."[17] But this analogy fails, though Gross does not appear to notice it, when applied to the case of blacks. For it isn't as if blacks are under-represented in the public school system, or in law, or in banking, or in the professions. They are under-represented in all of these fields. Consequently, though Gross may be right and that sociologically, certain groups are simply not represented in various jobs and at various levels in percentages closely approximating their percentage of the population, he fails to see that the case of blacks presents a matter of an altogether different order. Lack of interest—presumably culturally determined—in this or in that area may explain away the under-representation of a cultural group in one or two specific areas. However, unless we assume that some cultural groups have no interest in *any* of the traditional professional areas, we cannot explain a group's under-representation in all desirable positions by citing cultural differences.

The deeper and more serious implication of the claim that blacks are disadvantaged by their culture, not by discrimination, is that blacks, because of their culture, lack the discipline necessary for becoming qualified for desirable positions. But whether or not this is true, it cannot weigh against the argument for group compensation for blacks. For even if the traits which inhibit the success of blacks—supposedly a lack of appropriate work habits and discipline—are cultural traits it does not follow that they are not the result of wrongful harm. In order to survive and retain their sanity and equilibrium in impossibly unjust situations, people may have to resort to patterns of behavior, and consequently may develop habits or traits, which are debilitating and unproductive in a more humane environment. I see no reason why these cultural traits—which may be deeply ingrained and extremely difficult to eradicate—should not be classed as unjust injuries. This being the case, we have discovered another inconsistency in Sowell's argument. The cultural characteristics he blames for holding back blacks he considers to be the result of slavery and its aftermath. The "legacy of slavery," he declares, is "foot-dragging, work avoiding patterns," "duplicity and theft," and a "tragic hostility to menial jobs." Consequently, if it is blacks' culture which holds them back, then blacks deserve compensation for the culture which slavery imposed on them. Yet Sowell affirms the premise and denies the conclusion.

It is admittedly unusual to think of cultural traits as wrongful harms because we think of culture as, in an important sense, self-imposed. This is true of most cultures in the traditional sense of ethnic and national cultures. Such cultures come with built-in philosophical self-justifications. In the sense that participants in them therefore have elaborate resources with which to justify themselves, they may be viewed as self-imposed. Consequently, though such cultures may encourage development of traits which inhibit advancement in modern society, it would be philosophically hazardous to call such traits wrongful harms. At most, they might be considered self-imposed harms. But not all cultures are self-imposed, and certain cultures contain no mechanism of philosophical self-justification and self-definition. Thus, in describing what he calls the "culture of poverty," Oscar Lewis notes that though it is a genuine culture in the traditional anthropological sense, in that it provides human beings with a "design for living," it "does not provide much support . . . poverty of culture is one of the crucial traits of the culture of poverty."[18] Consequently, if we assume that the cultural legacy of slavery is of this nature and is harmful, inasmuch as it tends to block self-development, self-realization, and autonomy, as well as undermine self-respect and self-esteem, it follows that blacks have been wrongfully harmed, and therefore, according to the terms of the backward-looking argument, deserve compensation.

Moreover, there are other grounds on which the claim that blacks constitute a cultural group is not notably advantageous for the critics of preferential treatment. For, if it is true, it confounds the objection of some critics that blacks do not comprise a group in the sense required by the group compensation argument. For example, Goldman objects to treating blacks as a legitimate group eligible for compensatory treatment because they "do not qualify as genuine groups or social organizations in the sense in which sociologists generally use these terms." He goes on to point out that in genuine groups there is "actual interaction among members, each of whom occupies a certain position or plays a certain role in the group reciprocal to other roles, roles being reciprocal when their performances are mutually dependent.[19] But by that very account cultural groups do qualify as genuine groups. There is "actual interaction" among the members of a cultural group. That interaction is, of course, not specifically economic or political. Members of a cultural group do not, for example, necessarily buy from each other or employ each other or rule each other. Still, they do interact and that interaction is just as important as economic or political interaction.

Members of a cultural group share basic values and ideals—that is what we mean by culture—and they interact intellectually by exchanging ideas about these values and ideals; by clarifying, criticizing, and extending them; and by severing and drawing connections between them. In this way they come better to understand themselves. All prosperous and progressive peoples engage in this bustling process of self-clarification. W. E. B. Dubois thought that it was a condition of progress, and it was the basis of his theory of "the talented tenth." If a group is to progress, he argued, it must pay special attention to the cultural education of its talented tenth. If we make "technical skill the object of education," he observed, "we may possess artisans but not, in nature, men."[20] Other writers, Booker T. Washington particularly, have believed that cultural activity is the reward of progress.[21] In either case, it is obviously a great good. If, then, it is argued that blacks are underrepresented in positions of wealth and prestige because of culturally-induced differences, then they have been wronged as a group, and preferential hiring of qualified blacks is justified as a way of compensating the group. For, it needs no argument to show that the intellectually most active and advanced of a cultural group play a crucial role in the process of self-clarification. If, then, as seems likely, they will be among those qualified, and preferential hiring will give them the opportunity to play this crucial role, then preferential hiring is a way of compensating the group.

I am not, myself, altogether comfortable with the claim that blacks are a cultural group, or that they interact enough, and are sufficiently interdependent, to support the group compensation argument. These claims ultimately depend on empirical investigation, and even if the contention I made earlier is correct, and all blacks, whatever their class, are wronged, and have good reason to feel threatened by racial discrimination, the often cited disparity between the black middle, and the black under class still undermines the force of the group compensation argument. That point conceded, I must however reject certain other criticisms of the group compensation argument. For example, according to Fishkin the objection to compensating present-day blacks for slavery and past discrimination I discussed in Chapter 2—that were it not for these injustices, these individuals would not exist—can also be offered when the argument for compensating blacks is reformulated to rest on the premise that blacks deserve compensation as a group.[22] For, says Fishkin, just as it is impossible to return black individuals to the positions they would have held had there been no slavery and discrimination, because without these injustices present-day blacks would not exist, so also it is impossible to return the black group to the position it would have held had there been no slavery and discrimination, because had it not been for these injustices the group would not have the kind of inter-dependence among its members required by the group compensation argument. In support of this Fishkin reasons as follows: "had injustices to blacks not been committed, it is arguable that we might have a society in which race functioned the way eye-color does now. In a racially neutral society, blacks would not constitute a social group or natural class. Their status, identity, and welfare would not be tied to their group membership."[23] But if Fishkin's thesis is "arguable," it is, at best, barely so. Its gratuitous premise is that racial persecution is the only factor which binds blacks together as a social group. The slaves did not all share an identical culture and language, but their cultures and languages certainly had a family resemblance which, together with their common African origins, could well have operated to bind them together. Indeed, without slavery these factors would have operated more strongly than they did with slavery, since, as is well known, slave masters did their very best to destroy the slaves' cultures, languages, and traditions. Why does Fishkin write as if he believes blacks are different from other people? Many European minorities, without the benefit of slavery, manage to retain their identities. Why suppose that blacks would be so anxious to lose theirs? And, if Fishkin's observations are in any way correct, is it not likely that this is because of the very persecution which has served to bind them together in another way?

Having disposed of the first set of criticisms of the backward-looking argument—that the claims of the black beneficiaries of preferential treatment are unfounded or vacuously satisfied—I turn to the second set of criticisms, viz., that even if the claim to compensation of the black beneficiaries of preferential treatment is justified, it is outweighed by other, more urgent, claims. The first of these claims, according to critics, is the claim to compensation of the black and white lower classes.

Even if I grant the critics' assumption that the black beneficiaries of preferential treatment are middle class, they still cannot draw the conclusion that preferential treatment is unjustified. As I have demonstrated above, that conclusion depends on the assumption—which I do not grant—that the black middle class and the black lower class cannot both be compensated. However, when the white lower class is brought into the picture, this response is not adequate, because I do grant that the black middle and lower classes and the white lower class cannot all be compensated. Given this conclusion, the strategy of the critics is clear. Since compensating the most deserving is impossible, compensation in general is impossible, and so preferential treatment is impossible. Either that, or lower-class whites should be the ones getting preferential treatment, and Derrick Bell's dismal prognosis, that no sooner do blacks win an important concession than it is "rationalized" so that whites become the prime beneficiaries, is again confirmed.

The argument that the white lower class has more urgent claim to compensation than that black middle class is usually made, interesting enough, not on the grounds that the white lower class suffers wrongful harm, but on the familiar grounds that the black middle class suffers no wrongful harm.

Thus the late philosopher William T. Blackstone, noting that there is "no invariable connection between a person's being black or female and suffering from past invidious discrimination," leaps to the conclusion that there are lots of blacks who have suffered from no invidious discrimination. "There are," he writes, "many blacks . . . who are highly advantaged, who are the sons and daughters of well educated and affluent lawyers, doctors and industrialists. A policy of reverse discrimination would mean that such highly advantaged individuals would receive preferential treatment over the sons and daughters of disadvantaged whites . . . I submit that such a situation is not social justice."[24] Now this may seem like a commendable effort to define the groups deserving compensation in socioeconomic, rather than racial, terms. But why does Blackstone assume that "reverse discrimination" would mean that the "highly advantaged" blacks he speaks of would be getting preferred treatment over disadvantaged whites? It is more likely that being so advantaged they would be vying with their peers—the highly advantaged sons and daughters of white doctors, lawyers, and industrialists—leaving the sons and daughters of disadvantaged blacks to get preferred treatment in relation to the children of disadvantaged whites.

Furthermore, there is no warrant for Blackstone's assumption. Though critics who share his view are full of anecdotes to illustrate their point, they chose to over look the fact that minority applicants often fail to get preferred treatment precisely because they are believed to be middle class. According to Dr. Lindy Kumagai, chairman of the task force created to review minority applicants at Davis Medical School, "minority candidates from middle-class backgrounds were referred to the regular committee for evaluation." Furthermore, such students were often rejected and white students with lower scores accepted. Thus, Dr. Kumagai complains that the "regular committee often turned down well qualified minority applicants. . . . They would say he or she only has a 3.4 (G.P.A.) instead of a 3.6," he recalled. "I would point out that they were accepting whites with a 3.4 and much less."[25] Similarly, Thomas Sowell recalls that a black girl with an S.A.T. average of 750 was turned down by Cornell because she was "middle-class."[26] As it happens, the girl was far from middle class, the admissions committee apparently having made the invidious assumption that people with high scores are, necessarily, middle class.

But, apart from the way in which preferential admission does in fact operate, the more fundamental question is how it must operate. And here it is even clearer that there is no warrant for the claim that preferential treatment will prefer advantaged blacks over disadvantaged whites. Those who advance this claim argue that the scores and grades of the black middle class are in the same range as that of the white lower class, not in the range of the white middle class, thereby implying that the white middle class scores too well to be displaced by the black middle class, which can therefore displace only the white lower class if a policy of preferential treatment is instituted. But this is not a logical conclusion for several reasons. First, why assume, as Nagel does explicitly, that the preferentially treated blacks must displace those who score close to them? "Only candidates who in other qualifications fall on one or other side of the margin of decision," he writes, "will directly benefit or lose from" preferential treatment.[27] But he gives no reason why he believes this gratuitous claim must be true. And it does not have to be. Preferential treatment could deliberately prefer blacks over high-scoring middle and upper-class whites who do not score close to them.

Though Nagel does not give much weight to the argument that preferential treatment reduces the total efficiency of the society, he could object that displacing high-scoring whites in favor of blacks goes too far. This, he may argue, would exceed acceptable limits on inefficiency. But this argument is also flawed. Even if the white middle class generally outscores the black middle class, surely not all members of the white middle class score beyond the range of members of the black middle class, and surely not all the black middle class scores only in the range of the white lower class. Consequently, because the white middle and upper classes are so much more numerous than the black middle class, there seems ample scope for preferring middle-class blacks over only upper- and middle-class whites.

Furthermore, this is not mere speculation. Consider the Bakke case. Bakke complained that, although he had high scores, he was not admitted to medical school while blacks with scores below the official cut-off point were admitted. Although Bakke was certainly not disadvantaged, is it still necessarily true that the blacks who were admitted were admitted at the expense of lower-class, disadvantaged whites? Apparently not. As it turns out, the dean of the Davis Medical School "was allowed to select five admittees each year without reference to the screening process," and his choices were "invariably influential white applicants with ties to local or state politicians, wealthy businessmen, or campus administrators or faculty."[28] So much then, for Blackstone's outrage!

Other critics urge a similar objection in a more complicated way. They say that they are quite ready to endorse preferential treatment for blacks who can prove that they were discriminated against and harmed. Thus Goldman argues that, "for all those individuals discriminated against in the past in hiring or promotion reverse discrimination of the strongest type is owed by the institutions responsible, if those individuals are not still the most competent for the positions in question";[29] and to implement his proposal, Goldman proposes the "establishment of administrative boards" which would investigate and certify claims of discrimination and order compensation if the harms caused were "clear and measurable." The philosopher Barbara Baum Levenbrook has also come up with an apparently sturdier version of this argument. Even if blacks are harmed by racial injustice, she argues, "compensating for the difference in qualifications that racial injustice makes by preferring a black to a white applicant" may still be unfair because we may "thereby allow the differences in qualifications caused by other kinds of injustice to affect chances in ways they did not do before."[30]

But Levenbrook actually leans toward the view of Blackstone and Goldman that most blacks have not been harmed by racial injustice— at least in a way that supports preferential treatment. Thus, although she concedes the argument that discrimination can cause losses of self-confidence and self-respect, even when one is not actually discriminated against, she denies that these losses reduce opportunities. "It is clear," she writes, "that loss of self-confidence and self-respect handicaps people in future competitions. But there is a difference between something being made harder for one to do, and opportunities to do it being reduced."[31] If my analysis of the nature of opportunity is sound, this is mistaken. The reasoning behind the theory that obstacles reduce opportunities is that obstacles make it harder for people to do things. That is the rationale for the idea that unequal opportunities are unfair. Consequently, since Levenbrook concedes that lack of self-respect and self-confidence make success harder, I cannot see why she denies that they reduce opportunities.

It may be objected that considering lack of self-confidence and self-respect as obstacles involves the absurd notion that a thing can be an obstacle to itself, or in this case, a man to himself. This would be cogent if the lacks in question constituted such deep-seated, fundamental qualities of an individual that to try to improve his opportunities by restoring them would make him a different person. If lack of self-confidence makes Joan the person she is, we cannot increase Joan's opportunities by increasing her self-confidence, since doing so would mean that Joan would no longer exist. But it is absurd to conclude that a person's lack of self-confidence and self-respect makes him the person he or she is. People speak routinely of increasing *their* self-confidence and self-respect. Furthermore, when they succeed they do not say, except perhaps as a kind of dramatic overstatment, that they have become "different people." Would they, or should they have to give up valuable claims to things acquired by the persons from whom they have sprung?

But even if discrimination does cause a loss of self-confidence and self-respect, and even if these losses do reduce opportunities, we still have to deal with Levenbrook's argument that compensating for these losses through preferential treatment may be unfair because it may allow differences in qualifications caused by other kinds of injustice to affect chances for success. I confess that I am unable to see what Levenbrook finds so compelling about this argument. Perhaps it is well to recall here that the argument under consideration is the backward-looking argument, which calls for compensation for past injustice, *not* the forward-looking argument, which calls for ameliorating handicaps whether or not they are caused by injustice. We *know* that all blacks, lower class, middle class, and upper class, have been wronged by racial injustice. We do *not* know that all, or nearly all, or even most lower-class whites have been wronged by injustice. Unless justice is understood as so radically egalitarian a concept as to demand a classless society, being lower class does not necessarily mean being a victim of injustice. Thus we must be careful not to artificially swell the ranks of the unjustly treated white lower class. Just as it is a mistake to infer that middle-class blacks escape the effects of discrimination because they are middle class, it is a mistake to infer that lower-class whites are unjustly treated because they are lower class. Given that this is so, what objection can Levenbrook have to a policy that gives black candidates preference, but allows this preference to be voided if a white candidate can prove that he or she was the victim of a greater injustice? No advocate of preferential treatment—on the grounds of backward-looking argument—has asked, or could reasonably ask, for more than this. Moreover, as I have shown, it is the way many preferential admissions programs actually work. Levenbrook inadvertently admits the force of these considerations in the very example she uses to illustrate her argument. "If Brown is a middle-class black male and Smith is a lower-class white handicapped female," she writes, "she might be preferred."[32]

It may be objected that even a moderately egalitarian conception of justice supports the idea of preferential treatment for white lower-class students rather than for black middle-class students. For many critics of preferential treatment for blacks, for example, Fishkin, this is apparently so obvious that they see no need to advance an argument. But it is not obvious, and they do need to argue the case. This objection depends on the assumption that, because white lower-class students have lower incomes than black middle-class students, their opportunities are less and they suffer greater harms and injustices. But to imagine that this is obvious is to systematically underestimate the importance of the issue of race in America, and the effect that it has had on both white and black attitudes. Fishkin is guilty of this underestimating. Repeatedly he has described preferential treatment as based "merely" on race, sometimes even emphasizing *merely*.[33] But unfortunate a fact though it certainly is, a person's race is, at present never a mere fact about him like the color of his eyes. It is a fact about him which systematically determines his prospects, opportunities, and how he can expect those in power to treat him. Perhaps nothing illustrates this better than the saying, heard less often now than a few year ago, when people were more careless about black sensibilities and about admitting the advantages of being white—though it is still revealing—"I'm free, white, and twenty-one." The saying makes no mention of class. But it does mention race. And the attitude and confidence it expresses is that, because the subject is white, the world is his oyster, and with talent and effort—whatever his class origins—he can open it. And, of course, the saying also clearly implies that if a person is black he cannot have the same confidence.

It may be that Fishkin shares Goldman's view that the psychological effects of racism are too trivial to merit more than "vicarious compensation." But if this is so he is inconsistent, for he is quick enough to insist on the importance of the psychological effects of policies when he thinks those effects weigh *against* preferential treatment for blacks. Thus he warns that it may have a deleterious effect on the self-esteem of those it benefits.[34] (I take up this important question in Chapter 9.)

My point here is not that all or even most middle-class blacks lack self-confidence. This is clearly false. But we must distinguish between confidence in one's own abilities—self-confidence—and confidence in the fairness of one's fellow citizens and in the institutions of one's country. It is this latter kind of confidence that all blacks, middle class or lower class, have reason to lack. And, that lack of confidence, since it undermines self-motivation (why try when you fear you won't be rewarded even if you are the best?) is debilitating and can also indirectly sap self-confidence. But even so, my point is not that most middle-class blacks are debilitated by this, understandable, lack of confidence in their fellow citizens and national institutions. Many respond courageously to their predicament, and are moved to try even harder than they otherwise would, hoping that if they are not only the best, but far and away the best, they will be rewarded. But this is neither here nor there. It was Robert Nozick, certainly no radical egalitarian, who pointed out that men and women have a right not to reasonably fear that their other rights will be violated, and I submit that that right is violated even if they respond courageously to threats of transgression.[35] For these reasons I cannot countenance the notion that it goes without saying that the white lower class more deserves compensation than the black middle class. The claims of members of the white lower class *may* often be stronger than those of members of the black middle class. But they must bear the burden of proving this.

But the relative weight of different claims of compensation aside, it has seemed to many critics that preferential treatment, insofar as it involves preferential admissions and hiring, is unfair to young white males. For example, according to Robert K. Fullinwider, a research associate at the Center for Philosophy and Public Policy at the University of Maryland, the compensation argument for preferential treatment confuses the sound compensation principle—"he who wrongs another shall pay for the wrong"—with the "suspect" principle—"he who benefits from a wrong shall pay for the wrong."[36] To clinch the point, Fullinwider asks us to consider the following ingenious example: A neighbor pays a construction company to pave his driveway, but someone maliciously directs the workmen to pave Fullinwider's driveway instead. Fullinwider admits that his neighbor has been "wronged and damaged" and that he himself has "benefited from the wrong." However, since he is not responsible for the wrong, he denies that he is "morally required to compensate" his neighbor by "paying" him for it.

This example makes us see that not all cases where compensation may be due are straightforward, though one kind of case clearly is. If John steals Jeff's bicycle and "gives" it to me, however innocent I may be, I have no right to it and must return it to Jeff as soon as I discover the theft. Given that this example is unproblematic, in what way does it differ from Fullinwider's, which is problematic?

One difference is that, whereas I can simply hand over Jeff's bicycle to him, Fullinwider cannot simply hand over the pavement in his driveway. It will be objected that the proposal was not that Fullinwider should hand over the pavement, but that he should pay his neighbor for it. But this is a different case. I did not say that I had a duty to pay Jeff for his bicycle. I said that I had a duty to return the bicycle to Jeff. If Jeff told me to keep the bicycle but pay him for it, I do not admit that I would have a duty to do so. I could object fairly that when I accepted the bicycle I did not believe that I would have to pay for it, and if I had thought that I would have to, I might have not accepted it. Paying for the bicycle now would impose on me, because I might have preferred to spend my money in a different way and, being innocent of any wrongdoing, I see no reason why I should be penalized. The point is that though the beneficiary of an injustice has no right to his advantage, if he is innocent of the injustice, he does not deserve to be penalized. Thus, where compensation is concerned, the obligations of the innocent beneficiary of injustice and of the person responsible for the injustice are quite different. Though the former has no right to his benefits, the process of compensation cannot impose any losses on him over and above the loss of his unfair benefits. If compensation is impossible without such loss, it is unjustified. On the other hand, in the case of the person responsible for injustice, even if compensation requires him to give up more than he has unfairly gained, it is still justified.

But, though Fullinwider's example is cogent as far as it goes, it is irrelevant as an argument against preferential hiring. It is cogent as far as it goes because, as the above analysis shows, requiring young white males to pay women and minorities for all the unfair advantages they have enjoyed would indeed be unfair. The advantages cannot, as in my example of the bicycle, simply be transferred from their hands into those of the preferred group. Compensation of this kind would impose on young white males time and effort over and above the cost of the unfair advantages they are required to return. They could justly protest that they are being penalized, because they might not have accepted the advantages had they known what they would cost them—now they are "out" both the advantages and their time and effort. But preferential hiring does not require young white males to pay, at an additional cost to themselves, the price of their advantages. It proposes instead to compensate the injured with goods no one has yet established a right to and therefore in a way that imposes no unfair losses on anyone. And these goods are, of course, jobs.

It may be objected that, although a white male applicant may not have established a right to this or that job, he has a right to fair competition for it, and preferential hiring violates that right. But, on the contrary, by refusing to allow him to get the job because of an unfair advantage, preferential hiring makes the competition fairer. The white male applicant can still complain, of course, that, had he known that preferential hiring would be instituted, he would not have accepted his advantages in the first place. Since, if he knew that preferential hiring would be instituted, he would necessarily also have known that his advantages were unfair, his complaint would amount to his saying that, had he known his advantages were unfair, he would not have accepted them. But then, if he is concerned with fairness, and if preferential hiring makes the competition fairer, he should have no objections to it. Or to state the proposition somewhat less contentiously, preferential hiring imposes no unfair losses on him.

Thus, a fairer application of Fullinwider's example about the driveway to the case of preferential hiring would be as follows: Suppose an "improve-your-neighborhood group" offered a valuable prize for the best driveway on the block. Would Fullinwider be justified in insisting that he deserves to get the prize over his neighbor who has, at further cost to himself, built another somewhat inferior driveway?

To sum up my discussion of forms the backward-looking argument for preferential treatment, while I have insisted that all, or nearly all, blacks are victims of racial injustice, I have conceded that it has handicapped some blacks more than others, and that other kinds of injustice have handicapped some whites more than racial injustice has handicapped blacks. Consequently, although the backward-looking argument is the bedrock of the case for preferential treatment, to complete that case we must look forward.

## The Forward-looking Argument

Whereas the backward-looking argument tried to justify preferential treatment as compensation for past wrongful harms, the forward-looking argument tries to justify preferential treatment on the grounds that it may secure greater equality or increase total social utility. Moreover, the fact that blacks were slaves and the victims of discrimination is irrelevant to the forward-looking argument, which its proponents imply, would not lose force even if blacks had never been slaves and never discriminated against. All that is relevant to the argument is that blacks are often poor, generally less than equal to whites in education, influence, and income, and preferentially treating them will alleviate their poverty, reduce their inequality, and generally increase total utility.

The forward-looking argument has one very clear advantage over the backward-looking argument. As we have seen, a persistent criticism of the backward-looking argument is that, although some blacks deserve no compensation for discrimination because they have not been harmed by discrimination, they are precisely the ones benefiting from preferential treatment. I have tried to rebut this criticism, but this is unnecessary if the forward-looking argument is adopted. For that argument does not require the assumption that the beneficiaries of preferential treatment have been harmed by discrimination, or even that they have been harmed at all. Indeed, it does not require that they be less than equal to whites, and is consistent with their being relatively privileged. For it endorses a strategy of increasing the incomes and education even of blacks superior in those respects to most whites if, however indirectly, this will, in the long run, effectively increase blacks' equality and increase total social utility.

Now whether or not preferential treatment has such consequences is in the end an empirical question, but some critics, as I will show, insist on concocting specious a priori arguments to show that preferential treatment necessarily causes a loss in social utility.

Thus it has been argued that since, by definition, preferential treatment awards positions to the less qualified over the more qualified, and since the more qualified perform more efficiently than the less qualified, therefore preferential treatment causes a loss of utility. But suppose that less qualified blacks are admitted to medical school in preference to more qualified whites, and suppose the resulting black doctors practice in poor black neighborhoods treating serious illnesses, while if the whites they were preferred to had been admitted they would have practiced in affluent white neighborhoods, treating minor illnesses. In that sort of case, it is not at all necessarily true that preferential treatment causes a loss in utility. Some authors try to avoid the force of this argument by switching the basis of their criticism from the fact that preferential treatment may reward the less qualified to the false assertion that preferential treatment may reward the "unqualified." Thus, Goldman reminds us that "all will suffer when unqualified persons occupy many positions."[37] This is criticism of a straw man.

It has also been claimed that the forward-looking argument that preferential treatment increases utility is open to a serious philosophical objection. Thus philosopher George Sher writes that the utilitarian, or forward-looking, defence of preferential treatment is "vulnerable" to the "simple but serious" objection that "if it is acceptable to discriminate in favor of minorities and women when doing so maximises utility then it is hard to see why it should not also be acceptable to discriminate against minorities and women when that policy maximises welfare."[38] And against Thomas Nagel who argues that racial discrimination, unlike reverse discrimination, "has no social advantages . . . and attaches a sense of reduced worth to a feature with which people are born,"[39] Sher makes a similar objection. He says that Nagel gives us no reason to believe that "there could never be alternative circumstances in which racial, ethnic, or sexual discrimination had social advantages which did outweigh the sense of reduced worth it produced," and maintains that Nagel still has not shown us that such discrimination is illegitimate under "any circumstances at all."[40]

The serious utilitarian is likely to dismiss Sher's criticisms with the same impatience with which he dismisses the stock criticism that utilitarianism allows slavery. As R. M. Hare notes, it is the "strength" of the utilitarian doctrine that "the utilitarian cannot reason a priori that whatever the facts about the world and human nature, slavery is wrong. He has to show it is wrong by showing, through a study of history and other factual observation, that slavery does have the effects (namely the production of misery) that make it wrong."[41] In particular, he is not undone by the arguments of the intuitionist who thinks up "fantastic" examples which show slavery to be right according to the principles of utilitarianism, because these show only that the intuitionist has "lost contact with the actual world."[42] Much the same thing can be said about Sher's notion that there are circumstances in which racial discrimination would be legitimate according to utilitarian principles.

Finally, consider the way Sher deals with Dworkin's defence of preferential treatment. As we have seen, Dworkin's view is that if a policy is to be based on pure utilitarianism, which counts each person as equal, then it must consider only how personal preferences are affected. It cannot consider how external preferences are affected, and if it does, it fails to treat people with equal respect and concern. Dworkin's distinction between personal and external preferences may or may not be sound. I have offered emendations to the argument on which he bases it in my discussion of busing. But Sher accepts Dworkin's distinction because he thinks that even if he does, Dworkin's argument fails. "Neither, despite his bare assertion to the contrary has Dworkin produced any reason to suppose that such [racial] discrimination could never maximize the satisfaction of purely personal preferences," he writes.[43] But Sher seems to be confused by the ambiguous nature of the expression "racial discrimination."

If discrimination is taken to mean policies based on weighing the external preferences of whites that blacks be given less, then Sher has simply misunderstood Dworkin. Dworkin does not simply say that we must maximize the satisfaction of personal preferences. He also says that we must not give any weight to external preferences. Consequently, if we grant that Dworkin is right in his theory that racial discrimination gives weight to external preferences, then, contrary to what Sher says, that theory does not permit racial discrimination even if racial discrimination did maximize the satisfaction of personal preferences.

On the other hand, "racial discrimination" may, especially if one is careless, be taken to mean policies based on something like "reverse discrimination," which does not weigh external preferences. In that case, just as reverse discrimination can prefer blacks to whites, racial discrimination can prefer whites to blacks. Now, understood in this sense, racial discrimination may, of course, maximize the satisfaction of personal preferences without weighing external preferences, and certainly Dworkin's theory does not exclude it. But, what Sher seems to overlook is that such racial discrimination, not based on weighing external preferences, would be free of the insult of racial discrimination as we now know it.

Sher also attacks the argument that preferential treatment is justified because it conduces to equality. He allows that preferential treatment may reduce inequality between the races but points out that it does not reduce inequalities between individuals. "To practise reverse discrimination," he says, is ". . . merely to rearrange the inequalities of distribution which now prevail."[44] "What the defender [of reverse discrimination] needs to show," Sher declares, "is that it is consistent to denounce whichever inequalities follow racial, ethnic or sexual lines, while at the same time not denouncing those other inequalities which reverse discrimination inevitably perpetuates."[45]

There is a well-recognized ambiguity in the term "equality" that it is relevant to consider here. "Equality" may mean equality of opportunity, or equality of result, or equality of wealth. By his championship of direct redistribution of wealth, Sher assumes that the notion of equality advanced by the forward-looking argument is equality of wealth. In this way he saves himself the trouble of considering the argument for reverse discrimination that maintains that, although it sins against a present equality of opportunity, promotes a future equality of opportunity by providing blacks with their own successful "role models."

Sher's critique is made even weaker by the fact that he concedes to Nagel his point that racial inequalities are especially wrong because they are apt to "lead to further inequalities of self-respect."[46] He thinks he can safely concede this because even if he does the egalitarian defense of reverse discrimination fails decisively. "At best," he writes, this concession allows only that racial "inequalities would have first claim on our attention if we were forced to choose among inequalities—which as we have seen, there is no reason to think we are. It does not show, and no further argument *could* show, that any consistent egalitarian could ignore the import of the other inequalities altogether."

But on what grounds has Sher managed to conclude that the advocates of reverse discrimination, presumably consistent egalitarians, "ignore the import of the other inequalities altogether"? By what bizarre train of reasoning does it follow from the fact that the advocate of reverse discrimination thinks racial inequalities particularly harmful, that he must therefore "ignore the import of the other inequalities altogether"? And granting that other inequalities have a claim on our attention, how does it follow, as Sher says, that a policy of reverse discrimination is "dubious"? Even if, *contra* our assumption, racial inequalities are *not* more harmful than others, since we are *not* forced to choose among inequalities, why can't we attack all inequalities at once, racial inequalities through reverse discrimination, and other inequalities through other policies?

The only argument against this would be that the other policies might make reverse discrimination superfluous. But there are obvious weaknesses in it. Stigmas are not likely to be erased just because *incomes* are equalized. Apart from the extraordinary difficulties of equalizing incomes in a capitalist context—if this is possible at all—stigmas are likely to remain attached to members of groups because of the menial work many of them do, however equal their incomes. Preferential treatment is aimed at removing such stigmas.

In this chapter I have used more space in rebutting criticisms than in arguing positively for conclusions. This is because the main arguments for affirmative action are straightforward, and yet philosophers persist in concocting ever more desperately ingenious objections to it. Not that I believe that any one of the various backward- and forward-looking arguments is by itself sufficient to justify affirmative action. Affirmative action is justified by the combined force of these arguments and by the way they complement and support each other. The weaknesses in some are made up by the strengths of others. For example, the weakness in the case for compensation on an individual basis  is made up for by the case for compensation on a group basis, and the weaknesses of both these cases are strengthened by considerations stemming from the forward-looking argument. A society which tries to be just tries to compensate the victims of its injustice, and when these victims are easily identified, either as individuals or as a group less than equal to others, the case for treating them preferentially is overwhelming.

# 8

# Separation or Assimilation?

## Dubois's Dilemma

To assimilate, or not to assimilate. To black cultural nationalists, such as the poet Imamu Amiri Baraka (Leroi Jones), the political theorists Stokely Carmichael and Charles V. Hamilton, and, most important, W. E. B. Dubois, that has been *the* question in the race issue. Not, of course, that they imagined that blacks have had much of a choice about assimilation. Their question was and is about goals. Should the goal be to assimilate, to become as much like the white majority as possible, to blend in? Or should it be not to assimilate, to keep and even accentuate the differences from the majority, to stand out? These thinkers consider that question as crucial and fundamental as Hamlet's. They maintain that to choose assimilation is to choose self-obliteration, to choose, in some important sense, not to be. In their estimation, if black people are not to cave in under the slings and arrows of the majority, they must affirm, maintain, and even accentuate their distinctiveness. But their position has not gone unchallenged. There are black thinkers who have seen nothing crucial in the question of whether or not to assimilate, and no obligation to avoid assimilation. These so-called assimilationists, whose number included Henry Highland Garnet and Frederick Douglass in the 19th century and most of the leadership of the NAACP today, do not say that blacks must necessarily assimilate, though they usually believe that assimilation is inevitable. But they do say that black people are not obliged *not* to assimilate.

But even assimilationists concede that self-segregation may sometimes be desirable, if only as a temporary strategy. Thus, even Frederick,

Douglass, the most consistent and thorough-going assimilationist, conceded reluctantly that "although it may seem to conflict with our views of human brotherhood, we shall undoubtedly for many years be compelled to have institutions of a complexional character, in order to obtain this very idea of human brotherhood."[1]

Now, there is in this comment of Douglass's the suggestion of a paradox or dilemma. On the one hand, we must overcome segregation because it denies the idea of human brotherhood; on the other hand, to overcome segregation we must self-segregate and therefore also deny the idea of human brotherhood. Although Douglass evidently believed that this only "seemed" to be a problem, his great successor W. E. B. Dubois thought it a major dilemma. The "only effective defense" that a "segregated and despised group has against complete spiritual and physical disaster," he wrote, "is internal self-organization."[2] But internal self-organization, Dubois admitted, involves "more or less active segregation and acquiescence in segregation."[3] Consequently a paradox does seem to exist: To combat the evil of segregation blacks must acquiesce in the very evil they would combat. "The dilemma," Dubois declared, "is complete and there is no escape."[4]

## Cultural Pluralism

Why did Dubois believe that by self-segregating blacks would be acquiescing in racism? On the face of it, that idea seems as confused as the idea—which is nevertheless often put forward—that in defending oneself against aggression one acquiesces in the very aggression one condemns. But offence is not defence. Things one may not do in offence one may do in defence—and not thereby acquiesce in offence. And one could reason similarly in the case of racial segregation. In response to white segregation laws, the black community could conceivably have imposed its own segregation laws. This would have been as justifiable as one nation compulsorily "segregating" its citizens from another aggressive foreign nation. In neither case would there be any invidious "acquiescence." If Dubois believed that black self-segregation was in some sense an acquiescence to the segregation imposed by racism, he must have believed that, independent of the pressures of racism, there was some reason for self-segregation. Why did he believe that? The answer lies in his lifelong sympathy for the doctrine of cultural pluralism.

Cultural pluralism boils down to four main points: (1) Each race has its own distinct and peculiar culture. (2) Different races can accept a common conception of justice and can live together at peace in one nation-state. (For this reason cultural pluralism is to be distinguished from separatism, which maintains that the races cannot live together at peace in one nation-state.) (3) Individuals must develop more and closer ties to the other members of their own race in order to preserve and enhance those cultural traits which mark it off from others. (4) To forestall charges of chauvinism and exclusivity, the cultural pluralist hastens to add that he does not say that any particular culture is superior or inferior to any other, only that they are different, and that the members of each race must make a concerted effort to develop their own culture, not solely for their own self-realization, but also because each race must present its culture as a gift to the other races at "the meeting place of conquest,"[5] where all will benefit from, and participate as, equals in a universal world culture.

Many black thinkers have endorsed the idea of cultural pluralism. Even Booker T. Washington, with his feet planted so firmly on the ground—some would say trapped in the sand—toyed with it. It is "not too much to hope," he wrote, "that the very qualities which make the Negro different from the peoples by whom he is surrounded will enable him, in the fulness [sic] of time, to make a peculiar contribution to the nation of which he forms a part."[6]

And in Senegal and Martinique the poets and statesmen Leopold Sedar Senghor and Aimé Cesaire gave the theory powerful expression in the philosophy of Negritude, which favorably contrasted the communality and closeness to nature of African culture with the soullessness and materialism of European culture. However, Dubois was cultural pluralism's original architect, and had spelled out its essentials in the closing years of the 19th century. If "there is substantial agreement in laws, language and religion;" and "if there is a satisfactory adjustment of economic life, then," he wrote "there is no reason why in the same country and on the same street, two or three great national ideals may not thrive and develop."[7] And black people should develop their peculiar culture not only for themselves. ". . . other race groups," Dubois wrote, "are striving, each in its own way to develop for civilization its particular message, its particular ideal, which shall help to guide the world nearer and nearer that perfection of human life for which we all long, that one far off Divine event." The Negro race, he believed, has "not yet given to civilization the full spiritual message [it is] capable of giving."[8]

Although Dubois never again gave such eloquent and extended expression to the idea of cultural pluralism as he did in "The Conservative of Races," from which I quoted, he always clung to it. Thus, in 1934, nearly forty years after he wrote it, he cited the essay, observing "I am rather pleased to find myself still so much in sympathy with myself;"[9] and in 1954, nearly sixty years after the "The Conservation of Races" appeared, its shadow is still evident in his warning that the "price" of the desegregation promised by *Brown* was that black people "must eventually surrender race 'solidarity' and the idea of an American Negro culture."[10]

This last comment reveals why Dubois believed that self-segregation acquiesced in racism, and why it was his sympathy for cultural pluralism that made him believe this. For, according to the ideals of cultural pluralism, there is something positively good about self-segregation, independent of its function as a defensive response to imposed segregation. It is for this reason that Dubois could speak of the "price" of desegregation, although he was willing to pay that price. Moreover, it is quite clear that for the cultural pluralist the good offered by self-segregation is of such importance as to impose on blacks a duty to self-segregate. Since racists make precisely the same claim when instituting segregation, it is not surprising that to a cultural pluralist like Dubois, self-segregation seems to acquiesce in racism. The question we face then is whether cultural pluralism is a defensible doctrine.

Dubois offered three arguments for cultural pluralism: (1) It inspires black pride, (2) it maintains black cultural authenticity, and (3) it gives to the world the gift of black culture. I will address each argument separately.

## BLACK PRIDE

There is no quesiton that black pride is a necessary and desirable feeling. A person who lacks due pride in his race will probably lack self-esteem, self-respect, and autonomy, and racism has, of course, done all it can to undermine that pride in black people. But these are generalities. What exactly is black pride?

Black pride may mean several things. Cultural pluralism probably defines it as pride in being a member of a cultural group that has a particular "message" or "ideal" which, in Dubois's words, "shall help to guide the world nearer and nearer that perfection of human life for which we all long, that "one far off Divine event." At the other extreme, black pride may simply mean pride in being black, that is, pride in having a black skin and the other physical qualities typical of black people. Martin Delany was reported to have had black pride in that sense, and that is how Frederick Douglass understood—and condemned—it.

There is nothing wrong with black pride as the cultural pluralist understands it. There is nothing wrong in a Senegalese being proud that he participates in the culture which produced the "particular message" of the poetry of Leopold Sedar Senghor, just as there is nothing wrong with an Englishman being proud that he participates in the culture which produced Dickens, that most English of English novelists.

Also, despite Douglass's view, there is nothing wrong with being proud that one has a black skin. Douglass thought that the very idea of "race pride" was "supercilious nonsense." "The only excuse for pride in individuals or races," he wrote, "is in the fact of their own achievements," and, of course, a person's race or color is not his achievement. "If the sun has curled our hair and tanned our skin," Douglass remarked sardonically, "let the sun be proud of its achievement." He also thought that race pride was "mischievous" and a positive evil because it led to complacency. It was race pride, he believed, which led "The poorest and meanest white man, drunk or sober, when he has nothing else to commend him [to say] 'I am a white man, I am.' " Black race pride would endorse and justify "American race pride; an assumption of superiority upon the ground of race or color," and the "mountain devil, the lion in the way of our progress."[11]

But Douglass was mistaken. Race pride is not necessarily an assumption of superiority on the grounds of race or color. If, as Douglass observed, "Our color is the gift of the Almighty," race pride may simply be a rejoicing in the gift of the Almighty. No assumption of superiority need be implied. And since we can, and indeed *should* rejoice in these gifts, there is no impropriety in being proud—in that sense—of our color. Finally, in that sense race pride need not lead to complacency. On the contrary, it may be necessary in order to develop the only kind of pride Douglass countenances—pride in achievement. For it is not implausible to assume that, unless one rejoices in and appreciates one's natural gifts, one will achieve nothing.

Therefore, I do not object to the idea of black pride either in the sense of pride in one's physical being, or in the sense of pride in one's cultural being. But there is a third sense in which black pride can be interpreted which is distinct from these two, and which better enhances black self-esteem.

In this third definition of black pride, a person is simply proud of the fact that there are black people who have made great achievements. This kind of black pride is distinct from cultural or physical pride. If a black person is proud of the achievements of outstanding black people, his culture need not be their culture, and their achievements need not be exemplifications of a peculiar black culture. I am proud that St. Augustine was a black man, but I am sure that my culture is not his, and I am not less proud—for I do not really care—that his *The Holy City* shows no traces of Negritude. Of course, it goes without saying that pride in the achievements of black people can mean pride in black culture. Dubois was proud of the art of the ancient West African nation of Benin and well he might be. But he could be proud of these products of black cultures because these cultures and these products were the achievements of black people.

It may be objected that I have begged the question. I say that a person can be proud of the achievements of outstanding black people, but I do not say what I mean by black people. Dubois defined a race as a "vast family of human beings, generally of common blood and language, always of common history, tradition and impulses, who are both voluntarily and involuntarily striving together for the accomplishment of certain more or less vividly conceived ideals of life."[12] If he is right, then, since black Americans do form a race, the black American who is proud of the achievements of outstanding black people must share a culture with the people who make him proud.

But in fact it is Dubois who has begged the question. It is he who has defined a race as a family of human beings sharing a common culture. Armed with this definition it is possible to draw the tautological inference that every member of a race shares a culture. However, it is not possible to draw the substantive inference that every black American shares a culture. For since it is a false or at least controversial point, that black Americans are a family of human beings sharing a common culture, it is also false or controversial to maintain that they are a race as defined by Dubois.

In opposition to Dubois's cultural definition of race, I propose a physical definition of race. This definition is, for reasons which will presently emerge, the racist's definition. Individual differences in culture are supremely irrelevant to the way in which the racist classifies people into races. A man with blue eyes and blond hair who loves chitlins and jazz is still a white man, though perhaps a depraved one. A man with black skin and nappy hair who loves Shakespeare and ballet is still a black man, though certainly one who needs putting in his place. And when the black who "passes" is unmasked, it is not because he reveals a secret weakness for chitlins, but because it is revealed that he has black-skinned ancestors. The racist, we observe, takes a race to be a group of people distinguished either by their physical appearance or biology, or else descended from such a group of people, and since I have adopted their conception, I propose that, insofar as black people are a race, they are people who either themselves look black—that is, have a certain kind of physical appearance—or are, at least in part, descended from such a group of people.[13]

This definition of race better supports the idea of black pride and autonomy than the cultural definition and is more useful for an understanding of racism. Consider black pride. If to be black one must share in a particular culture, how can people who have black skins or black ancestors but who do not share in that culture have black pride? The cultural definition of race is evasive. When the racist tells black people that they can accomplish nothing because of their race, he is not telling them that they can accomplish nothing because of their culture. He is telling them that they can accomplish nothing because of their biological being. For racism is based predominantly on biology. Of course, it also maintains that black culture is degenerate, but it assumes that this is because blacks are biologically degenerate. Thus, to rebut racism's lie, to confront it directly, we must use words the way it uses words; we cannot use "race" to mean a cultural group. We must use "race," as racism uses it, to mean a group defined biologically. Only in this way can "race pride" mean "black pride" for all the victims of racism.

And Dubois's definition of race sometimes seriously misled him. It is, for example, what led him to define race prejudice as "nothing but the friction between different groups of people; it is the difference in aim, in feeling, in ideals of two different races."[14] If races are cultural groups this definition is plausible. There does tend to be friction between people with different aims and ideals. But that friction is not the friction between the races. The white racist does not hate blacks because they prefer jazz to country-and-western. He couldn't, because many prefer country and western to jazz. He hates them simply because they look black or are descended from people who look black. I do not deny that this hate may *arise* from a clash of cultures. But I am not describing here the origins of race prejudice. I am defining what it is. Neither do I deny that some, perhaps much, of the friction between blacks and whites is friction between people with different aims. Such friction is inevitable, given the difference in economic status of the two races. But the same kind of friction exists between the white lower class and the white middle and upper classes. It is not *racial* friction. And because Dubois's definition of prejudice is thus irrelevant it is also seriously misleading. It is often eminently reasonable to want to be widely separated from people with aims widely different from our own. When they pursue their aims, they are apt to prevent us from achieving our aims. Dubois's definition of race prejudice as a clash of cultures misleadingly allies it with this kind of reasonable attitude and thus obscures its utter irrationality.[15]

## CULTURAL AUTHENTICITY

To be authentic, and true to oneself, one must first know oneself. Dubois evidently thought that this was a special problem for black Americans. In a widely admired passage he wrote: "No Negro who has given earnest thought to situation of his people in America has failed, at some time in life, to find himself at these crossroads; has failed to ask himself at some time: What, after all, am I? Am I an American or am I a Negro? . . . "[16] But Dubois felt that he had the "reading of the riddle." He maintained that farther than birth, citizenship, political ideals, language, and religion, black "Americanism does not go. At that point we are Negroes, members of a vast historic race that from the very dawn of creation has slept, but half-awakening, in the dark forests of its African fatherland. We are the first fruits of this new nation, the harbinger of that black tomorrow which is yet destined to soften the whiteness of the Tuetonic today."[17]

But what of the assimilated black? Dubois's "reading of the riddle" does not really tell him much about what or who he is. Now, strictly speaking, in Dubois's definition of race a person with a black skin or ancestors, but who has assimilated, is white. But Dubois never let his ideas about race mislead him to that extent. He continued to accept the true, and commonsensical, view that such a person was black. However, he implied that a person with black skin or black ancestors *ought* to be culturally black if he wished to be authentic and true to himself. The destiny of black Americans, Dubois wrote, is "not absorption by the white Americans," nor "self-obliteration," nor a "servile imitation of Anglo-Saxon culture." It is a "stalwart originality which shall unswervingly follow Negro ideals."[18] If it is true, as these passages suggest, that cultural and individual authenticity, stalwartness, originality, and self-respect are undermined by acculturation, then, to the extent that blacks have a duty to be authentic, stalwart, original, and self-respecting, they have a duty to resist acculturation, that is, a duty to self-segregate.

It is widely believed that in some vague though deep sense, assimilated blacks are inauthentic, imitative, copy cats, unoriginal, ashamed of their color, morally flabby, so full of self-hate that they seek to be absorbed or obliterated, and, ultimately, servile. Thus, they are referred to derisively as "Afro-Saxons," or "oreos," black on the outside, white on the inside. If a person with a black skin writes a book or a poem, he must explicitly show his "blackness." Otherwise, he is trying to "pass," or, reverting inconsistently—since this view stresses color—to the cultural definition of race, he is not "really" black. Is there any basis to these extraordinary charges?

Attacks of this kind are sometimes based on the supposition that the assimilated black does not think of himself as black and therefore cannot be trusted as an ally. But this supposition begs the question. According to the cultural definition of race, the assimilated black will not, of course, see himself as black. But he is quite capable of seeing that he is black in the sense that racism puts him in the same boat as other people with black skins, and because he can see that, he can also see that he had better ally himself with them.

No doubt there are black people who are servile in part because they are assimilated. Indisputably, some aspects of white culture affirm that black people are inferior, and, to the extent that black people assimilate them, they will think of themselves as inferior. Some cultural pluralists go further and argue that the idea that white is superior and black is inferior is embedded in the very languages of Europe and North America, and, accordingly, that to speak those languages is to absorb a world-view which determines that one accept whites as superior to blacks.[19] But this theory is simplistic. Cultures are not seamless webs, their parts are not always consistent, and they are far more flexible than the theory supposes. For it is just as clear that some aspects of white culture affirm the equality of peoples, and black—and white—poets have not had to "destroy" English or European language before they could use them to say that black can be beautiful, and white can be ugly.[20]

And no doubt there are black people who pretend to a white culture which is not their own in order to "pass," or, if this is not possible, in order—they hope—to at least be accepted by that culture; and some black writers who imitate white writers because they believe that if they don't they won't be published, or the right people won't like their work, or simply because they despise themselves. The Martiniquan poet Étienne Léro delivered a scathing indictment of this kind of writer: "The very reason for his entire social and poetic existence," he wrote, "is to be a faithful copy of the pale-skinned gentleman. . . . In his poetry too he tries not to 'act like a Negro.' He takes a special pride in the fact that a white man can read his book without ever guessing the color of his skin."[21] Now, such people and such writers are certainly imitative, and possibly servile too, but it is false and vicious to infer that every assimilated black, or every black-skinned writer or poet who does not display "soul," is imitative and servile.

We do, I admit, have some grounds for suspecting a black poet or novelist—or moral philosopher—whose work appears to studiously avoid the question of the color bar. The color bar has caused too many tragedies, and raises too many personal and moral issues about the human condition—the subject of serious writing and philosophy—for one of its victims, who happens to be a serious writer or philosopher, to ignore it. But we must distinguish between writing about and protesting against the color bar, and displaying "soul," or, in Léro's words, "the black man's sensuous and colorful imagination." The serious black writer or philosopher sufficiently demonstrates his authenticity by coming to grips with, and condemning the color bar. He may, but need not do so with any particularly "black" style or diction.

But the world of white culture, it may be argued, is a world created by white-skinned people; black-skinned people feel like strangers in it, and white racism will make sure they continue to feel that way. In an essay significantly titled "Stranger in the Village," James Baldwin described this feeling of alienation when he visited an obscure hamlet in Europe. The inhabitants, Baldwin writes, "move with an authority I shall never have . . . the most illiterate among them is related, in a way that I am not, to Dante, Shakespeare, Michelangelo . . . Out of their hymns and dances come Beethoven and Bach. Go back a few centuries and they are in their full glory—but I am in Africa watching the conquerors arrive."[22]

I acknowledge the seductiveness of the feeling Baldwin describes. I deny, however, that it is rationally based, and deny therefore that we must cave in to it. The fallacy behind it is not that what is called "white culture" has been, to a considerable degree, created by black-skinned people, though, of course, this is true. The fallacy behind it is the assumption that people own cultures. Leaving aside the racist belief that a person's biology determines his culture or makes certain cultures more "natural" to him than others, only on that assumption does it even begin to make sense that blacks have any reason to feel "out of place" in white culture, or that whites have any right to make them feel that way. But the assumption is senseless. If the use or enjoyment of an object or idea by many different people causes a loss to someone, he may sensibly, and sometimes justifiably, claim ownership of it. But this does not apply to culture or the process of cultural assimilation. Except, perhaps as affronts to their racist beliefs—which count for nothing—assimilated blacks cause no loss to whites. Of course, many blacks do profess to feel truly ill at ease and out of place in white culture. But that may be simply because they are not assimilated. We succor the enemy if we let this unease be used to bolster the racist's argument that the assimilated black will inevitably still be alienated.

## THE GIFT OF BLACK CULTURE

According to Dubois, ". . . the Negro people, as a race have a contribution to make to civilization and humanity which no other race can make . . ." and ". . . it is the duty of the Americans of Negro descent, as a body, to maintain their race identity until this mission of the Negro people is accomplished. . . ."[23] This suggests that black people have an obligation to self-segregate because they have a duty to help make the race's cultural contribution to civilization and humanity. But on what sense of obligation is that duty based?

The most likely candidate is the obligation of reciprocity. Such an obligation does exist. Since each person benefits from the contributions to society of others, he or she has a duty to contribute to it as well. It is wrong, and a dereliction of duty, to be a parasite. Everyone has a duty to "pull his own weight." But although this is true, it does not imply that black people have a duty to self-segregate.

It is not necessary to deny that "the Negro people," if they were to retain their "race identity," would make a peculiar and worthy contribution to the world. Certainly their historical experience has been peculiar and ought to give us privileged insights into the human condition. And certainly, as John Stuart Mill noted, groups of individuals pursuing a way of life together are experiments in living and therefore furnish mankind with valuable information. Thus, I disagree with Harvard sociologist Orland Patterson, author of the widely-acclaimed *Slavery and Social Death*, who, in his critique of ethnic pluralism, professed to see no great value in a diversity of groups.[24] Neither is it necessary to deny that black people who choose to self-segregate for the purpose of helping to make the race's cultural contribution to humanity are fulfilling the duty of reciprocity, and fulfilling it in perhaps the most exalted way they can. Both these things will be true if the cultural contribution is likely to be, as I suspect it is, of great value.

What it is necessary and correct to deny is that black people—or white people—must fulfill the duty of reciprocity in the most exalted possible way, the way urged by Dubois. For although each person has a fundamental duty to reciprocate the contributions made by others to the world, each person also has an equally fundamental right to choose the way in which he or she will make that contribution. For example, a black person may choose to become a serious writer in order to distill and express the black experience, but he also may—and will commit no wrong if he does—choose to become a plumber. If he has literary talent we may fairly attempt to persuade him that writing is, for him, a worthier goal. But it is sleight of hand to convert goals into duties because they are worthy.

These conclusions dissolve Dubois's dilemma about the choice of separation or integration for blacks. For that dilemma exists only if we accept cultural pluralism's claim that, independent of the pressures of racism, black people have an obligation to self-segregate. It is that claim which makes black self-segregation seem to acquiesce in racism, for, as we have noted, racism makes the same claim about the need for cultural integrity. But when black people self-segregate they need not be acquiescing to the dangerous nonsense of racism and cultural pluralism.

They must admit, of course, that they have a common color or ancestry, and that they possess this commonality independent of separateness imposed by racism. And they may also admit that, independent of racist claims, they possess a common culture and that this makes it in some sense natural for them to self-segregate. But they may, and indeed should, deny that either of these identifications imposes on them an obligation to self-segregate. They should insist that the only circumstance that imposes such an obligation is the fact that they are all the victims of discrimination on the basis of their color or ancestry and that this commonality is not independent of racism, but, on the contrary, exists precisely because of racism. Consequently, since we have refuted the assumptions of pluralism, there is no dilemma. Black people may self-segregate in self-defense and may, simultaneously, and without the slightest inconsistency, protest the racism which makes this self-segregation necessary.

Nor does a dilemma reemerge if we grant that self-segregation may be necessary for the race to make a cultural contribution. Fighting and protesting against compulsory segregation does not mean fighting and protesting against every kind of segregation. It means precisely what it says: Fighting compulsory segregation. This is quite compatible with permitting, and even urging, black people to voluntarily self-segregate, and I see no reason why voluntary self-segregation cannot be a sufficient means of enabling the race to make its cultural contribution to the world.

Dubois's fear was that, if compulsory segregation were abolished, black people would *not* choose to self-segregate, but would assimilate as fast as they could. That was why he thought that the "price" of *Brown* would be the end of "American Negro culture." Perhaps his fears were well-founded. Perhaps blacks are assimilating as fast as they can, and perhaps the price of this is the disappearance of American Negro culture. I feel deeply the force of Dubois's concern. The price of desegregation may be high. And it may well be that, however much black people achieve in "white culture"—even if Keats, Dickens, and Newton had been black—black people would still not be esteemed as equals, unless they produced something peculiarly black, something completely and totally their own. People might still say—and are already saying—that, while blacks manage well among white people doing, and even improving, things white people started, they can't start anything or do anything at all by themselves. But even if we admit all this, and I don't think we have to, self-segregation and assimilation still pose no dilemma. For there is no dilemma about, no confusion between, securing justice and securing some other good, be it cultural integrity or maximizing welfare. Compulsory racial segregation is unjust. Even if its end means the end of "Negro culture" we seize no horn of a dilemma in striving to abolish it.

## Authenticity as Autonomy

The conclusions of the preceding section point to a further, more fundamental, flaw in cultural pluralism. "What am I?" the black person asks. Cultural pluralism's answer is: "I am a being who springs from a people with a certain history and tradition; because of this I share with them certain impulses and strivings, both voluntary and involuntary, and to be true to myself and to help fulfill the Negro mission, I have a duty to retain that identity." This is a false, or at least, not fundamental, answer. The true answer is, "I am a being capable and worthy of making my own choices; because of this, I have certain basic duties and rights; among my duties is a duty to contribute to society, but among my rights is a right to choose how I shall contribute; I must allow neither history, tradition, nor seer to make my choices for me; I may choose, consistent with performing my duties and exercising my rights, any identity I please; only if my choices are thus autonomous can I really be true to myself." Frantz Fanon may have expressed himself too succinctly, but it is all there in his words: "There is no Negro mission; there is no white burden . . . I have one right alone: That of demanding human behavior from the other. One duty alone: That of not renouncing my freedom through my choices—I am not a prisoner of history. I should not seek there for the meaning of my destiny."[25]

In Dubois's mind, the cause of the dilemma was that, while he felt an allegiance to cultural pluralism, he also felt an allegiance to the truths summarized by Fanon. The first seduced him into believing that blacks had a duty to self-segregate; the second showed him clearly that each person has a right to choose for himself. Fortunately, Dubois's allegiance to human autonomy and individual rights was stronger than his allegiance to cultural pluralism. Although he always believed that his proposal that blacks self-segregate and protest segregation involved a genuine dilemma, he also saw that self-segregation could be seen, and justified, as a purely defensive move against imposed segregation, and therefore as thoroughly consistent with protest. It was when he stressed this that he had his most significant insights into the nature of black self-respect—the subject to which I now turn.

# 9

# *Self-Respect*

## Racism and Self-respect

Racism has put black self-respect and self-esteem under siege. It has attacked with scientific theories about black inferiority, insults and insinuations, ridicule, overt and covert exclusion and discrimination, and self-fulfilling prophesies about black failure. And it has also deployed subtler devices. It has woven its poisonous threads into the very fabric of the language the besieged use to protest their plight, and it has set its boobytraps in the road to the truth—in history, psychology, sociology, and philosophy, as well as in genetics, art, and literature.

These combined onslaughts have, in many cases, achieved the desired end. That such names as "Uncle Tom" and "Sambo" have become standard invectives against blacks attests to this. And those blacks who have not succumbed still show the strain of the long seige. Though some defend their self-respect with panache, many are overly sensitive, thin-skinned, anxious, defensive, suspicious, and bumptious. Dubois recognized the scars of racism: "I admit, I am sensitive, I am artificial. I cringe or am bumptious or immobile. . . . I fear, quite craven in my fear, but the terrible thing is—these things do happen . . . Not all each day—but now and then . . . not everywhere, but anywhere . . . Imagine spending your life looking for insults or for hiding places from them."[1] If the philosopher A. I. Melden is right when he writes that, "What we label the dignity of a person is not a matter pertaining to some precious internal quality of his nature as a human being—his rationality or his autonomy—but that sense he displays of . . . the *expectation* that his rights will be honored,"[2] then what Dubois is describing here is racism's attack on his dignity.

Naturally, a question which has always been of deep concern to blacks is how they can maintain their dignity and self-respect in the face of racism's barrage, or, which is very much the same question: What is the self-respecting and dignified response to the injustice of racism? The answer Dubois gave is particularly interesting and insightful.

Dubois believed that he had an obligation to himself to protest injustice. "Whenever I meet personal discrimination on account of my race and color," he wrote, "I shall protest . . . I shall deem it my duty to make my grievances known, to bring it before the organs of public opinion. . . ."[3] And, he implied, this is the self-respecting response to discrimination. "I will walk my way, with uplifted head and level eyes," he declared "respecting myself too much to endure without protest studied disrespect from others."[4]

Frederick Douglass perceived a similar connection between self-defense and self-respect. This perception dawned on him after he defended himself against a man named Edward Covey. Covey was what was known as a "negro breaker," and was apparently very good at his work. Slave masters would send him their uppity slaves, and, through a liberal use of the whip, Covey would return them "well broken." Douglass's master sent him to Covey for that purpose. After being beaten every week for six months, Douglass, in desperation, finally defended himself. The act was, in Douglass's words, "a resurrection." "It recalled to my life," he recorded, "my crushed self-respect."[5]

But there is another side to the question. It may seem—and the claim would not be unsupported—that the kind of insistent protest Dubois urges blacks to make runs counter to dignity. Dignity, as the philosopher Aurel Kolnai tells us, denotes "composure, calmness, restraint, reserve . . . self-contained serenity . . . the dignified character is chary of emphatic activity. . . ."[6] And Dubois seems to give weight to this point: "Some people seem to think that the fight against segregation consists of one damned protest after another." But such a program, he granted, would be an "undignified and impossible attitude and method to maintain."[7]

And, of course, there is Washington's view to consider as well. Although he does at one point concede that a race should be swift to protest injustices done to it,[8] he certainly thought it was a waste of time to protest injustices that were violations of civil rights—the very opposite of Dubois's view—and seemed to condemn the kind of insistent protest urged by Dubois suggesting that it relied on sympathy.[9] If he was right about this, his qualms about protest are justified. Black spokesmen have always been anxious not to rely on sympathy in their struggle. "What I ask for the Negro," Douglass emphasized, "is not benevolence, not pity, not sympathy, but simply justice."[10] And for good reason. Unlike reliance on justice, reliance on sympathy, or pity, or benevolence shows a want of self-reliance, and there may even be a suggestion of servility about it. But, though the conceptual point is clear, a practical difficulty remains. Justice, on which one may presumably rely without endangering self-respect, is not always easy to distinguish from sympathy, pity, and benevolence.

For example, some black people reject certain strategies for the elevation of blacks, such as affirmative action, ostensibly based on the idea of justice, on the grounds that they actually arise from charity and sympathy, and are therefore destructive of self-respect. Thus, though conceding the possible advantages of affirmative action, Thomas Sowell maintains that it makes blacks into parasites and Uncle Toms, and undermines their self-respect. He argues that affirmative action, and the seeking of concessions in general, "gains some tangible benefits from whites, but exacts an exorbitant price from the black man who allows his aspirations to be oriented towards this basically subordinate and parasitic role." Thus, he thinks that, though it "works," it "works in the same way that Uncle Tomism worked—at a cost out of all proportion to what was gained by abandoning creativity and independence."[11] Sometimes, Sowell stresses particularly affirmative action's effect on black self-respect: ". . . here and there this program has undoubtedly caused some individuals to be hired who would otherwise have not been hired . . . even that is a doubtful gain in the larger context of attaining self-respect and the respect of others,"[12] and at other times he stresses its resemblance to charity. Preferential treatment, he writes, says "loud and clear that *black people just don't have it*, and that they will have to be *given* something . . . [competent blacks] will be completely undermined, as black becomes synonymous—in the minds of black and white alike—with incompetence, and black achievement becomes synonymous with charity or payoffs."[13]

This chapter will attempt to find the truth in these conflicting claims, beginning with the question of whether self-respect requires that we protest injustice.

## Self-respect, Self-esteem, and Protest

Philosophers differ fundamentally about the nature of self-respect. Some see it as a kind of self-confidence. Thus, John Rawls describes it as "a persons' sense of his own value, his secure conviction that his conception of his good, his plan of life is worth carrying out . . . and . . . a confidence in one's ability, so far as it is within one's power, to fulfill one's intentions."[14] But this definition includes both too much and too little. No doubt it is good to be securely convinced of the worth of one's plan of life, and to be confident of one's abilities. But surely these attitudes are not necessary to self-respect. It would then be beyond the reach of too many people. Self-respect is sparer, sterner, more fundamental; it has more to do with how we conceive of ourselves as human beings in our basic moral relations with others, and it is therefore within the reach of almost everyone. On the other hand Rawls's definition of self-respect is too confined. A person can be confident of his abilities and the worth of his life plan but still lack self-respect.

Self-respect has also been defined as a person's consciousness of his rights. Thus, Feinberg writes that to have a "minimal self-respect . . . is to think of oneself as the holder of rights;"[15] and Thomas E. Hill writes that the duty of self-respect is the duty "to understand and affirm one's rights."[16] These accounts of self-respect are an improvement on that of Rawls, for they deemphasize its relation to self-confidence, which he overemphasized. Thus, in describing the conditions of self-respect, Feinberg makes no mention of confidence in one's abilities or in the worth of one's life plan, and Hill is at pains to show that a person who "has in fact done poorly" and presumably has no reason to feel confident of his prospects or plans  can still have self-respect.

In the balance of the chapter I will adopt and further develop the definition of self-respect in terms of rights, following Lawrence Thomas, who maintains that Rawls's definition of self-respect is really a definition of self-esteem.[17] Although racism attacks both black self-respect and self-esteem, the distinction between self-respect and self-esteem is essential for a proper resolution of the problems I discuss in this chapter.

Now, even if one owes it to one's self-respect to protest injustice, or if protesting injustice is an expression of self-respect, there are, of course, often other reasons to protest. Sometimes protesting an injustice will stop it or prevent its perpetrators from repeating it, and sometimes, though probably less often, protesting an injustice will convert its perpetrators. Dubois was aware of these considerations and gave them due weight.[18] But he also thought that there was still a reason to protest even when there was no hope of obtaining these results: "even when bending to the inevitable," he wrote, "we bend with unabated protest."[19] The passage cited earlier indicates that he believed that this posture was justified by self-respect. What is the basis for this belief?

Dubois suggests that it is the obligation to be truthful. "May God forgive me," he wrote, "if . . . I ever weakly admit to myself or the world that wrong is not wrong, that insult is not insult, or that color discrimination is anything but an inhuman and damnable shame."[20] This response leads in the right direction, but is not complete. One has a duty to be truthful to oneself, and it may be a duty of self-respect. A man who is satisfied with falsehoods and half-truths, who deceives himself, and allows others to deceive him, does not acknowledge himself for what he is—a rational being—and therefore does not respect himself. One also has a duty to be truthful to others, and it, too, my be a duty of self-respect. A man who deceives or misleads others does not acknowledge himself for what he is—a moral being—and to that extent does not respect himself. But neither of these duties supports the idea that self-respect gives us a duty to protest. Failure to protest a wrong is not necessarily an admission, either to oneself or to the world, that the wrong is not wrong. Of course, sometimes it may be—sometimes silence speaks louder than words—but it need not always be. Sometimes to fail to protest injustice, to keep silent, is simply to say nothing. It is enough in such cases that the victim be sure in his own mind that he has been wronged. Why should he tell a cynical, uncaring and incorrigible world that he has been wronged? And, if he should for some reason, why should it be out of self-respect?

We need to postulate duty stronger than merely the duty to be truthful. It is not enough for our purposes, that a person be honest with himself; not enough that he refrain from deceiving or misleading others or from uttering falsehoods; not enough if he says nothing; not even enough if he corrects falsehoods; we need to conceive of a duty—at least where serious injustices are concerned—that each person has, to tell the world where he stands; a duty to deny others—especially the perpetrators of injustice—the possibility of ever misconstruing his position. Is there such a duty, and if there is, is it based on self-respect?

Respect can be understood in two senses. In the first, it is not *part of* respecting something to show respect for it. For example, in that sense a boxer can respect his opponent's left hook and, for strategic reasons—and at his peril—show no respect for it. In the second sense, it is *part of* respecting something to show respect for it. And in this sense, if a person respects the flag, part of his respect for it involves showing respect for it, for instance, by saluting it. Of course, in both cases, failure to show respect can be the basis of an inference that there is no respect. But in each case the major premise of such an inference would be different. In the first case, it would be the result of an empirical generalization—boxers who respect their opponents' left hooks normally take evasive action. In the second case, it would be based on the conceptual claim that people who respect their flag salute it. Where failure to show respect in the first case would call for *explanation*, failure to show respect in the second case would call for *excuse*.

In cases where having respect for something involves showing respect for it, the object of respect is of such paramount importance as to be owed an outward sign of allegiance.[21] Some people feel this way about the flag; others have the same attitude to a church or God; everyone should feel this way about morality, since it is morality that makes us more than brutes or automata. These things are, or ought to be, held in reverence. Reverence is partly an inward feeling, but also partly an outward one. A person who reveres God, for example, will protest the taking of God's name in vain, and if he fails to do so, he will look upon his silence not merely as *evidence* of a lack of reverence, but as *itself* a betrayal, as itself a failure to accord to God what He is owed, and, as itself, something for which he must beg forgiveness.

If this account of the nature of reverence is correct, and if morality is a proper object of reverence, then we have grounds for saying that a person with self-respect will protest violations of his rights. For, since his rights are derived from morality, their violation is its violation. His protest will not be self-centered, but will be both disinterested, and, at the same time, an expression of self-respect. It will be disinterested insofar as it is part of his reverence for morality, and it will be an expression of *self-respect* because it will affirm that *he* has the rights conferred by morality, and that he is thus a member of equal standing in the moral community.

If the argument above is sound, we do have a duty to protest injustice, and such protest is an expression of self-respect. However, it may be objected that this conclusion is based on the controversial premise that part of revering something is showing that one revers it. It may yet be argued that reverence is purely internal, and that the rituals associated with it are indeed more trappings. I think I have demonstrated sufficiently why ritual is part of the nature of reverence, but I maintain that, even if the objection can be sustained, the idea of a duty to protest injustice can still be based on the belief that we have duties of self-respect.

One obvious reason why countries require that citizens salute their flag, stand for their anthem, or make some other conventional sign of allegiance to their nation, is that national loyalties are important. Another, less obvious reason, also related to loyalty, is that shows of loyalty tend to strengthen loyalty. This idea, expanded, is the basis of my argument that we have duty to protest injustice.

The germ of this argument lies in Douglass's account of his moral resurrection. He recalled that Covey's repeated whippings had broken him. "Mr. Covey had succeeded in breaking me," he wrote, "in body, soul, and spirit. My natural elasticity was crushed; my intellect languished . . . the dark night of slavery closed about in upon me, and behold a man transformed into a brute."[22] But this transformation was reversed. "You have seen," Douglass continued, "how a man was made a slave; you shall see how a slave was made a man."[23] This reversal, as we noted, was effected by his fighting Covey. But precisely how did it work?

As Douglass notes, "the law of Maryland . . . assigned hanging to the slave who resisted his master."[24] In fighting Covey, Douglass therefore put his life on the line. This was the crucial factor. "I had reached," Douglass recounts, "the point at which I was not afraid to die. This spirit made me a freeman in fact, though I still remained a slave in form."[25] What this means, I think, is the following: Because Douglass fought Covey for his freedom, and placed his life on the line in doing so, his fighting Covey revealed to him that he valued his rights and freedom so much that he was ready to die rather than be denied them. A person who values his rights and freedom to that extent certainly has self-respect. Consequently, Douglass's fight with Covey revealed to him that he had self-respect.

And if Douglass had self-respect, this revelation would certainly be important to him. The self-respecting person's concern for his rights and freedom is not irrational. It is based on the conviction that they are objectively valuable because they are conferred by morality. Consequently, the self-respecting person will, necessarily, be concerned that he retain his concern for his rights and his obligations toward them, that is, he will necessarily be concerned that he retain his self-respect. At the same time, however, he will know that he can lose self-respect. It is a mistake to believe that only the confident, self-assured person who can take his self-respect for granted really does have self-respect. This is confusing self-respect with self-esteem and self-confidence. People sometimes do lose their self-respect. Thus, to the extent that he is reflective, a person with self-respect will concede the possibility of losing it. And, though he *may* be confident of retaining it, he *need* not be. Whether or not he has this confidence depends on matters outside his feeling of self-respect. Therefore, though he may not be servile, a person may properly fear that, because of what he is doing or because of what is happening to him, he will become servile.

He may also fear that he is already servile. If he has self-respect he will be aware that he entertains the belief that he has worth and that he should be convinced of it, though he need not be sure that he *is* convinced of it. For he will probably also know that servile people, too, can value self-respect and persuade themselves that they have that which they lack. Thus, not only may a person concerned about self-respect fear losing it; he may also fear that he does not have it. However, if he does have it, he will necessarily be concerned with retaining it. But no one is satisfied with the belief that he retains something of great value unless he has proof that he retains it. Hence, since the self-respecting person conceives of self-respect as of great value he necessarily wants proof that he is self-respecting—that is, it is important to him that his self-respect be revealed to him.

For this he needs strong, incontrovertible evidence of his self-respect. His need will be especially poignant when, to escape injury, he pretends to be servile. Observers often cannot agree on how to interpret such behavior. The "Sambo" character, for example, was supposed to typify the good-humored, ostensibly servile, black slave. Sambo was apparently very convincing. In *Slavery: A Problem in American Institutional Life*, the historian Stanley Elkins suggests that Sambo's "docility" and "humility" reflected true servility. On the other hand, some scholars suspect that Sambo was a fraud. Patterson, for example, argues that Sambo's fawning laziness and dishonesty was his way of hitting back at the master's system without penalty. Thus, Patterson perceives Sambo's clowing as a mask "to salvage his dignity," a "deadly serious game " in which "the perfect stroke of rebellion must ideally appear to the master as the ultimate act of submission."[26] Patterson is persuasive, but Sambo still might have been genuinely servile. Certainly every effort was made to make him so. There is, therefore, room for uncertainty. The master might have had reason to suspect that Sambo's antics were a pretense only if he had evidence that they were. But if he is to know that he is not really servile, Sambo too needs such evidence.

It may be thought that if Sambo's ostensible servility was his way of "hitting back," in this he *was* providing evidence of self-respect. But this idea must be qualified. Unless it is already known to be a pretense, apparent servility is evidence of servility. If Sambo gave a perfect imitation of servility, neither he nor his master could have any reason to think he was anything but servile. If the Sambo personality's pretense is to provide him with evidence of his self-respect, it must, to some discernible extent, betray him. Patterson may be right that the "perfect stroke of rebellion must seem to the master as the ultimate act of submission,"[27] but the deception must succeed, not because it is undetectable, but because the master is so blinded by his own arrogance that he cannot see that what is presented as abasement is really thinly-disguised affront.

If the argument above is sound, only consummate artistry can enable a person to continuously and elaborately pretend to be servile and still know that he is self-respecting. Unless this strategy is executed by a master, the evidence of servility will seem overwhelming and the evidence of self-respect too ambiguous. But, as I have argued, the self-respecting person wants to know he is self-respecting. He hates deception and pretense because he sees them as obstacles to acquiring the knowledge that he is self-respecting. If only occasionally, he must shed his mask.

And this may not be easy. Not only does shedding the mask of servility take courage, but, if a person is powerless, it will not be easy for him to make others believe that he has been wearing a mask. People do not take the powerless seriously. So, since he wants to know that he is self-respecting, the powerless but self-respecting person is driven to make others take him seriously. He is driven to make the evidence of his self-respect unmistakable. And what better way to do this than to put his very life on the line for his rights and freedom?

It does not follow, of course, that the person with self-respect will always risk his life to defend his rights, or, when he does risk his life to defend his rights, will do so just in order to discover his self-respect. In Douglass's case, for example, he risked his life only at the point of desperation, and he did not do so in order to discover his self-respect. However, it is sufficient for my purpose that risking one's life for one's rights or being willing to die for one's rights often allows one to discover one's self-respect. But even if this is granted, we still do not have proof that we have a duty to self-respect to defend and protest the violation of our rights. To obtain this proof, we must investigate the subtle interplay between self-respect and self-esteem.

If self-esteem is a sense that one's goals are worthy and a confidence in one's abilities to achieve these goals, then since people have all sorts of abilities, and all sorts of goals, they have all sorts of grounds for self-esteem. Given the appropriate goals and abilities, a person can esteem himself for being a good teacher, a good jockey, a good liar, a good thief, a good assassin, and a good slave. Of particular importance here is the idea that a person can esteem himself for having self-respect, and especially for keeping his self-respect in defiance of powerful attempts to destroy it. The exhilaration Douglass felt after his fight with Covey was the exhilaration of feeling a sudden surge of self-esteem. For he discovered that, despite his fears, and despite the massive efforts Covey had made to take away his self-respect and make him servile, he had, after all, kept his self-respect.

Now, as I noted, self-esteem is, in part, confidence in one's ability to secure one's ends. Consequently, the person who has self-esteem because of his self-respect has confidence in his ability to retain that self-respect, and, if he further enhances that self-esteem by discovering that he has kept his self-respect in defiance of powerful attempts to destroy it, he further enhances his confidence in his ability to retain his self-respect—one of his ends. Now a person's confidence in his abilities enhances these abilities, or at least enhances the effective use of his abilities. One competitor has often surpassed others of equal or greater ability because he had self-confidence and they did not. Consequently, self-esteem for one's self-respect enhances one's ability to retain self-respect. And the discovery that one can retain one's self-respect in the face of aggression is likely to enhance one's ability to retain one's self-respect in the face of further outrages But, since self-respect is, fundamentally, reverence for morality, and one has a duty to revere morality, one therefore has a duty to retain one's self-respect. Hence, especially in cases where powerful efforts have been made to destroy anyone's self-respect, where he has had to pretend to be servile and has begun to doubt his self-respect, he may have a duty, derived from his duty of reverence for morality, to do whatever is necessary to discover and confirm that he nevertheless has retained his self-respect.

It should be clear from Douglass's account of his fight with Covey how self-defense, especially when it risks death or retaliation, may be a way of fulfilling that duty. But since protest is often an act of defiance, as for example, when it is a case of saying, "I accuse you, and I defy you to make me shut up," it may sometimes serve as well.[28] Accordingly, at least when it is of this nature, protest is invulnerable to the charge that it is an appeal for sympathy. But what of the other common charge, that it is undignified?

## Dignity

Melden, as we have seen, described the person with dignity as displaying an "expectation that his rights will be honored." But this is not quite right. A person may have every reason to expect that his rights will *not* be honored and yet have the greatest dignity—we have only to think of Socrates and Jesus. Neither is it true, if we read Melden literally, that the person with dignity *displays*, if he does not really possess, an expectation that his rights will be honored. This would make dignity a kind of bluff, which is absurd. The sense which the person with dignity conveys is the sense that his rights are so plain that, though they may be violated, whoever does so disgraces himself. That is, though he need not expect that his rights will be honored, or still less display such an expectation, he radiates so serene a sense that his rights are manifest as to tacitly, but unmistakenly and eloquently, call shame on all who refuse to acknowledge them.

I believe it was to secure for each of us a minimum of dignity that early statements about human rights in this country—for example the Declaration of Independence—proclaimed those rights self-evident. For this does not mean merely that we contradict ourselves if we deny that people have human rights. It means that it is evident without proof, i.e., that it is manifest that people have human rights.

The importance of the idea that some human rights are manifest is often acknowledged, though inadvertently, in the way in which philosophers discuss flagrant wrongs. For example, in one of the most perceptive passages on the subject of rights Richard Wasserstrom writes, "a society that simply lacks any conception of human rights is less offensive than one which has such a conception but denies that some people have these rights. . . . This is surely among the greatest of all moral wrongs."[29] It would be more accurate, I think, to describe it as among the most flagrant of all moral wrongs. Though a wrong may be great, it may also be subtle. Considerable acuity may be necessary to perceive it. But though Wasserstrom's assertion that the denial of human rights to some people is "among the greatest of all moral wrongs," may be controversial, it is surely not controversial to describe it as among the most flagrant of all moral wrongs. Consider how Wasserstrom illustrates his point: "A lengthy account in a Southern newspaper about the high school band program in a certain city . . . emphasized especially . . . that . . . all high school students in the city participated. Negro children never were nor could be participants in the program. The article, however, saw no need to point this out. I submit that it neglected to do so not because everyone knew the fact, but because in a real sense the writer and the newspaper do not regard Negro high school students as children—persons, human beings—at all."[30] What makes this incident so outrageous is not simply that Negro children were denied the exercise of their rights. Rather, it was the fact that they were denied the exercise of their rights *as a matter of course*, as if there were nothing to weigh, nothing to consider—and in particular as if no reason had to be given for treating them unequally.

This fact makes the wrong a flagrant wrong because it denies something which is, in a fundamental sense, *self-evident*. It is almost like stating that a circle is a square. When confronted with such a statement there is little that one can say in the way of argument. In his example, this is exactly how Wasserstrom describes the predicament of black people when they see the newspaper article: "What is the Negro parent who reads this article to say to his children? . . . How does a Negro parent even begin to demonstrate to the world that his children are children too?"

But exactly what is it that is denied, and is self-evident? Not that human beings have rights. This requires a proof and such a proof, if indeed it has been adequately shown, is certain to be very complex. What is denied, and is self-evident, is the fact of humanity on which such a proof must inevitably be based. As, with some modifications, I earlier endorsed A. I. Melden's insight about dignity, here I endorse his belief that the basis of rights in the human personality must lie "open before us," and "cannot be given in terms of mysterious and hidden phenomena of human life."[31] Consequently, my position is not that human beings manifestly have rights, nor that it is a flagrant wrong to deny all human beings their rights. My position is that if some human beings have rights, all manifestly do; and it is a flagrant wrong to accord some human beings their rights and deny these same rights to others.

This analysis alone explains the *indignation* of those whose human rights are violated. For indignation is not merely, as Feinberg says, the general response to what is "offensive to reason," but, more precisely, its is a response to the violation of a *known* truth.[32] For that reason the indignant, and those whose basic human rights are violated, often find it difficult to say anything by way of argument. Shylock, we may recall, could only point to what was already obvious: "Hath not a Jew eyes? Hath not a Jew organs, dimensions, senses, affections, passions?" And when Frederick Douglass declared that "Common sense itself is scarcely needed to detect the absence of manhood in a monkey, or to recognize its presence in a Negro,"[33] he was not making a point about biology or psychology. He was making the *moral* point that what is distinctive about human beings that entitles them to human rights is as obvious in black people as in white people.

But the manifest fact of humanity on which proof of the existence of human rights must be based not only entitles each of us to human rights; it also establishes a manifest propriety in our having human rights.

This propriety is based more than on the fact that people are capable of exercising their basic rights. Melden writes that "even if the origin of natural or human rights is to be ascribed to the agency of God, this would be intelligible only if in endowing men with rights God also endowed men with a nature suitable to the possession of those rights."[34] This may mean that if our natures were not suited to the possession of rights, if for example we were unable ever to exercise those rights, our having them would seem unintelligible, or at least pointless. This is no doubt true, but it does not cover my whole point. It is clear that our natures are suited to the possession of rights in the sense that we could exercise them even if we were not worthy of exercising them. My point is that our natures are suited to the possession of human rights in the sense that we are, simply because we are persons, worthy of exercising our rights. Or, more precisely, that if some are worthy of exercising their rights, all manifestly are. This is based on the fact that a proof that we have human rights must rest on the assumption that there is an intrinsic value in our exercise of our human rights.[35]

The claim that human dignity is the sense that one's manifest humanity makes one manifestly worthy of one's human rights is upheld by the universal feeling that the arrogant and blatant violation of human rights is not merely unjust but is, in addition, an offense to dignity and an insult. For the arrogant, blatant violation of human rights has symbolic import—it repudiates the rights it violates—and, as I argued in Chapter 6, insult is often a form of denial of the self-evident.

But there are insults which are offensive to human dignity and which tend to undermine it, but which do not involve violations of human rights. An analysis of them provides us with a subtler confirmation of my account of the nature of dignity. I am speaking of those insults that make their point through ridicule. An examination of them should furnish us with a particular insight into dignity, for ridicule is the great enemy of dignity. Abuse and deprivation can indiscriminately obliterate self-esteem, self-respect, and dignity. But ridicule is aimed precisely at dignity. For ridicule intends to *belittle*, and our experience of dignity, as Kolnai reminds us, "is centrally an experience of "Height.""[36]

The belittlement that is part of ridicule comes in different forms. Sometimes it implies unworthiness in its object, and in that case the ridicule is suffused with contempt. Angus ridiculed and expressed contempt for Macbeth in this way:

Now does he feel his title
hang loose about him, like a
giant's robe upon a dwarfish thief.

On the other hand, sometimes belittlement does not suggest unworthiness, but a more general unfittness. Thus, in declaring his Negritude, Léon Damas, a poet from French Guiana, wrote,

I feel ridiculous
in their shoes, in their dinner jackets,
in their shirts, in their detachable collars.[37]

In both cases ridicule consists of alleging or displaying a conspicuous incongruity in the object of attack.[38] Damas does not say that Europeans are ridiculous in dinner jackets and detachable collars. He says that *he* is (or feels), quite clearly because he feels that as a black man he is conspicuously incongruous in such clothes. Similarly, the point of Angus's simile is that Macbeth's crimes make him conspicuously incongruous on the throne of Scotland. Something very similar can occur in relation to rights. We can accord a person his rights yet make him appear ridiculous by making it seem as if there were a conspicuous incongruity in the idea of his having and exercising rights. This occurs when blacks are portrayed, as they are, for example, in certain movies and novels, doing all the things other people do, but as if there were something funny about it, or more subtly, as if they cannot be taken seriously doing these things. The effects of this form of ridicule are not hard to predict. Unless black people are on guard, they begin to not take themselves seriously and to join in ridiculing themselves—occurrences Dubois often noted and deplored. They begin to feel that, although they have rights, there is something funny about their having rights because they are not worthy of their rights, and there is no value in their exericse of them. And when this happens to anyone, though the person may continue to affirm his rights and to protest their violation, he will do so without the economy of words and gestures that comes from a sense of his manifest fitness for the possession of them; he will insist too strenuously and ostentatiously, or too meekly. In short, only when a person has already lost his dignity will his protest be undignified.

## Preferential Treatment and Self-respect

As we have seen, Thomas Sowell believes that preferential treatment is a kind of "charity," undermines blacks' "self-respect," and encourages "parasitic roles" and "Uncle Tomism." Many white commentators have expressed similar or related fears about preferential treatment, though they do not express themselves as bluntly. Thus, Barry Gross writes that the beneficiary of preferential hiring "may come to feel himself inferior;"[39] Thomas Nagel, an advocate for preferential treatment, still warns us that preferential hiring "cannot do much for the self-esteem of those who know they have benefited from it, and it may threaten the self-esteem of those in the favored group who would in fact have gained their positions even in the absence of the discriminatory policy, but who cannot be sure that they are not among its beneficiaries."[40]

The charges boil down to two The first is related to self-esteem. According to Nagel, for example, once preferential treatment is instituted, those of the preferred groups can never be confident of their merits and achievements. Even if they get good positions they cannot be confident that they got them because of their merits and achievements. Knowing that there is a policy of preferential treatment being enacted, they must know that they may have gotten their positions for reasons other than their merits and achievements. Even if one of them happens to have been the best person for the job, he will never know, and *others* will never know, that he is the best. His doubt will be compounded by their doubt. In this way a policy of preferential treatment is likely to generate a class of individuals plagued by misgivings about their merits and achievements that must eventually undermine their self-esteem.

The second charge against preferential treatment concerns self-respect. If preferential treatment creates a class of people who do not know for sure whether they are the most qualified for the positions they hold, it also creates a class of people who know for sure that they are *not* the most qualified for the positions they hold. And their penalty is worse.

It involves not only a loss of self-confidence, but a loss of honor, and feelings of embarrassment and resentment. Addressing this subject, J. Harvie Wilkinson III, editor of the *Norfolk Virginian Pilot* writes of the "temptation" to accept preferential treatment and the "resentment" accepting it must arouse,[41] and professor of philosophy Michael Levin writes that a person who is "publicly known to be preferentially hired" must feel himself to be a "fraud" and intensely "embarrassed."[42] But the temptations one resents succumbing to are temptations to do what one believes to be shameful, or beneath one's dignity or "better self"; and embarrassment is close to shame, which is the feeling we experience when we do or suffer something inconsistent with what we conceive to be our self-respect. Consequently, what these authors imply is that those who accept preferential treatment offend and endanger their self-respect and dignity.

The charge, as I understand it, is not that preferential treatment gives its beneficiaries rational grounds for divesting themselves of their self-respect or dignity. These qualities are qualities people *ought* to have. There can be no rational grounds for divesting ourselves of them. The charge is that preferential treatment gives its beneficiaries rational grounds for inferring that they do not have the dignity they thought they had, and this loss of self-esteem could lead to a loss of self-respect. I demonstrated earlier how a person who esteems himself for successfully defending his self-respect is better able to defend it again if he has to. The opposite is also true. A person who disesteems himself because he fears—truly or falsely—that he has lost his self-respect, makes himself even less able to keep his self-respect; and the same is true of dignity. In the balance of this chapter I will not discuss further the first charge—Nagel's—that preferential treatment endangers self-esteem. Instead I will focus on the second charge—that preferential treatment undermines self-respect.

Why, according to this view, should the beneficiary of preferential treatment feel embarrassed? And why should he feel that he has succumbed to a temptation to do something shameful or underhanded? The idea seems to be as follows: Positions should be filled by those who best fit them; these are the most meritorious; but the beneficiary of preferential treatment is not the most meritorious; hence he does not fit, or best fit, the position he accepts. If this argument is sound, the beneficiary of preferential treatment, like the dwarfish thief tripping and blundering around in a giant's robe too big for him, makes himself ridiculous and ought to be feel embarrassed; and, if he has any self-respect, he will resent preferential treatment for seducing him into thus losing his dignity.

The implication of this last assumption is that one requirement of dignity is that one fit the position one holds, and that a person with self-respect should be concerned about this aspect of dignity. I have no quarrel with this. Indeed, it is a generalization based on the conception of human dignity discussed earlier. To fittingly hold a position is to have, and be worthy of, certain concomitant institutional rights. For example, if Ronald Reagan is president and this is fitting, then has he, and is worthy of, certain rights defined by the political institutions of the United States. So, just as basic human dignity involves a sense of being worthy of one's human rights, dignity in a more general sense involves a feeling of being worthy of one's institutional rights. Moreover, a person with self-respect will be concerned about this aspect of dignity. He need not, of course, be concerned about being worthy of all his institutional rights. For he may justly believe that some of these rights are frivolous. But he will value those institutional rights he believes are important to him, and among these rights for example, the right to vote, will, of course, be those which secure his human rights. Now, if he values such rights he will try to make himself able to exercise them well and properly. That is, when it is fundamentally relevant, the self-respecting person *will* be concerned about being worthy of some institutional rights.

This conclusion extends a position taken by Thomas Hill, Jr. in his essay, "Self-Respect Reconsidered." As Hill observes, beside the aspect of self-respect which involves valuing one's rights, there is an aspect which involves imposing standards on oneself.[43] The point I wish to make here is that the person who has the first aspect of self-respect will also have the second. For, as I said, if a person values his human rights he will also value, and try to make himself worthy of, some institutional rights. And this means, of course, that he will impose standards on himself.

When a person thus imposes standards on himself he does so in two ways. On the one hand, by an effort to make himself worthy of his acquired rights; on the other hand, by giving up those rights of which he cannot make himself worthy. This conforms to common intuition. We disesteem a person as lacking in self-respect for clinging to the rights and privileges attached to a position he is manifestly unworthy of, and he can redeem himself in our eyes only if he makes himself worthy of those rights or gives them up.

These remarks may appear to concede that preferential treatment undermines self-respect, for they grant that a person strikes a blow to his self-respect is he accepts a position he is unworthy of, and it may appear that the beneficiaries of preferential treatment are unworthy of their positions since they are not the most meritorious. Maintaining that preferential treatment is just may not answer this objection. A just practice may conceivably, in some circumstances, systematically undermine self-respect.

But there is a flaw in this objection. The flaw is not that a person who gives up his rights because he feels he is unworthy of them misunderstands what rights are. This is necessarily true of human rights, for, although no one earns or merits these rights, everyone is worthy of them. But it is certainly not necessarily true of institutional rights. In many cases these rights *are* earned, or are meant to be earned, and in such cases, it is the person who will not give up rights of which he is unworthy who misunderstands what rights are. For example, the rules which confer the rights and privileges associated with some important, well-paid administrative posts are designed to pick out the candidates who are most worthy of the posts. If an unworthy candidate gains a post through some loophole in the rules, he demonstrates either his misunderstanding of the nature of rights, or his opportunism—and in either case his want of self-respect—if he insists on holding the post.

The flaw in the objection is the assumption that the only way to be worthy of rights is to merit them in the sense of having certain knowledge and skills. This is clearly not true of human rights, for although we are worthy of them, that worthiness is not a question of having knowledge and skills, but it is also not true of certain institutional rights, like the right to vote. Other things being equal, the more a person understands democracy and the political system in which he lives, the more he merits his right to vote. But, more important than this kind of worthiness to vote is his concern for the freedoms that a properly constructed democratic system secures. If he hates these freedoms and studies them only to better suppress them, he is unworthy of the right to vote. And if he loves them, however ignorant he may be of the subtleties of democratic theory—and he is not likely to be too ignorant, for one tries to learn how to protect what one loves—he is worthy of his right to vote. Worth then, may consist simply of valuing one's rights—that is, of having self-respect. Washington's oversight in relation to this point is instructive. He often observed—and he was perfectly correct to do so—that it is more important that we be prepared for voting than that we vote. His oversight was that he did not see that part of being prepared to vote—that is, I assume, to be worthy of the right to vote— is valuing freedom enough to be prepared to fight for the power to exercise the right to vote, if this right is denied. As Douglass said, "One of the first things necessary to prove the colored man worthy of equal freedom is an earnest and persevering effort on his part to gain it."[44]

The fact that merit is not the only thing that makes us worthy of our rights becomes even clearer when we consider that the rights at issue in considering preferential treatment are the rights and privileges that go with places in universities and professional schools, and with jobs. Those most worthy of these places and jobs are presumably those who most contribute to the purpose for which these places and jobs exist. But that purpose is not the development, reward, exercise, or display of merit—if this is understood as pure knowledge, or expertise, or talent. It is the production or just distribution of goods and services of value to the world. These goods and services must not be construed in a narrowly utilitarian way. They may be such things as the directly useful knowledge of medicine, but they may also be the useless, but aesthetically pleasing mathematics esteemed by the Cambridge mathematician G. H. Hardy. What they cannot be is socially useless, or objectively valueless. Otherwise we should have jobs and places for those with a talent for twiddling their toes or counting grains of sand on the beach. Consequently, factors other than merit may contribute to making a person worthy of a university place position. In particular, if being black enables black doctors to do a better job treating black patients than white doctors would do, and thus contributes to the social good of a just distribution of medical treatment, then being black helps to make a black candidate worthy of a place in medical school. And, if, as I've shown, he also deserves compensation for past unjust disadvantages, and a place in a certain school provides him with that compensation, then he is all the more worthy of the place.

Merit-conscious objections to this view often do not appear to have been well thought out. For example, the philosopher John Cottingham argues that, although the needs of a community "may well be paramount in deciding whether there should be" schools of various sorts, admissions criteria for these schools "have nothing to do with that decision: they are fixed, not extrinsically but intrinsically by the nature of the subject."[45] By this I imagine he means that admissions criteria should focus exclusively on the mastery of certain disciplines, like science, for example, in the case of medicine. But this is absurd. It would allow the possibility that a community could decide to establish a medical school *because its members needed medical attention*, but rationally admit to that school talented scientists who had no intention of practicing medicine!

If these arguments are sound, then preferential treatment *is* just, and does not give its beneficiaries rational grounds for doubting their self-respect. For the crucial objection to it that we have been examining is that the sense of being unworthy of one's position undermines one's self-respect. But, as we have seen, just rules distribute places and positions to the most worthy. The belief that preferential treatment undermines self-respect depends on confusing it with cases in which some person without the qualifications for a particular position, through some loophole in the rules, gets that position and thus acquires rights of which he is unworthy. If such a person insisted on exercising these rights he would indeed show that he lacked self-respect. But this, as I have demonstrated in this chapter, is not the situation of the beneficiaries of preferential treatment. The rules which give them rights are *designed* to give them rights because it has been calculated that they are the most worthy.

# 10

# The Limits of Civil Disobedience

## Martin Luther King, Jr.

George Wallace first became governor of Alabama in 1962, running on a platform emphasizing segregation and promising, among other things, to "stand in the school house door" to keep blacks out. When two black students got a federal court directive requiring their admission to a summer session at the University of Alabama in 1963, he tried to keep his promise. Eventually, Wallace backed down when the National Guard was mobilized to secure the students' admission, but the confrontation apparently moved John Kennedy to deliver, on television that same evening, what Richard Kluger has described as "by far the most moving words on the deprivations of black Americans that had ever been heard in the land on the lips of a high federal official."[1] "We are confronted," Kennedy declared, "with a moral issue as old as the Scriptures and as clear as the Constitution," and suiting his actions to his words, a week later he sent Congress a new and broadened civil rights program.

Kennedy did not live to see his program made law—he was assassinated that November—but it was finally approved by Congress a year later, when Lyndon Johnson was president. The Civil Rights Act of 1964 was the most far-reaching law supporting racial equality Congress had ever enacted. Among other things, it outlawed discrimination in most public accommodations, established a federal equal opportunity commission, and authorized the termination of, or withdrawal of federal funds from, federally assisted programs which practiced discrimination. Over the years, the federal government has made considerable use of the law.

Now, it was the protest marches, the demonstrations, and the acts of civil disobedience then going on in the South, and particularly in Alabama, which, directly or indirectly, provoked George Wallace's stand and the displays of racial animosity of which it was an example. Since it was these displays which moved the nation to appreciate the injustice of the color bar in the South, and to do something about it, considerable credit for the 1964 Civil Rights Act should go to that strategy of protest, demonstration, and civil disobedience, and to its chief architect—Martin Luther King, Jr. I have argued in preceding chapters that many color-conscious policies used to combat discrimination are just. It is reasonable, therefore, to consider whether the strategy King used so successfully to combat unjust color-conscious policies twenty years ago are likely to be as successful in securing just color-conscious policies today.

After King's great civil victories many people began to say that the civil rights movement had to move into a new phase. They pointed out that it didn't do black people much good to have the right to go to a restaurant if they didn't have the money to buy a meal there. Civil rights, they concluded, were not enough. Education, jobs, and, in the end, money, were also necessary. And some of them suggested that the strategy of protest and civil disobedience was inappropriate for securing these goods. These sentiments echoed Booker T. Washington, who also argued that the strategy of protest Frederick Douglass had used so valiantly against slavery was inappropriate to the tasks of racial uplift after Abolition.[2] The necessity for, and the success of, King's strategy of protest and civil disobedience show that Washington retired it prematurely, and the view that this strategy is generally inappropriate for winning economic justice may also be mistaken. However, I will argue in this chapter that it is unlikely to be successfully used to secure just color-conscious policies.

When in the spring of 1963 the city of Birmingham obtained a court order directing the demonstrations organized by King to cease until the demonstrators' right to demonstrate had been argued in court, King and the other organizers, knowing that this was an attempt to completely obstruct legitimate protest (it might have taken two or three years before any disposition of the case was made) decided to disobey the court order. King knew his critics would make two main objections to this decision: first that it endorsed lawlessness and anarchy, second that it was inconsistent with his own view that the rulings of the Supreme Court and the federal courts should be obeyed.[3]

King's initial answer to these objections was, in effect, that the court order he decided to disobey was invalid because it denied blacks rights guaranteed by the Constitution. But, as he was aware, this answer was incomplete. Because the court order was invalid his disobeying it was lawful. But that was not why he disobeyed it. He disobeyed it because his conscience told him it was unjust. And this basis for his decision reinstates the objection that it seems inconsistent for King to have urged people to obey the courts while he accepted only the authority of his conscience. He should have invited them to do what he did, i.e., to obey only the laws that their own consciences assured them were just. But then, if everyone disobeyed laws their consciences told them were unjust, this would produce anarchy and chaos.

The solution to this apparent dilemma is that King did not believe that the consciences of the segregationists differed from his own. He knew, of course, that the segregationists opposed the policies he proposed. But he believed that they did this out of prejudice or self-interest, not from conscience. It was this belief that underlay his unshakable optimism. Like Frederick Douglass before him, King believed that Americans shared one conscience and that this conscience was good. He admitted, of course, that they regularly acted unjustly. But he believed that this was because they did not consult their consciences. He was sure that if they could be moved to consult their consciences, they would not promote and enact unjust laws. Because of this assumption King was sure that his following his conscience did not set segregationists an example that would lead to chaos. And since he also believed that his strategy of protest and civil disobedience was indeed successful in moving people to consult their consciences, he was also sure that he was not provoking violence and lawlessness that would consume the state.

Many objections can be raised to this view. The most radical is that the conscientiousness of the civil disobedient is irrelevant to his goal. His goal is to convince the community that a law should be changed because it is unjust, and what is relevant to that goal is the persuasiveness of his arguments. These arguments may have nothing to do with his motives for disobeying the law. His motives may be purely self-interested, vain, or even immoral. If they are, he is hardly sincere or conscientious. But that does not matter. All that matters is whether his arguments that the law he disobeys is unjust are persuasive.

## Ronald Dworkin and Civil Disobedience

Such a view is, I think, implicit in Ronald Dworkin's essay "Taking Rights Seriously."[4] According to Dworkin, "A man does not have the right to do whatever his conscience demands." Indeed, he affirms that the idea of "a right to conscience" is a "red herring drawing us away from the crucial political questions."[5] If so, we can ignore the issue of whether a man is acting out of conscience when we are trying to answer the question of whether he is acting within his rights. But whether or not he is acting within his rights is the crucial question the civil disobedient wants to raise when he disobeys a law. Hence we can ignore the question whether he acts from conscience or not.

This argument is sound, but it would be a mistake to infer that *in general* the sincerity and consciences of civil disobedients are not essential to the theory of civil disobedience. Dworkin makes that mistake. This has not been noticed because he has presented two intertwined theories that obscure each other's weaknesses. According to his first theory, justifiable civil disobedience consists of a significant number of people sincerely and conscientiously disobeying the law because of widely held moral views. This theory, which I call populist because of the confidence it evinces in the wisdom and virtues of the common people, makes Dworkin's views on civil disobedience appear attractively equalitarian, but it is incoherent—though its incoherence is obscured by a second, less prominent, theory. This second theory has none of the popular orientation of the first. It does not conceive of justifiable civil disobedience as necessarily involving significant numbers of people disobeying the law sincerely, out of conscience. Instead, it conceives of such civil disobedience as necessarily involving disobedients—and there need be only one—who can make a "plausible case" for their disobedience. However, this theory too has fatal weaknesses. It is conservative and elitist, and makes civil disobedience largely irrelevant to the black struggle. I will examine each of Dworkin's theories in detail below.


DWORKIN'S POPULIST THEORY

Dworkin's first populist theory can be summarized by three main propositions:

1. In the United States civil disobedience is always disobedience of doubtful laws.

2. Disobedience of doubtful laws should almost always be treated with leniency. Therefore:

· 3. Civil disobedience should almost always be treated with leniency.

The first proposition follows from Dworkin's claim that, in the United States, at least, almost any law a significant number of people are tempted to disobey on moral grounds is also doubtful on constitutional grounds.[6] For, given that civil disobedience always involves a signifcant number of people disobeying, or tempted to disobey, a law on moral grounds, it follows that civil disobedience is always disobedience of doubtful laws.

The second proposition follows from Dworkin's claim that it cannot be unfair not to punish a man for disobeying a *doubtful* law, and furthermore, that encouraging people to disobey doubtful laws is a good way to test hypotheses about the interpretation of laws and thus to clarify and improve the law. So strongly does Dworkin feel about the second proposition that at one point he goes so far as to say that "when the law is unclear citizens have the *right* to follow their own judgment."[7] Though he cannot mean this literally, for it would contradict his view that sometimes the state is justified in prosecuting the civilly disobedient, it does indicate how strongly he is drawn to a policy of leniency for civil disobedients.

According to this account, every American racial group possesses equally the moral and intellectual resources to identify doubtful laws and to engender full-fledged civil disobedients. For all it requires of civil disobedients is that their numbers be significant, that they share a conventional political morality, and disobey on the basis of sincerely- and conscientiously-held moral beliefs. It does not require esoteric reasoning or deep knowledge of the law or the Constitution on their part.

My objection to this theory is that while its argument for leniency depends on the identification of doubtful laws, it simultaneously renders unreliable the very criterion it proposes for identifying doubtful laws— the fact of disobedients acting out of conscience.

This incoherence begins to manifest itself when we ask how we are to know whether the disobedients are acting out of conscience. Dworkin complains that the common belief that the law should always be enforced does not distinguish the man who acts on his own judgment of a doubtful law from the common criminal. But one wonders whether his own proposal is any better. How does *he* distinguish the two? According to his populist theory a law is doubtful when significant numbers are tempted to disobey it on moral grounds, i.e., out of conscience. But how can we tell if they are really tempted to disobey the law on moral grounds? The fact that they protest that they are is unworthy of serious consideration. Dworkin suggests that sincere disobedients can be distinguished by the kinds of laws they disobey—they tend to disobey laws like draft laws, for example, while common criminals tend to steal and cheat. This implies that, if the common criminal dares to make moral protestations, we will be able to see through them to his true motives of self-interest. This is an argument for partisans. If there are self-interested motives for stealing, there are far greater self-interested motives for dodging the draft. After all, people get maimed and killed in wars, and even three years of service interrupts a blossoming career. There are too many advantages to breaking most laws, and the ubiquity and force of motive of self-interest in human beings, as well as their capacity for self-deception in the service of those motives, are too well established to permit taking anyone's moral protestations at face value. It makes no difference if significant numbers are protesting.

King and Rawls have argued that the civil disobedients' willingness to accept the penalty helps to show that they are sincere and conscientious. But Dworkin cannot appeal to this argument. For, given his support of a policy of leniency for the civilly disobedient, we cannot infer that even those disobedients who do not avoid arrest are willing to accept the penalty. They could be expecting leniency. It is true that a willingness to accept the penalty is not the only way a disobedient can show his sincerity. A member of a religious group that demands considerable sacrifices from its members—Dworkin mentions the Seventh Day Adventists—shows his sincerity by the fact that he accepts and has accepted these sacrifices. But Dworkin objects to the policy of granting leniency only to those who profess religious grounds for their disobedience of the draft laws, and apparently wants the policy extended to all who profess moral grounds for their disobedience.

But unless there is independent evidence of their sincerity, for example, a religious life, a policy or near-policy of leniency *subverts*—and is acknowledged to subvert—civil disobedience. It is not for nothing that authorities refuse to, as they say "make a martyr" of someone. They know that if they do the community is liable to take him seriously. For the person who cannot assure the community that he is conscientious will not be taken seriously to the same degree even if he has plausible arguments. As most people know, the possession of a repertoire of plausible arguments is too often only self-interest cloaked in sophistry. If they are given no reason to believe that the civilly disobedient person was conscientiously trying to discover what is just or right, but instead are allowed to believe that he has only looked for plausible arguments to justify his self-interest, then they will tend to take his professions as only self-serving insincerity.

Dworkin's second theory is revealed obliquely by the way in which he deals with the possibility that segregationists may claim, as he explicitly allows, to have moral reasons for disobeying civil rights laws. Must we consider these laws doubtful? And if we do, must we follow Dworkin's recommendations and treat segregationist civil disobedients with leniency?

Dworkin himself says no, and his argument is as follows: Some laws are supported by the proposition that the individuals protected have a moral right to be free from the harm proscribed. Other laws are not supported by any supposition of an underlying right. We may tolerate disobedience of the second kind of law, but not of the first. Civil rights laws are the first kind of law. Hence disobedience of such laws cannot be tolerated. Indeed, to tolerate such disobedience would be to violate the rights of the persons protected by these laws. As Dworkin puts it, "If we take no action against the man who blocks the school house door . . . we violate the moral rights, confirmed by law, of the schoolgirl he blocks. The responsibility of leniency cannot go this far."[8]

However, this argument contradicts the criterion he has suggested for telling whether or not a law is doubtful. Segregationists, whose numbers were significant in the 1960s, claimed to be tempted to disobey civil rights laws on moral grounds. Therefore, according to Dworkin's criterion, the civil rights laws were doubtful. But if the civil rights laws were doubtful, the moral rights they were alleged to protect must also have been doubtful. Furthermore, the existence of these moral rights cannot be "confirmed by law." As Dworkin repeatedly—and correctly—reminds us, neither the law nor the Supreme Court is infallible. That is, neither can "confirm" any moral right. The Dred Scott decision did not, and could not, confirm the property rights of slave masters over slaves, and regardless of what the Supreme Court said, a judge who took no action against a person who helped slaves escape would not be violating the "moral rights, confirmed by law" of slave masters. Consequently, when Dworkin refuses to extend leniency to the segregationist civil disobedient on the grounds that the Supreme Court has "confirmed" a right they violate, he accords to the Court precisely that moral authority which he had previously properly denied it.

DWORKIN'S ELITIST THEORY

It follows that, since Dworkin is right in maintaining that segregationist civil disobedients cannot be tolerated, but is unable to justify this argument with his populist theory, he must have another theory. This other theory, his elitist theory, differs from the first in its criterion for judging a doubtful law. A law is doubtful, according to this second account, if a "plausible case can be made on both sides" of it.[9] This second criterion certainly has advantages over the first. For example, it permits us to maintain, without any contradiction, that segregationists who disobey civil rights should not be tolerated. For we can argue that, however significant their numbers or sincere their claims, they do not have a plausible case and hence, the laws they disobey are *not* doubtful. Nevertheless, despite this agreeable conclusion, the second criterion is also worrisome.

The populist theory granted that every racial group was equally capable of engendering civil disobedients. This egalitarianism disappears in the second theory. Given that both justice and the law are complex, it follows that those most likely to come up with plausible arguments against a law that offends their sense of justice—or obstructs their self-interest—are the well-educated, those who can pay for legal expertise, and the well-connected. But according to the second theory, a doubtful law is one that people raise plausible arguments against. Hence, Dworkin's suggested policy of leniency for those who disobey doubtful laws would mean more leniency extended to the well-educated, the well-to-do, and the well-connected—usually white—than to the poor and black. And this points to another unfairness. Dworkin argues that a policy of encouraging disobedience of doubtful laws helps test hypotheses about what the law means and thus helps to clarify and improve the law. But given that these results are benefits, they will, if my criticism is sound, accrue mainly to the well-to-do, the well-educated, and the well-connected.

To sum up—my criticism of Dworkin's theory of civil disobedience is that it is really two theories, neither of which is satisfactory. The main tenet of the populist theory—that almost any law a significant number of people are tempted to disobey on moral grounds is doubtful—is true, but the theory is incoherent. The main tenet of the elitist theory—that laws are doubtful if plausible arguments can be raised against them—is also true, but the theory invites too many unfairnesses.

## John Rawls's Theory of Civil Disobedience

Having rejected both Dworkin's theories, I will now consider that of John Rawls, which stresses the importance of the conscience and sincerity of the disobedient and which, Rawls says, puts King's views in a "wider framework."[10] In order to comprehend his theory, we must first understand what is meant by conscience and sincerity.

CONSCIENCE

Martin Luther King, Jr., appealed to America's conscience because he believed everyone had the same conscience he had. It may be objected that people's consciences differ radically, and, in particular, that the consciences of most of the white Americans to whom King appealed did not acknowledge that blacks were morally equal to whites. Gunnar Myrdal's claim that the black condition conflicts with America's conscience, that "Americans are worried about it. It is on their minds and on their consciences,"[11] has been vehemently criticized on the grounds that it mistakenly assumes that whites think of blacks as moral equals. These criticisms would be more to the point if the assumption of a common conscience included the assumption that Americans, deep down, agree on all moral questions. This is certainly implausible. But King's assumption was only that, deep down, Americans agree on questions pertaining to the *justice of law*—a much less controversial view. Furthermore, though people often disagree on such questions, they are likely to do so less often if they tried to answer the questions conscientiously. This would involve that they scrupulously attend to all the arguments for and against the issue, check to see that they have all the facts straight, and, acknowledging the human capacity for self-persuasion and self-deception in the service of self-interest, make every effort to be sure that their judgment is really based on moral principle. Further, to ensure these ends the person who conscientiously seeks to know what is right often submits his initial findings to others for examination before he finally decides what it is that his conscience tells him is right. Thus, assuming that much of the disagreement over the justice of laws can be traced to self-interest, self-deception, and ignorance, it is not entirely farfetched to suppose that, if people conscientiously tried to decide what justice required of law, they would not infrequently find common ground.

Now, as I have argued, a person who has made a decision conscientiously has exhaustively considered the pros and cons of the issue at hand. If reasons and facts have anything to do with morality this suggests any judgment he offers could be right, or at least that, even if it is wrong, a consideration of his views is worthwhile because it could deepen and enrich our comprehension of morality.

Consequently, if the ultimate aim of the civilly disobedient person is to persuade the community that certain of its laws are unjust, clearly, his first step should be to convince it that he is conscientious. That is, he must persuade it that his claim that he is disobeying the law because of conscience is sincere. How can he do this? To answer this question we must understand clearly what it means to be sincere.

SINCERITY

Failure to mislead someone is not necessarily sincerity. Insincerity and hypocrisy can both be transparent. To be sincere, the agent must be concerned not to mislead. For example, a person is sincere if he intends his words or actions to express his beliefs. But he is not necessarily sincere just because we can accurately infer his beliefs from his words or actions. On the other hand, a person is not necessarily insincere just because we cannot accurately infer his beliefs from his words or actions. To be sincere, he must be concerned to mislead. For example, we cannot justly accuse a person of insincerity just because he deliberately conceals his motives and beliefs. Being poker-faced is not necessarily being insincere. To be insincere a person must try to mislead us about his motives and beliefs. Finally, the sincere person is not only honest with others. He is also honest with himself. Just as he is concerned that what he tells others does not mislead them about his beliefs, attitudes, and motives, he is concerned that what he tells himself does not mislead him about his beliefs, attitudes, and motives.[12]

If these considerations are sound, to have a reasonable hope of success, civil disobedients must demonstrate both their sincerity and their conscientiousness to the community. Both conditions are necessary: No community will consider altering its laws just because some people sincerely believe these laws unjust; and no community will seriously consider a disobedient's arguments if it thinks he does not take them seriously himself. But a demonstration of sincerity is the first desideratum. Without it the conscientiousness of civil disobedients will not be recognized and will avail them nothing.

How can the civil disobedient convince the community that his claim that he is conscientious is sincere? Normally, saying that he is will not be sufficient. As I've noted, it is always easy to impute a self-interested motive to those who break the law—even if it is only the desire to be noticed. Unless the civil disobedient can do something to rule out such motives, the community will suspect him of insincerity. And it must be admitted that it has reason to. For an act to be conscientious, the agent's motive must be that he believes the act is right, not that doing it is to his advantage. But there are almost always advantages to breaking the law. This is especially obvious when the civil disobedient breaks the law because he claims he has a right which it prevents him from exercising. Given that rights are usually to one's advantage, and that people usually have motives for doing what is to their advantage, it follows that neither the community, nor even the civil disobedient himself, will find it easy to know when his act of disobedience is really conscientious. For in order to know this, they must be certain that he would disobey the law even if he failed to have the self-interested motives which he in fact has.

This suggests that the civil disobedient can help establish his sincerity by acting on his conscientious belief in what is right even in situations in which he cannot plausibly have a self-interested motive for his actions. The problem with this is that such situations may not be easy to find or contrive.

As we've seen, one solution to the problem of recognizing sincerity maintains that the civil disobedient be willing to accept the penalty for his disobedience. The assumption is that a willingness to accept the penalty eliminates the motive of self-interest as the basis of the civil disobedient's actions since, presumably, accepting a penalty cannot be in his self-interest. But this argument has weaknesses. The civil disobedient who accepts the penalty for disobeying the law certainly goes some way toward showing that it is not in his immediate or short term interest to disobey the law. But he does not prove that his motive for disobeying the law was not self-interest. For, though it may not be in his short-term interest to break the law, it may yet be in his long-term interest to do so. This is especially obvious in the case of indirect civil disobedience. In such a case, the disobedient disobeys one law to protest another. If the law he chooses to disobey carries only a very minor penalty for transgression, and the law he protests disadvantages him considerably, self-interest alone may, plausibly, still be his motive.

The disobedient's attempt to demonstrte conscientiousness will also often be inconclusive. Being conscientious does *not* entail having arguments all will find plausible to support one's actions. Though a person may examine his conscience and decide that a law is unjust, his arguments may not seem plausible to the community. And because the community is liable to consider the absence of arguments it finds plausible as evidence of a lack of conscientiousness, it is liable to conclude that he is not conscientious.

The difficulty in demonstrating sincerity and conscientiousness will be especially grave for blacks attempting to urge the implementation of color-conscious policies. First, because these policies are in blacks' interest, the suspicion that claims of conscientiousness are a smokescreen for self-advancement is certain to be strongly aroused. Second, because the arguments for these policies are complex and raise hard questions, they are not likely to seem accessible and plausible to the community, and therefore the suspicion that those raising them are not conscientious is also likely to be strongly aroused. These points, taken together, suggest that civil disobedience is not likely to be a strategy much used by black Americans today to urge color-conscious policies. For, as the difficulty of demonstrating sincerity and conscientiousness rises, the penalties that must be accepted in order to demonstrate them become proportionately greater.

It may be objected that I have created the impasse above because I have ignored Rawls's warning that it civil disobedience is "a political act addressed to the sense of justice of the community then it seems reasonable, other things equal, to limit it to instances of substantial and clear injustice . . ."[13] With this qualification the impasse seems to disappear. If the injustice is "substantial and clear," or as Rawls also puts it, "blatant,"[14] then my fear that civil disobedients may have to accept excessively severe penalties in order to demonstrate their conscientiousness and sincerity seems unfounded.

This is true. But there are also costs in accepting Rawls's qualification: If we limit civil disobedience to cases of "clear" and "blatant" injustice, we limit drastically the conditions we can protest through civil disobedience; and since substantial injustices need not be blatant, there may be conditions that are substantially unjust to black people which cannot be protested by civil disobedience.

Furthermore, it is invalid to argue, as Rawls does, that because civil disobedience is an appeal to the community's sense of justice, it must be limited to clear and substantial injustice. If this were valid, then, since doubtful laws are, by definition, not clearly unjust, Dworkin's theory of civil disobedience, which allows disobedience of "doubtful" laws, could not involve an appeal to the community's sense of justice. But Dworkin's theory does involve such an appeal. The act of civil disobedience is designed to move the community to consult its collective conscience on the subject of the condition protested. It is not necessary for the injustice of the condition protested to be blatant. Indeed, if it were, I cannot see how Rawls can say, as he does, that civil disobedience is especially adapted to nearly just societies. I would have thought that in such societies blatant injustices would be eliminated simply by pointing to them.

The idea that civil disobedience should be limited to cases of clear and substantial injustice is not the only conclusion Rawls draws from the theory that civil disobedience is an appeal to the community's sense of justice. He also draws the conclusion that civil disobedience must be nonviolent. Violent acts, Rawls notes, are "incompatible with civil disobedience as a mode of address."[15] Furthermore, if civil disobedience were violent, because of the fear it would tend to arouse in people, not only would it be a threat and not an appeal, it would also, as Marshall Cohen notes in a discussion of Rawls in his essay "Liberalism and Disobedience," put "men beyond the reach of rational and moral persuasion,"[16] and would thus undermine appeals to their sense of justice.

Now, people feel threatened, not only by violence against their persons, but also by violence against their property. Consequently, if civil disobedience should not be threatening, it should be nonviolent not only toward people, but also toward their property. Rawls is usually interpreted as meaning just this. Thus, Cohen, in the essay just mentioned, grants that Rawl's views are persuasive when they are interpreted as a prohibition against "violence against other persons," but less persuasive "when violence against property is in question."[17] However, in keeping with the stipulation that civil disobedience should not threaten, Cohen restricts allowable violence against property to violence against public property.

Thus he writes, "violation of symbolically important property may be a dramatic and not truly threatening way of lodging effective protest."[18]

But it is invalid to argue, as Rawls does, that because civil disobedience is an appeal to the community's sense of justice it is incompatible with threat. If this view were valid, then King's practice of civil disobedience would have contradicted the premise Rawls shares with him—that civil disobedience is an appeal to the community's sense of justice. For, although King opposed violence, he did not oppose the use of threats. Thus, he wrote that he wanted to "bring pressure on the merchants" through a campaign of civil disobedience at Easter since after Christmas "this was the largest shopping period of the year."[19] And I think it is quite clear that on this point King was right and Rawls is wrong. Even if the civilly disobedient are appealing to the community's sense of justice, there is no reason why threats cannot sometimes serve their purpose by compelling the community to carefully consider their arguments and the condition they protest as being unjust.

## Justice and Harmony

These are not simply mistaken inferences of Rawls's. Nor are they explained by assuming that Rawls was proposing a form of civil disobedience for societies more nearly just than our own. The fact is, as numerous commentators have noted, Rawls seems to conceive of our society as nearly just and his form of civil disobedience is proposed for this society. Rawls's inferences about justifiable civil disobedience stem from his broad view of the nature of the just society, and of the harmony which, like Plato, he thinks is naturally associated with it. For Rawls uses his contracterian theory of justice to show that social harmony flourishes naturally in large complex and plural societies when justice is present. That is why he cannot conceive of civil disobedients, in a nearly just society, having to go to heroic lengths to establish their sincerity and having to use threats, and as King allows, "pressure" to compel the community into consulting its conscience. But I maintain that, except in small and simple societies, justice and harmony are not naturally associated, that Rawls overlooks the danger of people combining in stable and well-knit groups to exploit and injure outsiders, and that his view is, ultimately, conservative because it obscure the justification for the kind of pressure King's theory of civil disobedience calls for.

Not all social contract theorists overlook the danger of people combining to dominate others. For example, because Rousseau was aware of that danger he argued that there should be no "partial associations" in the state, or, if these were unavoidable, that they should be as numerous and as equal as possible.[20] He took this stand because he believed that human beings could, if appropriately socialized, acquire intense loyalties to groups and group ideals and that these loyalties are not always merely veneers for a crafty egoism. This confidence in the efficacy of socialization was the basis of Rousseau's recommendation that citizens regularly engage in public discussion and ratification of the law. He believed that this kind of political participation was an essential part of socialization and would give people an effective sense of justice and dispose them to act on principles which they would otherwise be incapable of willingly following.

But, if the theory that people can be socialized to the extent that they conquer their egoism shows why they can often be trusted to obey the law even when the law is not in their interests, it also shows why they often form stable, well-knit groups that exploit and dominate their fellow citizens. For, if people can grow out of their natural egoism and become loyal to a society, then perhaps they will even more readily grow out of their egoism and become loyal to lesser groups *within* a society. But, as I noted in Chapter 3, it is egoism which engenders free-riders, who in turn undermine groups and group loyalties. Consequently, if socialization can raise people above egoism, free-riders do not necessarily undermine groups, and while this means that people can often, in opposition to their self-interests, obey the law, it also means that people can form stable, enduring, and free-rider-resistant groups that treat their fellow citizens unjustly. Rousseau was well aware of this danger. He opposed smaller groups within society because he saw that, just as participation in the affairs of a society creates loyalties to that society, the *intenser* participation in the affairs of *smaller* groups *within* society creates *intenser* loyalties to those groups than to society at large, and, correspondingly, the danger of systematic and persistent group injustice.

Accordingly, realizing that large and complex societies are likely to harbor smaller groups within them, Rousseau concluded that for a society to forestall relationships of domination and subservience among its citizens, it must be small and simple. Modern social contract theorists reject this restriction and apply the theory of the social contract to large, complex societies. Rawls, for example, apparently sees no limit to the size and complexity of societies whose legitimacy can be established by a social contract. Indeed, seeing the advantages of such complexities, he insists on them, and shares none of Rousseau's misgivings.

Yet he assumes, as Rousseau did, that people undergo fundamental change because of socialization, have genuine loves and loyalties. But if this is so, and if the large and complex society he endorses is likely to harbor stable, well-knit, and probably even self-perpetuating groups, then, for the reasons outlined, Rawls's theory of justice and its relationship to society should fully acknowledge and be prepared to deal with the danger of group injustice.

But instead, Rawls develops his theory in such a way as to underplay that danger. For example, he argues that the principles of justice that should be applied to a society are principles that it would be rational for individuals to choose, behind the veil of ignorance. Now, among the principles of justice which he argues they would rationally choose is what he calls the "Difference Principle," a principle for the redistribution of wealth which demands that permissible inequalities be to the advantage of the least advantaged. But when Rawls derives from his theory principles of justice for societies or nations in relation to one another, that is, international justice, he introduces a dramatic variation of his argument for the social contract. In this case, the original position consists, he maintains not of individuals as such, but of representatives of *states*. Furthermore, although they too are behind a veil of ignorance, they agree only to adhere to principles of self-determination and non-aggression.[21] They do not agree to redistributive principles, and in particular, not to the Difference Principle. But why not? Rawls reasons that an individual choosing principles of justice for his society behind the veil of ignorance will be careful to maximize even the minimum position in that society since he knows it could be his position. Therefore he will particularly choose the Difference Principle. But exactly the same reasoning supports the conclusion that representatives of states *would* choose an international Difference Principle. Like individuals who know that their position in society could be the least advantaged, they know that their states could be the least advantaged. As the political scientist Brian Barry notes, there is no reason why the representatives should not agree to "some sort of international maximum."[22] Consequently, if nations are conceived of as persisting, self-perpetuating groups, Rawls's idea of the principle of international justice seems to ignore, and indeed to justify, group injustice.

The political scientist Charles R. Beitz has argued that Rawls's views on international injustice "make sense only on the empirical assumption that nation-states are self-sufficient."[23] And, somewhat similarly, the philosopher Thomas Scanlon has concluded that, "wherever there is systematic economic interaction between states, the Difference Principle would apply to the world economic system taken as a whole."[24] But while I endorse both argument and conclusion, I submit that, beside the empirical assumption that nation-states are self-sufficient, there is another, more likely, and more theoretically interesting reason why Rawls may have failed to apply the Difference Principle to the world economic system taken as a whole.

In the first place, it is very unlikely that Rawls makes the empirical assumption that nation-states are self-sufficient since that assumption is preposterous. Contemporary Third World demands for a new international economic order do not stem from any recent discovery of the fact and historical importance of international trade to the economic growth and well-being of nations. Consequently, we must, if we want to understand Rawls, find a better explanation for his shying from applying the Difference Principle world-wide.

One explanation lies in the fact that Rawls's rational contractors, whose choices determine the principles of justice, need not be prepared to choose redistributive principles such as the Difference Principle just because they acknowledge that they interact economically. According to Rawls, before they agree to such principles they must, knowing the facts of human psychology, anticipate that they will be able to freely honor what they agree to. Thus, he states that the contracting parties "cannot enter into agreements that may have consequences they cannot accept."[25] They know human nature and know that they have a "capacity for justice," but they also know that certain compacts "exceed the capacity of human nature" and cannot be "made in good faith."[26] So, though the parties may envision the prospect of world-wide economic interaction, according to Rawls it does not follow that they will agree that the Difference Principle should apply to the world. They may anticipate that this would exceed what they could actually implement. Thus, by stipulating that contracting parties must be able to freely do what they agree to, Rawls neatly undercuts any demands for redistribution among nations.

But is the requirement that the contracting parties agree only to what they can freely honor essential to the social contract theory? Rawls argues that it is because "for an agreement to be valid the parties must be able to honor it under all relevant and foreseeable circumstances."[27] But this is surely false if it means—as it must if it is to support Rawls's view—that for an agreement to be valid the parties must be able to *freely* honor it under all relevant and foreseeable circumstances. For then many, if not most, legal agreements would be invalid. When people marry, for example, the validity of their agreement does not depend on an assumption that the man and woman will always be able to freely keep their agreement. That is why the marriage contract which they sign empowers the state to compel each of them to do what they have agreed to do. Neither does either party prove the original contract invalid by demonstrating that he or she is psychologically incapable of freely fulfilling its terms.

It is true, of course, that if there is no provision for, or possibility of, compulsion, and a person makes an agreement he knows he cannot, and therefore will not, freely honor, then he acts in bad faith. But it is still false to conclude that his agreement was invalid, at least if this implies that he really made no agreement. It would be true to say simply that he made an agreement he knew that he could not keep. It would be true to say that he made no agreement only if the party to whom he said "I agree," knew that he could not freely do what he said he would do, and that he could not be compelled to do so. But these hypotheses are not germane to social contract theory. In the social contract the contractors explicitly provide for a sovereign who will compel them to do what they say they will do. Nor, if they agree to be compelled to do what they may not be able to do freely, does it follow that they have made no agreement. Such an inference begs the question and is unwarranted. What is essential to an agreement is that the contractors make provisions enabling them to do what they say they will do.

What is more, Rawls seems after all to concede all this. Thus, he allows that the contractors agree to a sovereign power which will enforce the principles of justice. ". . . to maintain public confidence in the scheme that is superior from everyone's point of view," he writes, "some device for administering fines and penalties must be established. It is here that the mere existence of an effective sovereign, or even the general belief in his efficacy has a crucial role."[28] It may be objected that this does not indicate that Rawls allows that principles of justice may be principles people cannot freely honor because the sovereign he postulates operates, not to compel people to do what they cannot do freely, but to enhance stability by compelling them to do what they may, from weakness or temptation, choose not to do freely. But this objection would be difficult to maintain. Rawls knows that there may be many people in society who are not at all disposed to act justly. This, however, does not move him to suggest that social contractors, who since they know human nature, also know this, might choose different, perhaps less stringent, principles. Instead, he says that "under such conditions penal devices will play a much larger role in the social system," insisting that this unfortunate possibility makes no difference either to the content or rationality of the contractors' choices. "None of this," he writes, "nullifies the collective rationality of the principles of justice; it is still to the advantage of each that everyone else should honor them."[29]

But while Rawls thus appears to concede that stability and justice may depend on compulsion, he underplays its role. "It is reasonable to admit certain constraining arrangements to insure compliance, but," he warns, "their main purpose is to underwrite citizens' trust in one another. These mechanisms will seldom be invoked and will comprise but a minor part of the social scheme."[30] He thinks that social stability and justice will depend much more on friendship, trust, and the public's sense of justice. Thus, while he admits that a general belief in the sovereign's efficacy may lead to stability, he adds that ". . . it is evident how relations of friendship and mutual trust and the public knowledge of a common and normally effective sense of justice bring about the same result."[31] But here Rawls understates the advantage of his own position. As Plato saw clearly, the stability brought about by mere law and order is not much to boast about. "A master passion," Plato wrote, "is enthroned in absolute domination over every part of the soul of the despotic man,"[32] but, though there is evidently law and order in such a soul, he did not admire it. Similarly, a sovereign can keep order among unwilling citizens. What Plato recognized as essential to his argument is that the citizens of the state willingly accept the role of its guardians,[33] and that the parts of the soul are trained to obey reason.[34] He insisted on this quality, which he called temperance, and likened to harmony, because it was essential to his argument that justice pays.[35] Likewise, when Rawls insists that people can acquire an effective sense of justice, and learn to willingly obey the dictates of justice, he is not merely describing an alternate way of securing stability. He is trying to persuade us that justice is associated with harmony, fraternity, and good fellowship; and that, ultimately, it pays.

Of course, if we want to be just more than anything else, justice pays. As Rawls notes, assuming a "settled desire to take up the standpoint of justice" in a sense makes the argument for the good of the sense of following justice "trivial,"[36] for those with a settled desire to take up the standpoint of justice "desire more than anything to act justly and fulfilling this desire is part of their good."[37]

But Rawls's requirement that we must be capable of freely honoring the principles of justice we agree to operates in a more substantial way to justify the claim that justice pays. Thus, as Rawls acknowledges, a more serious problem about the good of the sense of justice emerges when we ask whether being just is consistent with having other things generally considered to be good. And he grants that "Whether it is for a person's good that he have a regulative sense of justice depends on what justice requires of him."[38] Consequently, given the fact of worldwide economic interaction, we should expect him next to raise the question of whether being just is advantageous if it requires that the difference principle apply across national boundaries. But Rawls never even mentions this point. However, he does discuss another, very similar, question, and his response to it is revealing.

That question is whether or not being just is for a person's own good, if the requirements of justice are *utilitarian*. Now, according to Rawls, in requiring us to sacrifice our interests for "the greater happiness of all," utilitarianism is too "stringent" a doctrine. "A rational person," he writes, would hesitate to agree to a principle which would be "likely both to exceed his capacity for sympathy and to be hazardous to his freedom."[39] And he thinks this fact gives his "contract doctrine" a decided advantage over utilitarianism. What is significant about utilitarianism in the present context is that many theorists believe that one of its very prominent "stringencies" is its demand that rich nations share their wealth with poor ones; and what is revealing about Rawls's theory is that he thinks that it lacks such a demand. But it lacks such a demand only because of his requirement that we—the contracting parties—agree only to what we are capable of doing freely. Hence this requirement helps to justify the argument that justice pays by subtly restricting the demands of justice to such persons of whom it plausible to say that justice pays.

But why shouldn't the demands of justice not be *sometimes* too stringent to expect normal persons to freely comply? Why shouldn't it be possible that when justice demands that persons share with distant people they do not understand or with those they find it difficult to identify with, that justice is resisted? I do not see why not. Consider Rawls's contractarian derivation of principles of international justice. I submit that self-interested and rational beings acting behind a veil of ignorance which prevents them from knowing their countries would agree to an international Difference Principle, even if they knew that when the veil is lifted, those in rich countries would not honor the principle freely. The same prudential reasoning that would move them to agree to acknowledge the Difference Principle for a particular society would move them to agree to acknowledge the Difference Principle for the world.

It will be objected that, even according to my account of the requirement for agreement, the contractors would still not agree to an international Difference Principle because they would know that there is no sovereign international power able to compel compliance with such an agreement. But this would beg the question. Contractors agreeing to principles for a particular society would not fail to agree to follow the Difference Principle, nor would that principle fail to be a just one, just because that society does not have a sovereign power able to enforce it. Quite the contrary. The contractors would still choose the Difference Principle, and because that principle is a principle of justice, their agreement would also imply an agreement to provide for a sovereign power. Consequently, if the Difference Principle fails to be adhered to because there is no sovereign, then the disadvantaged are fully justified in feeling that they have been treated unjustly, and in agitating for a sovereign power. This argument also applies to the question of international justice. Unless it is proven that an international power capable of enforcing an international Difference Principle *cannot* exist, the fact that it *does not* exist does not support the argument that this principle is not a principle of internatioanl justice, nor, consequently, the argument that poor nations cannot agitate— on the grounds that they demand justice—for its implementation.

If this general line of argument is sound, it is unlikely that justice will be naturally associated with stability or, at least, with harmony. Since the Difference Principle can be applied world-wide, then, as the less advantaged come to realize this, more and more of them will demand its implementation, and since it is a principle of justice, will do so with all the resentment and urgency of people denied justice. At the same time, if Rawls is right about the limits of the human "capacity for sympathy," the more advantaged will meet these demands with ever stiffening resistance. In the end, a sovereign power, invoking penalties far more readily than Rawls had anticipated will be necessary, and while this may restore stability, it will hardly restore harmony.

Furthermore, this process is likely to proceed within states as well, especially if their societies are large, complex, and plural. For, according to the most plausible accounts of its nature, the sense of justice develops as the culmination of a psychological progression which includes love, friendship, loyalty, camaraderie, the various sentiments of the "morality of association" and pity.[40] Consequently, though persons with a sense of justice feel, at least to some degree, bound by sentiments of justice to all, they also feel bound, by more urgent and less intellectualized sentiments, only to some. And this suggests that the average person with a sense of justice is far less likely to transgress against friends, associates, fellow workers, and those of his own particular group than againt faceless, nameless outsiders, and that if he does transgress against the former his sense of justice will aggravate him more severely than it would if he transgressed against the latter. Similarly, people are far more likely to render justice to those they readily identify with, and far less likely to suffer for the injustice they do to those they do not readily identify with. For pity is the ally of the sense of justice, and pity is the "innate abhorrence to see beings suffer that resemble" one and is more potent when the one who "beholds the distress identifies himself with the animal that labors under it."[41] Finally, when we add to these points the fact that there are advantages in exploiting others, that human beings, to varying but always considerable degrees seek their own advantage, and that concerted group action is highly effective in extracting benefits from outsiders to the advantage of group members, we have to conclude that large, complex, and plural societies have a built-in tendency to engender systematic group injustice, and, accordingly, to be plagued by the instabilities and disharmonies of group conflict.

Rawls says that "if a conception of justice is unlikely to generate its own support, or lacks stability, this fact must not be overlooked. For then a different conception of justice might be preferred,"[42] and also observes that "other things being equal, the preferred conception of justice is the most stable one."[43] But why *must* this be so? Why assume that good things tend to come together? The danger is that, having the more visible good—in this case harmony—we may be deceived into believing that we also have the less visible but greater good—in this case, justice.

The subject of this chapter has been whether or not the strategy of civil disobedience which Martin Luther King used so successfully to secure blacks' civil rights is likely to be used successfully to establish and implement just color-conscious policies. I rejected certain theories about the nature of civil disobedience on the grounds that they were either incoherent or irrelevant, and considered at length Rawls's theory because Rawls presents it as being in some important sense similar to King's. I conceded that they are indeed similar insofar as they both stress that civil disobedients must demonstrate their conscientiousness and sincerity, though I also noted that the cost of such demonstrations on behalf of color-conscious policies is likely to be prohibitively high. However, I also argued that the theories of Rawls and King are not similar insofar as King's theory grants that civil disobedience could involve pressure, whereas Rawls's theory sees such pressure as inconsistent with civil disobedience as a mode of addressing society. The basis of Rawls's view, I argued, is his false linkage of justice with harmony, and his failure to see that, especially in large, complex, and plural societies, the two conditions are not likely to be found together. If I am right, then, rejecting the austerities of a small and simple society, where that linkage might obtain, we are compelled to recognize, on a theoretical level, the extreme improbability of the existence of genuine harmony and justice, which also implies that in large complex and plural societies, even when they are nearly just, pressure of the sort King described may have to be part of civil disobedience. But while this is true, in only strengthens the conclusion that black civil disobedients will have to accept severe penalties in order to demonstrate their sincerity and conscientiousness if their goal is the implementation of color-conscious policies, and consequently, that however just such policies are, civil disobedience is not likely to be much used to secure them.

# 11

# The Surrender to Injustice

The civil rights revolution and its resulting legislation led to a dramatic flourishing of the black middle class. More blacks were attending colleges and universities than ever before, many were attending the very best colleges and universities, and well-educated blacks were earning the same salaries as equally educated whites. All this and more was enthusiastically announced in books, scholarly journals, and the popular press, and it created the general impression that at last blacks were finally joining the American mainstream. Unfortunately this impression was misleading. Only a part of the black population was becoming better off. The black poor were becoming worse off at the same time that the black middle class was becoming better off. At first both policy-makers and the public were too dazzled by the advances of the black middle class to notice this, but then scholars who were aware of the condition of the black poor called on policy-makers to stop congratulating themselves for the success of the black middle class and to do something for the truly disadvantaged. Others tried to catch the attention of the public and to focus it on the new problem by inventing a disturbingly evocative name for the very poorest of the black poor—the "black underclass."[1]

A few conservative commentators interpreted the fact that the civil rights revolution was not a panacea as further support for their views. More sympathetic observers were surprised and disappointed. They should not have been surprised. It was not anomalous that black poverty rates remained high after the civil rights revolution. Despite its great wealth, a war on poverty, and an increasing commitment to the welfare state, poverty rates in general in the United States are "exceptionally high" compared with those of other industrialized nations.[2] However, what probably surprised the observers was that the poor were still disproportionately black. If so then observers must have been thoroughly nonplussed by the announcement that by the 1980s the much vaunted advance of the black middle class had been checked and even reversed.

The traditional explanation for the persistence of black poverty and the halted advance of the black middle class was that racism was still working its poison. According to this view, it was naive to imagine that racism could be foiled by the legal provisions of civil rights legislation; these only forced racism into subtler forms, where it remains a formidable barrier to black progress. But in the late 1980s and early 1990s certain black people became impatient with this argument. Obviously seeing themselves as challengers to tradition, they allowed that racism was in the past a great barrier to black progress but denied that this was still the case. Three of them achieved considerable prominence: a sociologist, William Julius Wilson; an economist, Glenn Loury; and an English professor, Shelby Steele.

However, they are not as original as they seem to think. Booker T. Washington anticipated some of their most characteristic claims by almost a century, and more recently, Thomas Sowell has tirelessly expounded and defended the view that racism is not a significant cause of black economic stagnation. But Washington's pronouncements have long been dismissed as cant and stratagem, and although Sowell's incantations enjoy a vogue in libertarian circles, they seem to have won him few black converts other than Walter Williams. To the contrary, those who now attack the orthodoxy are being taken seriously.

Although they are united in rejecting what they take to be the traditional preoccupation with racism, their recommendations for the advance of the black population are strikingly opposed. Loury and Steele emphasize that blacks must help themselves; Wilson, on the other hand, emphasizes that the federal government must help blacks. I will examine these recommendations and search out their deeper philosophical presuppositions. I will conclude that each of them is in its own way a retreat from the high ideals of the civil rights revolution and a surrender to injustice. If I am right, they must therefore be rejected or substantially altered. I begin with Wilson.

## William Julius Wilson

According to Wilson, the underclass emerged from those black people that racism had confined to the inner cities and had robbed of skills and education. These people were not at first an underclass, for they were regularly employed as unskilled laborers in the manufacturing sector in the inner cities and had fairly stable families. Two fateful developments combined to transform them into an underclass: first, they lost their jobs when the manufacturing sector contracted and second, they were left behind in the inner cities when de jure racial segregation in housing was outlawed, and the black middle and working classes that had shared their communities left for other neighborhoods. The combined effects of social isolation and joblessness transformed them from poor and unskilled people into poor and unskilled people with the cultural and behavioral traits alleged to characterize the underclass.[3]

Three aspects of this account deserve special notice. First, although Wilson insists that the effects of past racism are a major cause of the underclass, he denies that current racial discrimination is significantly implicated.[4] Second, although he includes social isolation as a cause of the underclass, it is the deleterious economic consequences of this isolation that seem to him really causative. Third, although he allows that the underclass has a distinctive culture, he firmly denies that this "ghetto-specific culture" is a cause of the poverty and joblessness of the underclass.[5] On his account the causal sequence runs the other way; that is, changes in the economy caused joblessness, and this, together with the social isolation caused by the exodus of black middle class from the black neighborhoods, caused the ghetto-specific culture.

This argument is plausible, and many people have been persuaded by it. It is also original, differing from both the customary liberal account of the origin of the underclass and from the dissenting conservative alternative. The liberal account insists that present-day racism is among the major causes of the underclass. The conservative account contends that the major cause of the black underclass is its distinctive culture that supports and sanctions traits like hedonism, fatalism, helplessness, dependence, and a strong present-time orientation with little disposition to defer gratification and plan for the future. In rejecting these competing conventional views, Wilson seems to rise above an ideological dispute and say something new and possibly true about an old issue.

There is another reason for the popularity of Wilson's account of the origin of the underclass. Although it challenges orthodoxies, it is nevertheless remarkably conciliatory. Observers have often noted approvingly that Wilson's account of the origin of the underclass avoids "blaming the victim." It is also true, although it is not so often noted, that he avoids blaming practically anyone. His argument that current racism is not a significant cause of the underclass lets current racists off the hook. And he emphasizes that the changes in the economy and society that caused the underclass are the unintended and largely unforeseen consequences of people acting in legitimate ways.[6]

The conciliatory quality of Wilson's explanation of the origin of the underclass carries over into his strategy for uplifting the underclass. Basically, this strategy requires that the federal government intervene in the economy to ensure that the underclass has decent jobs. This does not have the originality of his explanation of the origin of the underclass, but it is more amiable than the corresponding conservative and liberal strategies. The conservative strategy emphasizes policies aimed specifically and directly at getting the underclass to exchange its culture for that of the mainstream. This offends many people. They protest that for one group of human beings to set out to change the culture of another group of human beings implies that some cultures, and consequently some people, are superior to others. The liberal strategy of attacking racism offends almost as many people. On the one hand, most whites do not believe that they are racists and resent being told that they are responsible for black poverty. On the other hand, an increasing number of blacks claim to be tired of blaming racism and complain that doing so is demeaning.

In general then, Wilson's views are plausible, original, optimistic, and congenial. Moreover, they seem to rely on a positive conception of human nature and to contain no hidden assumptions or tendencies we should be wary of. But this assessment is mistaken; Wilson's conception of human nature is not as positive as it may seem, and it contains hidden assumptions and tendencies we should be wary of.

THE "HIDDEN AGENDA" OR JUSTICE THROUGH SUBTERFUGE

Let us begin by reexamining Wilson's strategy for the uplift of the underclass. Besides governmental intervention in the economy to create decent jobs for the underclass, it includes supplementary programs like compensatory job training, compensatory schooling, and special medical services. In accordance with his depreciation of racism as a cause of the underclass, he proposes that these programs should be class-specific rather than race-specific. This means that persons have to be classified as disadvantaged by their "economic class background" to qualify for the programs; the fact that they are black or have suffered racial discrimination would not be enough.[7] Similarly Wilson also launches into an extended attack on programs of race-based affirmative action. He allows that they benefit the black middle class, but he denies that the black middle class needs or deserves this special help. He also denies that the programs benefit the black poor, even in the form of trickle downs from the black middle class. Indeed, because he believes that they widen the gap between the black middle class and the black poor, he fears that they may harm the black poor by increasing its social isolation.[8]

Some commentators have therefore been surprised to find that Wilson's total strategy for uplifting the black underclass includes affirmative action policies based on race.[9] Liberals are pleasantly surprised because they take this to mean that Wilson is an ally. Conservatives are disappointed and complain that it is inconsistent with his attack on affirmative action. The conservatives are mistaken. Wilson's attack on affirmative action is directed at current programs that benefit mainly middle-class blacks. Presumably the programs he wants to include in his strategy would be designed to benefit mainly the black poor. The liberals are mistaken, too. Wilson is not their ally; indeed, his views contradict their most basic tenets.

Because Wilson claims that current racial discrimination is not a major cause of the black underclass but joblessness and social isolation are, he must hold that current racial discrimination does not cause either the joblessness or social isolation of the black underclass. He does not mean that racism is dead; indeed, he denies that he ever meant to imply that racism has even declined.[10] He means that because inner city blacks were unqualified for anything but unskilled jobs, no one had to racially discriminate against them to keep them jobless when unskilled jobs vanished from the inner cities, and that because poor inner city blacks could not afford to live outside the inner cities, no one had to racially discriminate against them to keep them socially isolated when the black middle class moved to other neighborhoods.

But if this is the argument, then given Wilson's concession that racism has not declined, it seems that we should expect a recrudescence of racial discrimination if underclass blacks became qualified for skilled work. It may be objected that antidiscrimination laws would prevent this. But there is a further difficulty. If the members of the underclass are unskilled and uneducated, the greatest barrier to their progress is not racial discrimination narrowly conceived—on this Wilson is correct; it is opposition to implementing programs designed to enable them to become qualified for skilled work. Given that racism is likely to provoke a recrudescence of racial discrimination if underclass blacks become qualified for skilled work, it would certainly provoke opposition to implementing such programs. We cannot reasonably expect current laws against racial discrimination to deal with this different problem.

Wilson seems aware of this difficulty. He says that President Reagan was able to cut taxes by persuading the middle class that their living standards fell because of tax-supported programs for the poor and "implicitly minorities."[11] The implication is not simply that the middle class opposes a drop in its living standard; it is that the middle class is especially opposed to a drop in its living standard caused by tax-supported programs for "minorities." And he suggests two stratagems for deflecting the opposition his race-based programs are likely to arouse. The first is standard liberal fare—for government to stimulate vigorous economic growth and full employment so that the majority does not feel the effects of his affirmative action programs.[12] The second is more unusual—for government to camouflage the programs so that the majority does not notice them. The "hidden agenda" for liberal policy-makers, he says, is to make race-specific programs (presumably programs like his race-based affirmative action for the underclass) "less visible" by constructing "an economic-social reform program in such a way that the universal programs seem as the dominant and most visible aspects by the general public."[13]

That Wilson proposes the second stratagem reveals that he is not confident about his claim that current racism is not a significant obstacle to the advance of the black poor. That claim suggests that the second stratagem is superfluous. But this inconsistency is only the tip of the iceberg. The real trouble is in the second strategy itself.

It is a basic liberal tenet that the laws of a society ought to satisfy a publicity requirement. There is nothing esoteric about this tenet. It simply requires that government should make no attempt to conceal, disguise, camouflage, or divert attention from any of its laws or policies, but on the contrary, should affirm and open them to scrutiny.[14]

Perhaps the most obvious consideration in favor of the publicity requirement is that it normally helps ensure that government not make unjust laws. Unjust laws overlook or ignore the interests of those concerned. Assuming citizens who know what the laws say will try to make sure that the government does not overlook or ignore their interests when it makes laws, the publicity requirement obviously helps prevent government from making unjust laws. This does not mean that laws that a government conceals are necessarily unjust. The publicity requirement helps to prevent government from making unjust laws, but if it is violated, the laws that are shielded from public scrutiny may be just. I emphasize this point because although Wilson's "hidden agenda" violates the publicity requirement, the race-specific programs it makes "less visible" are not therefore unjust. My objections to his hidden agenda are that it conceals the race-specific programs, not that these programs are unjust.[15]

If the publicity requirement normally helps prevent government from implementing unjust laws, a government that circumvents the publicity requirement implies that it does not want to be prevented from implementing unjust laws. This conveys the message that it cannot be trusted and that the laws it is implementing are unjust. As I have noted, this does not mean that the laws *are* unjust. But it does not matter only that the laws are just; it also matters that citizens believe that the laws are just. If they do not, they are likely to be rebellious, and the stability of the society and the benefits that depend on it will be threatened. These considerations suggest that if government adopted Wilson's "hidden agenda," it would send the message that the race-specific programs he recommends for the underclass are unjust—even if they are just.[16] This would be a great setback for the underclass. The majority already opposes race-specific programs. A message from government that these programs are unjust would imbue it with a sense of vindicated self-righteousness and make its opposition seem respectable.

Government may know citizens' interests and consequently may be able to frame just laws without consulting citizens. Nevertheless, if it makes just laws and conceals them from its citizens, it insults them by implying that they are morally immature and cannot be trusted with knowledge of the laws that regulate their society. This suggests that if Wilson's hidden agenda were attempted and the attempt were exposed, citizens would be inclined to feel that the government had insulted them to mollycoddle undeserving blacks.

It will be objected that my arguments assume that Wilson's "hidden agenda" will be exposed. I admit the assumption, but I believe it is justified. If racism is strong enough to make the "hidden agenda" seem necessary, it is strong enough to guarantee that the agenda will be detected. But suppose I am mistaken about this. In that case the majority would not notice the race-specific programs and consequently could not object to them. But what about those blacks the programs are supposed to benefit? Presumably they would have to know about the race-specific programs and that these programs were being shielded from public scrutiny. To what conclusions would this knowledge lead them?

There are two possibilities. First, underclass blacks could come to the same conclusion the majority would come to if it knew that government was trying to distract it from noticing the race-specific programs; that is, that the race-specific programs were unjust. But if underclass blacks believe that the race-specific programs are unjust and consequently that they are the secret beneficiaries of governmental injustice, their sense of being partners in underhanded dishonest dealings would probably have disastrous effects on their self-respect. Of course, dishonesty need not undermine self-respect if self-respect is conceived so as to include self-esteem.[17] The swindler who dupes others confirms his guile, and to the extent that he values and admires guile he may thereby gain in self-esteem. But underclass blacks benefiting from race-specific programs are not likely to feel that they are duping the majority. They are likely to feel that the government is doing so, and that it is passing the benefits of its injustice on to them because, although undeserving, they are pathetic and helpless. These considerations convince me that although the charge that affirmative action undermines the self-respect and self-esteem of its beneficiaries is false in general, it is decisive against affirmative action protected from public scrutiny by Wilson's "hidden agenda."

But underclass blacks may not feel that race-specific programs that are shielded from public scrutiny are unjust. They may feel that these programs are just and that the government shields them from public scrutiny because the majority is racist and unjust and would dismantle the programs if it knew about them. This would be the best outcome for Wilson's agenda. Yet it too has disturbing implications. For example, it implies that underclass blacks have a cynical attitude about the public sense of justice. Although that cynicism is probably justified, Wilson's hidden agenda would encourage and harden it, and I doubt that this is best in the long run. Worse, it implies that underclass blacks trust the government to manipulate the majority to give blacks justice. If the first attitude is cynical, the second is naive. I do not know whether underclass blacks have it, but I am certain that any strategy that encourages them to have it should be avoided.

If there are dangers in government shielding race-specific programs from public scrutiny, there are also advantages in government openly affirming these programs. Because just laws presuppose the positive equal worth of all persons, if government openly affirms such laws—as the publicity requirement demands—it declares its allegiance to the idea of the positive equal worth of its citizens and in this way powerfully supports their self-respect. Accordingly, given that the race-specific programs Wilson recommends are just, it follows that if government introduces such programs but fails to affirm them openly, it misses a great opportunity to declare that it is committed to the idea of the positive equal worth of its black citizens, and consequently, to support their self-respect.

When openly declared, just race-specific programs can have further symbolic importance. This is especially so in the case of affirmative action. The argument for affirmative action is not simply that it is a means to future goods such as greater economic equality between the races. This argument is radically incomplete because it ignores the injuries of past and current racism.[18] But the argument for affirmative action is also not simply that it is compensation for the injuries of past and current racism. This argument is better than the first, for it acknowledges the moral relevance of the injuries of racism, but it too is incomplete. Racism did not only injure black people; it was and is an open rejection of their moral equality and an insult.[19] It remains so even if it causes no further injury and even if Wilson is right that it is not a significant cause of the underclass. Consequently, it seems appropriate to supplement the usual arguments for affirmative action with the consideration that affirmative action is an unusually powerful way for society to send a message to black people, welcoming them into the society as equals and taking back the insults of racism.[20] But surely this message can be conveyed only if race-specific programs are openly affirmed. If they are veiled or camouflaged as Wilson recommends, a very different message will be conveyed. Even if they are just, the attempt to veil or camouflage them will say that the society is not ready to welcome blacks as equals and not ready to take back the insults of racism.

So far I have pointed to the dangers and missed opportunities inherent in any attempt to implement Wilson's "hidden agenda." But there is much more wrong with the agenda. As I now argue, it arouses the suspicion that Wilson has elitist and paternalistic views about how a society should be governed.

The publicity requirement is the minimal condition that must be satisfied if a society is to have any defence against elite control. If it fails to be satisfied, an elite will be in a position not merely to control, but also to manipulate the citizens.[21]

Manipulation is a special kind of control. It consists in controlling others by playing on forces that determine or strongly influence their behavior, while at the same time taking care that they do not know how this is being done or even that it is being done. Thus, it is generally imperative not to be in a position where one can be manipulated. This is especially so where the benevolence of the manipulators cannot be assumed, as for example, where they are the government. But whether a manipulative government is benevolent or not, its citizens cannot be free. By defending against manipulation, the publicity requirement is therefore a fundamental condition of political freedom. Political freedom does not require that there be no social control. This would make political freedom incompatible with law and consequently impossible in any society that needs law, for, of course, law is a form of social control. But political freedom requires that we at least not be prevented or distracted from knowing the laws that control us. John Locke was making this point when he stated that "Freedom of Men under Government" requires that we not be subject to the "unknown arbitrary will of another man."[22]

Now it seems that Wilson's "hidden agenda," with its schemes for diverting the public's attention from crucial government policies, is a proposal that government manipulates citizens. But it may be objected that merely diverting citizens' attention from governmental policies is not really concealing these policies and consequently that the "hidden agenda" is not manipulation. This is hardly compelling. If citizens are told bluntly that they will not be allowed to examine certain programs, they may not know how they are being manipulated, but they will at least know that they are in danger of being manipulated and can therefore take steps to defend themselves. The strategy of the "hidden agenda," essentially dangling goodies before citizens' eyes so that they do not notice what government is doing, leaves them defenceless and is simply more effective manipulation. Indeed, it is subterfuge, which is the sheerest form of manipulation.

It may be objected that although the "hidden agenda" proposes manipulation, this manipulation is justified because it is a means to a great good. I will not answer this objection with the platitude that the end does not justify the means. The platitude is false. Manipulating the majority to prevent it from blocking or undermining race-specific programs for the underclass may be an occasion when the end justifies the means. The end of this manipulation is a great good—the elevation of a whole population—and the manipulation itself is not objectionable, for its immediate purpose is to prevent the majority from acting unjustly by blocking or undermining programs demanded by justice. One could even mount an argument that the manipulation is not objectionable at all. There seems to be nothing objectionable about manipulating an armed robber to prevent him from committing the injustice of taking your wallet. Why then should there be anything objectionable about manipulating the majority to prevent it from committing the injustice of blocking race-specific programs for the underclass?

Conservatives would answer this question by arguing that blocking race-specific programs is not an injustice. I cannot give this answer because I believe that race-specific programs can be just and that blocking them may be unjust. My answer is that there are better ways to prevent injustice than manipulation.

Take the case of the robber. It is better to overpower him to prevent him from taking your wallet than to manipulate him for the same end, at least if it is possible to overpower him without excessive cost. Manipulating the robber to save your wallet also suffers by comparison with persuading him that he should not rob you because to do so would be unjust. Finally, if the losses are not likely to be excessive, it is also better to tell the robber that he is acting unjustly and let him take the wallet than to manipulate him and keep the wallet. If these views are sound, manipulating the majority to prevent it from blocking race-specific programs could be justified if it is a reasonable assumption that the majority cannot be compelled or persuaded to accept the programs or if openly avowing the programs and declaring their justice would be too costly.

It is difficult to know whether either assumption is true. But the dominant tradition in African-American political thought declares them false. It maintains that although the majority cannot be compelled to act justly, it may possibly be persuaded to do so, and that in any case, blacks do better to demand justice openly and risk not getting it than to get justice by subterfuge. That this was the position of Martin Luther King, Jr., and needs no argument. But it was also the position of Frederick Douglass and W. E. B. Dubois. Douglass openly denounced slavery in the heyday of slavery, and Dubois wrote in his debate with Booker T. Washington that "The South ought to be led, by candid honest criticism, to assert her better self and do her full duty to the race she has cruelly wronged and is still wronging."[23] Is the attitude expressed in these views obsolete because the majority has become intransigent and because the possible costs of demanding justice openly have become too great? I am not sure of the correct answer to these questions. The issues they raise are partly philosophical but also partly empirical. I do know, however, that Wilson cannot answer them in the affirmative; he cannot say that although Douglass, Dubois, and King were right to openly avow their reforms and insist that the public should accept these reforms because they were just, we must now resort to the sleight of hand of his "hidden agenda," because the majority has become intransigent. It is he who has become famous for announcing the declining significance of race.[24]

Accordingly, although Wilson's views on reform show a concern for the material welfare of the most disadvantaged, their cynicism about the possibility of public morality and their consequent elitism and paternalism are opposed to the philosophical presuppositions of the dominant tradition of African-American political thought. We must now search out the philosophical presuppositions of his own views. To do so let us now consider his view that the black underclass is a recent phenomenon.

THE PROBLEM OF GHETTO-SPECIFIC CULTURE

This view is controversial. Orlando Patterson argues that it relies heavily on studies that mistakenly conclude that the black family was intact during and after slavery and collapsed among the black poor only recently under the economic pressures of the 1960s. According to Patterson, the destruction of the black family and the creation of a black underclass occurred generations earlier during slavery. As he put it, the "black underclass has always been with us."[25]

This issue has deep theoretical implications if we suppose with Wilson that the underclass is characterized by a "ghetto-specific culture." Coupled with the view that the underclass is a recent phenomenon, that supposition suggests that Wilson believes that cultures can change quickly. On the other hand, Patterson's view seems to imply that cultures change only slowly. Thus although he agrees with Wilson that the underclass has a distinctive culture, he denies that this culture is of recent origin. He argues that we can detect its traits in the underclass of slaves. These individuals, he writes, were "idle," "compulsive liars," and in general "shiftless" and "economically and socially deviant."[26]

Wilson's view that cultures can change readily is a minority view. The traditional view is that cultures change slowly. Sowell states it clearly. Although he allows that cultures change, people "eventually" availing themselves of "the benefits of other cultures," he emphasizes that the change tends to be gradual.[27] Thus noting that Jewish peddlers followed the Roman legions and were found "on the American frontier or on the sidewalks of New York 2,000 years later," he concludes that "cultural patterns do not readily disappear, either with the passage of time or with social engineering."[28] If this theory of cultural change is correct, then if the underclass has a distinctive culture, it acquired this culture gradually and will lose it gradually. Sowell himself seems to take the view that blacks gradually acquired distinctive cultural traits under slavery and are only gradually losing these traits. "With many generations of discouragement of initiative and with little incentive to work any more than necessary to escape punishment," he writes, "slaves developed foot-dragging, work-evading patterns that were to remain as a cultural legacy long after slavery itself disappeared. Duplicity and theft were also pervasive patterns among antebellum slaves, and these too remained long after slavery ended."[29]

It may be objected that Wilson cannot hold that cultures can change quickly because he allows that racism, which is a cultural trait, is an enduring aspect of American life. But Wilson's view of cultural change is not simply that cultures can change quickly; it is that cultures change quickly when subjected to certain pressures. These pressures are specifically *economic*. In particular they are not moral, intellectual, or legal pressures; Wilson is clear that racism has survived and flourished in spite of being intellectually and morally exposed and in spite of a civil rights revolution. His position appears to be that when economic constraints force people to change their behavior, then if these changes in behavior become widespread and are socially isolated, they readily become acceptable and part of the culture.

The objection can now be answered. Wilson claims that most underclass blacks lack marketable skills. This implies that employers are under little or no economic pressure to change their racist hiring practices toward underclass blacks. But his account of the mechanics of cultural change implies that a change in these practices has to initiate the cultural change of a decline of racism.

There is much to be said for the theory of cultural change I have attributed to Wilson. Significant economic constraints do compel people to change how they behave. If I lose my job and income, I have no choice but to change how I live—at least if I was not a miser. Further when behavioral changes are widespread and isolated from other influences, they may easily come to seem inevitable and thus acceptable and even desirable; people have a useful capacity to be able to accept what they take to be inevitable and even to think it desirable. And customary behavior that people think is acceptable or desirable is a part of their culture.

Wilson's most characteristic explanations of the emergence of ghetto-specific cultural traits follow this pattern. Consider, for example, how he explains why illegitimacy and single parenthood became a part of underclass culture. According to Wilson, when job opportunities dried up in the inner cities, the economic constraints precluded marriage, and as a result single parenthood spread dramatically in the socially isolated areas of the inner cities, and then—apparently in short order—became acceptable and a part of ghetto-specific culture. Accounts of how other traits of ghetto-specific culture emerged are similar. The changes are assumed to have emerged readily because the widespread behavioral results of economic constraints on inner city blacks were socially isolated. For example, he argues that when jobs virtually disappeared from the inner cities in the 1950s and 1960s, the social isolation of inner city blacks made joblessness quickly acceptable and a part of underclass culture.

Now scientific theories are supposed to do more than enable us to explain past events; they are also supposed to enable us to predict, control, and perhaps bring about future events. Wilson proposes to bring it about that the underclass joins the mainstream. His strategy for doing this is basically to provide the underclass with decent job opportunities, and it seems to be informed by his theory of cultural change. That theory says that economic constraints caused inner city blacks to lose their mainstream culture and acquire a ghetto-specific culture. It may therefore seem reasonable that if these economic constraints were lifted, underclass blacks would as readily lose their ghetto-specific culture and reacquire a mainstream culture. If this is correct, Wilson's theory seems to support a far more optimistic outlook about the prospects of the underclass than the traditional view. The near cultural determinism of that view suggests that the underclass may not respond to economic incentives.

But empirical investigations of Wilson's claims about cultural changes in the underclass suggest that these claims may not be true. In the period Wilson cites to support his explanation of the spread of illegitimacy and single parenthood in the underclass, the marriage rate among black men with well-paid jobs declined almost as much as the marriage rate among all black men. As Christopher Jencks points out, this is not what one would expect if only economic constraints caused the behavioral changes in question. To explain these changes Jencks maintains that we must also bring in influences from the mainstream. One implication of this criticism is that the underclass may not be as socially isolated as Wilson assumes. But the more important implication is that Wilson's theory systematically ignores the role of culture and morality and intellectually held views in cultural change. According to Jencks, the mainstream influence necessary to explain the spread of illegitimacy and single parenthood in the underclass was a growing disenchantment with marriage and the traditional two-parent family. Moreover, although he allows that this was partly caused by economic changes, for example, better job opportunities for women, he believes that it was probably also partly the outcome of intellectually held positions such as a growing individualism and commitment to personal freedom.[30]

These considerations suggest that if Wilson concedes that the underclass has a ghetto-specific culture, this may not be because the facts about underclass behavior compel that concession but because his theory of cultural change compels it. For example, consider the alleged fact that underclass blacks disdain work even when it is available, whereas the mainstream works steadily. Even if this is true, it does not show that underclass blacks have exchanged their mainstream culture with a "work ethic" for a ghetto-specific culture with a "leisure ethic." It is fully consistent with the traditional view that the underclass retains its mainstream culture. The work underclass blacks allegedly disdain is menial work. This may reflect a negative attitude toward menial work, but it is an attitude blacks share with the mainstream. Most in the mainstream also disdain menial work and would not do it if it was the only option.

Further, the idea that Wilson's theory provides a more optimistic outlook of the fate of the underclass than the traditional view may be mistaken. It depends on Wilson's concession that inner city blacks exchanged a mainstream culture for a distinctive ghetto-specific culture when they became an underclass. But the traditional view would probably not make that concession and in that case supports as optimistic an outlook about the prospects of the underclass as Wilson's theory.

A more serious difficulty is that Wilson's theory of cultural change may not support his strategy for uplifting the underclass. The theory implies that economic constraints led inner city blacks to readily acquire a ghetto-specific culture, but it does not predict that they will as readily reacquire a mainstream culture if the economic constraints are lifted. Significant economic constraints compel me to change how I behave, if I was not a miser before the constraints, but economic opportunities do not similarly compel me to change how I behave. If I lose my income I must change how I live, but if I receive economic opportunities I need not change how I live. If economic constraints lead me to acquire a taste for idleness, I may not go back to my old way of living even if the economic constraints are lifted.

This difficulty could be avoided if we could assume that people almost always respond to economic incentives. It may even be argued that I am committed to that assumption. My argument that economic constraints compel people to change how they behave is valid only on the proviso that people are not misers. If people are misers, hoarding most of what they earn, they need not change how they behave even if significant economic constraints are imposed on them. But if people are not misers, that is, if, they spend more or less what they earn, it seems that they desire the things and services that money can buy and consequently will respond to economic incentives. However, this argument is invalid. The fact that people spend what they earn does not entail that they will try to earn more. They may be satisfied with what they earn or at least they need not be so dissatisfied with what they earn that they are ready to change how they live to earn more. I can show this to be the case.

There is an infamous theory popularized by Sowell and others that the market eliminates racial discrimination. It can be summarized as follows:

Firms that refuse to hire qualified black people because of their race will be at a disadvantage compared with firms that do hire qualified black people. By indulging their taste for discrimination the discriminators add to their costs and put themselves at a disadvantage compared with the nondiscriminators. Given competition in the market, this ensures that the discriminators will eventually be driven out of business.

Now empirical investigations have been conducted that show that Sowell's theory is false.[31] Apparently, many firms in the private sector discriminate against blacks but are not driven out of business. There are three ways to explain this: (1) All firms pass up the economic advantage of not discriminating against blacks. (2) Some firms pass up this advantage, but enough customers patronize them to keep them in business. (3) There are so few qualified blacks that there is no economic advantage in not discriminating against blacks in general.

The first two possibilities imply that many people are prepared to pay to indulge a taste for racial discrimination. This implies that many people do not respond to economic incentives, which contradicts the crucial assumption necessary to make Wilson's view of cultural change support his strategy for uplifting the underclass.

But suppose Sowell's theory fails because the third possibility is true; that is, suppose that qualified blacks are so few that there is no economic advantage in dismantling policies of racial discrimination against blacks in general. Because in that case people can indulge their taste for discrimination for free, the fact that they continue to discriminate is no reason to doubt that they would respond to economic incentives not to discriminate.

But can Wilson allow the third possibility to be true? As we have seen, he allows that it is true in part. His claim that current racism is not a significant cause of the black underclass relies on the assumption that underclass blacks are so lacking in marketable skills that employers have no economic incentive to stop discriminating against them. But he cannot allow that the third possibility is true in general. He maintains that past racism was a major cause of black backwardness and an important reason why the underclass is disproportionately black. This can be true only if past racism prevented a considerable number of qualified blacks from getting desirable jobs and positions. But if so, there must have been some economic incentive to dismantle policies of racial discrimination against blacks. The fact that few responded to that incentive suggests that people often do not respond to economic incentives.

It seems then that although Wilson's strategy for uplifting the underclass suggests that he thinks that people almost always respond to economic incentives, his claims about the effects of past racism commit him to the view that people often do not respond to economic incentives. Perhaps there is no contradiction. I have suggested myself that some behavioral traits and some cultural traits respond more readily to changes in economic constraints and incentives than do others. Racism could be a cultural trait that does not respond readily to changes in economic constraints and incentives, whereas a disposition to work could be a cultural trait that does. This could allow Wilson to keep his views about past racism and also to argue that his strategy is likely to succeed if an esteem for high material consumption is a cultural trait that resists changes in economic incentives. But why should an esteem for high material consumption be a cultural trait that resists changes in economic incentives? An esteem for marriage and a traditional two-parent family did not survive the economic constraints in the inner cities. Why should the esteem for high material consumption fare better? The likely answer to these questions is that the underclass shares the mainstream's culture or continues to be deeply influenced by its mores, but Wilson, of course, cannot give this answer.

Wilson could argue that although cultures change slowly in normal circumstances, even when there are economic incentives to change, they change quickly in response to economic incentives in circumstance of dire economic necessity. This would also enable him to keep his views about the effects of past racism and to remain confident that his strategy to uplift the underclass will succeed. But this attractive argument is not convincing. Poor people do not always change their tastes when doing so will make them better off. Poor whites have retained and indulged their racist tastes, opposing coalitions with poor blacks when such coalitions would have made them better off. Why then is it so clear that poor blacks would overcome their alleged opposition to work just because doing so would make them better off?[32] Of course, they would probably overcome their alleged opposition to work if they had to do so to survive. But although some conservative strategies recommend denying welfare benefits to able-bodied people who refused to work, Wilson gives no indication that he endorses such extreme measures.

THE EGOISTIC FOUNDATIONS

Perhaps no argument is needed to justify the assumption that, despite their ghetto-specific culture, underclass blacks will take decent, well-paying work if it is available. It is widely believed that it is human nature to try to better oneself economically and indeed that most human beings are avaricious.[33]

Unless one's own economic betterment is qualified in some way, for example, that one seeks economic advancement to be able to support charitable causes, it seems to be a good only for oneself. So if it is human nature to try to better oneself economically, whatever one's cultural attachments and commitments may be, it is human nature to try to secure one's own good whatever one's other attachments and commitments may be. This suggests that it is a feature of human nature itself, and not a contingent and acquired trait of character or culture, that the desire for one's own good invariably overwhelms all other desires. This is, of course, the central claim of egoism.

It should surprise no one that egoism lurks among Wilson's premises. Egoism is widely assumed to be true. Further, Wilson is a mainstream social scientist, and mainstream social science tends to assume that egoism is true. This is especially clear in mainstream economics, which the other social sciences emulate. As economics Nobel laureate George Stigler put it, economics assumes that "we live in a world of reasonably well-informed people acting intelligently in pursuit of their self-interests."[34] Further, according to Stigler, this widely held view stems from the father of economics, Adam Smith himself. Smith's *Wealth of Nations*, Stigler declares, "is a stupendous palace erected upon the granite of self-interest."[35]

Many mainstream economists seem to take it for granted that human avarice follows directly from egoism.[36] But argument is needed. Economic advancement may be good for a person, but it is not the only thing he must believe is good for him. Health, pleasure, honor, fame, and leisure are among the many things many people often believe are good for them besides economic advancement. So if egoism claims that the desire for our own good always overwhelms our other desires so that we always end up pursuing what we believe is good for us, some argument is needed to show that we always seriously pursue our own economic advancement.

Such an argument seems immediately forthcoming if people are not merely egoists, but—as Stigler's earlier comment implies—rational egoists. It seems that rational egoists will always pursue their economic advancement because money can be used to purchase the means to satisfy most desires. Karl Marx noted this basis of money's dominance as an object of desire. "Money," Marx wrote, "since it has the property of purchasing everything, of appropriating objects to itself, is, therefore, the object *par excellence*."[37]

But this argument is only suggestive, not compelling. For example, suppose that a rational egoist's main desire was to be idle; this seems possible because a desire to be idle may be an egoistic desire. Such a rational egoist would not seriously pursue his economic advancement, for his main desire does not take much money to satisfy. A rational egoist may be diverted from trying to get richer even if his desires are expensive. For example, suppose that his main desire was to practice racial discrimination; this too is an egoistic desire. But although he would be better able to satisfy it if he were richer, it would not always be rational for him not to practice racial discrimination and to hire the best candidates, even when they are black, just to get richer; on the contrary, this would be irrational, given his desires, for it would mean that he would never satisfy the desires he was trying to get rich in order to satisfy!

This difficulty suggests that to show that rational egoists seriously pursue their economic advancement we need an argument that they tend to have desires that move them to seriously pursue their economic advancement. Several such arguments can be derived from the writings of those who stress the egoism in human nature.[38] Let us consider that of Adam Smith. According to Smith, the egoistic desires for the "necessities of nature," or even for "ease" and "pleasure," cannot explain why people try to have more than a moderate income.[39] To explain this he appealed to a different kind of desire. The advantages we derive from wealth, he argued, are to "be observed, to be attended to, to be taken notice of with sympathy, complacency and approbation."[40] Now this desire for notice and approbation, or "vanity" as Smith called it, is a more complex desire than the simple egoistic desires for the "necessities of nature" and for "ease" and "pleasure." Unlike these desires it depends on the ability to be aware of and to delight in the approbation of others. But it too is an egoistic desire. The vain man epitomizes egoism.

This theory argues that human avarice is a consequence of a universal human desire for respect and approbation. And it seems to support Wilson's views about the consequences of economic opportunity, for given that underclass blacks seek respect and approbation like everyone else and that decent work is a means to economic betterment, the theory implies that underclass blacks will take decent work if it is available—precisely as Wilson's strategy to uplift the underclass assumes. The theory also seems to support Wilson's views about the cultural consequences of severe economic constraints. Consider the inner cities when jobs dried up. Jobs may have become so scarce that if inner city blacks were rational egoists they would save themselves the trouble of trying to get a job. Although they would still desire respect and approbation they would accept their joblessness and try to find means to respect and approbation other than economic betterment. In the context of the ghetto such means would be likely to include a reputation for violence.

But in that case money is not a means to respect and approbation in all cultures, and consequently although all people may desire respect and approbation, not all people in all cultures may be avaricious. So, if Smith's theory supports Wilson's view that violence and indolence are likely to become cultural norms in the underclass, it fails to justify Wilson's confidence in his strategy to uplift the underclass.

But Smith's theory also fails to support Wilson's view that violence and indolence are likely to become cultural norms in the underclass. This is because Smith's theory allows that people may have convictions that can determine how they respond to economic constraints. As Jencks's empirical research hinted, Wilson's views systematically underrate the role of such convictions in cultural change.

Although significant economic constraints compel us to change our behavior, they do not compel us to change our behavior in any particular way. If I have a good income and lose it, I certainly have to change how I behave, but although I may have to stop eating steak, I may not have to start eating hamburger. I may choose to eat chicken instead, or I may choose to become a vegetarian. What I choose depends on my tastes, values, and intellectually held positions. These can also block or slow behavioral changes that economic constraints would otherwise cause. If I lose my income I probably have to change how I behave, but I may not be compelled to change every aspect of how I behave. I have supposed that I change my eating habits, but I may choose to change something else instead. If I really loved steak, I could continue to eat steak and economize in other areas. These considerations suggest that we cannot explain how inner city blacks behaved when they lost their jobs simply by the fact that they lost their jobs, but we must also consider their tastes, values, and convictions—in short their culture and morality—before they lost their jobs.

Culture may not only determine how behavior changes in response to economic pressures; it can also determine whether behavioral changes lead to cultural changes. Wilson's view seems to be that when widespread behavioral changes are socially isolated they become acceptable and thus cultural changes. But the fact that behavior becomes widespread in an isolated group of people does not automatically mean that it will become socially acceptable among that people. Whether it does depends on the tastes, values, and convictions they have before the economic pressures that cause them to change their behavior. A people's tastes, values, and convictions give them a sense of who they are, and they may cling to these marks of their identity even if they are forced to change how they behave. Suppose that for reasons they find deep and intellectually compelling some socially isolated people become convinced that idleness is a disgrace. And suppose further that economic changes then impose such severe constraints on them that most of them are forced into idleness. Then although idleness may become widespread, and they may remain socially isolated, these people may continue to find idleness unacceptable. I do not mean that they will blame themselves for being idle, although this is possible. I mean that they may continue to be deeply dissatisfied with their idleness and to feel that the conditions that force them to it are evil, unjust and in some sense a violation of their identity. As long as they take that attitude, idleness will not become a part of their culture, however widespread it becomes and however isolated they remain.

I think that this concession to the force of human convictions and ultimately to the human need for self-identification lies behind the traditional view that cultures change very slowly, even in response to economic constraints. On the other hand, Wilson's view that cultures change readily in response to economic constraints gives little force to these convictions or to that need; indeed, it suggests that people do not have convictions but only habits that support behavior that maximizes economic returns when economic opportunities make the pursuit of economic advantage rational. They abandon these habits in hard times when economic constraints make the pursuit of economic advantage irrational but promptly recover them when good times return. On this account, human beings do not care who they are, or rather they always know who they are; they are essentially money-makers who desist from the pursuit of money when it is likely to fail but are ever ready to return to that pursuit when there is the slightest hope of success. If I am right, this crude and unsophisticated form of egoism, apparently shared by certain libertarian economists, is the crucial premise behind Wilson's account of cultural change and his strategy for uplifting the underclass.

It is also behind his "hidden agenda." If people are essentially money-makers and have no morals or other convictions, they certainly cannot have or be moved by a sense of justice. Justice must therefore be secured by the subterfuge of the "hidden agenda."

I do not mean that everyone who despairs of the majority's sense of justice must be driven to accept egoism; even Douglass, who certainly did not accept egoism, sometimes wearily complained that the South was almost beyond redemption. Similarly it may be argued that Wilson is driven to his hidden agenda because he despairs of the majority's racism. Earlier I suggested as much myself. Now, of course, this suggestion is inconsistent with his claim that current racism is not a significant cause of the black underclass. But there is a further difficulty. When Douglass complained of the South's intransigence, he meant that the South was corrupted for being blind to the injustice of the slavery. Further, it seems that anyone who rejects egoism, allowing that people can come to see and be moved by what justice demands, must also hold that those of mature years and reasonable intelligence who cannot or will not see or be moved by what justice demands are corrupted. But if Wilson believes that the majority is racist and incapable of giving justice, and as I have indicated this is a point he tends to understate, he gives no indication that he thinks that it is therefore corrupted. He seems to think that it is well adjusted and healthy, so much so that he wants to help the underclass join it. I conclude that he must assume that its insensitivity to justice is perfectly normal and consequently that his "hidden agenda" rests on egoism.

## Glenn Loury

Let us now consider the views of the economist Glenn Loury. It is important to distinguish his project from Wilson's. Wilson's project is to save underclass blacks, those he refers to as "the truly disadvantaged." He is not concerned with the black middle class. Loury's project too is mainly to save the black underclass, but he is also concerned with the black middle class in a way Wilson is not. This is partly because, unlike Wilson, he thinks that it has an essential role to play in the salvation of the black underclass and also because he conceives of the root problem interfering with black advancement somewhat differently from Wilson.

Not suprisingly, Wilson's and Loury's intended audiences are not the same. Wilson obviously addresses his work mainly to theoreticians and academics and sympathetic high-level policy-makers, most of whom are presumbly white. No doubt these are also included in Loury's intended audience, but it seems clear that his work is also addressed specifically to black intellectuals and the black middle class in a way Wilson's work is not.

If we keep this difference in mind we should avoid misunderstanding the superficially similar positions Wilson and Loury take on justice. As I noted at the beginning of this chapter, they both express impatience with the traditional argument that widespread ongoing racism is among the main causes of black poverty. And like Wilson, Loury too forbears from making the resulting stock claim that most blacks are the victims of societal injustice and that justice therefore demands that government introduce reforms for their benefit. But their reasons for this forbearance are different. Wilson's are strategic. He probably does not deny that underclass blacks—the truly disadvantaged—are the victims of societal injustice. He proposes to camouflage the race-specific programs for their benefit that he recommends to policy-makers, because the egoistic assumptions of his analysis, standard in mainstream social science, lead him to despair of the majority's capacity to give justice. Loury's views on these issues are different.

Although he is, like Wilson, a mainstream social scientist, he does not share the egoistic assumptions of his discipline, and he is not reticent about appealing to justice because he despairs of the majority's capacity to give justice. On the contrary, he believes that, whatever else may have been the case in the past, the majority is now ready to do the right thing. Thus he writes that "the historic cancer of racism has abated," and that white Americans are "now ready to welcome individuals of all races and creeds to make of their freedoms what they will."[41] Loury avoids appealing to justice because, unlike Wilson, he believes that justice no longer demands that government introduce any reforms to benefit blacks.

This belief follows from his views about the nature and limits of justice: the first concerns the relationship between justice and racial discrimination;

the second concerns the limits of compensatory justice. The first leads him to the conclusion that although justice at one time demanded governmental reforms for the benefit of blacks—he has in mind the chief civil rights legislation of the past—it no longer does, and consequently that "we now live in the 'past-civil rights' era."[42] The second leads him to the conclusion that although past white injustice inflicted serious injuries on blacks and that present-day blacks still suffer from the evil effects of these injuries, compensatory justice can do little to bring blacks to the condition they would have enjoyed if they had never been injured.

I begin with an examination of the first of his views about the nature and limits of justice.

## JUSTICE AND DISCRIMINATION

Justice condemns some racial discrimination, but it does not condemn all racial discrimination. It is unjust for an admissions officer at a school to reject applicants simply because they are black, but it is not unjust for that same admissions officer to choose not to invite blacks to her birthday party or to choose not to marry a black man simply because of his color. On the contrary, it would be unjust for anyone, including government, to try to force her to invite blacks to her birthday party or to marry someone she did not want to marry. This kind of consideration is the crux of Loury's first argument that justice now forbids any further governmental reforms for the benefit of blacks. He believes that the American "liberal political heritage," which he evidently takes to embody justice, provides legal protection to various freedoms and that any further governmental reforms to benefit blacks is likely to violate these freedoms. For example, consider governmental reforms to integrate schools and neighborhoods. Loury evidently believes that the object of this reform would be of significant benefit to blacks. He observes that research has established the "crucial importance of family and community background in determining a child's later success in life."[43] The trouble is that the American liberal political heritage protects freedoms that set limits on the reforms that government can legitimately introduce to integrate schools and neighborhoods, and Loury believes that these limits have been reached. As he puts it, housing laws cannot "prevent a disgruntled white resident from moving away if his neighborhood becomes predominantly or even partly black," and court-ordered busing cannot "prevent unhappy parents from sending their children to private schools."[44]

It would be a mistake to reject this argument on the ground that the freedoms in question should not be protected. If we took away freedoms whenever they secured and widened economic inequalities we would take away many of our most cherished freedoms. For example, consider, the freedom to choose whom one will marry. Protecting this freedom secures and widens economic inequalities. Few, however, would restrict or take it away simply because it has this consequence. Loury emphasizes this point.[45] And as he notes, it can be generalized.

This argument shows only that freedoms cannot rightly be taken away just because they secure or widen economic inequalities. It does not show that certain freedoms that secure or widen economic inequalities cannot rightly be taken away. The freedom to bash others on the head and abscond with their possessions would possibly secure and widen economic inequalities, but it is certainly rightly taken away! So the question is whether all the freedoms that secure or widen economic inequalities, and which Loury claims are protected by the American liberal political heritage, are in fact protected by that heritage. I believe that at least one of them is not.

As we have seen, Loury argues that government efforts to achieve integrated schools, which would be of great benefit to blacks, are routinely frustrated by white parents sending their children to private schools. The implication is that if government acted to block this way of frustrating its goals, it would act wrongly because the American liberal political heritage protects parents' freedom to send their children to whatever schools they please. I believe that this is false. As I argued in Chapter 5, parents' freedom concerning their children's schooling is restricted. Indeed, I think it is more felicitous to speak of parents' duties concerning their children's schooling rather than of their freedoms or rights in this regard. Parents have duties to their children to send them to schools where they will learn the skills necessary to earn a living later on, where they will acquire the right values, and where they will grow up with the appropriate respect for their fellow citizens and human beings. If parents fail to fulfill these duties, they violate their children's rights to a good education, and the state may step in to prevent these rights from being further violated. Now integrated schools may not benefit only blacks; in a multiracial society integrated schools are probably also necessary to help children grow up with the appropriate respect and appreciation for their fellow citizens who are of different races. If so, parents act wrongly if they try to segregate their children in racially exclusive schools, and government violates no sacrosanct freedom if it prevents them from thus giving their children an inferior education.

Another flaw in Loury's argument is that he fails to consider that government may be able to introduce reforms to achieve integrated schools and neighborhoods without violating protected freedoms. For example, suppose that my previous argument is mistaken and that parents do have a freedom, which government should not violate, to send their children to private schools. Even in this case, it does not follow that government can do nothing to integrate schools without violating parents' rights. One thing it can do, for example, is to make public schools so attractive that parents choose to send their children to such schools rather than to private schools. Similarly, without violating any protected freedoms, government may be able to induce people to stay in integrated neighborhoods by making such neighborhoods as attractive as possible, perhaps by lowering their property taxes and improving their schools, streets, and parks.

It will be objected that these strategies to achieve integration amount to penalizing people for exercising their freedom to take their children out of public schools or to move out of a neigborhood and consequently do violate their freedoms to do these things. Another way of putting this objection is to argue that the strategies avoid violating certain freedoms only to violate property rights. Making integrated schools and neighborhoods attractive enough to prevent white flight costs money. Government can get this money only by taxing whites. But it is a violation of their property rights to tax whites for this purpose.

There is an aura of plausibility to this objection. It may seem that there is little difference between making it illegal for people to exercise a freedom and taxing them with the result that they find it difficult or impossible to exercise the freedom. But in fact the objection is specious. If we object to some taxation because it reduces our ability to exercise some freedoms, we must object to practically every taxation because practically every taxation reduces our ability to exercise some freedoms. Assuming that we are not prepared to do this, the question then becomes to determine which taxation is justifiable even if it inevitably reduces our ability to exercise some freedoms. Suppose we argued that taxation to support strategies to achieve integration and thus reduce black poverty and the economic gap between the races was justified. Someone who took the position that the welfare state necessarily involves an unjustifiable violation of property rights could probably consistently object to this argument. But anyone who accepted the fundamental arguments for the welfare state would, I submit, meet with considerable difficulty in finding a principled objection to it.

If I am right about this, Loury's first argument against further governmental reforms to benefit blacks must be rejected. The American liberal political heritage which he endorses evidently supports the welfare state. But, as I have suggested, the fundamental arguments for the welfare state justify governmental reforms to achieve integration to benefit blacks.

THE LIMITS OF COMPENSATORY JUSTICE

Let us now consider Loury's second argument, that justice no longer requires governmental reforms for the benefit of blacks. As I noted, this argument depends on a view about the limits of compensatory justice. According to Loury, these limits imply that governmental reforms can do little or nothing to repair the most serious and crippling injuries traceable to past white injustice against blacks. Let us try to get clearer on the nature of these limits and on the arguments Loury gives for them.

Loury admits that the long history of racial oppression and discrimination in the United States is a considerable part of the cause of the black underclass and in general of the gap between black and white incomes, education, and achievements. This concession would seem to pave the way for an argument that principles of compensatory justice imply that white society has a reponsibility to repair the injuries that it has inflicted on the black community. But Loury rejects such an argument. Citing Orlando Patterson's essay, "The Moral Crisis of the Black American," he maintains that "fault and responsibility must not be presumed to go hand in hand." These are, he insists, separable.[46] In particular, although whites may be at fault for inflicting injuries on the black community, the responsibility for overcoming these injuries falls not on the white community but on the black community.[47]

The key premise in this argument is the claim that fault and reponsibility are separable. This claim is true in at least one sense. If a proxy is at fault, the person who authorized his actions may be held responsible for the injury he caused. But Loury does not have that kind of case in mind. His view is that those who are at fault for injuring others may not be responsible for repairing the injuries they caused; the responsibility for repairing these injuries may fall on the injured party.

Let us consider the first of these two claims, viz., that those at fault for injuring others—the injuring parties—need not be responsible for repairing the injuries they caused. For this claim to get off the ground Loury cannot mean that the injuring parties have no responsibility for repairing the injuries they caused. This would make justice an empty idea indeed. If I am at fault for destroying or stealing your bicycle, we mock justice if we say that it imposes on me no responsibility to replace or return your bicycle. Patently valid principles of compensatory justice—that I return or replace what I steal or destroy—clearly impose on me the responsibility to replace or return your bicycle.

Some philosophers have argued that a case for black reparations can be based on these same patently valid principles of compensatory justice. One statement of their argument goes as follows: "The slaves had an indisputable moral right to the products of their labour; these products were stolen from them by the slave masters who ultimately passed them on to their descendants; the slaves presumably have conferred their rights of ownership to the products of their labour to their descendants; thus the descendants of the slave masters are in possession of wealth to which the descendants of slaves have rights; hence the descendants of slave masters must return this wealth to the descendants of slaves."[48] If we acknowledge the principle of inheritance it appeals to, this argument seems to be as incontestable as the argument that I must return a bicycle I stole. If this is correct, Loury may be mistaken that blacks can make no claims of compensation against whites. But his mistake may be a small one. Although it may be a sound argument that blacks are owed compensation for their share of the profits of slavery that were stolen from them, blacks may not be owed much compensation. Many economists argue that slavery was not particularly profitable.

There is, however, a more ambitious argument for black compensation. This argument does not depend on the outcome of the debate over whether slavery was profitable. It rests on the injuries slavery inflicted on the bodies and minds of the slaves, such as the loss of life and limb, culture, traditions, language, self-esteem, morality, education, and achievement. This argument cannot be dismissed on the ground that the compensation it shows blacks are owed may be small. The injuries it rests on were tremendous, and they seem capable of grounding claims for compensation that are correspondingly tremendous. The trouble is that it cannot rest on the patently valid principle of compensatory justice stated earlier, that a person must return or replace what he stole or destroyed. How do you return or replace destroyed culture, traditions, language, self-esteem, morality, education, and achievement? It is the difficulty of answering this question that gives Loury's views of the limits of compensatory justice the plausibility they have. Nevertheless, I will show that these views are false.

The most straightforward cases of compensatory justice arise where the injury to be compensated is simple theft. In that kind of case, compensation may consist of simply returning what was stolen. The example of my stealing a bicycle cited earlier falls into this category. But there are often complications. For example, suppose that I lose or destroy the bicycle I have stolen. In that case, compensatory justice requires that I pay my victim enough to enable him to buy another bicycle of similar quality. Another complication is where the person from whom I stole the bicycle used it to earn money, for example, by making deliveries. In that case, compensatory justice requires that I return the bicycle to him plus the money I cost him when I had his bicycle and prevented him from making deliveries.

In these examples it was easy to see what compensation required because the losses to be compensated were losses of particular objects and of money that would have been earned were it not for the loss of the object. Further, the possibility of compensation seemed to depend only on the injuring party. If he returned the objects he had stolen or the money he had caused the injured party to lose, the demands of compensation seemed to be fully satisfied. The injured party only has to accept the objects or the money. But matters are often not so simple.

Suppose, for example, that the injury to be compensated is a permanent and serious debility. For example, how do we compensate a person for the loss of his sight? Simply paying him what he would have earned had he not been blinded seems grotesquely inadequate. But how do we determine what he is owed?

Robert Nozick says that "Something fully compensates a person for a loss if it makes him no worse off than he otherwise would have been; it compensates person X for person Y's action A if X is no worse off receiving it, Y having done A, than X would have been without receiving it if Y had not done A."[49] This is promising but incomplete. Suppose that the world's greatest runner lost the use of his legs. Assuming that this individual derived his greatest satisfaction from running, merely paying him the money he would have earned had he not lost the use of his legs will not make him no worse off than he would have been had he not lost the use of his legs. Further, if he indeed derived his greatest satisfaction from running, it seems that nothing anyone can do can make his life no worse than it would have been had he not been injured. If so, Nozick's account suggests that his loss may be impossible to compensate. But this seems premature.

Let us reconsider the injured champion runner. We assumed that his injury was permanent. But sometimes an injury may be permanent only because the way the injured party responds to it. For example, suppose that therapy could enable the runner to recover the use of his legs. If he chooses to apply the therapy, his disability will not be permanent; if he chooses not to apply the therapy, his disability will be permanent. Assuming that compensating a person for an injury involves making him no worse off than he would have been had he not been injured, it seems that the possibility of compensating him for his injury may depend as much on how he responds to it as on what the injuring party does.

Consider a more difficult case. Suppose that a person lives to see beautiful things. His only real joys are to see sunsets and the silvered sea under a full moon. And suppose further that someone maliciously blinds him, and that no therapy or procedure known to man can enable him to see again. Does it follow that his injury is incompensable? This may seem to be the case if compensation requires making the injured person no worse off than he would have been had he not been injured. But again this conclusion is premature.

The apparent impossibility of compensating a person for the loss of his eyes if he lives to see sunsets depends on the assumption that he retains the same desires and interests he had before he lost his eyes. On that assumption nothing his injurer does can make him no worse than he would have been had he not been injured. If his greatest desire continues to be to experience visual beauty, his injury will be incompensable. He will never stop lamenting his loss, and he may lapse into self-pity. However, suppose that the assumption is false and that the blinded man changes his desires so that he now lives to listen to Beethoven's music. In that case, if the pleasure or satisfaction of listening to Beethoven's music can be equal in quantity and quality to the pleasure or satisfaction of seeing sunsets, it seems that compensation of his injury may be possible.

I do not mean that every injury involving the loss of treasured abilities and faculties is compensable. There are probably some injuries that are so debilitating that no matter how much a person who suffers them changes his desires and interests, his life will always be much less rewarding and satisfying than what it would have been had he not been injured. Still, the central conclusion remains: In many injuries involving the apparent or real loss or diminution of a treasured ability or faculty, the possibility of compensating the injured party seems to depend as much on how he responds to his injury as on what the injuring party does.

This conclusion must, of course, be broadened. Compensating a person for the loss of a treasured object may, like compensating people for the loss of treasured abilities and faculties, depend on how he responds to his loss. If a person chooses to think that a particular bicycle is irreplaceable, its loss will be incompensable unless he is willing to find pleasure and satisfaction in another bicycle. This suggests that there may be few cases in which we can say with any confidence that the possibility of compensation depends only on what the injuring party does.

Such cases may occur where the injury to be compensated is a purely financial loss—assuming that no one is attached to particular dollar bills. But these cases may not occur as often as we think. Often injuries that seem to involve only financial losses also involve other losses. For example, suppose that I pride myself as a sophisticated wheeler and dealer, but a clever confidence man swindles me out of my life savings. My losses may seem purely financial, and compensating me for them may seem to depend only on whether the swindler returns my money with the appropriate interest. But this need not be the case. My injury may also involve a loss of standing and of self-esteem—remember, I prided myself as a sophisticated wheeler and dealer. How I respond to that loss may make my injury incompensable. If I insist on being consumed by shame, anger, and resentment for what the swindler did to me, unavoidably my life will be worse than it would have been had he not swindled me. In that case nothing he can do—even if he returns my money with interest, apologizes, and accepts punishment for his crime—can prevent me from making a shambles of my life. For my injury to be compensable, I must set aside my anger and resentment, and if I cannot forget his injury, I must at least forgive it.[50]

The difficulty with this analysis is that it implies that the same injury to different people could require the injuring parties to do different things to satisfy the demands of compensatory justice. Take the aforementioned case. The analysis implies that if I am disinclined to forgive the swindler, he will have to pay a lot to compensate me, whereas if he had swindled a more forgiving person, he would have to pay little. This seems to make compensatory justice unfair! Supposing this to be self-contradictory we must therefore find some way to make compensatory justice independent of individual idiosyncrasies.

In the straightforward cases of simple theft first considered, compensation depended only on what the injuring party did and consequently was independent of the idiosyncrasies of the injured party. This was because we made the tacit assumption that the injured person would respond to his loss in the way a normal and reasonable person would. We can avoid the drawback noted earlier if we extend this assumption to cover the more complicated cases. In those cases too we must assume that the injured party will respond to her injuries the way a normal and reasonable person would. In general then an injured person would be compensated for her injuries if, were she to respond to them as a normal and reasonable person would, the actions of the injuring party would enable her to make her life no worse than it would have been had she not been injured.

This account of compensation implies that an injured person could fail to be compensated for her injuries even if her life is no worse, and indeed possibly better, than it would have been had she not been injured. This would be the case if she responded to her injuries more positively than a normal and reasonable person would, so that, although the actions of the injuring party would not have enabled her to make her life no worse than it would have been had she not been injured, she was, despite his failure, able to get back on her feet and flourish. Conversely, the account of compensation also implies that an injured person could be compensated for his injuries even if his life is worse than it would have been had he not been injured. This would be the case if his life is worse than it would have been had he not been injured only because he failed to respond to his injuries as a normal and reasonable person would; if he had responded in this way, the actions of the injuring party would have enabled him to make his life no worse than it would have been had he not been injured.

Loury believes that governmental efforts to compensate underclass blacks will do them little good because they are not responding to their injuries the way normal and reasonable people would. Further, he also believes that this is because they lack the correct personal values and norms, and that this failing is traceable to past white injustice; he does not question "the existence of link between behavioral difficulties on the one hand, and the effects of racism on the other." Nevertheless, he warns that it is a "dangerous" argument that government can introduce reforms to give blacks the correct personal values and norms. Part of his objection to such an argument is that it is foolish to place "responsibility for the maintenance of personal values and norms among poor blacks on the shoulders of those who do not have an abiding interest in such matters."[51] But his more fundamental objection is that such reforms literally cannot succeed because personal values and norms "cannot be the gift of outsiders—they must derive from the thoughts and deeds of the people themselves."[52]

I will show that Loury's claims about the limits of governmental reform to benefit blacks are wildly exaggerated. I will not challenge the conclusions I have drawn about the limits of compensatory justice. Neither will I challenge his assumption that underclass blacks do not have the correct values. I have already commented on the difficulty of establishing that assumption, but here I will give it to Loury. I will focus on my criticism on the linchpin of the argument, viz., his assertion that the correct values cannot be the gift of outsiders but must come from the thoughts and deeds of a people themselves.

This assertion is clearly and absolutely true. If the correct values could be the gift of outsiders, a people could have the correct values simply by accepting a gift from outsiders. But this is false. Having the correct values involves being disposed to do what these values require. To become disposed to do what they require one must practice doing what they require. But it is a necessary truth that one's practice of the actions required by the correct values cannot be the gift of outsiders.

Further, to have the correct values it is not sufficient that one have a certain set of dispositions; it is also necessary that one feel the intellectual and emotional appeal of the correct values. Otherwise one's dispositions will be blind and insensitive and consequently may lead one to act foolishly and even wrongly. But one can get only a feel for the intellectual and emotional appeal of the correct values if one attends to the case for them. There is no other way to feel their intellectual and emotional appeal. But it is a necessary truth that one's attendance to the case for the correct values cannot be a gift of outsiders.

But if these two arguments show that the correct values cannot be the gift of outsiders, they also imply that the correct values cannot be the gift of insiders. If one must practice behaving in certain ways to have the correct values, no one, whether an outsider or insider, can make a gift of the correct values. If one must attend to the case for the correct values to have the correct values, no one, whether an outsider or insider, can make a gift of the correct values. Supposing that a people has the correct values only if most of the individuals who make up a people have the correct values, it also follows that neither insiders nor outsiders can give a people the correct values.

These results imply that with respect to the issue of giving people the correct values, Loury's distinction between outsiders and insiders is false and misleading. It is false insofar as it implies that there is a distinction between individuals with respect to giving a people the correct values, when in fact there is no such distinction. And it is misleading insofar as it insinuates that there are some, the insiders, who can give a people the correct values, when in fact no one, insider or outsider, can.

Now there is a way to make a meaningful distinction between outsiders and insiders with respect to how people acquire the correct values. But if we use it to make sense of Loury's assertion, it changes that assertion fundamentally.

The two arguments I used to show that neither outsiders nor insiders can give a people the correct values do not show that others, whether they are called outsiders or insiders, cannot *help* a people to acquire the correct values. Consider the first argument. Its key premise is that a person must practice behaving in accordance with the correct values if he is to acquire the correct values. This premise is true. But although it implies that others cannot give a person the correct values, it does not imply that they cannot help him acquire the correct values. For example, others can help a person become courageous by giving him opportunities and encouragement to practice performing courageous deeds; this is also the case for the other values. A person must work if she is to become hardworking, but others can help her become hardworking by giving her opportunities and encouragement to work.

Now consider the second argument for the view that others cannot give one the correct values. Its key premise is that a person must attend to the case for the correct values if he is to acquire them. Again this premise is true. But again, although it implies that others cannot give a person the correct values, it does not imply that others cannot help a person acquire the correct values by, for example, presenting the case for them in an especially accessible, vivid, and compelling way.

These arguments show that others can help a person acquire the correct values. They do not show, however, that just anyone can help a person acquire the correct values. Thus they permit a distinction between insiders and outsiders with respect to helping a person acquire the correct values. For various reasons, insiders can help a person acquire the correct values. Perhaps this is because they are particularly good at presenting the case for the correct values in an accessible, vivid, and compelling way, or perhaps it is because they are in a particularly good position to provide the person with opportunities to practice acting in accordance with the correct values. On the other hand, outsiders are those who, for various reasons, are unable to help a person acquire the correct values. Perhaps they are no good at arguing for the correct values or are likely to do so in ways that will not appeal to the person they are trying to help. Or perhaps it is because they are in no position to provide her with opportunities to practice acting in accordance with the correct values.

So it is possible to distinguish between outsiders and insiders with respect to how an individual, or a people, acquire the correct values. But if we use it to make sense of Loury's assertion, it changes that assertion fundamentally. The assertion is no longer that outsiders cannot give a people the correct values, but insiders can. It becomes instead that outsiders cannot help a person acquire the correct values, but insiders can.

But who are the insiders and outsiders in this case? Loury evidently believes that only blacks can be insiders, and all whites are outsiders. He calls on the black middle class, to help establish and maintain the correct values among underclass blacks, claiming that it has a special responsibility to help establish and maintain the correct values among underclass blacks. What is the basis of this responsibility? Common humanity and citizenship suggest that the members of a state owe obligations to each other. But this obligation is not the responsibility Loury is driving at. That responsibility is more specific; it is owed by the black middle class to the black underclass.

Loury argues that the black poor faithfully vote for black political leaders and get them elected into positions of power. Supposing that these politicians made promises to those who helped elect them, it follows that they have agreement-based obligations to their supporters. Further, elected politicians expressly commit themselves to working for their constituencies, and this too implies that representatives of black constituencies have special agreement-based obligations to the black poor. But these arguments are only about black politicians elected by the black poor. They are not about the black middle class in general. Consequently they fail to support the claim that the black middle class has a special obligation to the black underclass.

But Loury has a far more ambitious and provocative argument for that claim. He maintains that the black middle class uses the black poor as a "constant reminder to many Americans of a historic debt owed to the black community."[53] In this way, he says, the black middle class is able to sustain public support for race-specific programs like preferential treatment for blacks and minority business set-asides though these programs benefit the black middle class and not the black poor. On the basis of this claim Loury concludes that the black middle class owes a special obligation to the black underclass.

Several obvious objections can be raised against Loury's argument. For example, much of the black middle class does not owe its success to race-specific programs. After all, it did not suddenly materialize only after these programs were implemented. But I will give Loury his claim that the black middle class uses the misery of the black underclass to persuade government to implement programs that are to its benefit rather than to the benefit of the black underclass. I will show, however, that this claim does not justify the conclusions he draws.

Suppose, first, that the black underclass does not deserve the benefit of the programs in question. In that case, given Loury's strong implication that the black middle class dupes white society into bearing their cost, what his claim implies is that the black middle class owes a special obligation to white society to compensate it for the cost of the reforms. It does not imply that the black middle class has any special obligation to the black underclass except perhaps to apologize to it for using its misery to dupe white society.

But suppose that the black underclass deserves the benefit of the programs in question. This seems an attractive line, but it cannot save his argument if we remember the nature of the special obligation that Loury thinks that the black middle class owes the black underclass. According to Loury, this special obligation is to convince the black lower class of the advantages of hard work, discipline, and the possibility, and indeed moral necessity, of achieving success without special governmental intervention and charity. But Loury's views about the nature of the programs imply that they are likely to *prevent* middle-class blacks from performing their special obligation.

Consider, in particular, his views on preferential treatment. Loury believes that preferential treatment taints all black achievements because it "undermines the ability of people confidently to assert, if only to themselves, that they are as good as their achievements would seem to suggest." Further, according to Loury, preferential treatment hampers black achievement by "undermining the extent to which the personal success of any one black can become the basis of guiding the behavior of other blacks." Thus he complains that "fewer individuals in a group subject to such preferences return to their communities of origin to say, I made it on my own, through hard work, self-application, and native ability, and so can you."[54]

Given these views about preferential treatment, it is preposterous for Loury to argue that because the black middle class has benefited from preferential treatment, it is therefore obliged and especially well placed to preach to the black underclass about the values of hard work and making it on one's own. What does he want the black middle class to say to the black underclass? "I made it with special help, but you must make it on your own"? The claim becomes even more preposterous if we remember that Loury says that the black middle class exploited the misery of the black underclass to persuade white society to introduce programs of preferential treatment that the black middle class then used for its exclusive advantage. For now, if it is honest, the black middle class must say to the black underclass: "I made it with special help, and special help I used your misery to dupe white society into giving me, but you must make it on your own." Is Loury then urging the black middle class to continue its career of dishonesty, now by lying to the black underclass? Should the black middle class, which has accepted and benefited from preferential treatment, say to black underclass, "I made it on my own, and so can you"? This would be a cruel lie indeed.

Let us try to untangle Loury's confusions. On the one hand, he wants to claim that the black middle class is especially well placed to educate the black underclass about the values of hard work and making it on one's own. On the other hand, he wants to claim that the black middle class is especially obligated to do so. Now a good case can be made for claiming that the black middle class is especially, and perhaps uniquely, well placed to help educate the black underclass about how to succeed in America. It has at least partly overcome the barriers and disabilities of racism. The black underclass has failed to do this. Supposing that the black underclass must also overcome these barriers and disabilities, it may learn something from the black middle class. More particularly, the black middle class is the only class that can point to its own experience and achievement to validate the idea that the barriers and disabilities of racism can be overcome by hard work.

But if the black middle class is indeed uniquely well placed to educate the black underclass about the values necessary for success, a plausible case can be made for saying that it has an obligation to do so. I am not relying here on controversial nationalistic claims like Dubois's famous idea that the talented tenth of a race have a special obligation to save the masses. I am relying on the unexceptionable moral principle that if one can help a person in dire difficulties and no one else can, one may have a special obligation to help that person. If this is so, the acceptance by the black middle class of the benefits of preferential treatment is unnecessary and irrelevant to the argument that it has a special obligation to teach the black underclass the values of success. The black middle class has this obligation simply because it is in a unique position to do what the obligation requires.

Moreover, if Loury wants to continue claiming that the black middle class is well positioned to teach the black underclass about the importance of the right values, clearly he must recant his denunciations of preferential treatment and admit that it need not be unjust and need not taint black achievement. But in that case the lessons the black middle class will be in a position to teach underclass blacks will be different from the lessons Loury thinks it should teach them. It will continue to tell them that they must work hard if they want to succeed. But insofar as it has accepted preferential treatment and found this advantageous and just, it cannot tell them that they must reject outside help and try to make it on their own, at least if this is supposed to mean that they should disdain insisting on their rights and reject outside help that is demanded by justice. It must tell them that it is not demeaning or servile to demand justice; that, on the contrary, it is self-respecting to do so; and consequently that besides working hard, they must demand justice and be quick and proud to take advantage of every opportunity these demands bring.

There is another difficulty with Loury's position. As I have emphasized, people do not acquire the correct values simply by being persuaded, criticized, and preached at. To acquire the correct values they must also practice acting in conformity with these values. As we saw, this implies that persuasion, argument, criticism, and dialogue are not the only ways people can help others acquire the correct values. They can also help others acquire the correct values by giving them the opportunities to practice behaving in conformity with the correct values. In this respect, too, Loury evidently believes that whites are outsiders—that is, that whites cannot help underclass blacks acquire the correct values, by providing them with opportunities to practice behaving in accordance with the correct values. But he presents no argument for this position.

It may be suggested that Loury believes that white society has already paid its debt to the black underclass. In that case, although white society could provide the help for underclass values, it would have no obligation to do so. But widely accepted principles of liberal justice imply that because of their common citizenship, the better-placed members of society have obligations to underclass blacks to help provide them with the opportunities necessary to enable them to live materially and morally decent lives.

It will be objected that this is the point at issue. Loury rejects the principles of liberal justice that imply that white society owes the obligation in question to the black underclass. His individualism implies that people have only those obligations that they have created for themselves by their own voluntary actions. On this account, principles of compensatory justice imply that whites may owe obligations to the black underclass to the extent that they voluntarily engage in or voluntarily accept the benefits of unjust racial discrimination. The suggestion is that whatever obligations to the black underclass whites have thus created for themselves, they have already fulfilled these obligations.

This suggestion raises a number of important conceptual questions. Chief among these questions is what counts as unjust racial discimination. Certain black libertarians like Walter Williams claim that ordinary conceptions of unjust racial discrimination are too broad. For example, they say that it is not unjust for the owner of a business to refuse to hire or promote blacks simply because they are black. If these libertarians are correct, the obligations whites might owe the black underclass through their participation in unjust racial discrimination are probably very slight and are likely to have already been fulfilled. I will not take up Williams's claim here.[55] It does not seem to express Loury's view. Loury is clear that white racism and denial of opportunity are the main causes of the bad values he deplores in the black underclass and that racist whites may therefore be "at fault" for the grave injuries they cause.[56] So if he concludes that the obligations whites owe the black underclass through their participation in unjust racial discrimination are probably very slight, this is not for the same reason that Williams draws this conclusion. As we have seen, it is because he thinks that whites *cannot* compensate the black underclass for the injuries they cause it; they cannot do this because the correct values cannot be the gift of outsiders, and blacks must acquire these values for themselves.

There are two muddles in this. The first is the idea that because the correct values cannot be the gift of outsiders, whites can do little to help underclass blacks acquire the correct values. As I have shown, although whites cannot make a gift of the correct values to underclass blacks, they can do much to help blacks acquire the correct values. The second muddle is that compensatory justice cannot require the injuring party to help the injured party acquire the correct values. As we saw, the injured party must respond positively to her injuries if she is to be no worse off than she would have been had she not been injured. But although the injuring party cannot respond positively to the injuries of the injured party for the injured party, he can *help* the injured party respond positively to her injuries. Moreover, it seems that compensatory justice requires him to do so. If I blind someone through my faulty behavior, compensatory justice certainly requires me to do what I can to help him respond positively to his injury, even if, in the end, only he can do this for himself.

But if compensatory justice thus requires the injuring party to help the injured party respond positively to her injuries, it can require the injuring party to help the injured party acquire the correct values. This is so because the injured party needs the correct values to respond positively to her injuries. We need courage, fortitude, charity, and hope to respond positively to our injuries, the more so as our injuries are greater. But in that case Loury's concession that white injustice caused the loss of the correct values among underclass blacks implies that compensatory justice may require whites to help underclass blacks acquire the correct values. I have suggested that they cannot do this by criticizing underclass values. But as we have seen, whites can help underclass blacks acquire the correct values by providing them with the opportunities to practice behaving in accordance with the correct values. Given that opportunities to work and acquire skills are among the most important of these opportunities, it follows that compensatory justice may require whites to provide underclass blacks with decent work and educational opportunities.

As far as I can see, the only objection left for Loury to make is that whites have already provided the help for underclass values that compensatory justice requires of them. This objection is hard to take seriously. Compensatory justice requires that whites provide enough help so that if underclass blacks were normal and reasonable people, they would acquire the values they need to respond positively to their injuries. Normal and responsible people acquire the values associated with work by having decent opportunities for work. But by common agreement there are few decent opportunities for work for the underclass, and white society has been even more delinquent in making moral amends. It has passed legislation against racial discrimination, but it has frequently left loopholes in this legislation and failed to enforce it adequately. More generally, although it has changed, it often seems tempted to go back to its old ways. The uncertainty this must engender in a minority that has suffered cruelly by its hands is not such as would encourage normal and reasonable people to appreciate the satisfactions of society. And as David Hume admitted when he confessed himself unable to persuade the "sensible knave" to act morally, no attempt at such persuasion can be successful if the person to be persuaded fails to appreciate the satisfactions of society.[57]

## Shelby Steele

Let us turn finally to Shelby Steele. Steele is an English professor. Not surprisingly, his work differs in style and method from the work of Wilson and Loury, who are social scientists. Their work is impersonal and empirical, relying on carefully researched facts, statistics, and scientificallly cautious sociological and economic generalizations (Wilson's more so that Loury's). On the contrary, Steele's work is highly personal and intuitive, relying more on Steele's exercises in introspection than on the results of sociological and economic research and endeavoring to persuade with the telling anecdote rather than with a barrage of statistics.

Nevertheless, Steele's intuitive methods lead him to a basic agreement with certain of the scientifically derived views of Wilson and Loury. One of these is that many blacks exaggerate the role of current racism as a cause of black failure. But Steele's account of the true cause of black failure differs from the accounts of Wilson and Loury. Wilson says it is that blacks lack jobs and skills, and Loury says it is that blacks have the wrong values. Steele says it is that blacks have psychological problems. He lists three main problems: (1) racial anxiety makes blacks afraid to try, because trying involves the possibility of failure, and failure is seen as a confirmation of racial inferiority; (2) racial vulnerability makes blacks doubt their abilities and works and makes them apprehensive that they are inferior; and (3) many blacks see themselves as the victims of racial injustice. Although Steele admits that racism persists, he is convinced that these problems, not racism, explain black failure.

Steele blames past racial domination for these problems. Appealing to the psychological generalization that "oppression conditions people away from all the values and attitudes one needs in freedom—individual initiative, self-interested hard work, individual responsibility, delayed gratification, and so on,"[58] he argues that when oppressed people are freed, they are often plagued by psychological problems that prevent them from taking advantage of their freedom. He then applies this finding to blacks in

America and discovers that it explains why they have the psychological problems he claims to find in them. Thus, acknowledging that "we are not a people formed in freedom," he concludes that "we are still new to freedom, new to its challenges," and, in particular, new to the fact that "self-doubt," one of the listed banes of black happiness and advancement, "can be the slyest enemy of freedom."[59]

Although Steele is clear that blacks' psychological problems are the legacy of racial oppression, he insists they are not sustained by racial oppression. They cannot be, in Steele's view, because although racism persists, it has also declined markedly.[60] He suggests that it is the memories and imagined memories of racial oppression, not racial oppression itself, that sustains and feeds the psychological problems that hamstring middle-class blacks and explain their faltering advance.[61]

Steele also suggests that the problems in question persist because they pay. For example, when "blacks choose to believe in their inferiority," they gain "the comforts and rationalizations their racial inferiority" affords them. They hold their race to "evade individual responsibility."[62] Similarly, when blacks insist on seeing themselves as victims, they are spared "guilt" and "responsibility" for their condition and acquire "authority and power."[63] Often this authority and power can be used to wring preferential treatment and monetary concessions from guilt-ridden victimizers.[64]

The most impassioned criticism of Steele's book is that it places the blame for black failure on black shoulders rather than on racism and argues that further black progress therefore cannot come from governmental reforms or public policy solutions but can come only from black self-help measures.[65] Steele evidently thinks that at least the second half of this objection is unfair. He admits that he calls on blacks to show more individual initiative but strongly denies that he rejects governmental reforms to benefit blacks. Replying to a critic who had accused him of doing this, he asks rhetorically whether it is "impossible to imagine that I might simultaneously encourage more individual initiative among blacks and also support government programs and interventions that contribute to black uplift." And answering his own question he writes, "I especially favor programs that intervene in early childhood—earlier even than Head Start—to instill the attitudes and skills in parents as well as children that make it possible to break the cycle of poverty."[66]

What can we make of this? Does Steele oppose special programs for blacks, and is he changing his tune only when he is backed into a corner? This conjecture is false. When Steele discusses the black poor he is clear that he favors special programs for their benefit, although he thinks that these programs should be color-blind and designed to help the disadvantaged regardless of color.[67] It is preferential treatment as currently practiced that tends to "benefit those who are not disadvantaged—middle class white women and middle-class blacks," that he rejects.[68]

If this is indeed Steele's position, it is similar to Wilson's, who, as we have seen, also favors color-blind programs for the poor and condemns preferential treatment as currently practiced on the ground that it benefits middle-class white women and middle-class blacks who do not deserve special help. Why then has Steele's book aroused the animosity of some of the very people who enthusiastically praised Wilson's book?

Part of the answer is that critics have not noticed that Wilson and Steele are talking about different black people. As we have seen, Wilson is talking about underclass blacks; on the other hand, Steele is usually talking about middle-class blacks. Unfortunately, he does not make this clear, so when he condemns special treatment for blacks, his critics think he is condemning special treatment for all blacks, including poor blacks, when he is condemning only special treatment for middle-class blacks.

Clarity about Steele's subject takes much of the sting out of another criticism leveled at his book. Commentators have been outraged because they take him to be claiming that in general blacks fail mainly because of their own psychological problems rather than because of racism. This claim deserves their hostility. It implies that black poor fail mainly because of their own psychological problems. A person would have to be insensitive to countenance this view. I do not mean that it is clear that racism is the main cause of the failure of the black poor. This is not clear. Racism may not be the main cause of the failure of the black poor. Arguably the main cause of the failure of the black poor is that they lack jobs and skills, as Wilson says. What is clear is that the main cause of the failure of the black poor is *not* their psychological problems, even if they do have serious psychological problems. But Steele may not be making that claim. This follows if I am right that his subject is the black middle class, not the black poor. For in that case he may not be claiming that the main reason blacks in general fail is their own psychological problems rather than racism. He may be claiming only that the main reason *middle-class* blacks fail is because of their own psychological problems rather than racism. Now a critic may fairly think that this claim is false. I think it is false. But it is not so outrageously false that it deserves the virulence of the attack directed against Steele's views on the psychological causes of black failure. If I am right, the virulence of that attack is deserved by a claim Steele does not make.

But what about the claim that the main reason middle-class blacks fail is their own psychological problems rather than racism? I have said that I think this claim is false, but I have no way of proving that it is false. Neither have Steele's critics; they simply repeat that he underestimates the pervasiveness and destructiveness of racism. They are probably right, but they also overlook the more objectionable features of his analysis.

Consider again the claim that racism is not the main cause of black failure. This does not say that racism is not a significant cause of black failure. Steele is clear on this. His argument is that blacks can now succeed despite racism, if they gird their loins and make the extra effort. I propose to give Steele this argument. But it invites the following question: Given that blacks can succeed despite racism if they make the extra effort, is this fair? Steele has given us his answer to this question in the following imaginary dialogue between himself and an opponent. To the question whether the racist white man can hurt us, Steele answers "of course." And the questions and answers continue: "Can he stop us for long? No way. Will it be as easy for us to advance as it is for him? No. Can we advance anyway? Yes. Is this fair? Not at all. Is this reality? Absolutely."[69]

So there we have it. Even middle-class blacks, Steele admits, are disadvantaged by racism, and this is unfair. But we should not try to do anything about it. Injustice is here to stay. Steele has acknowledged his surrender to injustice at other places. "What I really believe," he writes, "is that we black Americans will never be saved or even assisted terribly much by others, never be repaid for our suffering, and never find that symmetrical, historical justice that we cannot help but long for. These things will never happen."[70]

## Conclusion

Like Wilson and Loury then, it appears that Steele too has wearied of the straightforward pursuit of justice. This weariness has overcome black thinkers before, but its previous appearances have always been followed by periods when blacks renewed their commitment to justice. If blacks are not to be disheartened by the current jadedness, they must understand this.

The history of blacks in the United States is in large part the history of a people preoccupied with winning justice for themselves from the more numerous and powerful people who had enslaved and oppressed them. Too few and too weak to obtain justice by force and too easily recognized to escape injustice, many resorted to moral suasion, including some of the greatest figures in African American history: Frederick Douglass, W. E. B. Dubois, and most recently, Martin Luther King, Jr. But there were always people who dissented from moral suasion. Martin Delany would have none of it; Booker T. Washington opined that Douglass's methods were obsolete and disparaged the claim of Dubois that blacks should demand justice; and more recently, the Black Power movement that arose in the wake of King's victories in the civil rights revolution expressed its dissatisfaction with his appeal to the nation's conscience. Wilson, Loury, and Steele are only the late-twentieth-century representatives of this tradition.

The dissenters from moral suasion do not necessarily dissent from its goal—justice for blacks. Most of them dissent only from the means moral suasion uses to reach that goal. They believe that the majority has no sense of justice as far as blacks are concerned and consequently that for blacks to appeal to its sense of justice to receive justice for blacks is profoundly wrongheaded. Indeed, their most rhetorically effective argument against moral suasion has always been that there is something paradoxical about blacks appealing to the sense of justice of the very people who deny them justice. Almost invariably they infer that therefore most blacks who claim to be appealing to the sense of justice of the majority cannot really be doing so but must instead be appealing to the pity and sympathy of the majority. Delany, Loury, and Steele make this inference. Disdaining appeals for pity and sympathy they therefore tend to disdain moral suasion.

Delany and Washington believed that the more honorable and self-respecting path to justice is self-help. They argued that when blacks became powerful and prosperous they would receive justice as a matter of course. They did not believe that this would be because the majority would develop a sense of justice toward blacks; they believed that this would be because the majority would find that treating blacks fairly pays. Washington also appealed to white self-interest to help blacks become powerful and prosperous. He reminded whites that they would be better off if they helped blacks become skilled and useful and consequently better off.

But Washington was too canny an observer of the human scene to believe that even enlightened self-interest always serves justice. So, having no confidence in the majority's sense of justice, he supplemented his overt appeals to its enlightened self-interest with covert attempts to manipulate it to obtain justice for blacks. The novelty and daring of his strategy has never been fully appreciated. The attempt to obtain justice by manipulation is not new; for example, it is Plato's strategy in *The Republic*. But Plato clearly stated that this was a strategy for the powerful. Washington tried to use it although he was far from powerful. If Plato's arguments are sound, Washington was doomed to failure.

Of our three authors, Wilson is the closest to Washington. Like Washington, although Wilson doubts the majority's sense of justice, he still wants to secure justice for blacks. But difficulties that are incipient in Washington become full blown in Wilson. Washington could, with some plausibility, argue that whites would be better off by helping blacks become better off. This argument is far less plausible today.[71] So whereas Washington could go some distance toward obtaining justice for blacks by appealing to white self-interest, Wilson has little chance of obtaining justice for blacks by this route. This is why he has recourse to his "hidden agenda."

But if the "hidden agenda" is necessary to save the underclass—if the public must be manipulated to obtain justice for the underclass—the manipulators at least must see what justice requires and be moved by the desire to obtain it. This approach is firmly in the tradition of Booker T.

Washington. As I noted, he supplemented his overt appeals to white self-interest with covert efforts to manipulate the masses to achieve the results he thought they were too morally blind to desire. This aspect of Washington's activities has sometimes been offered in extenuation of his ostensible concessions to injustice,[72] but I think it reveals a contempt for the moral powers of the average person and an elitism that is as disturbing as what it is supposed to excuse. And I submit that the same charge of elitism can be leveled at Wilson's strategy, with its "hidden agendas" and elaborate schemes to make needed reform "less visible." Nor does his admiration for the "corporatist democracies," with their associations with fascism and manipulative elites, give us reason to withdraw the charge.[73]

The views of Loury and Steele are more cynical. Wilson is weary of and pessimistic of the success of unveiled demands for justice, but he still tries to secure it. Loury and Steele give up the pursuit of justice altogether. But they do so in different ways. Loury says that blacks should no longer pursue justice because they have already been given justice; Steele says that justice is not worth pursuing. Steele's cynicism is the more profound. Only he has announced his outright surrender to injustice. Although Loury's proposals for black uplift represent a compromise with injustice, he cannot bring himself to admit this openly, for he tries to argue, although lamely, that justice demands nothing more for blacks.

And Steele is not satisfied with his own surrender to injustice. He maligns those who have not surrendered. As we have seen, he claims that blacks who denounce the unfairness of the gratuitous handicaps imposed by racism are playing the part of the victim to feel innocent and to win sympathy and special treatment. But Steele admits that justice has not done as much as it can for blacks. Why, then, does he criticize those who see fit to demand it?

Perhaps he would answer that such demands will fall on deaf ears and consequently those who make them are behaving pointlessly. But if that is his answer, he is mistaken. It is not necessarily pointless to demand justice, even if one knows that one's demands will not be met. One can demand justice in such circumstances as an expression of self-respect and of one's allegiance to justice, to remind oneself that one is dealing with someone who cannot be trusted, and to remind that someone that one knows exactly the sort of person he is.

Steele will reply that these are not the reasons blacks demand justice. But he cannot defend that claim. He declares his admiration for the methods used by Martin Luther King, Jr., in the civil rights movement, referring to King as "the most powerful and extraordinary black leader of this century,"[74] and as "our greatest leader."[75] In particular, he acknowledges that the movement "won so many concessions precisely because of its belief in the capacity of whites to be moral."[76] But those who now demand justice appear to be like King in appealing to the capacity of whites to be moral.

Steele argues that black leaders today have abandoned King's philosophy. Now it is true that black leaders today have abandoned some of King's methods. Black leaders no longer use his favorite strategy of civil disobedience, at least not on a large scale. But they may still be appealing to whites' capacity to be moral, just as Steele says King was. Civil disobedience is a means of persuading the majority that one's demands for justice are conscientious and sincere. Blacks do not have to use that means to appeal to whites' capacity to be moral.

Because even very moral people may reasonably ignore demands that seem insincere, blacks who want to appeal to whites' capacity to be moral have reason to persuade whites that they are conscientious and sincere. But civil disobedience may not be the appropriate means to do this any more: King used it against special injustices, clear violations of the basic liberties. King knew that the public did not need complicated arguments to be convinced that these injustices were injustices and consequently that it would be on his side if he could only persuade it to pay attention to what he was saying. Civil disobedience was therefore the ideal solution to his problem. But the injustices black leaders are trying to right today are different from the injustices King used civil disobedience to protest. Although current injustices are certainly injustices, they are not likely to be immediately acknowledged to be injustices; they are not clear violations of the basic liberties and depend on complicated and somewhat disputable claims about individual responsibility, economic distribution and contribution, property, and fairness. When black leaders argue against these injustices, emphasis shifts from their sincerity and conscientiousness to the cogency of the arguments they use to show that what they protest are injustices. This does not make their protests any less an appeal to whites' capacity to be moral. Their sincerity and conscientiousness help persuade whites to pay attention to their claims, but what makes their claims an appeal to whites' capacity to be moral is that they are supported by sound moral arguments and true factual claims. So, if Steele wants to discredit the methods and motives of blacks who now demand justice, he must show that their demands are unsupported by good arguments. But he does not do this; indeed, he does not show the slightest interest in what can be said to favor the various special programs for blacks that he condemns.

Steele also says that black leaders have adopted the Black Power philosophy. He says this because he thinks that they share what he takes to be Black Power's self-contradictory attitude to whites' "moral capacity," on the one hand denying that whites have such a capacity, and on the other hand demanding that "they be moral."[77] Steele is right about Black Power's attitude to whites' moral capacity. Black Power does question the capacity of whites, in the current circumstances, to treat blacks as morality requires. This follows from a broader agnosticism about the capacity of human beings generally to treat fairly those who are markedly different from themselves in outward appearance and markedly weaker. But Steele is wrong to suggest that black leaders today have adopted a Black Power philosophy. Many black leaders today urge blacks to acquire power and also appeal to enlightened white self-interest to speed black advance. But surely they can do this without sharing Black Power's skepticism about whites' capacity to treat blacks as morality requires. And Steele himself implies that they do not share this skepticism. How could they if, as Steele complains, they insist that blacks are victims of white injustice?

Steele's answer is that this insistence is really an exercise of power. By insisting that they are victims of white injustice, blacks make whites feel guilty, and this gives them power. Steele even insinuates that "white guilt" is the real basis of "black power."[78] But he cannot have it both ways. Guilt is a moral sentiment. People with no capacity to be moral cannot feel guilty. So, if blacks acquire power because whites feel guilty, whites must have a capacity to be moral. And if blacks deliberately try to make whites feel guilty by insisting that they are victims of white injustice, they must be appealing to whites' capacity to be moral.

Steele could dismiss these objections on the ground that blacks make whites feel guilty although they are not guilty. But Steele believes whites *are* guilty. He claims that "white guilt . . . springs from a *knowledge* of ill-gotten advantage,"[79] and that "white Americans *know* that their historical advantage comes from the subjugation of an entire people."[80] Perhaps Steele will say that blacks unfairly exploit whites' guilt feelings and that whites respond by assuaging these feelings in dishonest, evasive ways that fall short of true compensation. But if that is Steele's point, he should try to make it; that is, he should show that what seem to be black demands for justice are only pleas for a sop that blacks know whites are willing to throw to them to relieve their guilt feelings. But Steele does not do this. He pays no attention to the arguments for affirmative action. He simply dismisses affirmative action as subversive of black development and as obviously a sop.[81]

This suggests that Steele objects to the moral sentiment of guilt itself, not simply to its abuse, and consequently that he must also have reservations about justice. He puts it bluntly: "Even when it serves ideal justice, bounty from another man's guilt weakens."[82] To appreciate the radical implications of this declaration we must set aside Steele's distracting reference to the "bounty" from another man's guilt. Bounty suggests generosity, but what guilt moves us to do is to make reparations, not to be generous! So what, Steele is saying is that when someone is moved by guilt to compensate those he has injured, they "weaken" themselves if they accept what justice says they deserve. Given his view that affirmative action is ultimately subversive of black development, there should be no difficulty understanding what he means by "weaken." He means that accepting what justice says you deserve weakens you in the sense that it robs you of the qualities you need to get ahead. This goes a lot further than his surrender to injustice. That surrender showed only that he did not think that justice was worth pursuing. The current declaration suggests that he thinks that the pursuit of justice may actually subvert desirable qualities necessary for individual advancement. Callicles was not more contemptuous of justice.

I do not mean that the average person is usually ready to give justice, and I agree with Wilson that we should try to ease the burden of the costs of the reforms by making them part of a total package that includes vigorous economic growth. My objection is against the implication that all this is enough. Dubois took issue with Washington's programs, arguing that the exclusive emphasis on jobs and money would breed only money-makers. His concern was well founded and applies as well to the views of Wilson, and Steele, and to a lesser extent to those of Loury. A harmonious society cannot be based on money-making; it must be based on mutual respect and a public acknowledgment of the importance of justice, which do not arise spontaneously in a society devoted to money-making. At best, money-making will suffice when there is such vigorous economic growth that everyone is becoming better off. But what are we to do when economic growth slows and stops as inevitably it must? If we are only money-makers, we will tear each other apart.

# Notes

## Chapter 1: The Color-Blind Principle

1. Derrick A. Bell, Jr., ed., *Plessy v. Ferguson* in *Civil Rights: Leading Cases* (Boston: Little, Brown, 1980), 64–77.
2. Ibid., 71.
3. Ibid., 71–77.
4. Bill Russell and Taylor Brand, *Second Wind* (New York: Random House, 1979), 187.
5. Richard A. Wasserstrom, "Racism and Sexism," in Richard A. Wasserstrom, *Philosophy and Social Issues* (Notre Dame, Ind.: University of Notre Dame Press, 1980), 24, 25.
6. William Frankena, "Some Beliefs About Justice," in *Justice*, ed. Joel Feinberg and Hyman Gross (Encino, Calif.: Dickenson, 1977), 49.
7. Joel Feinberg, *Social Philosophy* (Englewood Cliffs, N.J.: Prentice-Hall, 1973), 49.
8. Frankena, "Some Beliefs About Justice," 49.
9. Ronald Dworkin, "Why Bakke Has No Case," *New York Review of Books*, 10 Nov. 1977, 14.

## Chapter 2: Black Progress and the Free Market

1. Booker T. Washington, "The Intellectuals and the Boston Mob," in *Negro Social and Political Thought 1850–1920, Representative Texts*, ed. Howard Brotz (New York: Basic Books, 1966), 430.
2. Ibid., 430.
3. Ibid.
4. Walter Williams, *Manhattan Report on Economic Policy*, vol. 2, no. 8 (New York: Manhattan Institute for Policy Research, 1982), 15.
5. Walter Williams, *The State Against Blacks* (New York: McGraw-Hill, 1982), 32.
6. Booker T. Washington, "Atlanta Exposition Address," in Brotz, 359.
7. Thomas Sowell, "Culture—Not Discrimination—Decides Who Gets Ahead," *U.S. News and World Report*, 12 Oct. 1981, 74.
8. Booker T. Washington, "The Educational Outlook in the South," in Brotz, 353.
9. Sowell, "Culture—Not Discrimination," 74.
10. It does not follow, however, that they stress education generally—at least if this is taken to include study of the humanities. The study of the humanities does not generally impart skills with significant market value, and the skills Washington and his followers would inculcate blacks with are those with significant market value—as it happens, technical and scientific skills. Washington is well known, of course, for his having been hostile to "schools of the strictly academic type", which emphasized Greek and Latin and ignored carpentry, farming and business. They graduate, he complained, students "who are not fitted to perform some definite service for the country or the community in which

they live," and who think that elevation will come through politics and protest rather than through hard work. Similarly, although Sowell argues that W. A. Lewis's classic criticism of black studies—that they are not "the way to the top "—"needlessly ties the criticism of black studies to a philosophy of integration and personal advancement," he too urges black students to "gain proficiency" in a wide range of "scientific and technical skills" which are "productive," and by implication, to deemphasize less productive fields like "black studies " and the humanities generally. See Washington, "The Mistakes and Future of Negro Education," in Brotz, 440; W. Arthur Lewis, "The Road to the Top Is Through Higher Education—Not Black Studies," in *New Perspectives on Black Studies*, ed. John W. Blassingame (Urbana: University of Illinois Press, 1973); Thomas Sowell, "The Plight of Black Students in America," *Daedalus* (Spring 1974), 192; and Thomas Sowell, "Economics and Black People," *The Review of Black Political Economy* (Winter–Spring, 1971): 12.

11. Thomas Sowell, "Assumptions versus History in Ethnic Education," *Teachers College Record* 83, no. 1 (Fall 1983): 58.

12. Thomas Sowell, "Educational Draftees," in Thomas Sowell, *Pink and Brown People* (Stanford, Calif.: Hoover Institution Press, 1981), 98.

13. Sowell, "Economics and Black People," 11.

14. Thomas Sowell, "Hype versus Higher Education," in *Pink and Brown People*, 103.

15. Thomas Sowell, *Ethnic America: A History* (New York: Basic Books, 1981), 203.

16. Washington, "Atlanta Exposition Address," in Brotz, 357.

17. Sowell, "Economics and Black People," 11.

18. Thomas Sowell, *Race and Economics* (New York: David McKay, 1975), 212.

19. Washington, "The American Negro and His Economic Value," in Brotz, 422.

20. Washington, "Democracy and Education," in Brotz, 364.

21. Sowell, "Culture—Not Discrimination," 74.

22. Washington, "Democracy and Education," in Brotz, 370.

23. Thomas Sowell, *Manhattan Report on Economic Policy*, vol. 1, no. 8 (New York: Manhattan Institute for Policy Research, 1981), 9.

24. Williams, *Manhattan Report on Economic Policy*, vol. 2, no. 8, 14.

25. Walter Williams, *Manhattan Report on Economic Policy*, vol. 2, no. 6 (New York: Manhattan Institute for Policy Research, 1982), 15.

26. Ibid.

27. Williams, *Manhattan Report on Economic Policy*, vol. 2, no. 8, 6.

28. Ibid.

29. Randall Rothenberg, "Philosopher Robert Nozick vs. Philosopher John Rawls," *Esquire*, March 1983, 202.

30. Robert Nozick, *Anarchy, State, and Utopia* (New York: Basic Books, 1974), 149.

31. For example, the ostentatious title of the article cited above in *U.S. News and World Report*: "Culture—Not Discrimination—Decides Who Gets Ahead."

32. Sowell, *Markets and Minorities*, 20.

33. Williams, *The State Against Blacks*, 21.

34. Sowell, *Markets and Minorities*, 28.

35. Williams, *The State Against Blacks*, 22.

36. Sowell, *Race and Economics*, 165.

37. Sowell, *Markets and Minorities*, 36–37.

38. Sowell, *Race and Economics*, 185.

39. Ibid., 182.

40. Ibid., 171.

41. Williams, *Manhattan Report on Economic Policy*, vol. 2, no. 8, 3.

42. Sowell, *Race and Economics*, 165.

43. William Julius Wilson, *The Declining Significance of Race*, 2d ed. (Chicago: University of Chicago Press, 1980), 165, 166.

44. Ibid., 153.

45. Sowell, *Markets and Minorities*, 29, 30.

46. Sowell, "Economics and Black People," 5, 7.

47. Williams, *The State Against Blacks*, 25.

48. Ibid., 23, 24.

49. Sowell, *Markets and Minorities*, 31.

50. Ibid., 32.

51. Ibid., 31.

52. Perhaps sensing the strangeness of this move, he tries to suggest that insisting that employers acquire more information about applicants for jobs is not merely inefficient, but unfair. The "presorting category" of race, he argues, "cannot be categorically eliminated for the benefit of ethnic minority individuals without increasing knowledge costs, thereby reducing efficiency and therefore imposing costs on other people who are no less real or important because they may not be a part of some readily recognizable group." This kind of argument is sometimes cogent. For example, philosophers have pointed out that requiring blacks to prove discrimination as a condition for preferential treatment, i.e., eliminating the "presorting category" of race for preferential treatment, would be unfair to blacks. But this consideration is inapplicable here. Whatever the loss of efficiency that would be caused by employers acquiring further knowledge, this loss is not unfair to whites.

53. Thomas Sowell, *Knowledge and Decisions* (New York: Basic Books, 1980), 118.

54. Nozick, *Anarchy, State, and Utopia*, 68.

55. Ibid.

56. See chapters 8 and 9.

57. Jeffrey Obler makes this point. See "Fear, Prohibition and Liberty," *Political Theory* 9, no. 1 (February 1981): 65–80.

58. Williams, *Manhattan Report on Economic Policy*, vol. 2, no. 8, 7.

59. Sowell, *Manhattan Report on Economic Policy*, vol. 1, no. 8, 7.

60. Sowell, *Markets and Minorities*, 100.

61. Ibid.

62. Ibid., 101.

63. James Fishkin, *Justice, Equal Opportunity and The Family* (New Haven: Yale University Press, 1983), 100, 101. See also Michael Levin, "Reverse Discrimination, Shackled Runners and Personal Identity," *Philosophical Studies* 37, no. 2 (February 1980): 143.

64. Sowell, *Ethnic America*, 187.

65. Thomas Sowell, "Blacker Than Thou," *The Washington Post*, 13 Feb. 1981, sec. A, 19.

66. John Stuart Mill, *On Liberty*, ed. Gertrude Himmelfarb (Suffolk: Penguin Books, 1974) 71. First published 1859.

67. Williams, *Manhattan Report on Economic Policy*, vol. 2, no. 8, 15.

68. Ibid., 8, 15.

69. Ibid., 3.

70. Ibid., 14.

71. Richard Wollheim, "John Stuart Mill and the Limits of State Action," *Social Research* 40 (1973).

72. Ibid., 9.

73. Ibid., 12.

74. Ibid., 14.

75. Ibid., 16.

76. Ibid., 19.

77. Ibid., 20.

78. Ibid., 18.

79. C. L. Ten, *Mill On Liberty* (New York: Oxford University Press, 1980), 22.

80. Wollheim, "John Stuart Mill," 20.

81. Mill, *On Liberty*, 70.

82. John Harris, "The Marxist Conception of Violence," *Philosophy and Public Affairs* 3, no. 2 (Winter 1974). See also John Kleinig, "Good Samaritanism," *Philosophy and Public Affairs* 5, no. 4 (Summer 1976).

83. Eric Mack, "Bad Samaritanism and the Causation of Harm," *Philosophy and Public Affairs* 9, no. 3 (Spring 1980): 230–59. See also Elazar Weinryb, "Omissions and Responsibility," *The Philosophical Quarterly* 30 (January 1980): 1–18.

84. Ibid., 242.

85. Ibid., 254.

86. Sowell, "Culture—Not Discrimination," 75.

87. Wilson, *The Declining Significance of Race*, 110.

88. Ibid., 152.

89. Ibid., 154.

90. Ibid., 166.

91. Wilson, cited in Carl Gershman, "A Matter of Class," *Current* (November 1980): 28.

92. Ibid., 28–32.

93. Ibid., 32.

94. Sowell, *Markets and Minorities*, 114.

95. Christopher Jencks, "Special Treatment for Blacks?" *The New York Review of Books*, 17 Mar. 1983, 12.

96. Ibid.

97. Sowell, *Markets and Minorities*, 107.

98. Ibid., 106.

99. Ibid., 113.

100. Sowell, *Race and Economics*, 52.

101. Ibid., 128.

102. Washington, "The Educational Outlook in the South," in Brotz, 352.

103. See Walter Rodney, *How Europe Underdeveloped Africa* (London: Bogle—l'Ouverture, 1972).

104. Washington, "The American Negro and His Economic Value," in Brotz, 418.

105. Martin Delany, "The Condition, Elevation, Emigration and Destiny of the Colored People of the United States," in Brotz, 42.

106. Ibid., 62.

107. Ibid., 41.

108. Douglass, "The Nation's Problem," in Brotz, 319.

109. Douglass, "The Claims of the Negro Ethnologically Considered," in Brotz, 242.

110. Washington liked to play the role of a Socrates. "If you kill the sort of man I say I am," Socrates warned his judges, "you will not harm me more than yourselves. . . . Meletus . . . may kill me . . . which he and maybe others think to be a great harm. I do not think so. I think he is doing himself much greater harm doing what he is doing now, attempting to have a man executed unjustly." When Washington played this role, he sometimes reminded white Americans that their injustice to blacks cost them in "dollars and cents." However, he often reminded them of a "higher" reason: "Unjust laws or customs that exist in many places," he wrote, "injure the white man and inconvenience the Negro. No race can wrong another simply because it has the power to do so without being permanently injured in morals. The Negro can endure the temporary inconvenience, but the injury to the white man is permanent." See Plato, "The Apology" in *The Trial and Death of Socrates*, ed. and trans. G.M.A. Grube (Indianapolis, Ind.: Hackett, 1981), 30; Washington, "Democracy and Education," in Brotz, 370.

## Chapter 3: Marxism, Justice, and Black Progress

1. W.E.B. Dubois, "The Negro and Communism" in *The Seventh Son: The Thought and Writings of W.E.B. Dubois*, ed. Julius Lester (New York: Vintage Books, 1971), vol. 2, 280, 281.

2. Dubois, "Marxism and the Negro Problem," in Lester, 294.

3. Ibid., 292.

4. Michael Reich, *Racial Inequality: A Political-Economic Analysis* (Princeton: Princeton University Press, 1981), 3.

5. Karl Marx, "Critique of the Gotha Program," in *Karl Marx: Selected Writings*, ed. David McLellan (Oxford: Oxford University Press, 1977), 569.

6. Karl Marx and Frederick Engels, "The Communist Manifesto," in McLellan, 231.

7. Dubois, "Marxism and the Negro Problem," 295.

8. Karl Marx, to S. Meyer and A. Vogt, 9 April 1870. In Karl Marx and Frederick Engels, *On Colonialism* (New York: New World Paperbacks International, 1972), 337.

9. Ibid., 337.

10. Edna Bonacich, "A Theory of Ethnic Antagonism: The Split Labor Market," *American Sociological Review* 41 (February 1976): 34–51.

11. Dubois, "Marxism and the Negro Problem," in Lester, 295.

12. Marx, to S. Meyer and A. Vogt, 337, 338.

13. Frederick Engels, to K. Kautsky, in *On Colonialism*, 341.

14. Alan Gilbert, "Marx on Internationalism and War," in *Marx, Justice, and History*, ed. Marshall Cohen, Thomas Nagel and Thomas Scanlon (Princeton: Princeton University Press, 1980), 185.

15. Ibid., 193.

16. Frantz Fanon, *The Wretched of the Earth* (New York: Grove Press, 1963), 106.

17. Reich, *Racial Inequality*, 268.

18. Ibid., 311.

19. Sowell, *Race and Economics*, 169.

20. Reich, *Racial Inequality*, 94.

21. Ibid., 184, 185.

22. Ibid., 185.

23. Perhaps Reich believes that an interracial coalition of workers would still stand because workers can sacrifice their individual interests for their class interests, but a cartel involving capitalists would fall because capitalists are so greedy they will always play the free-rider. But he has implied that this idea embodies one of the fundamental errors of neoclassical economics. According to Reich, neoclassical economics implies that "competition among economic agents should be expected to break down structures of racial discrimination"—even when the discriminating agent is the "individual capitalist" (*Racial Inequality*, 306). Since this has not happened there must be an error in neoclassical economics. Reich locates that error in the neoclassical view of human rationality. He concludes, we must "jettison the view that individuals are only self-interest maximising individuals who rarely engage in coalitions" (*Racial Inequality*, 307). But since this conclusion is clearly meant to apply to the "individual capitalist" as well as it to workers, it implies that capitalists are not so greedy that they will always play the free-rider. Also, we must not exaggerate the difficulty Reich notes of policing a white cartel against blacks. This is apt to be especially easy since most blacks are so *visible*.

24. Marx and Engels, in "The Communist Manifesto," McLellan, 223.

25. But suppose that individual capitalists must either break the coalition or go under. Marx's law of the falling tendency of the rate of profit implies that this will happen. If it does, perhaps nothing can prevent individual capitalists from cheating. The problem with this assumption is that the law of the falling tendency of the rate of profit, on which the objection rests, is highly controversial. Even Paul Sweezy, the doyen of American Marxist economists, admits that it is "not very convincing." And the pauperization of the workers, which the law implies, is not necessarily conducive to their unity. Paupers might fight among themselves for scraps, rather than unite. Dubois was very favorably inclined to Marxism, but even in the Great Depression, which he said "levels all in mighty catastrophe," he saw no signs of interracial unity. "Race antagonism, and labor group rivalry," he complained, "is still undisturbed by world catastrophe." See Paul M. Sweezy, *The Theory of Capitalist Development* (New York: Modern Reader Paperbacks, 1942), 104; and Dubois, "Marxism and the Negro Problem," in Lester, 295.

26. Reich, *Racial Inequality*, 94.

27. Ibid.

28. Ibid., 14.

29. Sometimes Marx wrote as if ideas developed and changed as a direct result of changes in modes of production. Thus, in *Capital*, vol. 1, he wrote that the working

class becomes "disciplined, united, organized by the very mechanism of the process of capitalist production itself" (*Karl Marx: Selected Writings*, 487). Moreover, this way of looking at the process seems to follow from the basic principle of Marx's materialist conception of history—that our ideas are determined by how we produce the material conditions of our existence. "We begin with real active men," he wrote in "The German Ideology," "and from their real life process show the ideological reflexes and echoes of this life process" (*Karl Marx: Selected Writings*, 164). But this is not very plausible nor, probably, does it reflect Marx's more considered view. Alan Gilbert has pointed out that this economic determinism is unrealistic because only through political struggle can the working class come to understand that class unity alone serves its interests and, moreover, that Marx was aware of and emphasized this ("Marx on Internationalism and War," in Cohen, 185).

30. *Karl Marx: Selected Writings*, 228.

31. Ibid.

32. Ibid., 569.

33. See the discussion in Dennis C. Mueller, *Public Choice* (Cambridge: Cambridge University Press, 1979), 148–70.

34. David McLellan, *The Thought of Karl Marx* (New York: Harper & Row, 1971), 99, 100.

35. Allen Wood, "The Marxian Critique of Justice," in *Marx, Justice and History*, ed. Marshall Cohen, Thomas Nagel, and Thomas Scanlon (Princeton: Princeton University Press, 1980), 37. There are reasons for not countenancing this theory. There is much that suggests that Marx believed that workers' major motive for toppling capitalism was material self-interest. According to the materialist conception of history, men's attitudes and ideas arise from the modes of production, and Marx maintained, of course, that capitalism made men materialistic and self-interested. This is the beauty of his claim that what capitalism "produces, above all, is its own grave-diggers": Capitalism produces materialistic and self-interested people, and precisely because they are materialistic and self-interested they will overthrow capitalism. That materialistic self-interest would be the motive for the revolution is also strongly suggested by the importance Marx placed on his theory of the pauperization of the proletariat. For, out of sheer need, material self-interest must constitute a powerful motive for paupers; and if they see others wallowing in wealth, it is surely that motive which most urgently impels them to dispossess the wealthy. And, even though Marx subsequently replaced the pauperization theory with the theory that in a capitalist system the gap between the proletariat and the bourgeoisie widens, nothing changes. That theory also strongly suggests that the workers' major motive for revolting is material self-interest. Furthermore, the writings of Marx's disciples seems to confirm this. It is not for nothing that Reich devotes a whole book to trying to prove that interracial unity is in the material self-interest of workers. For Reich acknowledges that, although workers may have motives other than material self-interest, they will not unite for any cause that will undermine their material self-interest. "To succeed," he writes, efforts to achieve racial coalitions must "indicate to whites that racial economic equality need not occur at their cost" (*Racial Inequality*, 311).

Finally, although the domination and lack of freedom of the worker is the cause of his miseries, he may not realize that this is so, and may not be motivated to revolt in order to be free. Frantz Fanon was convinced of the distinction between the materially self-interested motive for revolution, and the unintended beneficial result—freedom—of revolution. Thus, although he is famous for the dictum that the colonized "thing—becomes man during the same process by which it frees itself," he did not say that the "thing" revolted because it wanted to become "man." On the contrary, Fanon, like Marx, attributes the revolution to pure and simple self-interest. "The look that the native turns on the settler's town," Fanon wrote, "is a look of lust, a look of envy; it expresses his dreams of possession" (*The Wretched of the Earth*, 39).

36. *Karl Marx: Selected Writings*, 589.

37. McLellan, *The Thought of Karl Marx*, 176.

38. This argument was directed very forcefully at me at the conference "Marxism: One Hundred Years After," held in Baltimore in April 1983.

39. *Karl Marx: Selected Writings*, 246.

40. Exactly what Marx meant by the "increasing misery" of the proletariat is a controversial subject. McLellan says that Marx "would have wished to modify" his "simplistic statements on immiseration" in the *Manifesto* (*Karl Marx: Selected Writings*, 221), meaning, presumably, his assertion that the proletariat is absolutely immiserated. Yet there are passages in *Das Capital* that suggest the same idea. See Thomas Sowell's useful essay "Marx's 'Increasing Misery' Doctrine," *American Economic Review* (March 1960): 110.

41. Mathew Edel, "A Note on Collective Action, Marxism and the Prisoner's Dilemma," *Journal of Economic Issues* (September 1979): 762.

42. Gregory S. Kavka, "Two Solutions to the Paradox of Revolution," *Midwest Studies in Philosophy* (1982): 457.

43. Dubois, "The Negro and Communism," in Lester, 281.

44. John E. Roemer, "Mass Action Is Not Individually Rational: Reply," *Journal of Economic Issues* 13, no. 3 (September 1979): 763.

45. John E. Roemer, "Neoclassicism, Marxism, and Collective Action," *Journal of Economic Issues* 12, no. 1 (March 1979): 147.

46. Roemer, "Mass Action," 765.

47. Roemer, "Neoclassicism," 158.

48. Kavka, "Two Solutions," 460.

49. Ibid., 461.

50. Roemer, "Neoclassicism," 154.

51. David Lyons, *Forms and Limits of Utilitarianism* (London: Oxford University Press, 1965), p. x and Chapter V.

52. *Karl Marx: Selected Writings*, 176.

53. Harold Cruse, "Behind the Black Power Slogan," in Harold Cruse, *Rebellion or Revolution* (New York: William Morrow, 1968), 232.

54. Ibid., 236.

55. Ibid., 239.

56. Ibid., 242.

57. Ibid., 240.

58. Ibid., 238.

59. W.A. Lewis, "The Road to the Top," in *New Perspectives on Black Studies*, ed. John. W. Blassingame (Urbana: University of Illinois Press, 1973), 146.

60. Cruse, "Black Power Slogan," 240.

61. Ibid.

62. Martin Kilson, "The Black Bourgeoisie Revisited," *Dissent* (Winter 1983): 93.

63. *Karl Marx: Selected Writings*, 467.

64. Nancy Holmstrom, "Exploitation," *Canadian Journal of Philosophy* 7, no. 2 (1977): 353–69.

65. Wood, "The Marxian Critique of Justice," in Cohen, 37.

66. Allen Buchanan, *Marx and Justice* (Totowa, N.J.: Rowman & Littlefield, 1983), 59.

67. Karl Popper, *The Open Society and Its Enemies*, vol. 2. (New York: Harper Torch Books, 1962), 138.

68. Cruse, "Revolutionary Nationalism and the Afro-American," in *Rebellion or Revolution*, 93.

69. Gerald Cohen, *Karl Marx's Theory of History: A Defense* (Princeton: Princeton University Press, 1978), 337.

70. Cohen, 343.

71. See note 29 above.

## Chapter 4: Busing: The Backward-looking Argument

1. Ross Mackenzie, "Time to Admit Busing Doesn't Work," *The Tampa Tribune*, 2 Aug. 1983, 6A.

2. Shirley Chisholm, speech at University of South Florida, reported in *Oracle*, 21 Feb. 1983, 1.

3. Derrick A. Bell, Jr., ed., *Brown v. Board of Education of Topeka* in *Civil Rights: Leading Cases* (Boston: Little, Brown 1980), 113.

4. As reported in Richard Kluger, *Simple Justice* (New York: Vintage Books, 1977): 714.

5. Derrick Bell, "The Burden of Brown on Blacks: History-Based Observations of a Landmark Decision," *North Carolina Central Law Journal* 7, no. 1 (1975): 25.

6. Kluger, *Simple Justice*, 714.

7. Thomas Sowell, *Knowledge and Decisons* (New York: Basic Books, 1980), 264.

8. Bell, *Brown v. Board of Education*, 112.

9. Edmond Cahn, "Jurisprudence," *New York University Law Review* 30 (1955): 161.

10. Ibid., 158.

11. Charles L. Black, "The Lawfulness of the Segregation Decisions," *Yale Law Review* 69, no. 1 (Jan. 1960): 424.

12. Herbert Wechsler, "Toward Neutral Principles of Constitutional Law," *Harvard Law Review* 73, no. 1 (1959): 34.

13. Ronald Dworkin, "Social Science and Constitutional Rights," *The Educational Forum* (March 1977): 271–80.

14. Ibid., 277. Dworkin's fear is that if he is right, and if busing is justified only when de facto segregation is caused by de jure segregation, advocates of desegregation will have to prove that every case of de facto segregation they oppose is caused by de jure segregation, and this will be difficult. But he has exaggerated the difficulty. In anticipation of such an objection, the court argued in *Swann* that whenever there are one-race schools in districts that once practiced de jure segregation, the school authorities must prove that these one-race schools are not the result of past de jure segregation and that this is a plausible position.

15. For a general discussion, see Derrick A. Bell, Jr., *Race, Racism, and American Law* (Boston: Little, Brown, 1980), 382, 383.

16. See, for example, Justice Brennan's discussion of *Keyes* in Bell, *Civil Rights: Leading Cases*, 314, 315.

17. Bell, *Civil Rights*, 316, 317. Critics object to this presumption on the grounds that the burden of proof it places on the school authorities is unfair, and that it tends to make them responsible for too much. But this objection can be met. Suppose we know X to be an intentional killer, and that he intentionally delivered the blow that killed Y. Surely we can reasonably presume that he intentionally killed Y and reasonably place the burden of rebutting this accusation on him. See Justice Brennan's comments in Bell, *Civil Rights: Leading Cases*, 316.

18. Bell, *Civil Rights*, 322.

19. Owen Fiss, "School Desegregation: The Uncertain Path of the Law," in *Equality and Preferential Treatment*, ed. Marshall Cohen, Thomas Nagel, and Thomas Scanlon (Princeton: Princeton University Press, 1977), 178.

20. Ibid., 187.

21. Owen Fiss, *Federal Rules Decisions*, vol. 74 (St. Paul, Minn.: West Publishing Co., 1977), 278.

22. Ibid., 279.

23. Ibid., 280.

24. Owen Fiss, "The Supreme Court 1978 Term Foreword: The Forms of Justice," *Harvard Law Review* 93, no. 1 (Nov. 1979): 23.

25. H.L.A. Hart, "Intention and Punishment," in H.L.A. Hart, *Punishment and Responsibility* (London: Oxford University Press, 1968), 120.

26. George Graham, "Doing Something Intentionally and Moral Responsibility," *Canadian Journal of Philosophy* 11, no. 4 (Dec. 1981): 672.

27. Anthony Duff, "Intention, Responsibility and Double Effect," *The Philosophical Quarterly* 32, no. 126 (Jan. 1982): 3.

28. This kind of argument is suggested by Anthony Kenny, "Intention, Purpose and Law," in *Essays in Legal Philosophy*, ed. R. S. Summers (London: Oxford University Press, 1968), 156.

29. Fiss, *Federal Rules Decisions*, 279.

30. Ibid., 278.
31. Ibid.
32. John Stuart Mill, *Utilitarianism*, ed. Oskar Piest (New York: Bobbs-Merrill, 1957), 24, n. 3. First published 1861.
33. Fiss, "The Supreme Court 1978 Term Foreword," 22.
34. Fiss, *Federal Rules Decisions*, 278.
35. Bell, *Keyes v. School District No. 1. Denver Colorado Civil Rights: Leading Cases*, 324.
36. Fiss, "School Desegregation," 187.

## Chapter 5: Busing: The Forward-looking Argument

1. Mill, *On Liberty*, 68.
2. Kenneth B. Clark, "The Effect of Prejudice and Discrimination on Personality Development" (Midcentury White House Conference on Children and Youth, 1950).
3. As reported in Kluger, *Simple Justice*, 319.
4. Cahn, "Jurisprudence," 161.
5. Ernest Van den Haag, "Social Science Testimony in the Desegregation Cases—A Reply to Professor Kenneth Clark," *Villanova Law Review* 6 (Fall 1960): 69, 77.
6. Bruno Bettelheim, "Discrimination and Science." (Review of *Prejudice and Your Child* by Kenneth B. Clark), *Commentary* 21 (Apr. 1956): 386.
7. Van den Haag, "Social Science Testimony," 77.
8. As reported in Kluger, *Simple Justice*, 356.
9. Frantz Fanon, *Black Skin, White Masks* (New York: Grove Press, 1967), 100.
10. Nathan Glazer, *Affirmative Discrimination: Ethnic Inequality and Public Policy* (New York: Basic Books, 1975), 106.
11. As reported in Kluger, *Simple Justice*, 530.
12. Thomas Sowell, *Knowledge and Decisions*, 301.
13. Ibid., 264.
14. As reported in Kluger, *Simple Justice*, 354.
15. As reported in Derrick A. Bell, Jr., *Race, Racism and American Law*, 2nd ed. (Boston: Little, Brown, 1980), 370.
16. As reported in Kluger, *Simple Justice*, 492–98.
17. Charles V. Hamilton, "Race and Education: A Search for Legitimacy," *Harvard Educational Review* 38, no. 4. (Fall 1968): 669, 670.
18. As quoted in Kluger, *Simple Justice*, 498.
19. Hamilton, "Race and Education," 678.
20. As quoted in Kluger, *Simple Justice*, 498.
21. Hamilton, "Race and Education," 673.
22. R. M. Hare, "Wrongness and Harm," in R. M. Hare, *Essays on Moral Concepts* (London: Oxford University Press, 1972), 97, 98.
23. R. M. Hare, "Reply to Liberals, Fanatics and Not-So-Innocent Bystanders," in *Jowett Papers 1968-69*, eds. B. Y. Khanbhai, R. S. Katz, and R. A. Pineau (Oxford: Basil Blackwell, 1970), 52.
24. Joel Feinberg, "Harm and Self-Interest," in *Rights, Justice, and the Bounds of Liberty* (Princeton: Princeton University Press, 1980), 45.
25. Feinberg, *Social Philosophy*, 26.
26. Feinberg, "Harm and Self-Interest," 47.
27. David Miller, *Social Justice* (London: Oxford University Press, 1976).
28. Ibid., 133, 134.
29. Ibid., 131.
30. Joel Feinberg, "The Child's Right to an Open Future," in *Whose Child*, eds. William Aiken and Hugh LaFollette (Totowa, N.J.: Littlefield, Adams, 1980), 127.
31. John Rawls, *A Theory of Justice* (Cambridge: Harvard University Press, 1971), 178.
32. Ibid., 179.
33. Plato, *Republic*, trans. Francis Cornford (London: Oxford University Press, 1975), Book IX: 582–87.

34. Mill, *Utilitarianism*, 14.
35. Feinberg, "Harm and Self-Interest," 48.
36. Plato, *Republic*, Book VI, 496.
37. Feinberg, *Social Philosophy*, 30, 31.
38. Stokely Carmichael and Charles V. Hamilton, *Black Power* (New York: Random House, 1967), 166, 167.
39. Hamilton, "Race and Education," 666.
40. See, for example, Thomas Sowell, *Black Education: Myths and Tragedies* (New York: David McKay, 1972), 234.
41. Hamilton, "Race and Education," 666.
42. Wechsler, "Toward Neutral Principles," 34.
43. Antony Flew, *The Politics of Procrustes* (New York: Prometheus Books, 1981), 86.
44. Milton Friedman and Rose Friedman, *Free to Choose* (New York: Harcourt, Brace, Jovanovich, 1979), 164.
45. Ira Michael Heyman, "The Chief Justice, Racial Segregation and the Friendly Critics," *California Law Review* 49 (1961): 108, 109.
46. Derrick A. Bell, Jr., "*Brown v. Board of Education* and the Interest Convergence Dilemma," *Harvard Law Review* 95 (1980): 519.
47. As reported in Godfrey Hodgson, "Do Schools Make a Difference?" in *The Inequality Controversy*, eds. Donald M. Levine and Mary Jo Bane (New York: Basic Books, 1975), 22.
48. Christopher Jencks, *Inequality* (New York: Harper & Row, 1972), 256.
49. Ibid., 49.
50. Ibid., 30.
51. Ibid., 265.
52. Aimé Cesaire, *Return to My Native Land* (Paris: Présence Africaine, 1971), 138.
53. J. R. Lucas, "Equality in Education," *Education, Equality and Society*, ed. B. Wilson (London: Allen & Unwin, 1975), 45.
54. John W. Gardner, *Excellence: Can We Be Equal and Excellent Too?* (New York: Harper & Row, 1971), 74, 75.
55. Jencks, *Inequality*, 109.

## Chapter 6: Ronald Dworkin and Busing

1. Hodgson, "Do Schools Make a Difference?" 25.
2. Cahn, "Jurisprudence," 150–69.
3. Kenneth B. Clark, "Social Science, Constitutional Rights and the Courts," *The Educational Forum* (March 1977): 288.
4. Ronald Dworkin, "Social Science and Constitutional Rights," *The Educational Forum* (March 1977): 271–80.
5. See Chapter 4.
6. Dworkin, "Social Science and Constitutional Rights," 276.
7. Ibid.
8. Ibid.
9. Ibid.
10. See Chapter 5.
11. Ronald Dworkin, "What Rights Do We Have?" in Ronald Dworkin, *Taking Rights Seriously* (Cambridge, Mass.: Harvard University Press, 1978): 273.
12. Dworkin, "Social Science," 276.
13. Dworkin, "A Reply to Critics," in *Taking Rights Seriously*, 365.
14. Dworkin, "Why Bakke Has No Case," 15.
15. Ronald Dworkin, "Reverse Discrimination," in *Taking Rights Seriously*, 231.
16. Ibid.
17. Ibid., 238.
18. Ibid., 234.
19. Dworkin, "What Rights Do We Have?" 276, 277.
20. Fiss, "School Desegregation," 165.

21. Feinberg, "Noncomparative Justice," 296.

22. Justin Leiber, "Insulting," *Philosophia* 8 (Oct. 1979): 556.

23. Ibid.

24. Feinberg, "Noncomparative Justice," 298, 299.

25. J. L. Austin, *How to Do Things With Words*, William James Lectures at Harvard, 1955 (Cambridge, Mass.: Harvard University Press, 1962), 30, 31.

26. Leiber, "Insulting," 551.

27. Zeno Vendler, "Shadow Performatives," appendix I to *Res Cogitans* (Ithaca, N.Y.: Cornell University Press, 1972), 207, 208.

28. Leiber, "Insulting," 552.

29. Yet there is a difference between insulting and hinting—the difference between metaphor and hint. In the case of hinting, the person to whom the hint is directed must exercise some ingenuity or imagination in order to arrive at what is being hinted. Thus, it is possible to say that the hint does not, literally or figuratively, say what it hints. But if I call the greedy man a pig I am saying figuratively what I want him to say literally. Consequently, though the hinter can always truthfully deny that he *said* what he hinted, the insulter can make a corresponding disavowal only by an insincere appeal to the literal sense of his words.

30. Cahn, "Jurisprudence," 258.

31. Bell, *Plessy v. Ferguson*, 70, 71.

32. Dworkin, "Social Science," 279.

33. Glazer, *Affirmative Discrimination*, 129. This claim of Glazer's betrays incredible naiveté. As every writer on democracy has stressed, its great and obvious weakness is that it does not adequately protect minorities from majorities. This generalization applies to blacks' situation. See Derrick A. Bell, Jr., "The Referendum: Democracy's Barrier to Racial Equality," *Washington Law Review* 54, no. 1 (1978): 1–29. Or does Glazer know all this? See Kenneth B. Clark's comment on Glazer's claim in "Social Science, Constitutional Rights and the Courts," 282.

34. Dworkin, "Social Science," 279.

35. Ibid., 280.

36. Ibid.

37. Dworkin, "Reverse Discrimination," 235.

38. Dworkin, "What Rights Do We Have?" 277.

39. Marshall Cohen, "He'd Rather Have Rights," *New York Review of Books*, 26 May 1977, 38.

40. H.L.A. Hart, "Between Utility and Rights," in *The Idea of Freedom: Essays in Honour of Isaiah Berlin*, ed. Alan Ryan (Oxford: Oxford University Press, 1979), 93.

41. Ibid., 95.

42. Ronald Dworkin, "Liberalism," in *Public and Private Morality*, ed. Stuart Hampshire (Cambridge: Cambridge University Press, 1978), 127.

43. Hart, "Between Utility and Rights," 95.

44. Dworkin, "A Reply to Critics," 358.

## Chapter 7: Affirmative Action

1. Michael Kinsley, "Equal Lack of Opportunity," *Harper's*, June 1983, 8.

2. Alan Goldman, "Reparations to Individuals or Groups," in *Reverse Discrimination*, ed. Barry Gross (New York: Prometheus Books, 1977), 322.

3. Thomas Nagel, "A Defense of Affirmative Action," *Report from the Center for Philosophy and Public Policy* 1, no. 4 (Fall 1981): 7.

4. Ibid.

5. Goldman, "Reparations to Individuals," 322, 323.

6. Goldman, *Justice and Reverse Discrimination* (Princeton: Princeton University Press, 1978), 90, 91.

7. James S. Fishkin, *Justice, Equal Opportunity and the Family* (New Haven: Yale University Press, 1983), 92.

8. Ibid., 97.

9. Judith Jarvis Thomson, "Preferential Hiring," in *Equality and Preferential Treatment,* 36.

10. Alan Goldman, "Reverse Discrimination and the Future: A Reply to Irving Thalberg," *The Philosophical Forum* 6, nos. 2–3 (Winter–Spring 1974–75): 324.

11. Alan Goldman, "Affirmative Action," in *Equality and Preferential Treatment,* 206.

12. 438 U.S. 265 (1978).

13. Sowell, *Markets and Minorities,* 110.

14. See the table in Christopher Jencks, "Discrimination and Thomas Sowell," *New York Review of Books,* 3 Mar. 1983, 34.

15. See Chapter 2.

16. Sowell, "Culture—Not Discrimination," 74.

17. Barry Gross, "Is Turn About Fair Play?" 381.

18. Oscar Lewis, "The Culture of Poverty," *Scientific American* 215, no. 4 (Oct. 1966): 25.

19. Alan Goldman, "Limits to the Justification of Reverse Discrimination," *Social Theory and Practice* 3, no. 3 (1975): 292.

20. Dubois makes this point about the talented tenth of every group. See Dubois, "The Talented Tenth," in Brotz, 518.

21. See, for example, his "address delivered at Hampton Institute" in Brotz, 372.

22. See Chapter 2.

23. Fishkin, *Justice, Equal Opportunity and the Family,* 117.

24. William T. Blackstone, "Reverse Discrimination and Compensatory Justice," *Social Theory and Practice* 3, no. 3 (1975): 268.

25. Reported in Joel Dreyfuss and Charles Lawrence III, *The Bakke Case: The Politics of Inequality* (New York: Harcourt Brace Jovanovich, 1979): 42.

26. Sowell, *Black Education,* 142.

27. Nagel "A Defense of Affirmative Action," 7.

28. Allan P. Sindler, *Bakke, DeFunis and Minority Admissions: The Quest for Equal Opportunity* (New York: Longman, 1978), 69.

29. Goldman, *Justice and Reverse Discrimination,* 120.

30. Barbara Baum Levenbook, "On Preferential Admission," *Journal of Value Inquiry* 14 (1980): 269.

31. Ibid., 258.

32. Ibid., 270.

33. Fishkin, *Justice, Equal Opportunity,* 88, 89, 105.

34. Ibid., 94.

35. See the discussion of this point in Chapter 2.

36. Robert Fullinwider, "Preferential Hiring and Compensation," *Social Theory and Practice* 3 (Spring 1975): 316, 317.

37. Goldman, *Justice and Reverse Discrimination,* 29.

38. George Sher, "Reverse Discrimination, the Future and the Past," *Ethics* (Oct. 1979): 83.

39. Ibid.

40. Ibid.

41. R. M. Hare, "What Is Wrong with Slavery?" *Philosophy and Public Affairs* 8, no. 2 (Winter 1979): 118.

42. Ibid.

43. Sher, "Reverse Discrimination," 84.

44. Ibid., 85.

45. Ibid., 86.

46. Ibid., 85.

47. Ibid., 86.

## Chapter 8: Separation or Assimilation?

1. Douglass, "An Address to the Colored People of the United States," in Brotz, 211.

2. Dubois, "Separation and Self-Respect," in Lester, 237.

3. Ibid., 247.
4. Ibid., 237.
5. Cesaire, *Return to My Native Land,* 138.
6. Washington, "On Making Our Race Life Count in the Life of the Nation," in Brotz, 380.
7. Dubois, "The Conservation of Races," in Brotz, 488.
8. Ibid., 487.
9. Dubois, "Counsels of Despair," in Lester, 254.
10. W.E.B. Dubois, "Two Hundred Years of Segregated Schools," in *W.E.B. Dubois Speaks: Speeches and Addresses 1920–1963,* ed. Phillip S. Foner (New York: Pathfinder Press, 1970), 283.
11. Douglass, "The Nation's Problem," in Brotz, 316, 317.
12. Dubois, "The Conservation of Races," in Brotz, 485.
13. Dubois often objected to definitions of this sort on the ground that they were imprecise. "Physical characteristics," he pointed out, "are not so inherited as to make it possible to divide the world into races" ("The White World," in Lester, 501). But though this is true, it is also irrelevant. First, all definitions of physical phenomena are imprecise; no matter how carefully we frame our definitions, new phenomena can always arise which elude them. Second, as Dubois himself was certainly aware, these theoretical problems in defining race did not matter one whit to practical racism. Third, they can be applied with even greater force against his cultural definition of race.
14. Dubois, "The Conservation of Races," in Brotz, 488.
15. That he would have agreed with me is indicative of Dubois's ambivalence. Thus, in the same essay in which he emphasized the theoretical problems in a definition of race, he also acknowledged the practical irrelevance of these problems. To the question of how he would differentiate the "black" race from others when he admitted it was "not black," he answered: "the black man is a person who must ride 'Jim Crow' in Georgia" ("The White World," in Lester, 512). And this also acknowledges, of course, the complete irrelevance of culture to race. Similarly, when Dubois tacitly employed the physical definition of race, he was as clear as anyone of racism's irrationality. "I refuse," he wrote "to assent to the silly exaltation of a mere tint of skin or curl of hair" (Dubois, "A Philosophy for 1913," in Lester, 380).
16. Dubois, "The Conservation of Races," in Brotz, 488.
17. Ibid., 489.
18. Ibid., 488.
19. This idea is suggested by some of the poets of negritude and by James Baldwin. See, for example, his "Stranger in the Village," in *What Country Have I? Political Writings by Black Americans,* ed. Herbert J. Storing (New York: St. Martin's Press, 1970), 219.
20. The necessity to "destroy" European language is suggested by J. P. Sartre in *Black Orpheus* (Paris: Présence Africaine, n.d.), 26.
21. Quoted in "Negritude Black Poetry From Africa and the Caribbean," ed. and trans. Norman R. Shapiro (New York: October House, 1970), 7.
22. Baldwin, "Stranger in the Village," 218.
23. Dubois, "The Conservation of Races," in Brotz, 491.
24. Orlando Patterson, "Ethnic Pluralism," *Change* (March 1975): 10.
25. Fanon, *Black Skin, White Masks,* 228, 229.

## Chapter 9: Self-Respect

1. Dubois, "On Being Black," in Foner, 3, 4.
2. A. I. Melden, *Rights and Persons* (Berkeley and Los Angeles: University of California Press, 1977), 194.
3. Dubois, "A Philosophy for 1913," in Lester, 379.
4. Ibid., 380.
5. Frederick Douglass, *The Life and Times of Frederick Douglass* (New York: Collier Books, 1962), 143. First published 1892. (Notice how Frantz Fanon too makes a similar

claim. "Violence is a cleansing force . . . it makes him [the native] fearless and restores his self-respect" [*The Wretched of the Earth*].)

6. Aurel Kolnai, "Dignity," *Philosophy* 51, no. 197 (196): 253, 254.

7. Dubois, "Counsels of Despair," in Lester, 253.

8. Washington, "On Making Our Race Life Count in the Life of the Nation," in Brotz, 380.

9. Washington, "The Intellectuals and the Boston Mob," in Brotz, 429.

10. Douglass, "What the Black Man Wants," in Brotz, 283.

11. Sowell, "Economics and Black People," 18, 19.

12. Sowell, "Affirmative Action Reconsidered," in Gross, 130.

13. Sowell, *Black Education*, 282.

14. Rawls, *A Theory of Justice*, 440.

15. Joel Feinberg, "The Nature and Value of Rights," *The Journal of Value Inquiry* 4, no. 4 (Winter 1970): 252.

16. Thomas E. Hill, Jr., "Servility and Self-Respect," *The Monist* 57, no. 1 (Jan. 1973): 103.

17. Laurence Thomas, "Self-Respect: Theory and Practice," in *Philosophy Born of Struggle*, ed. Leonard Harris (Dubuque, Iowa: Kendall/Hunt, 1982), 174–89.

18. Dubois, "Our Own Consent," in *The Seventh Son*, 8.

19. Dubois, "The Parting of the Ways," in *W.E.B. Dubois*, ed. William M. Tuttle, Jr. (Englewood Cliffs, N.J.: Prentice-Hall, 1973), 43.

20. Dubois, "A Philosophy for 1913," in Lester, 379.

21. This discussion is indebted to Hill, "Servility and Self-Respect."

22. *The Life and Times of Frederick Douglass*, 124.

23. Frederick Douglass, *Narrative of the Life of Frederick Douglass* (New York: Anchor Books, 1973), 68. First published 1845.

24. *The Life and Times of Frederick Douglass*, 124.

25. Ibid.

26. Orlando Patterson, "Toward a Future That Has No Past—Reflections on the Fate of Blacks in the Americas," in *The Public Interest* 27 (Spring 1972): 43.

27. Ibid.

28. Dubois's words suggest the defiance and challenge in protest: "protest, reveal the truth and refuse to be silenced." From "Our Own Consent," in Lester, 8.

29. Richard Wasserstrom, "Rights, Human Rights and Racial Discrimination," in *Rights*, ed. David Lyons (Belmont, Calif.: Wadsworth, 1979), 57.

30. Ibid.

31. Meldon, *Rights and Persons*, 199.

32. But the offense to reason that arouses indignation is narrower than Feinberg allows. For example, he asks us to consider a "typical example" of a child who "has direct possession of the truth and cannot prove it to anyone." The child knows that he knew the answer to a question but no one believes him and he cannot prove that he knew it. According to Feinberg, the child will be indignant because "the truth itself has been injured."

I do not find this persuasive. Given, as Feinberg, assumes, that the others have no independent reason to believe that the child knew the answer to the question, I think it is more plausible to suppose that the child will be frustrated because he cannot *prove* a truth that is important to him, rather than indignant because the truth has been injured. Consider the boy who cried "Wolf!" when there was no wolf. When at last the wolf appeared could he have reasonably been indignant when no one believed him? Would he not rather more reasonably have been frustrated that he could not *prove* the truth? And yet in this case, too, the truth would have been injured. Contrast his case with that of the boy who has always been scrupulously responsible about sounding the alarm. He certainly might be indignant if no one believed him. But then it would not be merely because the truth was injured, but rather because of his long history of accuracy, honesty, and responsibility—all presumably well known to the others, was being repudiated. And I think that on consideration Feinberg would concede this. Thus, he approvingly cites the "dizziness" that Albert Camus reported as his response to the "*murder* of the truth." For

Feinberg's discussion, see Joel Feinberg, "Non-Comparative Justice," in *Rights, Justice, and the Bounds of Liberty*, 293.

33. Douglass, "The Claims of the Negro Ethnologically Considered," in Brotz, 228.

34. Melden, *Rights and Persons*, 194.

35. This does not imply or assume that we have basic rights just because there is inherent value in our choosing and acting. I am ready to allow that we have basic moral rights because a world with such rights is more just, less dangerous, and more elevated and civilized than a world without such rights. My point is only about dignity and respect. But in a critique of Charles Fried's *Right and Wrong* (Cambridge, Mass.: Harvard University Press, 1978), W.A. Parent argues that a system of rights can be justified without any appeal to the notion that human beings have inherent worth, solely on the grounds that it is necessary for human well-being. I allow that this may be true. My reservations center around the fact that Parent rejects the idea of inherent human worth, but obviously thinks that even without this assumption his account of rights provides for dignity, self-respect, and respect for persons.

Consider, first, Parent's utilitarian defense of rights. Anticipating the obvious objection that a system of rights does not necessarily maximize total utility, he emphasizes first that a sound utilitarianism is concerned with "everyone's well-being," not simply with maximizing total well-being, and second that such a utilitarianism does not "engage in hasty generalizations about the source of human welfare." Human welfare presumably can involve more than simply pleasure or happiness. These remarks, coupled with Parent's claims that the notion of moral worth "emerges" and "evolves" in a society which respects rights, suggest that this notion is one of the good things which is secured by, and which justifies, a system of rights. The fact that we have rights does not mean that we are fit for them. If we have rights we qualify for them according to rules, but we can qualify for rights in this way and still be unfit for them. This is obviously true of legal and institutional rights, but it may seem false in relation to basic moral rights. Everyone, it may seem, is fit for at least these rights. But though this is the case, if we assume that human beings have intrinsic worth there is no reason why it has to be the case if we don't make that assumption. If basic rights are justified for forward-looking utilitarian reasons, they are in that respect just like legal and institutional rights, which are also usually justified on utilitarian grounds. If persons can have citizenship and legal rights they are unfit for, in the sense that they cannot or will not use these rights properly, they can have basic rights and in a similar sense be unfit for them.

But it may be argued that people are always fit for their human rights on a utilitarian account of these rights, in the sense that however badly a person exercises his rights there is always some good that results from his having them that could not otherwise result. But what is this good? Self-realization, say many philosophers. But their argument is invalid. I grant the utilitarian argument that a system of universal rights may be necessary for the self-realization of as many individuals as possible. What I do not grant is that a system of universal rights is sufficient for the self-realization of every individual. If, as must be allowed, some people consistently misuse their rights, then a system of universal rights is consistent with some people using their rights to turn themselves into drunkards and dope addicts. If this is self-realization, then self-realization is not always a good. It may be objected that such men are, at least, self-made. Now, a man is self-made if he is what he is because of his own choices. Thus, it seems that the mysterious good in being self-made comes from the intrinsic good in making one's own choices. But this is exactly what the utilitarian defense of rights denies. For Parent's discussion, see W. A. Parent, "Fried on Rights and Moral Personality," *Ethics* 90, no. 1 (Oct. 1979): 141–56.

36. Aurel Kolnai, "Dignity," 252.

37. Léon Damas, "Put Down," in *Black Poetry of the French Antilles*, trans. Seth L. Wolitz (Fybate, 1968), 27.

38. See D. H. Monro, *Argument of Laughter* (Cambridge: Cambridge University Press, 1951).

39. Barry Gross, "Is Turn About Fair Play?" 383.

40. Thomas Nagel, "Equal Treatment and Compensatory Discrimination," in Cohen, 17. See also Midge Decter, "On Affirmative Action and Lost Self-Respect," *New York Times*, 6 July 1980, sect. IV:17.

41. J. Harvie Wilkinson, III, *From Brown to Bakke* (New York: Oxford University Press, 1979), 297.

42. Michael Levin, "Reverse Discrimination, Shackled Runners and Personal Identity," *Philosophical Studies* 37, no. 2 (Feb. 1980): 147.

43. Thomas E. Hill, Jr., "Self-Respect Reconsidered," in *Respect for Persons*, ed. O.H. Green, Tulane Studies in Philosophy, vol. 31 (New Orleans: Tulane University, 1982), 129–37.

44. Frederick Douglass, "What Are the Colored People Doing for Themselves?" in Brotz, 205.

45. John Cottingham, "Race and Individual Merit," *Philosophy* 55 (1980): 525–31.

## Chapter 10: The Limits of Civil Disobedience

1. Kluger, *Simple Justice*, 756.

2. Washington, "The Intellectuals and the Boston Mob," in Brotz, 425.

3. Martin Luther King, Jr., "Letter from Birmingham City Jail," in *Revolution and the Rule of Law*, ed. Kedward Kent (Englewood Cliffs, N.J., Prentice-Hall 1971), 12–29.

4. Ronald Dworkin, "Taking Rights Seriously," in *Taking Rights Seriously*, 184–205.

5. Ibid., 190.

6. Dworkin, "Civil Disobedience," in *Taking Rights Seriously*, 208.

7. Ibid., 208.

8. Ibid., 218.

9. Ibid., 215.

10. Rawls, *A Theory of Justice*, 364, n. 19.

11. Gunnar Myrdal, *An American Dilemma* (New York: McGraw-Hill, 1964), 26.

12. This may lead us to the supposition that we can depend on the sincere not to mislead us. But this is an error. The sincere person is concerned not to mislead himself or others about his beliefs. That is, he is careful to ensure that, by word or action, he does not lead himself or others to believe that he has beliefs he does not have. But though he is thus concerned that his beliefs about his beliefs are true, it does not follow that he is concerned that his beliefs about the world are true. That is an altogether different matter: he may or he may not. If he does not he may be very misleading.

Antony Flew has proposed a subtly broader conception of sincerity. According to Flew, the sincere person is not only concerned not to mislead others about his beliefs, he is also, *necessarily*, concerned that his beliefs are true. Thus, in Flew's account, a person who claims to hold some moral position or to believe in some policy or theory is insincere if he does not test the truth of his position, theory, or policy. This account is, however, mistaken. For example, consider the deeply religious person. Surely it is outrageous to question his sincerity because he does not weight the arguments for or against the existence of God, or even refuses indignantly to do so. His sincerity is established, as well as sincerity can be established, by the consistency of his life with the belief he professes to hold as fundamental.

Flew has, in fact, conflated sincerity and conscientiousness. The conscientious person, as I have described him, takes considerable pains to test the truth of his beliefs and the soundness of his principles, and if he finds that he holds inconsistent beliefs, he will not be satisfied until the inconsistencies are resolved. The person who is merely sincere does not go nearly as far. He will take care to report the state of his mind truthfully, and may thus honestly acknowledge the possibility that he is self-deceived and confused. But, though he will not deliberately mislead, or deliberately avoid the truth in order to mislead, he need not be concerned about whether his facts are true and his principles sound. Similarly, he need not share the concern of the conscientious person with resolving inconsistencies in his beliefs. He may be satisfied with announcing honestly that he believes p and, though q contradicts p, that he also believes q.

Flew claimed that sincerity would not deserve the respect it received if it were merely the absence of deliberate falsehood, and to make it more deserving he inflated it until it became conscientiousness. He would be correct if sincerity were indeed only the absence of deliberate falsehood. But if I am right, sincerity is much more than the absence of deliberate falsehood. It involves concern and an effort not to mislead about the contents of one's mind, and so fully deserves the moderate respect it receives. Sincerity therefore is not conscientiousness nor, incidentally, is conscientiousness sincerity. For, though the conscientious person never tries to hide the truth from himself, he may try to hide the truth from others. Consequently, to that extent he need not be sincere. See Antony Flew, "Sincerity, Criticism, and Monitoring," *Journal of Philosophy of Education*, 13 (1979): 141–47.

13. Rawls, *A Theory of Justice*, 372.

14. Ibid.

15. Ibid., 366.

16. Marshall Cohen, "Liberalism and Disobedience," *Philosophy and Public Affairs* 1, no. 3 (Spring 1972): 298.

17. Ibid.

18. Ibid.

19. King, "Letter from Birmingham City Jail," 14.

20. Jean-Jacques Rousseau, *The Social Contract*, ed. Roger D. Masters; trans. Judith R. Masters (New York: St. Martin's Press, 1978), bk. II, 61, 62.

21. Rawls, *A Theory of Justice*, 378.

22. Brian Barry, *The Liberal Theory of Justice* (London: Oxford University Press, 1978), 133.

23. Charles R. Beitz, "Justice and International Relations," *Philosophy and Public Affairs* 4, no. 4 (1975): 361.

24. Thomas Scanlon, "Rawls' Theory of Justice," in *Reading Rawls*, ed. Norman Daniels (New York: Basic Books, n.d.), 302.

25. Rawls, *A Theory of Justice*, 176.

26. Ibid.

27. Ibid., 175.

28. Ibid., 270.

29. Ibid., 576.

30. Ibid., 577.

31. Ibid., 497.

32. Plato, *Republic*, Book IX, 572.

33. Ibid., Book IV, 431.

34. Ibid., 443.

35. Ibid., 431.

36. Rawls, *A Theory of Justice*, 569.

37. Ibid.

38. Ibid., 572.

39. Ibid., 573.

40. Ibid., 426–79.

41. Jean-Jacques Rousseau, "Discourse on Inequality," in *Social Contract and Discourses*, ed. L. G. Crocker (New York: Washington Square, 1967), 203.

42. Rawls, *A Theory of Justice*, 573.

43. Ibid.

## Chapter 11: The Surrender to Injustice

1. William Lawson points out that the name was actually introduced in the 1960s. See his Introduction, *The Underclass Question*, ed. William Lawson (Philadelphia: Temple University Press, 1992). The name became widely used only in the 1980s.

2. See Paul E. Peterson, "Urban Underclass and the Poverty Paradox" in *The Urban Underclass*, eds. Christopher Jencks and Paul E. Peterson (Washington, D.C.: The Brookings Institution, 1991), 3–8.

3. William Julius Wilson, *The Truly Disadvantaged* (Chicago: University of Chicago Press, 1987), 140–46.

4. Ibid., 11, 12.

5. Ibid., 137.

6. Adolph Reed, Jr., has expressed his doubts about this. See his "The Liberal Technocrat" in *The Nation* (February 6, 1988), 246, 167–70.

7. *The Truly Disadvantaged*, 117.

8. Ibid., 118.

9. Ibid., 154.

10. See his "Response to Hochschild and Boxill" in *Ethics*, 101, no. 3 (April 1991): 604.

11. *The Truly Disadvantaged*, 120.

12. Ibid., 124.

13. Ibid., 115, 154.

14. See E. Kant, "Perpetual Peace" in *Kant: Political Writings*, ed. Hans Reiss (New York: Cambridge University Press, 1991), 126. See also John Locke, *Two Treatises of Government*, ed. Peter Laslett (New York: Cambridge University Press, 1988), bk. II, secs. 136, 137, 142.

15. Jason DeParle describes Wilson's "hidden agenda" as a "sneak attack." See his "And Start Helping the Underclass" in *The Washington Monthly*, March 1988, 55.

16. Ibid.

17. The important distinction between self-respect and self-esteem was first emphasized by Laurence Thomas in his seminal essay "Self-Respect: Theory and Practice" in *Philosophy Born of Struggle*, ed. Leonard Harris (Dubuque, Iowa: Kendall/Hunt, 1982), 174–89.

18. See Howard McGary, "Reparations, Self-Respect and Public Policy" in *Ethical Theory and Society*, ed. David Goldberg (New York: Holt, Rinehart, and Winston, 1988), 280–89.

19. See pages 132–40.

20. For this point I am indebted to Thomas E. Hill, Jr.'s, fresh and insightful essay, "The Message of Affirmative Action," *Social Philosophy and Policy* 8 (Fall 1991), and reprinted in Hill, *Autonomy and Self-Respect* (New York: Cambridge University Press, 1991), 189–211.

21. On the relationship among manipulation, publicity, and paternalism, see Adrian M. S. Piper, "Utility and Manipulation," *Ethics*, 88, no. 2 (January 1978): 189–206.

22. Locke, *Two Treatises of Government*, bk. II, chap. IV, sec. 22, p. 284.

23. W. E. B. Dubois, "Of Booker T. Washington and Others" in Dubois, *The Souls of Black Fold* (New York: Vintage Books, 1990), 47, 48.

24. The title of one of his earlier books was *The Declining Significance of Race*.

25. Orlando Patterson, "Toward a Study of Black America," *Dissent* (Fall 1989): 480. Wilson may at one time have given greater weight to the consequences of slavery. See his review of *Time on the Cross* in *American Journal of Sociology*, 81, no. 5 (March 1978): 1198.

26. Ibid.

27. Thomas Sowell, *The Economics and Politics of Race* (New York: Morrow, 1983), 138.

28. Thomas Sowell, *Civil Rights: Rhetoric or Reality* (New York: Morrow, 1984), 29.

29. Thomas Sowell, *Ethnic America* (New York: Basic Books, 1981), 187.

30. Christopher Jencks, "Deadly Neighborhoods," *The New Republic*, 198, no. 24 (June 13, 1988): 30. See also Jencks, "Is the American Underclass Growing?" in *The Urban Underclass*, 89.

31. For example, the Urban Institute recently conducted a test of hiring practices in Chicago and Washington and found that when equally qualified blacks and whites applied for 476 randomly selected private-sector jobs, whites received favorable treatment, including job offers, three times more often than blacks; Raleigh (N.C.) *News and Observer* (May 15, 1991): p. 1A. See also John Kirschenman and Kathryn M. Neckerman, "We'd Love to Hire Them; But . . .: The Meaning of Race for Employers" in *The Urban Underclass*. The authors affirm that their findings "suggest that racial discrimination deserves an important place in analyses of the underclass" (p. 204).

32. J. David Greenhouse also raises this question. See his "Culture, Rationality and the Underclass" in *The Urban Underclass*, 403.

33. According to David Hume, for example, "Avarice, or the desire of gain, is a universal passion, which operates at all times, in all places, and upon all persons." Hume, "The Rise of Arts and Sciences" in *David Hume: Essays Moral, Political and Literary*, ed. Eugene F. Miller (Indianapolis: Liberty Classics, 1987), 113.

34. George J. Stigler, "Economics or Ethics?" in *Tanner Lectures on Human Values*, vol. II, ed. S. McMurrin (Cambridge: Cambridge University Press, 1981), 190.

35. George J. Stigler, "Smith's Travel on the Ship of the State" in *Essays on Adam Smith*, eds. A. S. Skinner and T. Wilson (Oxford: Clarendon Press, 1975), 237.

36. This is true not only of economists like Milton Friedman who apparently originated the argument that the market eliminates racial discrimination. See his *Capitalism and Freedom* (Chicago: University of Chicago Press, 1962), especially the essay "Capitalism and Discrimination," 108–18. It is also true of other mainstream economists who do not have that axe to grind. See, for example, Stigler's "Economics or Ethics?" Stigler explicity states his assumption that people are rationally self-interested and throughout the essay writes as if this implies that people are singlemindedly interested in making more money. Thus he says that he will believe that ideology moves people to act in non-self-interested ways if the proponents of "small is beautiful" *earn less* than comparable talents urging the "National Association of Manufacturers to new glories" (p. 188). Some economists are more careful. According to Ludwig von Mises, "Praxeology is indifferent to the ultimate goals of action—the proposition: man's unique aim is to attain happiness—does not imply any statement about the state of affairs from which man expects happiness"; see von Mises, *Human Action: A Treatise on Economics* (London: Hodge, 1949), 15.

37. Karl Marx, *Early Writings*, trans. and ed. T. B. Bottomore (New York: McGraw-Hill, 1963), 189, 190. See also Plato, *The Republic*, trans. G. M. A. Grube (Indianapolis: Hackett, 1974), 581A.

38. Thomas Hobbes, *Leviathan*, ed. Richard Tuck (Cambridge: Cambridge University Press, 1991), chap. 11, p. 70. According to Hobbes, "all mankind" has a "perpetual and restless desire to Power after power, that ceaseth only in Death." This desire, which is a consequence of egoism, can be shown to lead to a perpetual and restless desire for money given that money is power.

39. Smith's argument here depends on a distinction similar to J. J. Rousseau's distinction between *amour de soi* and *amour propre*. See Rousseau, "Discourse on the Origin and the Foundations of Inequality among Men," note XV, in *The First and Second Discourses* and *Essays on the Origin of Languages*, trans. and ed. Victor Gourevitch (New York: Harper, 1986), 326.

40. Adam Smith, *The Theory of the Moral Sentiments*, eds. D. D. Raphael and A. L. Macfie (Indianapolis: Liberty Classics, 1982), 50.

41. Glenn C. Loury, "Who Speaks for American Blacks?" *Commentary* 83, no. 1 (January 1987): 35.

42. Glenn C. Loury, "The Moral Quandary of the Black Community," *The Public Interest* 79 (Spring 1985): 13.

43. Glenn C. Loury, "Beyond Civil Rights," *The New Republic* 3690 (October 7, 1985): 22.

44. Ibid.

45. See ibid. or " 'Matters of Color'—Blacks and the Constitutional Order?" *The Public Interest* 86 (Winter 1987): 115, 116.

46. Loury, "The Moral Quandary of the Black Community," 11. Patterson's essay "The Moral Crisis of the Black American" was published by *The Public Interest* 32 (Summer 1973): 43–69.

47. Ibid.

48. Bernard Boxill, "The Morality of Reparation," *Social Theory and Practice*, 2 no. 1 (Spring 1972): 120.

49. Robert Nozick, *Anarchy, State and Utopia* (New York: Basic Books, 1974), 57.

50. On the question of forgiveness see Howard McGary's important discussion in "Forgiveness," *American Philosophical Quarterly*, 26, no. 4 (1989): 343–51. See also his "Forgiveness and Slavery" in *Between Slavery and Freedom: Philosophy and American Slavery*, eds. Howard McGary and William Lawson (Bloomington: Indiana University Press, 1992).

51. Loury, "The Moral Quandary of the Black Community," 10, 11.

52. Ibid., 11.

53. Ibid., 20.

54. Loury, "Beyond Civil Rights," 25.

55. I have already dealt with it in Chapter 3.

56. Loury, "The Moral Quandary of the Black Community," 10, 11.

57. David Hume, *Hume's Moral and Political Philosophy*, ed. Henry Aiken (London: Macmillan, 1984), 261.

58. Shelby Steele, *The Content of Our Character* (New York: St. Martin's Press, 1990), 68.

59. Ibid., 54.

60. On the decline in racism, see *The Content of Our Character*, 27, 29, 31. On the persistence of racism, see Steele's exchange with Amiri Baraka in "A Race Divided," *Emerge* (February 1991): 48.

61. On this see especially his essay "The Memory of Enemies" in *The Content of Our Character*, 149–65, where he speaks of the "enemy-memory" of blacks.

62. Ibid., 28.

63. Ibid., 67.

64. Ibid., 118.

65. See, for example, Martin Kilson, "Realism about the Black Experience," *Dissent*, 37 (Fall 1990): 519, and Adolph Reed, Jr., "Steele Trap," *The Nation*, 252 (March 4, 1991): 274, 275.

66. Shelby Steele, "Shelby Steele Replies," *Dissent*, 37 (Fall 1990): 523.

67. Ibid., 124.

68. Ibid.

69. Steele, "A Race Divided," 48.

70. Steele, *The Content of Our Character*, 172, 173. See also 174.

71. William A. Darity, "The Managerial Class and Surplus Population," *Society*, 21, no. 1 (November/December 1983): 54–62.

72. Sowell, *The Economics and Politics of Race*, 131.

73. See Frank Kirkland, "Public Policy, Ethical Life and the Urban Underclass" in *The Underclass Question*.

74. Steele, *The Content of Our Character*, 19.

75. Ibid., 175.

76. Ibid., 18.

77. Ibid., 19.

78. Ibid., 81.

79. Ibid., 80.

80. Ibid., 81, emphasis in original.

81. Ibid.

82. Ibid., 80.

# Index

# Index to Chapter 11

# About the Author

Bernard Boxill is professor of philosophy at the University of North Carolina at Chapel Hill since 1986. Before that he taught at the University of South Florida, the University of Kentucky, and U.C.L.A. He has published articles on compensatory justice and on the moral and philosophical issues raised by racism. His main interests are in the history of African American political thought and the history of political thought.